FOUNDATIONS OF COMPARATIVE POLITICS
A Policy Perspective

FOUNDATIONS OF COMPARATIVE POLITICS
A Policy Perspective

Charles F. Andrain
San Diego State University

Brooks/Cole Publishing Company
Monterey, California

Consulting Editor: Bernard Hennessy

Brooks/Cole Publishing Company
A Division of Wadsworth, Inc.

© 1983 by Wadsworth, Inc., Belmont, California 94002. All rights reserved. No part of this book may be reproduced, stored in a retrieval system, or transcribed, in any form or by any means—electronic, mechanical, photocopying, recording, or otherwise—without the prior written permission of the publisher, Brooks/Cole Publishing Company, Monterey, California 93940, a division of Wadsworth, Inc.

Printed in the United States of America
10 9 8 7 6 5 4 3 2 1

Library of Congress Cataloging in Publication Data

Andrain, Charles F.
  Foundations of comparative politics.

  Includes bibliographical references and index.
  1. Comparative government. 2. Policy sciences.
I. Title.
JF51.A65   1983   320.3   82-17791
ISBN 0-534-01377-5

Subject Editor: *Marquita Flemming*
Production Editor: *Marlene Thom*
Production Assistant: *Penelope Sky*
Manuscript Editor: *Sylvia Stein*
Interior and Cover Design: *Katherine Minerva*
Typesetting: *Boyer & Brass, Inc., San Diego, California*

PREFACE

In the concluding chapter of *Walden*, Henry David Thoreau wrote: "If you have built castles in the air, your work need not be lost; that is where they should be. Now put the foundations under them."* The task Thoreau suggests also seems appropriate for the political scientist. Just as the architect designs the foundations that undergird a castle, so the political scientist analyzes the basic dimensions that shape the operation of a political system. This book explores three foundations (dimensions) undergirding the comparative study of politics. One foundation focuses on the political power of social groups—the effects of social groups on political decision making as well as the impact of public policies on the group's power, wealth, and status. A second foundation deals with political beliefs about public policies, especially the ranking and interpretations that different ideologies ascribe to freedom and equality. A third foundation revolves around the power of political organizations, such as government institutions and parties in the public process. The first three parts of the book delve into these three foundations. Part IV analyzes the impact of policy performance on political stability in the United States, Britain, Germany, and Russia. In this concluding section, I seek to explain how the power of social groups, attitudes toward the political system, and the role played by governments and political

*Henry David Thoreau, *Walden*, ed. J. Lyndon Shanley (Princeton, N.J.: Princeton University Press, 1971), p. 324.

parties mutually affect the degree of systemic change in these four countries.

Viewing different nations from a comparative perspective, this book uses a systemic approach.† First, the systemic approach highlights the importance of policy analysis. The policy orientation of this book stresses several key issues: (1) the role of social groups, government institutions, and political parties in the public policy process, (2) the importance of political beliefs on policy formulation and implementation, and (3) the effect of public policies on political system performance, especially on its degree of continuity and change over time.

Second, the systemic approach adopts a theoretical overview of political systems. Facts accumulated from several countries never speak for themselves. Instead, the comparative analyst must attribute theoretical significance to these descriptive data. Rather than merely describing government institutions, defining esoteric political terms, and constructing typologies of political systems, I have stressed general theoretical principles that *explain* individual political behavior and political system operation. Theories are sets of generalizations that explain the relationships among variables. A theoretical perspective requires that we explain the general significance of isolated bits of specific information, synthesize discrete empirical findings into a general whole, and link abstract concepts to concrete cases. Policy theory focuses on politically relevant issues that affect the empirical world—issues such as the causes of homicide, the strength of the nation-state, the causes of voting behavior, the impact of political ideologies on income equality, and the reasons for stability and change in political systems.

Third, the systemic approach uses explicit variables to compare nations. I have concentrated on nine countries: the United States, Canada, Britain, West Germany, Sweden, France, Italy, the Soviet Union, and the People's Republic of China. Rather than describe each nation in sequential order, I compare several political systems according to such variables as the power of the nation-state, the degree of group polarization in voting behavior, and the policy priorities of political leaders.

Fourth, comparative analysis impels us to compare not only across geographic space but also across time; thus, a historical orientation becomes essential to understanding the changes taking place within political systems. The parts of a political system hardly remain in static equilibrium; rather, these parts—social groups, political organizations, political beliefs, public policies—change over time. As

---

†For "the logic of systemic analysis," see Morris Janowitz, *The Last Half-Century: Societal Change and Politics in America* (Chicago: University of Chicago Press, 1978), pp. 18, 53–81.

certain circumstances change, politicians articulate different interpretations of such beliefs as freedom and equality. When one set of rulers replaces another, the new leaders may change their value priorities. The power of social groups and government institutions also changes over time. As these structural transformations occur, they often stimulate changes in the content and impact of public policies. By adopting a historical framework, we can better explain the reasons for political changes—specifically, how past events shape present conditions.

Producing a book, like making public policies, is a collective enterprise. I appreciate the contributions of the following individuals. I wrote this work while a research associate at the Institute of International Studies, the University of California, Berkeley. Dr. Carl G. Rosberg, director of the IIS, facilitated my research at the university. Bernard Hennessy, Alexander Groth, Jack Parson, and Hugh Stevens reviewed the manuscript for Brooks/Cole Publishing Company. Several editors at Brooks/Cole helped me prepare the book for publication: Henry Staat, Marquita Flemming, Marlene Thom, and Sylvia E. Stein. Peggy McCroskey efficiently typed the manuscript.

CONTENTS

INTRODUCTION 1

1   **Comparing Political Systems: The Causes of Homicide in the United States, Sweden, and Japan**   2

Purposes of Comparison   3
  Description and Enlargement of Knowledge   4
  Explanation   5
  Evaluation   5
  Interdependence of the Objectives   6

Methods of Comparison   7
  Statement of Analytical Puzzle   7
  Formulation of Tentative Answers   10
  Collection of Information   15
  Analysis and Interpretation   19

The Dilemmas of Comparative Analysis   33
  The Problems of Causal Analysis   34
  The Individual Observer and the Social Context   37

Conclusion   39

Notes   40

PART I SOCIAL STRUCTURES AND THE EXERCISE OF POLITICAL POWER 45

2 Social Groups 47

The Group Concept 49
  Categoric Groups 50
  Membership Groups 50
  Reference Groups 50

Dimensions of Social Groups 51
  Objective Dimensions 51
  Subjective Dimensions 53

Types of Social Groups 53
  Ethnic Groups 53
  Religious Groups 55
  Economic Groups 60

Notes 66

3 Social Stratification 69

Dimensions of Social Stratification 69
  Political Power 69
  Wealth 71
  Status 73
  Congruence of Political Power, Wealth, and Status 75

Social Stratification under Feudalism, Capitalism, and State Socialism 78
  Feudalism 79
  Capitalism 82
  State Socialism 85

Change in the Social Stratification System 89
  Types of Social Changes 89
  Political Mobilization for Social Change 92

Notes 98

PART II POLITICAL BELIEFS 101

4 Political Ideology: The Meaning of Freedom and Equality 103

Dimensions of Political Ideology   105
  Style of Reasoning   105
  Functions   106
  Content   107

Classical Conservatism   112
  Monist and Pluralist Interpretations   113
  Contemporary Conservative Ideologies   117

Classic Liberalism   117
  Classical Liberal View of Freedom   119
  Classical Liberal View of Equality   121
  Contemporary Liberal Ideologies   122

Democratic Socialism   124
  Tawney's Interpretation   125
  Corporate Socialism   129
  Welfare State Socialism   129
  Market Socialism   130

Communism   130
  Marx's Views   131
  Lenin's Views   134
  Anarcho-Communism   139
  Structural Pluralism   140

Fascism   141
  Beliefs of Hitler and Mussolini   143
  Military Fascism in Latin America   147

Summary   149

Notes   152

5   Political Ideology and Public Policy   157

Commitment to Civil Liberties   158

Commitment to Economic Equality   160
  Communism   160
  Fascism   161
  Democratic Socialism   161
  Classical Liberalism   165
  Conservatism   165

Notes   166

PART III POLITICAL STRUCTURES 169

6 Governments 171

The Concept of Government 173

Emergence of the Nation-State 176

Structural Dimensions of State Power 178
  Monopoly of Coercive Force 179
  Centralization of Power 179
  Coordination of Government Activities 179
  Specialization and Autonomy from Social Groups 180
  Comprehensive Scope of Power 180

Types of Nation-States 181
  Personal Autocracies 181
  Bureaucratic Dictatorships 186
  Constitutional Governments 191
  Summary 200

Reasons for the Power of Nation-States 202
  Involvement in War 202
  Rigid Social Structure 204
  Political Beliefs 209
  Conclusion 212

Notes 215

7 Government in the Economy 219

Capitalism 220

Corporatism 222

State Socialism 224

Market Socialism 225

Notes 227

8 Political Parties in Constitutional Systems 229

Party Ideologies 231
  Partisan Attitudes toward Equality 231
  Partisan Attitudes toward Freedom 233
  Partisan Ideological Conflicts over Public Policies 236

Voting Behavior of Social Groups 244

Political Parties and Social Cleavages 245
Ethnic Voting 246
Religious Voting 249
Class Voting 250
Political Parties and Group Support 256

Party Activities 259
Political Education 260
Political Recruitment 261
Interest Aggregation 261
Management of Government 262
The Declining Influence of Political Parties 268

Notes 269

PART IV POLITICAL LEGITIMACY AND SYSTEM STABILITY 279

9 The Concept of Political Legitimacy 281

Sources of Legitimacy 283

Political Alienation 285

Challenges to Legitimacy: Political System Stability 286

Notes 288

10 Puritanism and Madisonianism in America 290

Puritanism and Madisonianism 291

The Revolutionary War: Emergence of an American Civil Religion 295

The Civil War: Crisis of Political Legitimacy 297

Economic Crisis of the Depression 300

Political Legitimacy in Contemporary America 301
Race Relations 303
Vietnam War 304
Watergate 304
Economic Stagnation 306

Political Stability in America 306

Notes 310

11 The Mixed Constitution in Britain 314

The Dignified and Efficient Institutions 315

Decline of Deference and Rise of Political Alienation 317

Political Stability in Britain 320

Notes 321

12 Pragmatism and Absolutism in Germany 324

Rise and Fall of the Second Reich 325
  Group Conflicts 325
  Value Conflicts 326

Political Illegitimacy of the Weimar Republic 330

Third Reich: The Cult of the Führer 333

Federal Republic of Germany: The Economic Foundations of Political Legitimacy 335

Notes 339

13 Orthodoxy and Revolution in Russia 342

Political Legitimacy in Czarist Russia 343

Downfall of the Czarist State and the Provisional Government 344
  Disaffection of Key Groups 344
  Disintegration of State Control 347
  Mobilization of Key Groups 347

Stability of the Soviet Union 349
  Coercive Power 349
  Consensual Power 351

Notes 354

14 Conclusion: Political Legitimacy, Policy Performance, and System Change 355

Structural Crises and Political Legitimacy 356

Political Change in Four Nations 358

Notes 362

Index 363

Introduction

CHAPTER

1

Comparing Political Systems
The Causes of Homicide in the United States, Sweden, and Japan

> *Not to compare is not to reason, not to wonder, not to know if we like* fromage à la crème *better than rat cheese.*
> —HARRIET VAN HORNE

Juan lives in the South Bronx, an area of New York City plagued by high crime. A junior at Brooklyn Technical High School, he wants to become an engineer. Yet he faces obstacles to getting a good education. Murders, rapes, and knifings occur daily. Violence pervades Bronx Park. Whereas in the past families enjoyed lunch there every Sunday, now the park remains empty. Teenagers have broken the benches and cut off the heads of the statues. Juan's family, who made the trip to New York from Puerto Rico five years ago, now lives in a cramped apartment with three locks on the door. Last week his grandmother was robbed and beaten while waiting for a bus. Taxicabs rarely venture into the district. Police cars cruise through the South Bronx like an occupying force. No rules restrain violent behavior, and the citizens feel abandoned by their political authorities.[1]

A resident of Tokyo, Setsuko does not feel so threatened by urban violence. She rarely fears going to the movies at night with her boyfriend, Mitsuo. Despite the densely populated city life, little interpersonal violence takes place in the streets. Muggings are rare. Her grandparents enjoy visiting the nearby park each day. They frequently go on bus rides to other parts of Tokyo. Rather than riding around in a patrol car armed with powerful spotlights, the police usually walk their beats. Indeed, Setsuko and her friends call their neighborhood policeman "Omawari-san"—Mr. Walkabout. At least once a year, he visits her home and also the office where she works in downtown Tokyo as a secretary. For these reasons, Setsuko regards the patrolman as a part of her family's local community.[2]

Similarly, in Stockholm, Erik feels relatively free from murder and mayhem. Although recently the homicide rate has increased slightly, it remains far below New York City figures. A first-year student at the University of Stockholm, Erik also works part-time as a laboratory assistant for the KemaNord Chemical Company. Each night from 6 to 10 o'clock, he works at the plant; yet he has no fear of coming home to his apartment late at night. The bus system offers frequent, safe, and convenient transportation. Few slum areas dot the Stockholm landscape. The gap between the rich and the poor seems far less apparent than in the United States. Although the police carry weapons, they rarely use them. Even when a police officer has been shot, his or her colleagues on the force first try to persuade the killer to surrender peacefully. Only when persuasive attempts have failed will they decide to storm the house where the cop killer is located. However, these incidents of tension between police and murderers occur infrequently.[3]

Purposes of Comparison

These three vignettes compare New York City, Tokyo, and Stockholm. Comparison involves pointing out the similarities and differences among units, such as cities in the United States, Japan and Sweden. When we compare, we rank order units according to certain variables—that is, particular aspects of behavior that are common to individuals, groups, or societies. In this case, we have compared the homicide rates (a variable) found in three cities. Whereas two cities—Tokyo and Stockholm—have similar homicide rates, New York City's crime pattern is different. The murder rate— the number of victims per 100,000 people—is nearly ten times higher in New York City than in Tokyo or Stockholm. Why? Perhaps the explanations lie in (1) cultural beliefs (attitudes toward authority and the exercise of violence), (2) the operation of the criminal justice system (the activities of the police, courts, and prisons), and (3) social-structural variables such as economic relationships (the degree of income inequality and unemployment), population patterns (the heterogeneity of a society, the proportion of young men in a nation), and small-group interactions. All these variables may have some impact on the different homicide rates found in the United States, Japan, and Sweden.

According to Harriet Van Horne, "Comparisons are odious, runs the cliché, ignoring the fact that we all make them every day. How else are we to draw valid conclusions? Not to compare is not to reason, not to wonder, not to know if we like *fromage à la crème* better than rat cheese."[4] This passage suggests three purposes of comparison: accurate description and an enlargement of our knowledge, explanation, and evaluation.

DESCRIPTION AND ENLARGEMENT OF KNOWLEDGE

By engaging in comparative analysis, we expand our descriptive knowledge. Before we can explain how individuals behave and how political systems operate, we need accurate information about both the effect (homicide rate) and the assumed causes (cultural beliefs, criminal justice policies, and patterns of social interaction). Specific descriptive statements provide information about the aspects of particular individual and systemic behavior. For example, table 1-1 records the homicide rates per 100,000 persons in the United States, Sweden, and Japan between 1965 and 1978. These national rates correspond to the different murder rates that plague New York City, Stockholm, and Tokyo. From this table, we can compare three nations over both time and space. Although the U.S. homicide rate increased during most of this period, in Japan the murder rate declined a bit. From a cross-national perspective, the United States showed a far higher homicide rate than either Japan or Sweden. Until 1976, Sweden had a slightly lower homicide rate than Japan. As table 1-1 suggests, comparative descriptive statements point out the similarities and differences among different societies at certain time periods.

TABLE 1-1 Homicide rates

Year	United States	Sweden	Japan
1978	9.4	1.0	1.1
1977	9.2	1.2	1.2
1976	9.1	1.3	1.3
1975	10.0	1.1	1.3
1974	10.2	1.2	1.3
1973	9.8	1.0	1.3
1972	9.4	1.1	1.3
1971	9.1	0.9	1.3
1970	8.2	0.8	1.3
1969	7.7	0.9	1.4
1968	7.3	0.7	1.4
1967	6.8	0.9	1.4
1966	5.9	0.8	1.4
1965	5.5	0.7	1.4

Note: *Homicide rate* refers to the number of murders and non-negligent manslaughters for every 100,000 persons in the society.
SOURCE: The *World Health Statistics Annual* (Geneva, Switzerland: World Health Organization, 1965–1981).

EXPLANATION

Comparative analysis facilitates the task of explaining individual behavior and systemic performance. Why are some individuals more likely to murder than others? Why does the United States have a higher homicide rate than Sweden and Japan? Explanatory statements posit general relationships among variables.[5] They take the form of if/then statements. If certain conditions are present, then what consequences will follow? The consequence is the effect, the "dependent variable"—in this case, the homicide rate. Explanations for this effect may stem from several different sources or "independent variables": aggressive cultural beliefs, lenient criminal justice policies, unequal economic conditions, and the patterns of rewards and punishments in small groups, such as the family and the neighborhood gang. For example, deterrence explanations assume that individuals seek to maximize their gains and minimize their losses. Under this assumption, the greater the ease of committing homicide, the lower the probability of apprehension by the police, the lower the probability of conviction if caught, and the less certain, immediate, and severe the punishment if convicted, then the higher the homicide rate in a particular country. All these variables are highly general. They presumably pertain to all societies, not just a few specific ones. These explanatory statements posit the direction of a relationship among variables; for instance, if the certainty of punishment increases, then the homicide rate will decline. If the police in a country demonstrate a high probability of catching a murderer, then that country will have a low homicide rate. These hypotheses have been investigated mainly in the American context. Cross-national comparisons enable us to test their credibility in other societies.

EVALUATION

Comparisons help us evaluate political systems and clarify our standards of evaluation. The evaluation process involves three steps:

1. Political scientists specify the criteria of worth—the standards used to judge different systems. If they assume that the United States has a better criminal justice system than Sweden, what values (standards of desirability) are used to make this evaluative judgment? Justice, individual freedom, and police efficiency are a few possibilities.

2. Analysts next devise some empirical indicators to measure abstract values such as justice, freedom, and efficiency. Because these criteria are general and ambiguous, different observers will probably choose diverse ways to measure them. For instance, certainty of punishment—the number of admissions to prison on sentence for homicide divided by the total number of homicides—may

serve as one rough indicator of procedural justice. Individual freedom may refer to the opportunities for defense attorneys to gather the evidence needed to defend their clients charged with murder. An observer may also evaluate different societies according to their police efficiency. If police officers in a nation quickly apprehend a high proportion of actual murderers at a relatively low economic cost, then they rank higher on a police efficiency scale than those police who spend more money and take a longer time to catch a lower percentage of murderers.

3. Political scientists finally match the empirical observations to the criteria of desirability, thereby rank ordering different societies on these evaluative standards. For example, how do political systems rank on the freedom of lawyers to gather evidence and to challenge the state prosecutor? If we have the empirical evidence on rights to present evidence, then we can rank various nations on an individual freedom scale. Hence, we can ascertain to what degree the United States government operates a "better" criminal justice system than do other governments.

The process of making evaluative comparisons arouses controversy among political scientists. Two problems seem crucial. First, not all observers agree on the specific values that should constitute the criteria of worth. Some attach the highest value to personal freedom; thus, if a country demonstrates a high amount of freedom for its citizens, it is a better society. Others believe that public order and personal security are primary values. According to their logic, if individuals live in a violent country characterized by the war of all against all, then individuals have little opportunity to realize their freedom. In this sense, the freedom to challenge the established authority of police officers and court judges may come into conflict with public order. These analysts believe that a balance between public order and individual freedom should be achieved.

Second, disagreements arise about the best ways to measure such abstract values as freedom and justice. Among democratic societies, analysts have the opportunities to choose diverse operational indicators. In dictatorial societies, however, government officials deny political scientists the right to carry out "dangerous" research on freedom and justice. Thus, virtually no information may be available about the behavior of the police, the operation of the courts, and treatment within prisons.

INTERDEPENDENCE OF THE OBJECTIVES

Description, explanation, and evaluation constitute three primary purposes of comparative analysis. Each one depends on the others: Just as valid explanations depend on accurate descriptive information, so evaluations rest on valid description and explanation. Political scientists find it difficult to achieve accurate descriptive comparisons, particularly outside the United States. Today more than 150 different political systems operate in the world. We know far more about homicide in North America, West Europe, and Japan than in other countries where government leaders erect obstacles to political research. Yet without accurate descriptive information for a wide range of systems, we cannot be sure that explanatory statements about the causes of homicide really are general—that is, applicable to all societies, not just two or three.

Evaluation also requires descriptive knowledge and explanations that specify relationships among individual, cultural, and structural variables. If we have not examined a large number of countries, then we are hardly in a position to proclaim that Sweden or the United States has a better political system than any other. If we fail to explain the linkages between homicide and criminal justice policies (behavior of police, court officials, and prison officers), then we cannot claim that public policies in Sweden and Japan more effectively reduce the murder rate than do American policies. The conclusions political scientists reach thus rest on a tentative foundation. As new information is accumulated, theoretical assumptions undergo revision. This constant interaction between theoretical generalizations and empirical statements helps us better understand the performance of individuals and systems in different countries.

Methods of Comparison

How do social scientists compare different political systems? Appropriate methods involve several steps:

1. Stating the analytical puzzle to be resolved
2. Formulating hypotheses or explanatory generalizations that suggest the reasons behind a particular condition, such as homicide rates
3. Collecting information about the dependent and independent variables—the effect and assumed "causes"
4. Analyzing and interpreting the data, a task that involves matching the degree of correspondence between the hypotheses and the empirical observations

STATEMENT OF ANALYTICAL PUZZLE

Before finding the answers to individual behavior and systemic operation, we must pose theoretically interesting questions. The questions are often more important than the tentative answers. Robert

Coles, a Harvard psychologist, interviewed the maid of a wealthy girl in New Orleans. The maid told Coles:

> Remember that you're put here only for a few seconds of God's time, and He's testing you. He doesn't want answers, though. He wants you to know how to ask the right questions. ... I'm poor but at least I know that I should ask myself every day, Where's your destination, and are you going there, or are you getting sidetracked?[6]

Because nobody can possibly compare all aspects of two or more political systems, posing the "right questions" becomes important to avoid getting sidetracked in a wilderness of factual minutiae. Political scientists must compare a *few aspects* of individual behavior and systemic performance, not the whole system. If someone asked you to compare the United States, Japan, and Sweden, where would you begin? What aspects of these three countries would you explore? Cultural values? Economic conditions? Individual perceptions and motivations? The possibilities are limitless. Even a study of only three individuals in different countries—Juan, Setsuko, and Erik, for example—poses difficulties. Individuals, like societies, are complex entities performing several different activities. We need to focus on a few key features of their behavior, such as strength of self-esteem, intensity of frustration, and degree of aggressive behavior. Because of these complexities of individual behavior and societal performance, political scientists engaged in comparative research must make explicit their analytical problems.

The analytical problem should pose a puzzle to solve, a series of questions to explore. For example, why does the United States have a higher homicide rate than Japan or Sweden? What is the impact of public policies—expenditures for police, lengthy prison sentences, the abolition of capital punishment—on the murder rate? Why does Japan have a higher degree of social solidarity than America? To what extent does national participation in war increase aggressive tendencies among individuals living in that country? All these questions specify a behavior pattern, a structural condition, or an event that needs explaining.

The analytical problem should posit some relationships among two or more variables. Types of relationships take the following forms:

1. *What variables explain some effect?* For example, what variables explain political assassinations, homicide rates, and participation in war among different countries?
2. *Is there a relationship between two variables?* For instance, does a highly centralized, coercive state make life less nasty, brutish, and short, as the English philosopher Thomas Hobbes implied? What association exists between the centralization of police forces

and murder rates? Does punitive, lengthy treatment in prison reduce the homicide rate? Does the abolition of capital punishment increase or decrease homicidal behavior?

3. *What variables explain the relationship between two factors?* Say that a political scientist found a high correlation between ethnic heterogeneity and the homicide rate; that is, those countries characterized by many ethnic groups have a higher murder rate. What are the reasons for this assumed relationship? Do the diverse ethnic groups hold divergent cultural beliefs about the exercise of violence? What are the unemployment rates and degrees of income inequality among ethnic groups? To what extent do members of various ethnic groups feel alienated from the political power structure, especially the police? What is the extent of family disintegration within each ethnic group? Among all these variables—cultural beliefs, economic conditions, political alienation, and family cohesion—which ones best explain the relationship between ethnic heterogeneity and homicide across several countries?

Sources of information about the analytical problem should be available. At least some of the variables should be empirically observable. For instance, few contemporary political scientists would choose to explore this question: How many demons in the human body are needed to stimulate a person to commit murder? Although we can observe a murder, most social scientists cannot empirically observe demons; therefore, the counting process becomes difficult. Unfortunately, some of the most theoretically interesting variables cannot be easily measured in most parts of the world. For instance, cultural values undoubtedly affect human behavior, including homicides. Yet we do not observe values directly but infer them indirectly through the overt behavior of individuals and the activities of social structures. Verbal responses to sample surveys represent one technique for ascertaining the extent to which people in a society share a certain belief. Observing rituals and festivals, reading folk tales, listening to popular songs, and peering at art objects also give clues about societal values. By observing all these behaviors, comparative analysts impute values to societies. However, they often lack the information to understand the precise ways values shape individual behavior. Some values, such as freedom, equality, and achievement, are so general that they can be interpreted to justify any behavior, whether violent or nonviolent. For these reasons, the political scientist needs to gain information about individual attitudes toward authority and toward the use of violence to attain goals. Yet in most parts of the world, the information is difficult to obtain. Information about patterns of small-group interaction within the family, work group, and neighborhood gang also remains elusive.

Finally, the analytical problem should pose questions of moral and theoretical significance. Politics, like religion, concerns moral values—that is, questions of freedom, equality, justice, virtue, order, and equity. Since the time of Plato and Aristotle, political theorists have explored the conditions under which a political system will best realize some of these moral values. Rank-and-file individuals also share a public interest in the ethical conditions of their societies. Most people prefer living in a society where few homicides threaten personal security. Certainly, murder victims and their families would like to see governments take effective steps to reduce the homicide rate.

Not only moral significance but also theoretical criteria should guide the selection of analytical topics for investigation. Theories are sets of generalizations that explain relationships among variables. Because individual behavior and system performance are so complex, theories are needed as a conceptual map for exploring the political universe. By specifying particular variables as crucial, theories establish criteria of significance (that is, the aspects of sociopolitical life most important to examine). Theoretically derived variables represent guideposts that organize complex information into simpler categories for investigation. Because theories posit certain similarities (regularities of behavior) and direct our attention to departures from these similarities, they facilitate comparative analysis. Most important, theories help explain individual behavior and system performance. Theoretical statements usually make assumptions about the relationships among social conditions (cultural beliefs, sociopolitical structures), individual motives, personal actions, and the consequences of behavior on the wider social system. By so doing, theories can help us understand the reasons for the varying homicide rates among different individuals and societies.

FORMULATION OF TENTATIVE ANSWERS

After selecting a theoretically interesting topic, the comparative analyst must formulate a series of hypotheses that provide tentative answers to the puzzles under investigation. Hypotheses, which assume a certain relationship among variables, derive from general theories. The social-learning theory sketched by Albert Bandura provides an appropriate theoretical perspective for explaining the causes of homicide.[7]

Social-learning theory. Social-learning theorists assume that all behavior, including homicidal behavior, results from the interaction between individual and environmental variables. Although specific individuals, not general society, commit murders, individuals live in a particular social context. The causes of crime thus do not stem from inborn aggressive instincts or XYY chromosome patterns. Rather, as Bandura has pointed out, aggression, crime, and violence are socially learned behaviors. True, individuals partly create their own environments. Yet environmental factors such as cultural values, small-group pressures, and various rewards and punishments emanating from authority figures shape individual behavior. According to Bandura, human behaviors "result from reciprocal interaction of external circumstances with a host of personal determinants, including endowed potentialities, acquired competencies, reflective thought, and a high level of self-initiative."[8]

The social-learning theory of aggressive behavior makes the following assumptions about the interaction among beliefs, the means used to realize these values, and the outcomes of the activities. Beliefs serve several functions: They shape goals, encourage specific activities, restrain other actions, and justify choices. According to social-learning theorists, cultural beliefs legitimate violence, including murder, in several ways. First, individuals justify violence in terms of high moral principles. Violence against evil people is regarded as morally good. Political ideologies and religious beliefs have legitimated unusual cruelty and murder by linking barbaric practices to righteous principles. For example, Hitler viewed aggression against the Jews and Marxists as ethically righteous; it embodied the ultimate realization of German manhood. Other fanatics may also perceive the murder of "evil" people as a normative end.

Second, beliefs often justify homicide not as a valuable end in itself but as the most functionally useful means to secure a concrete benefit. It has functional value for survival in a world filled with scarce resources and violent conflicts to obtain these resources. Under certain conditions, such as armed robbery, murderers justify their crimes as functionally necessary to attain the economic rewards.

Third, some beliefs encourage people to deny responsibility for the effects of their aggressive actions. Murderers often claim that they lack control over their actions: "The devil made me do it." Aggressive individuals also deny the harmful consequences of their actions on others; they selectively forget or ignore the fate suffered by the victims and their relatives.

Fourth, individuals often justify homicide by blaming the victims rather than themselves. By acting in a bad or objectionable way, the victim of murder supposedly "deserved" to die. A high proportion of homicides occur against close relatives or friends of the murderer, who may excuse his crime by accusing the victim of mistreating him.[9]

Individuals learn to attain goals through both direct experience and the observation of others. People who grow up in a violent environment directly experience ways to use guns and commit murders. Yet for most people, modeling—the observation and imitation of others—constitutes the main mode of learning. By observing other persons perform certain activities, individuals gain the information and the motives (the valued incentives) to commit violent crimes.

Social-learning theory stresses the actual and anticipated consequences of behavior; these outcomes represent "reinforcements" that strengthen a behavioral pattern. Criticizing the "frustration–aggression" formulation behind violent behavior, Bandura observes:

> Behavior is extensively controlled by its consequences. Responses that cause unrewarding or punishing effects tend to be discarded, whereas those that produce rewarding outcomes are retained and strengthened.... A culture can produce highly aggressive people, while keeping frustration at a low level, by valuing aggressive accomplishments, furnishing aggressive models, and ensuring that aggressive actions secure rewarding effects. Since aggression does not originate internally and its social determinants are alterable, social learning theory holds a more optimistic view of man's capacity to reduce the level of human destructiveness.[10]

According to social-learning theory, behavior can have rewarding, punitive, or neutral consequences. When individuals receive rewards, they gain access to valued resources, including weapons, material benefits, approval, and information. "Punishment" refers to the deprivation of resources. Not all rewards and punishments are directly experienced. To gain compliance to established authority, political leaders can promise future rewards as well as threaten to deny valued resources; in the latter case, these threats of punishment act as a *deterrent* to future behavior. Thus, fear of punishment restrains homicidal tendencies.

Bandura distinguishes among three types of rewards and punishments.[11] First, some are *concrete* and others are more *symbolic*. Although many people in industrial societies seek concrete benefits, such as income and property, not everyone places priority on these material payoffs. Some persons actually behave according to symbolic values, including moral principles and normative restraints. They avoid committing murder not because they coolly weigh the relative rewards and punishments on a utilitarian calculus but because they regard law-abiding behavior as an ethical end in itself. For them, human life as a moral value takes precedence over the presumed tangible payoffs from murder.

Second, we can distinguish *extrinsic* from *intrinsic* consequences. Extrinsic rewards and punishments arise from other persons. Approval from others represents a valued reward; condemnation from others brings punishment. Other reinforcements, however, are self-produced. For example, self-esteem and self-respect are internal rewards; similarly, self-blame and self-censure constitute intrinsic types of punishment. Often a conflict arises between the external outcomes and the self-produced consequences. Prison treatments stressing external material rewards but minimizing the importance of internal rewards such as self-esteem may not deter future aggressive behavior.

Third, reinforcements can be *directly experienced* or *anticipated*. Not all rewards and punishments are directly experienced. More frequently, individuals vicariously observe the consequences that arise from other people's behavior. Depending on their rationality, they can also anticipate the possible outcomes of taking a specific action. The deterrence theory of homicidal behavior assumes that most people have the cognitive ability to anticipate future punishments, to evaluate the relative costs of engaging in murder, and to take appropriate actions. If the anticipated punishment is certain, severe, and immediate, then presumably the individual will not commit murder.

Social-learning theory assumes that as a deterrent to homicide, rewards are generally more effective than punishments. Deterrence works best when high risks of punishment result from committing a violent crime. Those persons at the top of the social stratification system—that is, individuals with the most political power, wealth, and status—have the most to lose if their homicides lead them to prison. In contrast, persons at the bottom of the stratification totem pole have less to lose if apprehended and convicted for murder.

Most murderers come from a punitive environment; they often experienced harsh discipline as children. Rather than deterring future violent crime, these punitive agents—fathers, gang leaders—serve as models for violent behavior. Through observing those who punish them, individuals gain information about ways to act aggressively—for example, methods for using a handgun or a knife. They also become motivated to commit violence if they see that the punitive agents justify their use of force as either morally good or functionally useful.

Frequent experiences of harsh, arbitrary punishment may develop feelings of injustice in the victims. Particularly if authority figures exercise inconsistent punishment over time and do not act according to settled rules, people may act in a violent way to right real or imagined wrongs.

Punishment tends to weaken moral restraints; people come to comply out of fear. Because deterrence works most effectively when a supervisory agent is always present to monitor behavior, the political regime needs to employ a high degree of coercion. Yet democratic government can hardly station a police officer in every home, business, or street. Hence, democratic societies depend on internal moral restraints, rather than punitive agents such as police, to discourage murder.

Finally, not everybody seeks to avoid punishment; some actually pursue it. Each individual attributes a distinctive meaning to the consequences of his or her behavior; some persons may even subjectively perceive a supposedly objective punishment as a reward. Rather than deterring murder, capital punishment may actually relieve a murderer's feelings of guilt. Execution in the gas chamber may bring public notoriety, which the murderer may interpret as a reward.[12]

Social-learning theorists do not assume that punishment exerts no effects on the reduction of homicide. To the extent that it highlights the disadvantageous consequences of murder and also stimulates fearful attitudes, punishment may "work." Especially if punishment is certain, severe, and immediate, it may inhibit tendencies to commit murder. Of course, punishment also isolates a murderer from the rest of society, either temporarily or permanently, as is the case with capital punishment. Imprisonment may bring moral condemnation to murderers. Stigmatized for their crimes, they may not only lose their personal freedom but also suffer disapproval of their friends, separation from their families, and loss of their jobs.[13] In all these ways, punishment may restrain potential murderers. Yet for most persons, rewards for nonviolent behavior seem a more effective strategy for reducing the homicide rate.

In summary, according to social-learning theory, an individual's tendency to engage in homicide depends on three types of controls: moral restraints, state punishment, and small-group pressures. First, some individuals have internalized cultural beliefs that restrain the use of violence; for these people, moral restraints embedded in the conscience inhibit violent crime. Second, the decision to commit homicide is affected by the political controls of the state manifested in the actions of the police, judges, and prison officials. In this case, fear of punishment by government agencies motivates nonviolent behavior. Third, the values articulated by small-group leaders, as well as the rewards and punishments meted out in such small groups as the family, neighborhood, youth gang, or work mates, also shape the expression of aggression. Individuals may either gain acceptance from the group by acting violently or else lose small-group approval when they commit violent actions. Some social scientists assume that because individuals directly participate in small groups, the values, rewards, and punishments experienced in the group setting more effectively restrain potential homicidal behavior than do state sanctions.[14] By the same reasoning, if individuals never develop any internal normative restraints against homicide and remain isolated from nonviolent group pressures, they may become deranged and act out their aggressive fantasies in murderous deeds.

Specific hypotheses. From these general theoretical perspectives of the social-learning paradigm emerge the following specific hypotheses that help explain the higher homicide rate in the United States than in Japan or Sweden. I classify the hypotheses around three general dimensions: cultural beliefs, operation of the criminal justice system, and social-structural conditions (degrees of economic inequality and unemployment, large-scale population patterns, and small-group interactions). These dimensions correspond to the three types of controls on individual behavior—moral restraints, state sanctions, and small-group pressures. According to these hypotheses, a nation will show a high homicide rate if the following conditions occur:

1. *Cultural beliefs:* (a) Cultural beliefs strongly justify the use of violence for "good" ends. (b) A distrustful attitude toward political authority characterizes the relations between citizens and police.
2. *Operation of the criminal justice system:* (c) People can easily commit homicide: Weapons are widely accessible. Understaffed police fail to restrain violent behavior. (d) The probability of arresting a murderer is low. (e) Punishment is distant, not immediate; a long time elapses between a person's arrest for murder and conviction for homicide. (f) A person convicted of homicide receives uncertain and lenient punishment.
3. *Social-structural conditions:* (g) High economic inequalities separate the poor citizens from the rich. (h) A society faces high unemployment, especially among young men between fifteen and twenty-four years of age. (i) The society is highly urbanized; collective solidarity, shared norms (rules of behavior), and established agents of social control remain weak in the cities. (j) A high percentage of young men between fifteen and twenty-four live in the society; the traditional social controls of family, school, and church exercise a weak restraint over their behavior. (k) High heterogeneity divides different ethnic groups, which show divergent degrees of wealth, political power, and family disintegration. (l) Strong informal social controls by small groups reward the expression of aggression and fail to punish violent behavior.

COLLECTION OF INFORMATION

Only through the collection of information about the independent and dependent variables (the assumed causes of the effect—homicide) can we determine the relative plausibility of these hypotheses.

Presumably, not all these hypotheses are equally valid. Data collection involves two steps: choosing the units for comparison and then selecting the techniques for gathering information about these units.

Although this chapter compares the homicide rate in three national societies—the United States, Japan, and Sweden—several other units remain open for comparison. These include individuals, groups, neighborhoods, cities, states or provinces, and regions. For example, social-learning theory makes assumptions not just about social conditions but about individuals' behavior. Because individuals, not society or the unemployment rate, commit specific murders, we need information about the personalities, attitudes, beliefs, perceptions, and motives of particular individuals and the ways they respond to environmental conditions—unemployment, economic inequalities, peer group pressures, and police sanctions. Although few social scientists have carried out this research, a random sample survey of nonmurderers and persons convicted of homicide in different countries could shed light on the interaction between individual characteristics and social conditions.

Groups also offer worthwhile comparisons. Either within a nation or among different countries, political scientists can compare diverse social groups, neighborhoods, cities, and states or provinces. For instance, why do Mexican Americans have a lower murder rate than do Blacks? Why do Tokyo and Stockholm experience lower homicide rates than New York City? Why does the state of North Dakota have a lower murder rate than the state of Nevada? (The rate for 100,000 persons in 1976 was 1.4 in North Dakota, compared with 11.5 for Nevada.)[15] Why are the homicide rates for North Dakota, Sweden, and Japan roughly similar? What social conditions do they share? We may also want to compare regional clusters of nations and discover if capitalist nations have higher homicide rates than communist or nonaligned countries. Do Asians face greater murder threats than Latin Americans?

Comparative analysts have used four primary techniques for collecting information: examination of written and visual records, observation, oral interviews and written questionnaires, and laboratory experiments. When examining written documents or observing what people say and do, political scientists record information that already exists. However, using the techniques of oral interviews and experimentation, they exercise greater initiative in creating new data that formerly did not exist for analysis.

Written and visual records constitute the primary source of information for most political scientists. The *World Health Statistics Annual* contains cross-national data about homicide rates. By examining economic reports, statistical yearbooks, census reports, police records, and court proceedings across several countries, they can gain indicators of unemployment rates, ethnic heterogeneity, age-group patterns, the percentage of homicides reported to the police cleared by arrest, the number of persons sent to prison for homicide as a proportion of the total number of offenses for homicide, and the median time spent in prison by convicted murderers prior to parole. Newspapers report the number of political officials assassinated each year. Through these press accounts, we can ascertain in several nations the proportion of officials actually murdered or against whom assassination attempts were made. A content analysis of motion pictures or television programs provides information about the percentage of characters involved in the overt expression of violent behavior and the number of aggressive incidents, especially killings, taking place during each minute of film.

The observation of behavior can proceed in a relatively detached or else participant manner. David Bayley investigated Japanese police behavior by riding with Tokyo police officers in their patrol cars.[16] Some American social scientists become police officers to gain a greater understanding of police values and behavior. Others go to prison to observe the types and extent of punitive treatment. Anthropologists used to live several years in a village observing small-group behavior; they could see in a specific context the impact of family pressures, youth group controls, and workplace sanctions on individual behavior. Observation of rituals, festivals, and child-rearing practices may give clues about basic values in a society, particularly attitudes toward authority and justifications of violence. Outside the United States, American social scientists find it more difficult to act as participants than detached observers. For this reason, since the Second World War, they have engaged in collaborative research projects with foreign social scientists.

Similarly, oral interviews and written questionnaires require close interaction between American and foreign researchers. A particular verbal response makes sense only in a broader context. An interviewer may talk to individuals about their attitudes toward authority, their dependence on small groups, and their perceptions about the certainty of punishment. The analyst may distribute a written questionnaire to ascertain the prevalence of authoritarian personalities in a group. But the researcher needs to interpret these verbal responses to oral interviews and written questionnaires according to the distinctive linguistic context of each society. Compared with Americans, Japanese social scientists will likely have more perceptive insights into both the denotative and the connotative meanings of words; that is, they better understand the literal, explicit meanings and, more important, the vaguer implications behind verbal responses.[17]

Although laboratory experiments are the least widely used technique for gathering information, they offer the best means to test the causal validity of certain hypotheses. Naturally, ethical considerations preclude the choice of murder as a dependent variable for laboratory experimenters to manipulate. Yet experiments can probe explanations for the aggressive behavior of individuals and small groups. The experimenter randomly assigns individuals to two groups. The *experimental* group is exposed to some independent variable, such as aggressive stimuli in a highly violent film. The *control* group watches a nonviolent film. By randomizing the assignment of individuals to these two groups, the experimenter controls for *extraneous variables* (factors other than the independent variables) that affect an outcome such as aggressive behavior. The experimental and control groups are alike except that the experimental group becomes exposed to the independent variables—violent TV stimuli.

Later the investigator measures the behavioral responses of individual members within the experimental and control groups. Possible indicators of interpersonal aggression include the intensity of electric shock the subjects administer to a presumed "victim." These shocks may range from zero to 450 volts (the highest possible voltage on a shock generator). Finally, the experimenter compares the responses of the two groups. If subjects within the experimental group administer a higher aggregate voltage level than do members of the control group, we assume that the violent film "caused" the aggression because the experimenter found a high correlation between exposure to the violent film and personal aggression. The independent variables (aggressive stimuli in the film) came before the dependent variable (interpersonal aggression as measured by intensity of electric shock). The random assignment of individuals to the control and experimental groups controlled for other extraneous variables that may have produced the aggressive behavior; that is, before exposure to the films, the two groups presumably were alike. By maximizing comparability, the experimenter isolated the precise causal impact of an independent variable.

Despite these advantages for causal analysis, experimental designs have certain deficiencies that limit their applicability to the comparative study of large-scale political systems. Most important, the contexts of the laboratory and the political world differ. First, political activity involves *macro* concerns—the issues of power, authority, legitimacy, a common identity, the distribution of wealth, and the societal impacts of public policies. Citizens' role expectations diverge from those of a subject in an experiment. If a Japanese citizen violates the law against murder, he or she may incur the death penalty. The laboratory experiment deals with more *micro* concerns. Power relationships among subjects and the experimenter differ from power relationships in the wider political order. The sanctions for disobeying the experimenter's legitimate authority are less severe in the experimental situation. Although experimental subjects may receive an electric shock, they will hardly be sent to the electric chair.

Second, the political and experimental worlds have a different orientation toward time. The decisions political leaders and citizens make are based partly on historical considerations; historical events, values, and power relationships shape current choices. However, such historical experiences are usually factored out of a laboratory experiment; the time span of the typical experiment rarely extends beyond a year.

Third, analysts comparing large-scale political systems, such as nations or even cities, can rarely if ever find two societies that are identical except for one or two features. Because they, unlike the experimenter, cannot control for extraneous factors, valid causal statements become difficult to make.[18] In short, experimental designs provide the best instrument for testing causal hypotheses. Yet the findings reached in the experimental situation show only a weak correspondence with explanations for behavior in political contexts across nations.

ANALYSIS AND INTERPRETATION

After collecting information about the independent and dependent variables, the comparative political scientist analyzes the data. Facts rarely speak for themselves; rather, they must be interpreted in terms of some theory. The analyst plays a creative role in attributing general significance to specific findings. Several questions become important: To what extent do the data confirm the hypotheses? Why do some hypotheses seem more valid than others across different countries? What qualifications should be made about their validity? The analyst usually lacks information about all the independent variables. Often the theory used for analyzing the data cannot account for all the precise interactions among the variables. For this reason, we cannot fully explain some phenomena, such as the cross-national causes of homicide. Comparative investigations thus remain open-ended; the most theoretically useful studies suggest future questions to probe and avenues of inquiry that need more exploration. The following sections highlight some generalizations about the reasons behind the higher homicide rate in the United States than in Sweden or Japan. Like most cross-national generalizations, these conclusions remain tentative, subject to further investigation and revision.

Cultural beliefs. As social-learning theorists assume, the higher homicide rate in the United States than in Sweden or Japan stems from certain values that justify aggressive means to attain desired ends. Americans consider the ends more important than the means. As the late football coach Vince Lombardi once commented, "Winning is not the main thing; it's the only thing." Despite the legalistic framework of American political life, Americans historically have shown a stronger commitment to success than to nonviolent, legal means to reach goals. Perhaps reflecting the frontier tradition, interpersonal relations often seem brusque and aggressive; individuals are anxious to assert their personal will against other people, who are treated as means toward the individual's success.

In contrast, although both the Swedes and Japanese value self-achievement, they place greater priority on the rules of the game than do Americans. For them, playing by the rules becomes just as important as winning: "It's not whether you win or lose, it's how you play the game." In Japan and Sweden, decorum and ritual pervade social interactions. Adhering to norms of politesse, people act with caution, reserve, and restraint toward others. Even radical Japanese students opposing government policies carry out their protests in a decorous, restrained manner. The Swedes probably feel a greater horror of violence than do the Japanese. They depend on proper norms of etiquette to regulate interpersonal behavior, as one Scandinavian joke illustrates: If two Danes, two Norwegians, and two Swedes found themselves shipwrecked on a deserted island, the Norwegians would go swimming, the Danes would set up a cooperative, and the Swedes would wait for the others to introduce them to the group.[19]

Attitudes toward authority, which reflect beliefs about the most appropriate means to attain goals, partly account for the three countries' different homicide rates. Both the Japanese and the Swedes display greater respect for authority; they more readily accept the legitimacy of the existing governmental institutions, including the police agencies. For citizens in these two nations, an agreement to show self-discipline and abide by the law seems necessary to preserve public order. Rather than challenging the state and the wider community, the individual realizes his or her goals through cooperating with the government and social groups.

In contrast, the typical American expresses more distrustful attitudes toward political authority. Taking a more assertive, aggressive view of governmental authority, he or she interprets freedom to mean the right to remain independent of bureaucratic government control and to achieve success regardless of community restraints. According to this American perspective, authority figures and governmental rules appear as obstacles to individual success, rather than as facilitators to eventual goal attainment. Whereas Americans have traditionally perceived an antagonism between individual freedom and state authority, Japanese and Swedes have tried to reconcile freedom and authority.

These divergent attitudes toward authority appear particularly striking in the relationship between citizens and police. Compared with Japanese, Americans show greater willingness to challenge police authority. As David Bayley points out:

> In both Japan and the United States the characteristic stance of offenders in the face of authority complements the role-definition of the police. An American accused by a policeman is very likely to respond "Why me?" A Japanese more often says, "I'm sorry." The American shows anger, the Japanese shame. An American contests the accusation and tries to humble the policeman; a Japanese accepts the accusation and tries to kindle benevolence.[20]

Although Swedish citizens probably do not take such a deferential view of the police, they too, like the Japanese, perceive the police officer as a helpful authority figure in the community. National sample surveys taken during the early 1970s revealed that over 90 percent of Swedish citizens found the police a likable, helpful presence. In Sweden, the police carry out a greater variety of social services than in America. They organize youth clubs, assist the unemployed, help the aged, present puppet shows for children, teach bicycle and motorcycle courses to teenagers, collect Christmas parcels for older people, establish hobby clubs, provide transportation to the local market, and even set up crime prevention clinics. Highly trained and professionally organized, the Swedish police perform as efficient, helpful civil servants. Citizens respect them for their expertise, specialized skill, technical competence, and scientific knowledge used to assist the community and to solve crimes.[21]

Less pressured by challenges to their authority, Japanese and Swedish police rarely use violence. Most Japanese police officers carry no guns. Although Swedish police officers wear a gun, they rarely shoot to kill; instead, they usually fire shots in the air to warn a suspected criminal. In contrast, American police officers have more openly displayed their coercive power. All officers wear guns. Few regulations limit the use of force. The local district attorney rarely prosecutes a police officer who has killed a civilian. Grand juries usually do not indict police charged with using excessive coercion. Even if charged, an officer rarely gets convicted. Armed with the means of coercion and subject to fewer legal restraints than in Sweden or Japan, the American police exercise their authority in a more violent manner. Young males from ethnic minority groups, especially Blacks and the Spanish-speaking, receive the greatest verbal and physical harassment from American police officers. As expected, national sample surveys reveal that Blacks under thirty-five years of age have far less respect for the local police than do white citizens of all ages. The resentful attitudes toward the police thus parallel the coercive treatment meted out to them.[22]

In sum, living in a violent, antiauthority society where legal restrictions fail to limit the use of guns by both police and civilians, the American police exercise their authority in a comparatively coercive manner. Swedish and Japanese police feel less challenge to their authority; as a result, they emphasize the more consensual aspects of their authority role.

Social-learning theorists' hypotheses suggest some reasons behind the correlation between a higher homicide rate and more severe treatment shown by police authorities. First, severe punishment by police officers may help legitimate the exercise of violence in general. Second, people learn by observing others' behavior; for some individuals, police violence serves as a model of behavior to imitate. Third, especially if the police treat some groups more coercively than others for the same type of behavior, police coercion may stimulate anger and a sense of injustice. That anger may be channeled into aggressive actions. Fourth, punishment operates most effectively when the punitive agent is present. Because punishment produces greater changes in outer conformity than in internal norms, the political elite needs a vast police state apparatus to regulate behavior.[23] Although dictatorial states can frighten their citizens into nonviolent submission to political authority, few democratic regimes seem willing to rely on extensive repression as the primary means to maintain order.

Criminal justice system operation. Despite the reliance on consensual power in a democratic society, a rise in the homicide rate may provoke support for a greater use of coercion by "cops, courts, and corrections." According to this view, if more police are hired, police officers restrict access to handguns, police officers arrest a high percentage of suspected murderers, and judges sentence convicted murderers to long prison terms or execution, then the homicide rates will be lower. To what extent do the criminal justice policies enacted in the United States, Japan, and Sweden support these assumptions of deterrence theory?

One reason the United States has a higher homicide rate than Sweden or Japan may stem from the greater availability of guns in America. Although people, not guns, commit murder, those persons with a will to injure others need appropriate ways. Widespread access to firearms makes homicide an easier, more convenient, and more efficient activity. The distribution of weapons per person is higher in the United States than in Sweden or Japan; as a result, deaths from firearms occur more frequently. For example, in 1971, the gun homicide rate for every 100,000 persons was 5.5 in America, 0.2 in Sweden, and close to zero in Japan. Whereas only about 5 percent of Japanese murderers used a gun, about two-thirds of American murder victims died from gunshot wounds.[24]

Both the Swedish and Japanese governments have enacted strict gun control legislation. In Japan, only hunters and police own guns; laws forbid citizens the right to possess handguns. The police register firearms, knives, swords, and ammunition. Similar regulations in Sweden restrict guns to hunting purposes. By contrast, the United States has far more permissive laws about the importation, sale, and possession of firearms. The widespread availability of guns makes it easy for murderers to act out their aggressive impulses.

Yet a comparison with Swiss gun control policy suggests that attitudes toward the use of weapons, rather than mere availability, lead to a high American homicide rate. Like the early American settlers, Swiss men participate in a citizen-soldier force or militia. Nearly all men between twenty and fifty years of age serve in the citizen army; they keep rifles, revolvers, and occasionally automatic weapons with them in their homes. However, the Swiss homicide rate is slightly lower than the Swedish and Japanese rates. The few homicides that do occur rarely involve handguns.

Unlike the Swiss, American police and citizens identify guns with independence, manhood, and the assertion of authority. As B. Bruce-Briggs points out, the opponents of gun control assume as their model "the independent frontiersman who takes care of himself and his family with no interference from the state. They are 'conservative' in the sense that they cling to America's unique premodern tradition—a nonfeudal society with a sort of medieval liberty writ large for everyman. To these people . . . life is tough and competitive. Manhood means responsibility and caring for your own."[25] Americans have historically romanticized the use of a gun. Such interest groups as the National Rifle Association have convinced lawmakers to oppose strict controls on gun possession. Therefore, neither state nor national legislators have taken effective steps to restrict the ownership and sale of firearms.

Although the addition of more officers to the police force may facilitate apprehending a suspected murderer, cross-nationally the homicide rate does not seem to depend on the size of the police force. During the mid 1970s, the United States had a higher police–citizen ratio (around 30 police officers for every 10,000 persons) than did Japan or Sweden, where about 18 police officers served each 10,000 individuals. Yet the two less well staffed nations had lower homicide rates. Probably the performance of the police and their location in particular geographical areas of large cities, rather than their ratio to the national population, more accurately account for violent crimes.[26]

The certainty of arrest seems to exert a stronger deterrent effect on potential murderers than the mere ratio of police to citizens. The Japanese police clear by arrest a higher proportion of reported murders than do American police; for instance, during the late 1970s, the "clearance rates" were 96 percent for Japan and 76 percent for the United States.[27] Although precise data are unavailable for Sweden, the Swedish figures probably more closely approximate the Japanese clearance rates.

Compared with American police officers, the Japanese and Swedish police officers operate a more professionalized force; they receive higher education and more specialized training. Living in smaller, more centralized political systems, they can more effectively apprehend a suspected murderer. In contrast, American police must perform within a large territorial area populated by diverse groups. Because of the decentralized American federal system, overlapping jurisdictions are common. The specific responsibilities of the Federal Bureau of Investigation, the state police, and the city or town police remain vague. These law enforcement agencies often fail to coordinate their activities. A murderer may flee from one jurisdiction to another in which the chances of apprehension remain less certain. In short, because different police agencies throughout the country practice diverse degrees of efficiency in arresting suspected murderers, the certainty of apprehension serves as a less effective deterrent in America. However, in Sweden and Japan all the police forces function within a single national, centralized agency. National police agencies secure more uniform, coordinated, and efficient police operations throughout their countries.[28]

As variables explaining the homicide rates in Japan, Sweden, and the United States, the immediacy of punishment has greater impact than either the certainty or the severity of punitive treatment. In Sweden and Japan, a relatively brief time elapses between an arrest for homicide and conviction by a court. This period usually lasts no more than a year; most often, the criminal justice personnel imprison a convicted murderer within three to six months after the commission of the crime. By contrast, in the United States, the prosecution of an individual arrested for homicide takes a longer time, averaging from eighteen months to two years.

In the United States, Sweden, and Japan, greater certainty of imprisonment is linked to higher, not lower, homicide rates. During the mid 1970s, nearly 30 percent of Japanese convicted for murder received a suspended sentence. Over the same period, most Swedish murderers—around 75 percent—were placed in closed psychiatric care. The National Board of Health and Welfare, not the National Prison and Probation Administration, administered this psychiatric treatment. About one-fourth of the murderers went to prison. In the United States, the courts sentenced about 80 percent of convicted murderers to prison; approximately one-fifth won probation.[29] Thus, the country in which murderers faced the greatest likelihood of imprisonment had the highest homicide rate.

Criminologists studying the causes of violent crimes focus on three aspects of severity of punishment: (1) the length of the sentences, (2) the degree of punitive treatment within the prison, and (3) the use of capital punishment. Contrary to expectations of deterrence theory, the length of a prison sentence fails to explain the different homicide rates between the United States and the other two nations. In Japan and Sweden, fewer than 1 percent of all criminals are sent to prison for life, compared with 9 percent in the United States. Most Japanese found guilty of homicide remain imprisoned for fewer than five years. Only about half the Swedish murderers receive a legal prison sentence lasting over four years. Even those few sentenced to life imprisonment gain their freedom after eight to ten years. The homicide offenders who receive closed psychiatric treatment usually serve shorter sentences than the convicted murderers sent to prison. Despite the shorter sentences for homicide in Japan and Sweden, these two countries have a lower homicide rate than the United States, where murderers spend a longer time in prison before their release on parole—a national median average of five years, two months from 1971 through 1977.[30]

The lower Japanese and Swedish homicide rates also do not stem from the harsher treatment received in prison; on the contrary, prisoners endure less severe punishment in Japan and Sweden than in the United States. Especially since the close of World War II, Swedish and Japanese political leaders have attempted to establish a nonpunitive prison environment. They do not stress isolation from society but instead prepare a prisoner for reemergence into the outside world.

The Swedish government officials have concentrated the greatest attention on developing nonpunitive programs. Prison officials there consider an inmate's loss of freedom the main punishment. They exercise a relatively low degree of coercive power. Guards carry no weapons. Corporal punishment is rarely used. No prisoners experience solitary confinement. One-third of all Swedish prisoners stay in open prisons, where few restrictions regulate their personal behavior. No bars or high walls intimidate the inmates. The main form of punishment is the threat of a return to a closed prison if the prisoner misbehaves.

The Swedish political system allows a high degree of civil and personal liberties for prisoners. Inmates have the right to join unions to articulate their demands. An organization of prisoners, exprisoners, and intellectuals named KRUM (The Association for the Humanizing of the Penal System) has actively campaigned for penal reform since 1966. Several prisoners have witnessed the formation of staff–prisoners' councils to discuss the inmates' specific grievances. Prisoners can appeal to the national judicial ombudsman for a redress of grievances. They have the right to vote in national elections; political party leaders visit the prisons campaigning for votes. Although prison officials do search incoming mail for drugs and weapons, they generally avoid censoring outgoing mail. Prisoners enjoy not only considerable and extensive civil liberties but also personal freedoms, especially in the open prisons. Most can take home leaves and furloughs six times a year. Some prisons even pay the inmates the market wage for constructing houses and working in light engineering.

Rather than isolating prisoners from the rest of society, Swedish prison officials have tried to develop some ties between the prisoners and those outside the penal institution. Prisoners have the opportunity to leave the prison every three or four months to visit an ill relative, to hunt for a job, and to take a paid vacation. Even more serious criminals in the closed prisons participate in this furlough system. Many Swedish prisoners work outside the prison, where they can participate in trade union activities. Leaders in the local area maintain frequent contacts with inmates. For example, local ministers, instead of special prison clergy, offer religious guidance. Local educational authorities provide prison education. Prison libraries are a part of local public libraries. In all these ways, Swedish prison officials try to integrate prison life with the local communities, thereby hoping to expose the inmates to a continuous pattern of noncriminal reinforcements.[31]

In Japan as well, the correctional institutions operate a comparatively nonpunitive program. Officials stress work and educational activities. Prison industries employ about 90 percent of inmates, who learn woodcraft, molding, printing, and tailoring trades. Through vocational training, correspondence courses, and library services, prisoners have the opportunity to gain an education. As in Sweden, the Japanese correctional system emphasizes the need for small-group interaction within the prison and for greater integration between inmates and citizens in the local communities. Prisoners are encouraged to become involved in work groups and club activities. They perform various civic services in the local areas, including repairing bridges, painting lamp posts, tending village shrubs, and helping farmers. Family members and other citizens frequently visit the prisoners, who talk about personal problems, learn a hobby, or plan for life outside the prison when released. In contrast to the American situation, prison officials exercise virtually no supervision of these encounters between inmates and outside visitors.[32]

The American prisons function in a more punitive manner than either the Japanese or especially the Swedish ones. Most prisoners, especially those in local jails and state prisons, must endure severe punishment. Physical brutality from both guards and other inmates is common. Compared with Swedish prisons, the American correctional institutions feature greater overcrowding and higher staff–prisoner ratios. The Swedish government operates small prisons. Whereas the maximum size is 435 inmates, most hold from 20 to 40 prisoners. For every prisoner, there is one staff member. However, the prisoner–staff ratio in most American prisons approaches five inmates for every staff person. City and county jails as well as state prisons are overcrowded. Some contain as many as 1,600 inmates. Under these crowded conditions, there are few opportunities for humane treatment. Corporal punishment and solitary confinement often occur. Guards wield high-powered weapons to maintain order.

American prisoners enjoy few civil or personal liberties. Indeed, during 1977, the Supreme Court even ruled that prison administrators need not necessarily grant prisoner unions the rights to conduct meetings and solicit members within the prison. Because of the need to "preserve order and authority," these unions were denied opportunities to hold meetings and to receive union literature from outside sources. Prison officials suppress political conflicts dealing with legitimacy of prison rules and practices. Violations of petty rules bring severe punitive treatment. For example, in a northeastern youth reformatory for men, the rule book forbade the exchange of library books with other inmates. Any prisoners who violated this edict were sent into solitary confinement, where they had to eat a restricted diet and could read only the Bible and the *Reader's Digest*. Not surprisingly, the inmates viewed the prison environment as a Hobbesian war of all against all. In their opinion, the goal of the prison was to frighten people and force them to behave. They perceived the staff as vengeful people who showed no concern for the prisoner's welfare.[33] Despite these punitive conditions existing not only in the northeast but to a greater extent in other parts of America, the severe punishment has largely failed to deter either those already in prison or those outside thinking about committing a violent crime. As we have seen, Sweden and Japan, with a more nonpunitive prison environment, have lower homicide rates.

Why does a punitive prison system fail to deter homicide? The deterrence principle best applies to those who commit crimes for rational reasons—that is, persons who coldly calculate the relative costs and gains of engaging in criminal behavior. However, most murders seem to occur for less-rational reasons stemming from anger or passion. Indeed, some murderers may even seek to undergo punishment, rather than avoid it. For this reason, increasing the severity may not deter homicides.

Capital punishment represents the severest type of punitive treatment; it too has not operated as an effective deterrent to homicide. Between 1930 and 1980, American state prison authorities directed the execution of nearly 4,000 individuals. William C. Bailey examined several variables associated with capital punishment and the homicide rate. According to his findings, neither the severity of imprisonment (the length of time served in prison for homicide) nor the certainty of the death penalty (the number of executions performed as a percentage of the total number of homicides) was statistically correlated with the homicide rate among different states. Indeed, for 1950 and 1960, the homicide rate was actually slightly lower in states that had abolished the death penalty. Historical studies investigating the impact of capital punishment on homicide rates have found an ambiguous relationship that varies with different time periods. Between 1920 and 1939, the United States had a higher murder rate and more executions than between 1940 and 1959, when both executions for murder and the homicide rate decreased. During the twenty-year period from 1960 through 1979, however, as the risk of execution became lower, the homicide rate rose.[34]

Similarly, in Japan and especially in Sweden, the use or nonuse of capital punishment shows little relationship to the homicide rate. The last execution in Sweden took place in 1910; yet the annual homicide rate per 100,000 persons was higher between 1810 and 1880 than after 1910. Unlike Sweden, Japan has retained the death penalty; from 1973 through 1977, only two to four people were executed each year. Although more yearly executions occurred before than after 1950, the homicide rate has actually declined since 1950.[35] A lower murder rate has thus accompanied less reliance on capital punishment as a deterrent.

Why has capital punishment exerted only a limited impact on the deterrence of murder? The largest percentage of murders occurs against relatives or close friends. Presumably, most of these murderers do not rationally assess the costs and benefits of homicide before they commit aggression; instead, impassioned rage motivates their behavior. Some may be mentally deranged. Others may have an unconscious desire to be punished. Many murderers commit suicide or else want to die for their misdeeds. In sum, the deterrence theory has greater applicability for professional economic crimes; robbers, burglars, and auto thieves seem to behave according to more rational strategies.[36] Yet few people in the Western world recommend that robbers, burglars, or even street muggers receive the death penalty for their crimes.

Social-structural conditions. Even if punitive treatment by the criminal justice system exerts only a weak deterrent impact on the homicide rate, what are the effects of social-structural conditions? *Social structures* refer to the patterns of interaction among individuals, such as economic relationships, demographic patterns, and small-group networks. I will first explore the effects of unemployment rates and income inequalities across nations. Next, I will analyze such demographic variables as the proportion of urban residents, young men, and ethnic minorities in each country. Finally, I will consider the relationship between homicide and the small-group interactions found among families, neighborhoods, youth gangs, and work associates.

Although most homicides do not stem from rational cost–benefit calculations, the economic conditions within a nation do affect the tendencies for particular individuals to commit murder. If a country faces high unemployment and high income inequality, the unemployed and the poor may feel alienated from the existing economic system. The resulting frustration may lead to several possible responses: the unemployed may physically withdraw from one nation and migrate to another in search of work. They may psychologically withdraw from their economic woes, seeking compensation in drugs, alcohol, or religious mysticism. Some of the poor and unemployed may double their efforts to increase their wealth and job prospects at home. Others will express aggression, directed against either the self or other persons. The probabilities of engaging in aggressive homicide depend on early patterns of social learning, especially the rewards and punishments received for violent behavior. Particularly if the poor and unemployed reject cultural beliefs justifying nonviolent responses to economic inequalities, then relative deprivation may become expressed in homicide. Perhaps murder will occur during an armed robbery. Or feelings of low self-esteem and anger will motivate an unemployed person to kill a friend or relative.[37]

Economic conditions within the United States, Japan, and Sweden suggest an association among unemployment, income inequality, and the homicide rate. As table 1–2 indicates, compared with Japanese and Swedes, Americans face a greater unemployment rate and a lower degree of income equality. They must also contend with a higher homicide rate. In most countries, youth between the ages of fifteen and twenty-four show an especially high tendency to commit murder. Significantly, the American jobless rate in 1976 for this age group was over three times the Swedish or Japanese level. Of course, the national unemployment rate and the relative gap separating poor people from the average income earner are variables linked to collectivities rather than to individuals. Not all unemployed or poor persons murder. The cognitive makeup of the individual, the models for law-abiding behavior, and the reinforcement patterns affecting particular individuals shape the responses to deleterious economic stimuli. Yet economic conditions form part of the individual's social context. Particularly if the government takes active steps to reduce unemployment and income inequalities, then economically deprived

TABLE 1-2 Unemployment rates, income inequality, and homicide

Country	Unemployment rates[a]		Gini index for posttax income[b]	Homicide rate[c]
	Total	Youth 15-24		
Japan	2.0%	3.2%	.34	1.3
Sweden	1.6	3.8	.27	1.3
United States	7.7	14.7	.37	9.1

[a]The unemployment figures represent the average number of unemployed persons in 1976 as a percentage of the civilian labor force.
[b]Low *ginis* indicate low income inequality (high income equality). The figures refer to 1972 in the United States and Sweden and to 1969 in Japan.
[c]The homicide rates are the number of murders and nonnegligent manslaughters in 1976 for every 100,000 persons.
SOURCES: Constance Sorrentino, "Youth Unemployment: An International Perspective," *Monthly Labor Review* 104 (July 1981): 4–5; Malcolm Sawyer, "Income Distribution in OECD Countries," *OECD Economic Outlook: Occasional Studies* (Paris: Organisation for Economic Cooperation and Development, July 1976), p. 19; *World Health Statistics Annual*, vol. 1 (Geneva, Switzerland: World Health Organization, 1978, 1979).

individuals may feel less incentive to engage in homicide. As chapter 5 will show, Swedish officials have demonstrated greater enthusiasm than American leaders about implementing tax and spending policies that secure greater income equality. Along with Japanese business executives, Swedish industrialists have enacted more numerous programs designed to maintain the employed worker's job security. These programs have undoubtedly brought order, self-esteem, and security to citizens within Japan and Sweden. As a possible consequence, their homicide rates are lower than in the United States.

Three demographic variables—the degree of urbanization, the proportion of youth between the ages of fifteen and twenty-four, and the extent of ethnic heterogeneity—may affect national homicide rates. Nations ranking high on these three population indicators will presumably experience the greatest danger from murderers. To what extent are these assumptions valid for the United States, Japan, and Sweden? Table 1–3 indicates that the age and ethnic structures seem to account for a greater variance in the homicide rate than does the degree of urbanization. Both the United States and Japan are highly urbanized. Yet the murder rate in 1975 was far lower in Japan than in the United States. Compared with urbanization, age profiles appear more closely correlated with homicide. Americans, who are a younger people than either the Japanese or especially the Swedes, face the greatest danger from murderers.

Sweden and particularly Japan are more ethnically homogeneous societies than the United States. Except for a few Koreans, most individuals in Japan comprise the same ethnic stock. In Sweden during the late 1970s, about 7 percent of the population was born outside

TABLE 1-3 Population patterns and homicide

Country	Percentage of population living in cities over 100,000 persons[a]	Population aged 15–24 as percentage of population aged 25–64[b]	Ethnic homogeneity[c]	Homicide rate[d]
United States	51	37	82nd	10.0
Japan	57	30	5th	1.3
Sweden	43	26	29th	1.1

[a] The urbanization rates refer to the percentage of the national population inhabiting cities of 100,000 and more people in 1975.
[b] These national age profiles indicate the population aged fifteen to twenty-four as a proportion of the population aged twenty-five to sixty-four in 1975.
[c] Ethnic homogeneity means the degree of ethnic and linguistic unity in a nation. Out of 136 countries, Japan has the fifth highest degree of ethnic homogeneity, Sweden ranks twenty-ninth, and the United States has the most ethnic diversity.
[d] The homicide rates are the number of murders and nonnegligent manslaughters in 1975 for every 100,000 persons.
SOURCES: *Demographic Yearbook: 1976*, 28th ed. (New York: United Nations, 1977), pp. 242–248; U.S. Bureau of the Census, *Statistical Abstract of the United States: 1977*, 98th ed. (Washington, D.C.: Government Printing Office, 1977), p. 22; *Statistical Abstract of Sweden: 1980*, vol. 67 (Stockholm: National Central Bureau of Statistics, 1980), p. 39; *OECD Observer* no. 87 (July 1977), p. 32; Charles Lewis Taylor and Michael Hudson, *World Handbook of Political and Social Indicators*, 2d ed. (New Haven, Conn.: Yale University Press, 1972), pp. 271–274; *World Health Statistics Annual*, vol. 1 (Geneva, Switzerland: World Health Organization, 1977, 1978).

the Swedish nation, mainly in other northern European countries, such as Finland, Denmark, Norway, and West Germany. Of all these foreign-born persons, over two-fifths have become Swedish citizens. From the beginning of its history, however, America has experienced greater ethnic diversity. Native Americans, Asians, Latin Americans, Africans, and people from all parts of Europe have settled the country. Particularly when these diverse ethnic groups underwent divergent degrees of family disintegration and faced differential access to wealth, political power, and status, they showed varying homicide rates. For example, during the 1970s, Blacks were more involved in homicides than either Whites or Hispanics. In the late 1970s, Blacks, mainly young black men, made up nearly half the murder victims. Just under half the persons arrested for homicide were black.[38]

Why do urban residents, young men between fifteen and thirty, and American Blacks reveal a high homicide rate? The reasons probably stem from the values and reinforcements found within the small-group structures surrounding these individuals. Economic conditions also shape the tendencies to engage in homicidal behavior. All these groups feel less well integrated into the existing community. The traditional social controls of family, school, and church exert a weaker restraint over their behavior. They often participate in small groups, such as youth gangs, that reward violence and disdain nonviolent responses to frustration. Lacking a general solidarity with the larger community, they seem more likely than others to challenge traditional authority figures such as the police. Unemployment and economic inequality may hinder their economic prospects. For example, young American Blacks face bleaker employment opportunities than do either Whites or Spanish-speaking youth. In 1977, among youth sixteen to nineteen years old, 15.4 percent of Whites, 22.8 percent of Hispanics, but 41.1 percent of Blacks were unemployed. That year, whereas the median income of Mexican American families averaged about 72 percent of the white median income, the median black family's income reached only 57 percent of the white family income. These economic conditions, combined with the family disintegration and the heritage of violence used by Whites to keep Blacks in their place, may account for the greater homicide rate among Blacks than among the Spanish-speaking.[39]

Small-group patterns explain not only different homicide rates among groups but also the variations across nations. Japan and Sweden may face lower homicide rates because small-group controls more effectively restrain their citizens from engaging in aggressive behavior. Especially in Japan, the individual functions within a tight group network. Family associations, neighborhood clubs, crime prevention associations, and vocational unions for crime prevention all establish informal social pressures that restrain aggressive behavior. Like the Japanese, the Swedes belong to a variety of groups, including labor unions, cooperatives of producers and consumers, sports federations, study circles, civic associations, and political parties. Providing solidarity, these groups also reinforce the norms of law-abiding behavior.[40] In contrast to Japan and Sweden, America is a more mobile society. Community solidarity seems weaker. American values stress the need for individuals to assert themselves against existing authority. Less influenced by informal small-group pressures to act nonviolently, Americans thus experience a higher homicide rate.

Conclusion. The degree of coercive treatment administered by the police, court judges, and prison administrators fails to explain the varying homicide rates among different countries. According to Ted Gurr, who studied the 150-year history of crime in London, Stockholm, and Sydney, Australia, after 1840 the police force grew larger and the prison environment became less punitive. Violent crimes declined. From 1950 through 1970, however, these two aspects of the criminal justice system accompanied a rising murder rate. Gurr concludes: "Public order depends more on basic socioeconomic and political circumstances than on conditions controlled by the law, the police, the courts, or the prisons."[41]

My brief examination of the homicide rate in Japan, Sweden, and the United States has reached a conclusion similar to Gurr's. Although an analysis of just three countries can hardly "prove" the general validity of hypotheses, the evidence suggests that features other than the criminal justice system operate more effectively to restrain homicidal behavior. These "basic socioeconomic and political circumstances" include cultural values justifying aggression, combative attitudes toward authority, the degree of unemployment and economic inequality, and especially the informal social controls small groups exert.

Under pressure to lower the crime rate, public policymakers face a dilemma: the conditions most directly under the control of political leaders appear least responsible for homicide. Public officials can more easily add police officers to the force, increase the legal sentence for homicide, and restore capital punishment than they can change cultural values or small-group rewards and punishments. Yet the attitudes justifying the use of violence originate in the family and other small-group settings. The more violence children observe, the more violently they behave toward others. Children who have experienced the most violence express the strongest approval of interpersonal and political violence in later adulthood. As social-learning theory assumes, through direct experiences and observations of interpersonal relations, a person comes to learn whether or not violence "pays off"—that is, represents a functionally useful tactic for attaining desired goals.[42] Unfortunately, because most individuals learn these attitudes in a small group, public policies, at least in democratic societies, can exert only a limited impact on reshaping the reinforcements and cultural beliefs that stimulate aggression. Particularly in the United States, most individuals resent government attempts to interfere with family life and small-group interactions. David Bayley points out: "The levels of criminal behavior that Americans find so disturbing may be the inevitable consequence of aspects of national life that Americans prize—individualism, mobility, privacy, autonomy, suspicion of authority, and separation between public and private roles, between government and community."[43]

The Dilemmas of Comparative Analysis

As Harriet Van Horne reminds us, comparisons are odious. Why? To the friends of homicidal victims, political scientists who use impersonal, detached, "scientific" methods to compare homicide rates across different countries appear insensitive to human suffering. To citizens frightened by the high murder rates, the focus on the limits of public policies in reducing violent crimes implies a resigned, fatalistic attitude toward the status quo. They associate theoretical analysis of homicide with political paralysis to change existing conditions. Indeed, the contemporary stress on the limitations of public policies recalls the famous lines of the German philosopher Hegel, who wrote 150 years ago: "One word more about giving instructions as to what the world ought to be. Philosophy in any case always comes on the scene too late to give it. . . . The owl of Minerva spreads its wings only with the falling of the dusk."[44] In this observation, Hegel assumed that political theorists can more easily explain past events than predict future conditions or change the existing world. Only after events have actually occurred can political theorists begin to interpret past conditions. Yet even if comparative analysts want to play the role of Minerva, they must recognize the difficulties of understanding past experiences, let alone the future scenario. Two related dilemmas plague comparative analysis. One deals with the problems of reaching valid causal generalizations. Another revolves around the difficulties of understanding the whole social context from the perspective of only a part of the system.

THE PROBLEMS OF CAUSAL ANALYSIS

Like any causal analysis, inferences about the impact of public policies on homicide involve three steps.[45] First, some correlation must exist between the presence of a policy and its effect. For instance, if long prison sentences really do reduce the homicide rate, then we must discover a correlation between these two variables. Second, the independent policy variables should precede the effect. If we assume that increasing the number of police personnel produces a lower murder rate, the additions to the police force should come before, rather than after, indicators for a reduced homicide rate. Third, although a high association and the proper time sequence may exist between two variables, the relationship may be spurious—that is, caused by other antecedent factors. Social scientists have uncovered a positive correlation between the number of storks in an area and the number of children born, but probably we would not conclude that the storks produced the babies. Instead, both the birth rate and the stork rate are higher in rural areas; conditions in the rural context account for the spurious correlation between babies and storks. To take an example from the political world, although the proportion of persons owning handguns may be associated cross-nationally with homicide rates, both variables may depend on cultural attitudes toward authority and the use of violence. In those countries where people are suspicious of authority and hold beliefs justifying the use of violence, both handgun possession and homicide rates may be high.[46]

Unfortunately, political scientists who engage in comparative studies across nations have found it difficult to meet these three conditions and thereby discover valid causal generalizations. What are the difficulties? First, most correlations in the policy sciences reveal weak, rather than strong, statistical relationships, indicating that public policies exert only a limited effect on such social conditions as crime. In some cases, situational variables not subject to policy control may have a stronger impact on social change than do policy variables. At least in the short run, it is easier for officials to control the lengths of prison sentences than to change individual attitudes, family backgrounds, or peer group interactions. Yet these three situational variables may better explain homicide rates than does a policy variable.[47]

Second, comparative political scientists also face problems disentangling the temporal occurrence of policy variables and those effects that stem from a public policy. In some cases, the effects may cause the policy, rather than vice versa. Although a high correlation exists between the percentage of people owning a handgun in different nations and cross-national homicide rates, perhaps a high murder rate leads more people to buy guns.

Third, the investigation of several diverse countries expands the complexity of conditions affecting some outcome. These complex situations make it difficult to control for all the variables that may explain a certain effect, such as the homicide rate. It is easier to generate a strong statistical correlation and to specify a temporal order among variables than to discover all the antecedent factors accounting for a spurious relationship. Even if we uncovered a statistical association between peer group interactions and homicide and demonstrated that participating in a violent group setting preceded the murder, we still do not know the other variables causing peer group rewards for violent behavior.

Many social scientists remain skeptical about the possibilities of developing a cross-national "policy science" that accurately specifies causal generalizations. Public policies constitute only one variable shaping national homicide rates. Other relevant factors, including the heterogeneity of a population, distinctive cultural beliefs, and patterns of small-group interaction, also explain this effect. If several countries have a similar crime policy, other nonpolicy variables may diverge. Faced with these varied conditions, the comparative analyst finds it difficult to trace the precise interaction among distinctive policy and nonpolicy variables. We can find few cases for comparison that share all traits except a different policy content or implementation method. Aaron Wildavsky points out the dilemma faced by analysts who seek theoretical explanations for policy impacts: "If the predictive variables are too few, the theoretical models are too simple; and if there are too many, it is extremely difficult to understand their interaction."[48] Hence, to understand social complexities, we need theoretical simplicity. Yet by concentrating on a few variables, especially ones linked to policy decisions, we ignore other relevant factors that may explain the effects. Efforts to assess the causal impact of public policies across nations become risky.

Another dilemma facing the comparative political scientist involves the confusion between the individual and group levels of analysis. Although specific individuals commit murders, most hypotheses about the causes of homicide rely on aggregate data about collectivities—for example, police personnel per 10,000 citizens, prison–staff ratios, percentage of persons owning a handgun, unemployment rates, and the degrees of economic inequality. The units employed are not individuals but collective entities such as cities, states, provinces, and nations. The correlations among these aggregate data do not explain the reasons for specific individuals engaging in homicidal behavior. Social-learning theorists assume that individual and environmental variables reciprocally shape human behavior. Individuals' perceptions, motivations, attitudes, and personalities interact with such environmental conditions as cultural values and sociopolitical structures. In turn, individual behavior influences the environment.

According to these assumptions, not everyone in a roughly similar environment responds in an identical manner. When social scientists uncover a correlation between a nation's unemployment rate and its homicide rate, we cannot thereby assume that the jobless level "causes" murder. The vast majority of unemployed persons do not commit homicides. Even if economic inequality and unemployment provide a context that increases the likelihood of murders occurring during an armed robbery, these economic conditions do not have exactly the same effect on all the poor and unemployed. The specific stimuli and reinforcements affecting each particular individual, as well as unique motives and cognitive processes, determine a person's response to the aggregate conditions. Statistical data about the length of prison sentences, the certainty of execution for murder, and unemployment rates give no evidence about individual motives or individual perceptions of the certainty and severity of punishment, variables the theorist considers important.

In sum, comparison involves this dilemma: The information regarded as the most theoretically useful remains the most difficult to obtain cross-nationally. Whereas the explanatory hypotheses make assumptions about individuals' attitudes, beliefs, motives, and

CHAPTER 1 COMPARING POLITICAL SYSTEMS 37

perceptions, the aggregate data refer to collective entities, not individuals. Therefore, the causal validity of these hypotheses becomes difficult to prove.

THE INDIVIDUAL OBSERVER AND THE SOCIAL CONTEXT

Another dilemma revolves around the difficulty of understanding the operation of whole political systems. Comparative political scientists seek to explain the interaction between the various concrete parts of a system—government institutions, social groups, and individuals. How do government policies toward crime affect social groups, such as ethnic groups, young men, the unemployed, and poor persons? How in turn do ethnic, religious, and economic groups shape government decision making? To what extent can the will of a powerful individual overcome the limitations posed by cultural beliefs and social structures? All these questions concern the relationship between the parts of a system and the functioning of the whole system.

In trying to answer these questions, comparative analysts face this problem: Despite the desire to understand systemic performance in its entirety, observers are involved in a part of the whole system. How do they transcend their limited concrete perspectives to gain analytical insights into the whole system? Whatever their pretensions, no observers are theoretically all-knowing. Political scientists who have grown up in the United States often have difficulties understanding the behavior of foreign systems, especially those in Africa and Asia. Even those who carry out field research in a city such as Tokyo cannot easily explain the effects of each police post (*koban* in Tokyo), court, prison, youth association, and family on the operation of the whole system. In short, observation must necessarily begin from the part. Yet this partial perspective confounds efforts to understand the interaction among all the parts of a system and the precise way that the behavior of the parts affects the functioning of the whole system.[49]

How have political scientists dealt with this dilemma? Especially since the Second World War, two styles of comparison have characterized the study of foreign political systems. Whereas the *holistic* approach wants to understand systems in their entirety, the *cross-national analytical* approach compares many different societies by examining a few analytical parts or dimensions. Each style makes divergent assumptions about the relationship between the parts and the whole. The holistic approach assumes that a system is a complex, interrelated whole. No observer can understand the parts without a knowledge of the whole. The overall context shapes the behavior of particular individuals and social groups. Political scientists who adopt a country-by-country strategy of comparison view societies as organisms. The goal is to understand the relationships among the parts, the functioning of the whole system, and its growth over time. Thus, historical comparisons of one country or city become important. How did Japanese police practices evolve over time? What factors caused the police to change their mode of operation through the centuries? Due to the tendency to take a historical perspective, holistic comparisons use mainly qualitative methods of analysis, because precise quantitative data rarely exist before the twentieth century. Examining written records, directly observing contemporary systems, and synthesizing others' accounts become the primary strategies for interpreting information.

The cross-national analytical approach assumes that the investigator can break down a complex system into its simpler parts, which can be measured. Political scientists preferring this style try to compare a large number of cases in both time and space. Rather than studying the United States first, then Sweden, and finally Japan, they investigate a few features—homicide rates, police–citizen ratios, court convictions for 1,000 persons, length of prison sentences, unemployment rates, and levels of income inequalities—in scores of different countries. Because historical data are not widely available for most nations, the comparisons usually do not extend beyond the last two centuries. Whatever the problems of data collection, the goal is to ascertain if the empirical generalizations true at one time period also remain valid at other periods. As these assumptions imply, the cross-national analytical approach views societies largely as machines. The investigator can isolate the parts of the system for detailed examination. Complex computer routines make it possible to carry out quantitative analyses of over one hundred different societies.[50]

In summary, the two styles differ on the possibilities of comparing different systems. According to the holistic approach, valid comparisons of several diverse societies are difficult to achieve, mainly because to know the parts (the trees), we must understand the whole (the forest). Because each society is unique and different from any other, generalizations about the functioning of systems in general are infeasible. Few observers can penetrate the minds of the observed, except by lengthy field experiences; thus, they cannot easily gain an objective understanding of political behavior across several nations. The cross-national analytical approach takes a different position on each of these points. If investigators choose theoretically significant variables found in all units, they can compare a wide variety of different systems. Although each society is unique, it is not totally dissimilar to all others. All political systems share some aspects—the political power of social groups, the importance of political beliefs in the policy process, and the role of political organizations in public policymaking. From this perspective, generalizations about the interactions among these variables are possible across several societies. Finally, despite the difficulties of observing political behavior in different contexts, the comparative political scientist can gain an objective understanding of diverse political systems.

Conclusion

This book blends features of both the holistic and the cross-national analytical styles of comparison. Rather than taking a country-by-country approach, I compare political systems according to their analytical dimensions. I assume that a political system makes and carries out public policies that have a binding effect on the society. Hence, I use an explicit policy focus that highlights the interactions among three foundations of a political system: (1) the impact of social groups on the exercise of political power, (2) the beliefs about public policies, and (3) the power of governments and political parties over the policy process. Like the holistic approach, this strategy of comparison relies more on qualitative than quantitative analyses. Instead of comparing one hundred different societies, I concentrate on nine: the United States, Canada, Britain, West Germany, Sweden, France, Italy, the Soviet Union, and the People's Republic of China. Although each chapter does not compare all these systems, I analyze the similarities and differences among a few of them on several different variables: political stratification (part I), political beliefs (part II), and the power of government institutions and political parties (part III). Part IV analyzes the effect of policy performance on the degree of system continuity in the United States, Britain, Germany, and Russia. This section explores how political beliefs, the power of social groups, and the role played by governments and parties explain patterns of political stability and change in the four nations. This analytical strategy best enables us to make cross-national comparisons yet still show a proper regard for the impact of the whole context on the performance of a part of that system.

In sum, the main goal of this book is to explain the behavior of individuals in political situations and the performance of political systems. Unlike the skeptical Hegel, I assume that accurate description and valid explanation lay the groundwork for changing public policies and systemic operation. Although the complexity of social systems makes prediction difficult, explanations seem more feasible. Whatever our attitudes toward specific policies, only by understanding how and why political systems operate can we effectively change existing situations, such as a high crime rate. From this perspective, the owl of Minerva can serve as a partial guide to our political choices.

Notes

1. See Robert Scheer, "Bronx–Landscape of Urban Cancer," *Los Angeles Times*, August 6, 1978, pp. 1, 30–33.
2. David Bayley presents the most probing accounts of crime in Japan and the United States. See his *Forces of Order: Police Behavior in Japan and the United States* (Berkeley: University of California Press, 1976); "Learning about Crime—The Japanese Experience," *The Public Interest* no. 44 (Summer 1976): 55–68.
3. For an account of crime in Stockholm, see Ted Robert Gurr, *Rogues, Rebels, and Reformers* (Beverly Hills, Calif.: Sage, 1976); Ted Robert Gurr, "Contemporary Crime in Historical Perspective: A Comparative Study of London, Stockholm, and Sydney," *Annals of the American Academy of Political and Social Science* 434 (November 1977): 114–136.
4. *New York Post*, January 11, 1974, p. 36. Quoted with permission of the author, Harriet Van Horne.
5. According to Morris Zelditch, Jr., "A sentence is *explanatory* if it asserts a relation between two or more variables." He gives the following statement as an example: "A democracy is stable if its wealth is equally distributed." Democracy, stability, wealth, and equal distribution are all general terms. See his "Intelligible Comparisons," *Comparative Methods in Sociology: Essays on Trends and Applications*, ed. Ivan Vallier (Berkeley: University of California Press, 1971), p. 270.
6. Robert Coles, "The Children of Affluence," *Atlantic* 270 (September 1977): 66.
7. See Albert Bandura, *Aggression: A Social Learning Analysis* (Englewood Cliffs, N.J.: Prentice-Hall, 1973); Albert Bandura, *Social Learning Theory* (Englewood Cliffs, N.J.: Prentice-Hall, 1977).
8. Bandura, *Social Learning Theory*, p. 207. See also his *Aggression*, pp. 39–59.
9. See the following four works of Albert Bandura: *Aggression*, pp. 210–216; *Social Learning Theory*, pp. 155–158; "Behavior Theory and the Models of Man," *American Psychologist* 29 (December 1974): 861–862; "Institutionally Sanctioned Violence," *Journal of Clinical Child Psychology* 2 (Fall 1973): 23–24. In *Why Men Rebel* (Princeton, N.J.: Princeton University Press, 1970), pp. 155–183, Ted Robert Gurr analyzes the normative and utilitarian justifications of violence.
10. Bandura, *Aggression*, pp. 47, 59.
11. Ibid., pp. 183–243; Bandura, *Social Learning Theory*, pp. 97–158.
12. Bandura, *Aggression*, pp. 297–308.
13. Jack P. Gibbs, "Preventive Effects of Capital Punishment Other than Deterrence," *Criminal Law Bulletin* 14 (January–February 1978): 34–50.
14. See Bayley, "Learning about Crime," esp. pp. 61–68; David H. Bayley, "Ironies of American Law Enforcement," *The Public Interest* no. 59 (Spring 1980): 45–56.
15. United States Bureau of the Census, *Statistical Abstract of the United States: 1979* (Washington, D.C.: Government Printing Office, 1979), p. 169.
16. See Bayley, *Forces of Order*, pp. xi–xv.
17. See the essay in Robert T. Holt and John E. Turner, eds., *The Methodology of Comparative Research* (New York: Free Press, 1970): Frederick W. Frey, "Cross-Cultural Survey Research in Political Research," pp. 295–341.
18. See John B. McConahay, "Experimental Research," in *Handbook of Political Psychology*, ed. Jeanne N. Knutson (San Francisco: Jossey-Bass, 1973), pp. 356–382; Stanley Milgram, *Obedience to Authority: An Experimental View* (New York: Harper & Row, 1974), esp. pp. 23–24, 174–178.
19. See Richard F. Tomasson, *Sweden: Prototype of Modern Society* (New York: Random House, 1970), pp. 276–290; M. Donald Hancock, *Sweden: The Politics of Postindustrial Change* (Hinsdale, Ill.: Dryden Press, 1972), pp. 37, 44; Harry Eckstein, *Division and Cohesion in Democracy: A Study of Norway* (Princeton, N.J.: Princeton University Press, 1966), p. 94; Bayley, *Forces of Order*, pp. 149, 174. For an analysis of American instrumental values and the high orientation toward success, see two books by Seymour Martin Lipset: *Revolution and Counterrevolution: Change and Persistence in Social Structures* (New York: Basic Books, 1968), p. 42; *The First New Nation: The United States in Historical and Comparative Perspective* (New York: Basic Books, 1963), pp. 248–273.
20. Bayley, *Forces of Order*, p. 150.
21. "What the Swedish People Think of Their Police," *International Criminal Police Review* 28 (May 1974): 132–133; George E. Berkley, *The Democratic Policeman* (Boston: Beacon Press, 1969), pp. 89–107.
22. Berkley, *The Democratic Policeman*, pp. 107–118; Bayley, *Forces of Order*, pp. 160–

183; Charles W. Peek, Jon P. Alston, and George D. Lowe, "Comparative Evaluation of the Local Police," *Public Opinion Quarterly* 42 (Fall 1978): 370–379; *Gallup Opinion Index* no. 98 (August 1973): 34.
23. Bandura, *Aggression*, pp. 221–229.
24. Edward M. Kennedy, "The Need for Gun Control Legislation," *Current History* 71 (July–August 1976): 27; Irvin Block, *Gun Control: One Way to Save Lives*, Public Affairs Pamphlet No. 536 (Washington, D.C.: Public Affairs Committee, 1976), p. 20; United States Bureau of the Census, *Statistical Abstract of the United States: 1977* (Washington, D.C.: Government Printing Office, 1977), p. 175; Minoru Shikita, "Prevention of Crime in Japan: An Integrated Approach," *Proceedings of the Third International Search Symposium on Criminal Justice Information and Statistics Systems*, May 24–26, 1976, Philadelphia, Penn., ed. John Laucher and Martha Casey (Sacramento, Calif.: Search Group, 1976), p. 434; Ruth A. Ross and George C. S. Benson, "Criminal Justice from East to West," *Crime and Delinquency* 25 (January 1979): 85.
25. B. Bruce-Briggs, "The Great American Gun War," *The Public Interest* no. 45 (Fall 1976): 61. See also Marshall B. Clinard, *Cities with Little Crime: The Case of Switzerland* (New York: Cambridge University Press, 1978), pp. 114–115.
26. See *European Marketing Data and Statistics*, 10th ed. (London: Euromonitor Publications, 1973), p. 259; *European Marketing Data and Statistics;* 13th ed. (London: Euromonitor Publications, 1976), p. 235; Harold K. Becker and Einar O. Hjellemo, *Justice in Modern Sweden* (Springfield, Ill.: Thomas, 1976), p. 72; Bayley, "Learning about Crime," p. 59.
27. Shikita, "Prevention of Crime in Japan," p. 437; United States Department of Justice, *FBI Uniform Crime Reports: Crime in the United States, 1978* (Washington, D.C.: Government Printing Office, 1979), p. 177.
28. Gordon Fraser, "The Swedish Police," *Police Review* 85 (December 2, 1977): 1672–1673; Haruo Ueno, "The Japanese Police: Education and Training," *Police Studies* 2 (Spring 1979): 11–17; Walter L. Ames, "The Japanese Police: A General Survey," *Police Studies* 2 (Spring 1979): 6–10; Ross and Benson, "Criminal Justice from East to West," pp. 79–80; Shikita, "Prevention of Crime in Japan," p. 438; Bayley, *Forces of Order*, pp. 56–57; Berkley, *The Democratic Policeman*, pp. 76–78, 178–181; George E. Berkley, "Centralization, Democracy, and the Police," *Journal of Criminal Law, Criminology and Police Science* 61 (June 1970): 309–312; George Berkley, "How the Police Work in Western Europe and the U.S.," *New Republic* 161 (August 2, 1969): 15–18; Becker and Hjellemo, *Justice in Modern Sweden*, pp. 50–54; A. J. Bilek, "Regionalization as a Response to the Problems of Fragmentation in the Criminal Justice System," *Journal of Forensic Sciences* 17 (July 1972): 399–408; Erik Beckman, "Police Education and Training: Where Are We? Where Are We Going?" *Journal of Criminal Justice* 4 (Winter 1976): 315–322.
29. Ross and Benson, "Criminal Justice from East to West," pp. 81–82; Michael S. Serrill, "Profile/Sweden," *Corrections Magazine* 3 (June 1977): 18; personal communication from Leif Lenke, Department of Criminology, University of Stockholm, April 2, 1979; Shikita, "Prevention of Crime in Japan," p. 439; *Statistical Abstract of the United States: 1977*, p. 186.
30. Serrill, 'Profile/Sweden," p. 20; personal communication from Leif Lenke; Bayley, *Forces of Order*, p. 143; Government of Japan, *Summary of the White Paper on Crime, 1969* (Tokyo: Research and Training Institute of the Ministry of Justice, 1970), pp. 25–26; Jonathan M. Winer, "Huge Disparities in Jail Time," *National Law Journal* 3 (February 23, 1981): 1, 28–30.
31. See John R. Snortum, "Sweden's 'Special' Prisons: Correctional Trends and Cultural Traditions," *Criminal Justice and Behavior* 3 (June 1976): 151–163; Norman Bishop, "Developments in Criminal Law and Penal Systems, 1976: Sweden," *Criminal Law Review* (July 1977): 410–413; David A. Ward, "Inmate Rights and Prison Reform in Sweden and Denmark," *Journal of Criminal Law, Criminology, and Police Science* 63 (June 1972): 240–255; Gunnar Marnell, "Comparative Correctional Systems: United States and Sweden," *Criminal Law Bulletin* 8 (November 1972): 748–760; Gunnar Marnell, "Penal Reform: A Swedish Viewpoint," *Howard Journal of Penology and Crime Prevention* 14, no. 1 (1974): 8–21; Hero Buss, "In for Repairs," *Sweden Now* 4 (March 1970): 34–39; Ruth Link, "Where Prisoners Are People," *Sweden Now* 7, no. 2 (1973): 34–41.
32. *Correctional Institutions in Japan* (Tokyo: Correction Bureau, Ministry of Justice, 1970), pp. 11–18; F. Lovell Bixby, "Two Modern Correctional Facilities in Japan," *Federal Probation* 35 (September 1971):

13–15; *Criminal Justice in Japan* (Tokyo: Ministry of Justice, 1978), pp. 29–33.
33. Peter L. Scharf, *Moral Atmosphere and Intervention in the Prison: The Creation of a Participatory Community* (Ph.D. dissertation, Graduate School of Education, Harvard University, 1973), pp. 14–38; Philip Hager, "Supreme Court OKs Limits on Prisoner Unions if Deemed Necessary for Security," *Los Angeles Times*, June 24, 1977, p. 14; Marnell, "Comparative Correctional Systems" pp. 758-759; Serrill, "Profile/Sweden," p. 14.
34. United States Department of Justice, National Criminal Justice Information and Statistics Service, *Capital Punishment 1976*, National Prisoner Statistics Bulletin SD-NPS-CP-5, November 1977, p. 13; William C. Bailey, 'Imprisonment v. the Death Penalty as a Deterrent to Murder," *Law and Human Behavior* 1, no. 3 (1977): 239–260; Thorsten Sellin, *The Penalty of Death* (Beverly Hills, Calif.: Sage, 1980), pp. 157–179. For a contrary interpretation that assumes an inverse correlation between the number of executions and the homicide rate, see Isaac Ehrlich, "The Deterrent Effect of Capital Punishment: A Question of Life and Death," *American Economic Review* 65 (June 1975): 397–417; Isaac Ehrlich, "Capital Punishment and Deterrence: Some Further Thoughts and Additional Evidence," *Journal of Political Economy* 85 (August 1977): 741–788. Critiques of the Ehrlich research appear in Daniel Glaser, "The Realities of Homicide versus the Assumptions of Economists in Assessing Capital Punishment," *Journal of Behavioral Economics* 6 (Summer–Winter 1977): 243–268; Stephen J. Knorr, "Deterrence and the Death Penalty: A Temporal Cross-Sectional Approach," *Journal of Criminal Law and Criminology* 70 (Summer 1979): 235–254.
35. Ezzat Abdel Fattah, *A Study of the Deterrent Effect of Capital Punishment with Special Reference to the Canadian Situation* (Ottawa: Department of the Solicitor General, Canada, Information Canada, 1972), pp. 56–57; *Japan Statistical Yearbook 1967* (Tokyo: Statistics Bureau, Prime Minister's Office, 1968), p. 598; *Japan Statistical Yearbook, 1978* (Tokyo: Statistics Bureau, Prime Minister's Office, 1978), p. 633; Government of Japan, *Summary of the White Paper on Crime, 1978* (Tokyo: Research and Training Institute of the Ministry of Justice, 1979), p. 24.
36. Reynolds Farley, "Homicide Trends in the United States," *Demography* 17 (May 1980): 183; Richard Sparks, "Crime," *New Society* 36 (June 24, 1976): 694; Lynn A. Curtis, *Criminal Violence: National Patterns and Behavior* (Lexington, Mass.: Heath, 1974), pp. 48–58; Fattah, *A Study of the Deterrent Effect of Capital Punishment*, p. 26; Richard J. Gelles and Murray A. Straus, "Family Experience and Public Support of the Death Penalty," *American Journal of Orthopsychiatry* 45 (July 1975): 601; Phillip H. Ennis, "Crime, Victims, and the Police," *Trans-action* 4 (June 1967): 38; Vijay K. Mathur, "Economics of Crime: An Investigation of the Deterrent Hypothesis for Urban Areas," *Review of Economics and Statistics* 60 (August 1978): 459–466; George F. Soloman, "Capital Punishment as Suicide and as Murder," *American Journal of Orthopsychiatry* 45 (July 1975): 701–711; Michael Geerken and Walter R. Gove, "Deterrence, Overload, and Incapacitation: An Empirical Evaluation," *Social Forces* 56 (December 1977): 424–447.
37. See three essays in *Unemployment and Crime: Hearings before the Subcommittee on the Judiciary, U.S. House of Representatives, 95th Congress, 1977–1978* (Washington, D.C.: U.S. Government Printing Office, 1978): M. Harvey Brenner, Impact of Economic Indicators on Crime Indices," pp. 20–37; G. D. Woods, "Unemployment and Crime—A General Perspective," pp. 923–925; John D. Braithwaite, "Unemployment and Adult Crime: An Interpretation of the International Evidence," pp. 925–933. See also Marvin D. Krohn, "Inequality, Unemployment and Crime: A Cross-National Analysis," *Sociological Quarterly* 17 (Summer 1976): 303–313; Steven Fredrick Messner, *Income Inequality and Murder Rates: A Cross-National Analysis* (Ph.D. dissertation, Department of Sociology, Princeton University, 1978); Steven F. Messner, "Income Inequality and Murder Rates: Some Cross-National Findings," in *Comparative Social Research*, vol. 3, ed. Richard F. Tomasson (Greenwich, Conn.: JAI Press, 1980), pp. 185–198.
38. *Statistical Abstract of Sweden: 1980*, vol. 67 (Stockholm: National Central Bureau of Statistics, 1980), pp. 44–47; Charles E. Silberman, *Criminal Violence, Criminal Justice* (New York: Random House, 1978), pp. 119–123; E. Terrence Jones, "Crime Change Patterns in American Cities," *Journal of Criminal Justice* 4 (Winter 1976): 333–340; *Statistical Abstract of the United States: 1979*, pp. 181, 186.

39. Morris J. Newman, "A Profile of Hispanics in the U.S. Work Force," *Monthly Labor Review*, 101 (December 1978): 7, 8, 10; *Statistical Abstract of the United States: 1979*, p. 448; U.S. Bureau of the Census, *Statistical Abstract of the United States: 1978* (Washington, D.C.: Government Printing Office, 1978), p. 401; U.S. Department of Labor, Bureau of Labor Statistics, *Handbook of Labor Statistics* (Washington, D.C.: Government Printing Office, 1980), p. 71; Silberman, *Criminal Violence, Criminal Justice*, pp. 123–132.
40. Bayley, "Learning about Crime," pp. 61–68; Shikita, "Crime Prevention in Japan," p. 436; Tomasson, *Sweden*, pp. 242–270; Hancock, *Sweden*, pp. 55–59; Clinard, *Cities with Little Crime*, p. 154.
41. Gurr, *Rogues, Rebels, and Reformers*, p. ix. See also his "Contemporary Crime in Historical Perspective," pp. 118–135.
42. David J. Owens and Murray A. Straus, "The Social Structure of Violence in Childhood and Approval of Violence as an Adult," *Aggressive Behavior* 1, no. 3 (1975): 193–211.
43. Bayley, "Learning about Crime," p. 68.
44. G. W. F. Hegel, *Philosophy of Right*, p. 12, quoted in Shlomo Avineri, *Hegel's Theory of the Modern State* (London: Cambridge University Press, 1972), p. 128.
45. See Arthur L. Stinchcombe, *Constructing Social Theories* (New York: Harcourt Brace and World, 1968), pp. 28–38.
46. Charles W. Turner, Lynn Stanley Simons, Leonard Berkowitz, and Ann Frodi, "The Stimulating and Inhibiting Effects of Weapons on Aggressive Behavior," *Aggressive Behavior* 3, no. 4 (1977): 357.
47. James S. Coleman, *Policy Research in the Social Sciences* (Morristown, N.J.: General Learning Press, 1972), pp. 5–6.
48. Aaron Wildavsky, review of *Politicians, Bureaucrats, and the Consultant*, by Garry D. Brewer, in *Science* 182 (December 28, 1973): 1335.
49. See David E. Apter and Charles F. Andrain, eds., *Contemporary Analytical Theory* (Englewood Cliffs, N.J.: Prentice-Hall, 1972), esp. pp. 11–18.
50. See Hartmut Grewe, *Comparative Politics and Political Development* (Ph.D. dissertation, Department of Political Science, Duke University, 1973), esp. pp. 79–80, 155–156.

PART

I

Social Structures and the Exercise of Political Power

The political power of social groups represents a basic analytical foundation of all political systems. In most societies, various social groups—ethnic associations, religious institutions, economic organizations—play a role in shaping public policies. A group's success in transforming its policy preferences into government decisions depends on the interactions within a group, the relations among diverse groups, the ties between group leaders and government officials, and the group's position in the social stratification system. If a group maintains high solidarity based on shared political preferences and tightly organized communications networks, then the chances for realizing its political goals increase. Furthermore, if a group allies with other groups and establishes dominance over competing social organizations, it can more effectively maximize its political power. Close ties between group leaders and government officials also increase the likelihood that a group will see its objectives realized by public policymakers. Finally, social groups with the greatest wealth and status can potentially exercise the most political power.

The two chapters in part I explore these general themes

about the links between social groups and political organizations. Chapter 2 highlights the importance of social groups—primordial, religious, and economic—in political struggles. Chapter 3 deals with three dimensions of social stratification—political power, wealth, and status—and theorizes about the reasons for changes in the social stratification system.

CHAPTER
2

Social Groups

> *When Adam delved and Eve span,*
> *who was then the gentleman?*
> —JOHN BALL, a leader of
> England's Peasants' Rebellion (1381)

At the beginning of the twentieth century, English women lacked political power, wealth, and status. With a few exceptions, such as Queen Victoria, most women held a subordinate position to men in the social stratification system. No women enjoyed the right to vote. Their prestige usually depended on the status of their husbands or fathers. Even when men and women performed the same work, women earned lower wages.[1] Although equal rights under the law remained the ideal, women failed to receive equal treatment with men.

Faced with these conditions, women began to organize political movements demanding the right to vote. The suffragettes did not expect that gaining the franchise would secure only political power; rather, they hoped that the suffrage would bring increased status for women and greater economic equality with men. Annie Kenney, a worker in a Lancashire textile factory and one of the early leaders of the women's suffrage movement, expressed the following aspiration: "Poverty would be practically swept away; washing would be done by municipal machinery! In fact, Paradise would be there once the vote was won!"[2]

To attain these comprehensive goals, the suffragettes strove to organize a powerful movement that would mobilize the apathetic behind a cause, coordinate formerly isolated activities, and overcome the resistance of government leaders opposing women's right to vote.

From 1903 through 1918, the most important organization campaigning for the suffrage was the Women's Social and Political Union. Led by members of the Pankhurst family—Emmeline, the mother, and her two daughters, Christabel and Sylvia—the WSPU tried to rally support from all social classes. Although upper- and middle-class women played the dominant role in the organization, it also gained support from working-class women such as Annie and Jessie Kenney. Sylvia Pankhurst, a member of the upper-middle class, made special efforts to organize women in the East End of London, the poorest section of the city.

The tactics devised by the suffrage movement partly depended on the type of resistance government leaders mounted. Initially, the tactics were relatively peaceful. As early as 1870, Dr. Pankhurst, Emmeline's husband, convinced a member of Parliament to introduce a Women's Disabilities Removal Bill granting the suffrage to women. The governing party of England at that time, however, refused to place the bill before Parliament for a vote. After the WSPU was formed, women demonstrated in the streets, lectured at meetings, wrote magazine articles, published pamphlets, sent petitions to Parliament, and negotiated with cabinet ministers in the government.

Despite all these attempts to mobilize political support for their cause and to coordinate diverse suffragette activities behind a common movement, England's male leaders still refused to enfranchise women. Aggressive resistance to the women accompanied the refusal to consider their demands. When the Pankhurst family members peacefully demonstrated outside the House of Commons, the police arrested them and judges sent them to prison. The police also raided the offices of the WSPU. Encouraged by the police, mobs attacked suffragettes trying to question England's political leaders about voting rights.

Responding to government resistance, the WSPU implemented more militant tactics. Women in prison went on hunger strikes. Suffragettes outside prison smashed windows. Some set fire to theaters. Others planted bombs in public buildings. Emily Wilding Davison, a graduate of London University and a former honors student at Oxford University, died for the cause of women's suffrage. In 1913 at the Derby, she threw herself in front of King George's horse and died with the WSPU colors sewn inside her coat. But English political leaders still denied women the vote.

At the start of World War I, a split emerged in the suffrage movement. In 1914, Emmeline and Christabel Pankhurst rallied to support the government in its war efforts against Germany. They assumed that if women played an equal role with men in winning the war, the government would have to grant women the suffrage after hostilities ceased. Sylvia Pankhurst, however, remained more committed to pacifist and socialist ideals. In her view, English participation in the war threatened to bring even greater deprivations to the poor people of London's East End. Unlike Christabel, who wanted only the "strongest and most intelligent" women to lead the suffrage movement as generals command an army, Sylvia wanted both poor men and poor women to play a democratic role in the campaign for the vote. During the war, she worked in the East End to provide free meals for the poor, to uphold civil liberties, and to institute a health clinic, day nursery, and Montessori school.[3]

After the war ended in 1918, the electoral objectives of the suffrage movement triumphed over the socialist ideals. Fearful of postwar WSPU militancy and recognizing women's wartime contributions, the English Parliament granted voting rights to women over thirty who met certain property qualifications. Ten years later the government agreed to enfranchise all women aged twenty-one and above, regardless of their property holdings. Through the activities of the WSPU and other feminist organizations, women had gained greater electoral equality with men, higher status, and perhaps more equal economic opportunities.

Yet the more comprehensive ideals of the suffrage movement remained unfulfilled. Enfranchisement hardly brought the abolition of poverty, as Annie Kenney had anticipated. Those people at the bottom of the social stratification totem pole, both poor men and poor women, still experienced an inferior status, economic deprivation, and unequal access to political power. Working through social groups and political organizations, later generations would carry on the movement to secure public policies bringing a more equalitarian social stratification system to England.

The Group Concept

As the WSPU experience suggests, social groups play a key role shaping government decision making. A group is an entity composed of two or more individuals. Social scientists distinguish between "concrete" and "analytic" groups. Different concrete groups can be empirically observed and physically separated. We can observe the activities of primordial organizations (the Women's Social and Political Union), religious institutions (the Roman Catholic church, the Church of England), and economic associations such as the Transport and General Workers Union in Britain. We can physically separate these groups from each other. Analytic groups, however, can neither be observed nor physically separated. From the observable behavior of concrete groups, we infer the existence of such analytic structures as categoric, membership, and reference groups. For example, certain women in London may simultaneously form a statistical category, a participatory membership association, and a reference group with which to identify. Although we can draw analytical distinctions among these three groups, they cannot be physically separated.[4]

CATEGORIC GROUPS

Categoric groups are aggregates or categories of people who share some characteristic yet do not necessarily interact with each other. For example, survey analysts often compare the political attitudes of men and women in several different countries. Compared with men, do English women give stronger support to conservative parties than French women? In both countries, what different attitudes do men and women take toward governmental payments for abortions? This focus on the political attitudes of men and women does not imply that all English women interact with all other women; rather, the analyst isolates all the males and females in the sample for investigation to ascertain the extent to which they share certain attitudes.

MEMBERSHIP GROUPS

Membership groups comprise persons who share a relatively long-lasting interaction with each other. They communicate with one another, make demands, offer support, negotiate, trade, bargain, and perhaps exercise coercion. Because political life revolves around social interactions, membership groups play a more significant role than categoric groups in political decision making. During the early part of the twentieth century, England's male political leaders did not worry about the attitudes of all women aggregated in a public opinion survey, but they did have to confront women organized in the Women's Social and Political Union. To exert effective power, individuals with a common characteristic must become members of an organized group.

REFERENCE GROUPS

Like membership groups, reference groups assume an important position in political life. Individuals may identify with a reference group even though they are not necessarily members or do not share attributes. For example, despite her wealthy, middle-class origins, Sylvia Pankhurst identified with the working-class poor of London's East End. For her, the working class constituted a valued reference group. Although women dominated the leadership roles of the Women's Social and Political Union, some men, such as Frederick W. Pethick-Lawrence and Keir Hardie, a Labour member of Parliament, actively supported the WSPU. They identified with the movement for women's suffrage and regarded it as a positive reference group. As we have seen, the political importance of social groups partly depends on leaders' success in strengthening group identifications. Not all trade union members identify with the union movement. Not all women identify with the women's movement. Yet if unionists and women are to play an effective role in political decision making, they must become organized in a membership group and also develop strong identifications with it.

Dimensions of Social Groups

Both the objective and subjective dimensions of groups shape their relative importance in political life. These dimensions give distinctiveness to a social group; they signify the ways one group differs from some other group. Objective dimensions refer to the aspects that can be empirically observed, including a group's physical attributes, resources, behavior, and treatment by others. The subjective dimensions indicate the beliefs group members hold, such as their identification with the group, their agreement on shared values, and their motivation to work for a group's welfare.[5]

A Buddhist story illustrates the difference between the objective and subjective dimensions. Two Buddhist monks were arguing about a flag waving in the wind. One monk said, "It is the flag that is waving." The other retorted, "No, it is the wind that is waving." Because they could not agree, they went to see the abbot of the Zen monastery, who told them: "You are both wrong. It is the mind that is waving."[6] In this case, the group's flag and the wind represent the objective features; individuals can empirically see the flag and feel the wind. The mental picture or perception of the flag waving in the wind represents the subjective aspect of reality. As the sociologist W. I. Thomas once said, "If people define situations as real, they are real in their consequences."[7]

OBJECTIVE DIMENSIONS

The distinctiveness of certain "primordial groups"—ethnic, sex, and age groups—stems partly from their physical attributes. People are born into these groups; it is difficult for them to change their ethnic membership, sex, and age. Others recognize these groups by their inherited biological characteristics. Throughout the world, old men have dominated political life. Where several different ethnic groups populate a country, one usually exercises decisive political power. Particularly in the Republic of South Africa, an individual's ethnic group membership, as indicated by physical attributes, determines status, wealth, and access to political power. Within South Africa, four ethnic groups struggle for resources: Africans make up 72 percent of the total population, Whites make up 16 percent, Coloureds (a mixture of Blacks and Whites) constitute 9 percent, and Asians (mainly Indians) comprise 3 percent.

The ruling Afrikaner white elite has decreed that physical characteristics determine a person's position in the social stratification system. Thus, Whites govern the nation, hold the highest prestige, and enjoy the highest average monthly household income. The Asians are somewhat worse off, followed by the Coloured population. At the bottom of the social stratification system is the black African majority, whose members play virtually no role in political decision making, live in the most inferior status, and earn the lowest incomes. South Africa is a "pigmentocracy" because skin color determines one's cultural status, economic resources, and political power.[8]

As the South African case illustrates, the political significance of social groups, such as ethnic groups, depends partly on how other individuals and organizations treat the group. The degree of exclusion from the right to wield political power, possess wealth, and enjoy high status forms a fundamental objective condition. Within most societies, the political elite grants some groups the right to participate in the exercise of political power but denies this right to others. In the economic sector, the rich and poor receive different treatment. Particularly in nondemocratic societies with elitist values, the political leaders may divide social groups into those with pure and defiled status. Over the long run, the degree of discrimination or exclusion meted out to a group may create a sense of injustice, thereby reinforcing the members' objective solidarity.

The resources a group possesses constitute a basic objective dimension. Six resources seem especially important for the effective exercise of political power:

1. Weapons, such as guns
2. Wealth, including tangible economic goods and more intangible services
3. Normative righteousness, as manifested in political authority (the justified right to rule) and religious virtue
4. Personal charm and attractiveness
5. Knowledge, information, skills, and technical expertise
6. Social approval based on either ascription or achievement.

A group's status may derive from ascribed (inherited) personal qualities, such as ethnic origin, sex, or age. Alternatively, the prestige a group enjoys may stem from its achievements: warrior skills and the possession of weapons, wealth and economic accomplishments, virtuous performance demonstrated in a political or religious authority role, charm shown by group members in their personal interactions with others, and various types of knowledge. Groups that possess these resources, become motivated to use them to attain political goals, and effectively use these resources to shape public decisions will play an objectively powerful role in the political sphere.[9]

SUBJECTIVE DIMENSIONS

Whatever the objective conditions group members experience, subjective beliefs also affect the group's political power. Although rituals, customs, and work experiences can solidify group interactions, the members must share attitudes, identifications, perceptions, motives, and awareness if they want to play an effective role in political decision making. Identification with an ethnic group, church, or class seems especially important. Groups obviously exert a greater impact when individuals are aware of the group's situation, sensitive to the group's prospects for improving its position, and conscious of the relationship between the group's fate and their own personal fortunes. When group members achieve high agreement on shared values, such as the interpretation of freedom and equality, this value solidarity will strengthen their power in the political process.

A group's effectiveness in realizing its goals also depends on the translation of beliefs into organized action. Individuals must become motivated to work for the group's welfare in such organizations as ethnic associations, churches, trade unions, peasant leagues, and political parties. Through these concrete structures, members struggle to realize their common values, motives, and perceptions of desirable conditions.

Types of Social Groups

In all parts of the world, three social groups play a significant part in political life: primordial, religious, and economic groups. We can define these groups by their objective and subjective dimensions. Primordial groups include ethnic, sex, and age groups. By and large, individuals involuntarily become members of them; that is, they are born into them. It remains difficult, if not impossible, to change one's primordial group membership. Membership in religious and economic groups is more voluntary; individuals have greater freedom to join or leave these groups.

ETHNIC GROUPS

From the standpoint of objective characteristics, members of an ethnic group share certain physical attributes arising from biological inheritance. Particularly in societies where little intermarriage occurs between members of different ethnic groups, individuals of a particular ethnicity may inherit distinctive physical qualities that separate them from others. These physical differences assume special importance in such countries as South Africa, where Whites, black Africans, Asians, and Coloureds comprise a heterogeneous national population.

From the subjective perspective, ethnic groups reveal varying degrees of shared beliefs. Ethnic group members usually perceive that they have all descended from a common ancestor and now share a common heritage. These distinctive cultural beliefs give them a sense of peoplehood, a common identity different from other ethnic groups. In their view, the beliefs associated with the ethnic group assume mystical value.

Yet ethnic groups also demand concrete payoffs from government policy. Although modern societies have become more industrialized, ethnic groups still retain a significant attraction over members. Their influence stems partly from their importance as a political interest group. As governments expand social services to citizens, ethnic associations pressure government leaders to provide more jobs, educational opportunities, public health facilities, and housing for their group. To realize these objectives, they demand greater representation in national political institutions and perhaps greater political autonomy for the region where most members of the ethnic group live. Since the Second World War, the Basques in Spain, the Bretons in France, the Scots and Welsh in Great Britain, the Flemings in Belgium, and the French-speaking citizens of Quebec have sought not only greater resources from the central government but also increased political autonomy, even secession.

A major reason for the continuing importance of ethnic groups in political life stems from their close links with nationalistic sentiments. The term *ethnic group* derives from the Greek word *ethnos*, meaning people or nation. In the new states of Asia and Africa, which became politically independent after World War II, middle-class occupational groups, such as intellectuals, teachers, authors, journalists, lawyers, and even priests, led nationalist movements for independence from European domination. Justifying the need for national independence, these leaders articulated the distinctive cultural contributions of non-European peoples. Ethnic heritage translated into national grandeur. Yet in contrast with Europe, where one ethnic group resides in such nations as Iceland, Ireland, Luxembourg, and Portugal, most countries in Asia and Africa contain several ethnic groups, Thus, after political independence, ethnic cleavages threaten to disrupt the territorial integrity of the new state as ethnic leaders seek greater political autonomy, even a separate nation-state, for their group.

As the examples of Wales, Scotland, Northern Ireland, Spain, Belgium, and Canada demonstrate, the more industrialized, secularized societies of the Western world have not escaped the trend toward greater ethnonational assertiveness. Here, too, as in Afro-Asian countries, middle-class representatives affirm the distinctive cultural values of the ethnonational group and demand greater government resources that will upgrade the objective position of the ethnic group.[10] If the established central government leaders fail to implement public policies benefiting the group's members, then some within the ethnic community will rally behind a movement for national independence.

RELIGIOUS GROUPS

Religious groups often establish close ties with ethnic and national movements. For instance, the Jewish citizens of Israel perceive themselves in ethnic terms. They have all descended from a common ancestor, Abraham, experienced a common historical struggle against various Gentile groups, and speak the same language, Hebrew. Yet their distinctive religious values—the belief in one transcendent God and in the covenant between God and the Jewish people—also give Israelis their sense of national identity. Within China, Confucian beliefs provided solidarity to the Han Chinese and the Chinese nation. Similarly, Shintoism strengthened the national unity of the Japanese people. The Russian Orthodox church historically strove to consolidate the national political integration of all the Russians.

When a people live under foreign oppression, a religious organization often becomes the center of the movement for national independence. Between the two world wars, British colonialists and white settlers dominated the East and Central African territories. Because the colonial power forbade overt political activity by Africans, separatist churches and prophetic movements expressed the African demand for an end to European colonial rule. In Iran, the Shah, allied with Britain and the United States, autocratically governed the nation. Suppressed by the Shah's military and secret police, Iranians rallied behind Moslem leaders in their demand for a nationalistic Islamic republic and for an end to American-British dominance over military affairs and economic investment. In Poland as well, the church has historically articulated nationalistic sentiments. Threatened by Germany and Austria on the west and by Russia on the east, the Polish nation-state disappeared between 1795 and 1918. During this time, the Roman Catholic church in Poland kept alive the spirit of Polish nationalism. Today, under challenge from Soviet officials, the Polish Catholic church not only proclaims the universal values of the Catholic faith but also the need for Poland to remain free from Soviet domination.

Particularly where ethnic and religious ties reinforce each other, national unity remains fragile. In contemporary Yugoslavia, the different ethnic groups share divergent religious attachments. The Serbs, Macedonians, and Montenegrins are members of the Eastern Orthodox church. Some Croats and Slovenes identify with Catholicism. Ethnic groups within Bosnia practice Islam. Similar ethnoreligious cleavages threaten Sri Lanka. Whereas the majority Sinhalese follow Buddhism, the ethnic Tamils are Hindus. Since 1968, ethnic and religious conflicts have brought civil war to Northern Ireland. Over two-thirds of the Catholics identify with the Irish ethnic group; the same percentage of Protestants see themselves as members of the British or Ulster ethnic group. Under these reinforcing religious and ethnic identities, a peaceful reconciliation of differences becomes difficult to achieve.

Despite these close attachments between a religious and an ethnic group, membership in the religious group is somewhat more voluntary. Although most Moslems and Catholics are born into the Islamic and Christian faiths, these missionary religions seek to convert the unchurched. It is easier to change one's religious affiliation than to change one's ethnic group membership. Thus, in Africa, several former "animists," those who worshiped gods in their local villages, have converted to either Islam or Christianity.

Both objective and subjective features characterize religious group members. Objectively, devotees participate in ritual behavior and sacramental ceremonies. They attend a church, temple, or mosque. Religious authorities, such as Buddhist monks, Moslem ulama, Jewish rabbis, and Catholic clergy, usually wear distinctive vestments. From the subjective standpoint, individuals within religious groups share a sense of ultimate ends that transcends the empirical world. The sacred values embodied in the spiritual faith provide a meaning behind history, a purpose for living, reasons for suffering, and guidelines for moral behavior.

Sacred and secular values. Besides articulating transcendental values, religious groups have historically played a key role in politics because their sacred values have justified the exercise of political power and shaped specific policy preferences. Politics and religion have both dealt with general, common concerns affecting the whole community—that is, with notions of the public well-being. Like the religious vocabulary, political discourse has focused on concepts of justice, virtue, equality, freedom, and the public interest. Before the nineteenth century, few political systems distinguished between sacred religious values and secular political beliefs. Kings and emperors claimed to rule by the grace of God. For example, in West Europe before the emergence of the nation-state during the sixteenth century, the pope of the Roman Catholic church consecrated the kings, thereby legitimating their rule. In East Europe, however, the emperor gained greater power over the Orthodox churches. In Russia, the Orthodox church regarded the czar as the appointee of God, the representative of Christ on earth. The czar himself claimed that his decisions directly reflected God's commandments.

In the late twentieth century, the more "secular" values of statehood, nationalism, and economic development comprise the dominant political beliefs; yet political leaders still justify their rights to rule on the basis of sacred values. In revolutionary societies, secular values of industrialization and the socialist transformation of society assume ultimate significance, with Marxist-Leninist ideology representing a new form of secular political religion. Even in democratic societies that have preserved the autonomy of the church from state control, elected officials appeal for support in terms of moral–religious values such as justice, freedom, and pursuit of the common welfare. In short, despite the declining political power of orthodox religious organization, religious beliefs still shape the pursuit of political power.

When religious groups affirm certain guidelines for moral behavior, they often strive to translate these moral values into concrete policies. For example, during the twentieth century, Catholic groups in West Europe, North America, and South America have pressed government officials to grant increased funds for Catholic schools and to exempt church property from taxation. Catholic leaders have also opposed legislation legitimizing divorce and authorizing expenditures for abortion. In their view, these policy stands reflect the moral guidelines of church teachings.

Religious group struggles. Throughout the world, political struggles have involved conflicts among three types of religious groups. Especially before the nineteenth century, most religious conflicts occurred between opposing orthodox groups. Catholics and Moslems fought for supremacy in Spain. In sixteenth-century France, Protestant Huguenots battled with Catholics. On the eve of political independence in 1947, the conflict between Hindus and Moslems in India caused over a million deaths. The impossibility of reconciling these religious differences led to the formation of the Moslem state of Pakistan.

A second type of religious struggle, particularly in Islamic and Catholic societies, centers around the conflicts between believers and nonbelievers who remain indifferent to the creeds and rituals of a traditional orthodox religion. For instance, in many Catholic countries, such as Spain, France, Italy, and Chile, women maintain a strong adherence to the Catholic faith, but their husbands and sons adopt an indifferent attitude toward Catholic theology and attendance at mass. These religious divisions translate into political conflicts; the women strongly support Christian Democratic parties, but the men align themselves with anarchists, Socialists, or Communists.

Third, as the world has become more secularized and industrialized, movements have arisen to articulate a secular political religion. Rejecting identification with an orthodox faith, these groups worship the party, state, nation, and national leader. During the early 1790s, the French revolutionary Jacobins ordered some Catholic churches closed and turned into temples of reason. These Jacobins instituted a number of national ceremonies that resembled religious rituals. At the Jacobin clubs, the citizens took part in quasi-religious ceremonies. The official scripture became the revolutionary Declaration of the Rights of Man. Jacobins gave sermons or moral discourses, sang national anthems, such as the Marseillaise, and took an oath of loyalty to the French republic. In one oath, the citizen pledged to have no "other temple than that of Reason, other altars than those of the Fatherland, other priests than our legislators, no other cult than that of liberty, equality, and fraternity."[11]

In all these nationalistic ceremonies the Jacobins established a worship of *la patrie*, the nation or fatherland. Whereas in medieval times the Latin word *patria* had meant either the City of God or particular localities and provinces, now *la patrie* referred to the whole nation. Whereas before the revolution children had received a Catholic education, now they went to public schools, where nationalist propaganda replaced the indoctrination formerly carried out by the church. In the public schools, the teachers propagated the national doctrines of patriotism and citizenship. Whereas in the past, people had lived and died for the church, now they were encouraged to die for the nation. "Mort pour la Patrie"—Death for the Fatherland—became the rallying cry.

Similarly, during the twentieth century, secular political religions have dominated political life in Nazi Germany, the Soviet Union, and the People's Republic of China. Before he came to power in 1933, Adolf Hitler appealed for support from German Christians; he himself had been educated in Catholic schools. Yet after consolidating his rule, he began to curb the activities of the churches, especially if they opposed his anti-semitic policies. Indeed, nationalism soon superseded universal religion. Hitler replaced Christ as an object of worship. His close followers called him "savior" and perceived themselves as apostles spreading the gospel of national socialism.[12]

In the Soviet Union, the party, nation, and leader assumed sacred value under communist rule. Although Lenin criticized those party members who made an analogy between the Communist party and a church, his doctrine of party primacy and the need for the Bolsheviks to play a vanguard role in the new Soviet state later led to the institution of a comprehensive political religion. The Communist party played a political role performed by the Russian Orthodox church under the czarist regime. The Party became viewed as a charismatic organization. Like the Orthodox church, it fulfilled religious needs, giving its members meaning, purpose, and a common identity. Educating the populace, it spread both nationalist and socialist values. The struggle to construct a communist society paralleled the early Christian efforts to accelerate the coming of the Kingdom of God. During the 1930s and 1940s, the veneration of Stalin resembled a religious cult.

Today Soviet leaders use political saints, secular rituals, and holy traditions to cement national solidarity. Lenin, not Stalin, serves as the political saint. By observing busts of Lenin, placing flowers at memorials to Lenin, and visiting his mausoleum in Moscow, citizens are reminded that "Lenin lived, Lenin lives, and Lenin shall live." Secular rituals such as the Festive Registration of the New-Born Child, special wedding ceremonies, and funeral rites mark an individual's passage through life. By encouraging participation in holy traditions that honor the Soviet revolution of 1917, the Great Patriotic War (World War II), and May Day (a holiday dedicated to working-class solidarity), Soviet leaders try to strengthen citizens' attachments to the political regime.[13]

In China under Mao Zedong, Communist party leaders also practiced a form of secular political religion. Maoist beliefs blended aspects of both ancient Confucian beliefs and more modern doctrines voiced by the Presbyterian church, the dominant Protestant group in China before the revolutionaries gained political power in 1949. Mao's stress on austerity, asceticism, rule by moral example, and the supremacy of the collective identity over individual self-interest all derive from Confucianism. The affirmation of the need for hard work, organization, sacrifice, and the confession of political sins resemble some key Presbyterian beliefs.

During the Cultural Revolution (1966–1969), Maoist study meetings functioned like religious sects. Each meeting opened with the singing of a hymn, such as "Song of the Helmsman." (Mao was seen as the Great Helmsman guiding China to national glory and socialism.) Members renounced their former feudal and capitalist sins, such as corruption, luxury, class oppression, and the pursuit of self-interest. After confessing guilt, the member gained absolution from the Communist party by agreeing to engage in manual labor on a rural commune.

Work for the Chinese national and socialist cause paralleled religious sacrifices. Mao and his associates urged young party members—the Red Guards—to emulate the sacrificial spirit displayed by Communist party officials on the Long March from Kiangsi to northern China in the 1930s. As Mao reminded his followers, out of temporary defeat experienced by the Red Army during that march emerged eventual victory and the founding of a communist regime throughout the Chinese mainland.[14] In short, despite their belief in historical materialism, communist leaders in power have relied not only on economic self-interest to motivate the masses but also on more transcendent spiritual values embodied in secular political religions.

ECONOMIC GROUPS

Like religious groups, economic groups reveal distinctive objective and subjective features. From the objective standpoint, they occupy different relational positions in both the productive and distributive process. For example, in a highly industrialized capitalist society, the capitalists own the physical means of production (equipment, machinery, plants, and technological devices to increase productivity). They control the investment of money and capital, as well as the allocation of scarce resources. Supervising the labor force, capitalists also have the authority to dictate pay, working conditions, and promotions. Except where trade unions play a significant role in collective bargaining, workers do not directly control investments, wages, working conditions, and promotions. These differential positions within the productive process lead to divergent shares of the scarce resources. Compared with workers, capitalists receive higher incomes, hold more personal property, and enjoy more fringe benefits.[15]

Distinctive subjective beliefs and interest claims also characterize economic groups. They seek from other classes and from government officials concrete benefits or material payoffs. For example, capitalists strive for higher profits, more government expenditures for investment, and reduced corporate taxes. Labor unions seek higher wages, healthier, safer working conditions, increased fringe benefits (pensions, health care, life insurance), and perhaps greater control over the workplace. More radical unions advocate the need for a transformation of a capitalist economy into a socialist economy. Farmers want higher prices for their agricultural produce, lower interest rates, and greater access to fertile land. All these interest claims reflect a preference for government actions to increase the economic group's wealth and status.

Yet even if a group shares similar economic interests, it will not play an effective role in the political system unless it develops a subjective feeling of community solidarity. To exercise decisive political power, members of an economic group must develop an awareness of the group's common interests, especially a heightened realization of how the individual's wealth depends on the group's economic standing. Generally, economic leaders try to strengthen the individual's group identification. Their task lies in transforming a category of individuals with similar economic resources into both a membership and a reference group.

Group classifications. The most useful classifications of economic groups derive from their occupation or mode of work. In most societies, individuals work within the agricultural, manufacturing, and service sectors of the economy.[16] That is, they extract produce from the sea or land, produce tangible commodities, or provide intangible services.

At the earliest stages of economic development, persons worked primarily in agricultural pursuits. They picked berries, planted crops, fished, or hunted wild game.

Beginning in late eighteenth-century England, the Industrial Revolution focused economic activities on the manufacture of tangible commodities. Some individuals produced capital goods, such as electrical equipment, machine tools, dams, and railroads. Others manufactured consumer goods, such as clothes, cooking utensils, and books.

During the twentieth century, the service sector has become the dominant part of industrial economies. This sector encompasses a wide variety of occupations with diverse political power, wealth, and status. The following are the most important components of the service sector:

1. *Professional and technical services:* jurists, scientists, educators, health personnel, computer programmers, engineers, authors, artists, journalists, popular entertainers, and religious officials
2. *Coordination services:* managers, administrators, clerical personnel (typists, word processors, stenographers, cashiers), and individuals engaged in protective services, such as military, police, and prison work
3. *Distribution and exchange services:* the allocation of tangible goods (truck drivers, wholesale and retail traders, salespeople), money (bankers, financiers, insurance agents), and information (telephone operators)
4. *Domestic and quasi-domestic personal services:* hairdressers, barbers, launderers, maids, janitors, and workers in hotels, bars, and restaurants

What changes in occupational roles occur as a society becomes more industrialized? Generally, the initial change involves a decline in persons engaged in the agricultural sector. Factories begin operations in the urban areas, and farmers often flee the land seeking work in the new manufacturing industries. As seen in the experiences of the United States, Germany, England, and Sweden, when a country reaches a fairly high level of industrialization, workers in the manufacturing sector, especially unskilled laborers, decline as a percentage of the total labor force. Professional, technical, and managerial occupations become more economically important. Professionals and technicians play a greater role in decision making. Theoretical knowledge and technical expertise partially guide the formulation of public policies. Whereas the early industrializing society experienced conflicts between the capitalists and factory workers, a key struggle in a highly industrialized society revolves around disputes between professionals oriented toward specialized knowledge and populist leaders who articulate the general demands of "the people" against the claims of "the experts."[17]

Occupation and political recruitment. Throughout all political systems, an individual's location in the occupational network largely shapes his or her chances for recruitment to political office. Those who occupy high-status jobs, especially professional and technical ones, have the greatest opportunities for securing a government position. For example, in the democratic, industrialized societies of the United States, France, Britain, West Germany, Sweden, and Italy, legislators and bureaucrats hail from upper-status social backgrounds. A fairly high percentage have fathers who were executives, managers, and professionals. The fathers of the others held middle-class positions as clerks, salespersons, and lower-ranking employees. Except in Germany and Italy, few governmental leaders have fathers who worked as manual laborers. The legislators themselves represent even higher occupational prestige than their fathers. Most legislators come from professional, managerial, and executive business positions. A rather high proportion of the legislators, and especially the bureaucrats, have a university education. Hence, individuals from middle- and upper-class occupations dominate the political process; the workers are highly underrepresented in recruitment to political office.[18]

A comparison of legislators' occupations in France, Britain, and the United States suggests that even the left-wing parties contain few members with a working-class background. True, during the early 1970s, working-class legislators were most likely to belong to a leftist party—the British Labour party and the French Communist party. Yet in both societies, working-class representation has declined since the 1930s. A higher proportion of French Communist and British

Labour party members hailed from working-class backgrounds during the 1930s than in the early 1970s. In 1975, only three members of the United States Congress had labor union affiliations; all three identified with the Democratic party. The left-wing parties have experienced the rise of professional, university-educated persons. The French socialists are mainly university professionals, such as teachers, civil servants, and writers. Similarly, a large percentage of British Labourites are teachers, lawyers, journalists, and engineers. In 1975, about twice as many Democrats as Republicans in Congress came from the professions of education and journalism.[19]

The historical trends for nearly all Western democratic countries reveal a growing "embourgeoisement" of the legislatures. France and England have seen the declining influence of the aristocratic nobility in their parliaments. Members from the factory working class now hold a lower representation in left-wing parties than before World War II. The old nineteenth-century struggles between the "proletariat" and the "bourgeoisie" have largely waned. The new political disputes over government policy revolve around conflicts within the middle class. Whereas professionals aligned with a left-wing party usually support a more equalitarian role for the government, most managers and executives employed by business corporations belong to right-wing parties and favor less-equalitarian public policies.

Although Soviet officials claim to head a proletarian, socialist state dedicated to social, political, and economic equality, leaders within the Communist party and the Soviet government come from highly educated managerial, technical, and professional occupations. During the early 1970s, about two-thirds of the members in the Politburo, the top decision-making organ of the Communist party of the Soviet Union, had attained a higher technical education. Nearly all party secretaries operating at the district level and above were college graduates; most originally held occupations as engineers, technicians, agronomists, and economists. Along with these managerial, technical, professional, and scientific personnel, other segments of the "intelligentsia"—artists, writers, and musicians—also play a dominant role in the Party. The least-educated segments of the population, especially collective farmers, have the lowest access to government and party structures. In sum, compared with the general population, the Communist party overrepresents highly educated, urban, and white-collar occupations.[20]

Occupation and support for revolution. Middle-class professionals also form the nucleus of revolutionary movements dedicated to establishing a regime furthering the interests of the proletariat and peasantry. The radical intelligentsia, including lawyers, lower-ranking bureaucrats, teachers, doctors, and university students, have played the dominant leadership roles in these revolutionary movements. For example, Lenin, Vo Nguyen Giap (Vietnamese revolutionary leader), and Fidel Castro, Cuba's president, were lawyers. Che Guevara, Castro's associate; Frantz Fanon, intellectual advocate of the Algerian revolution; and George Habash, leader of the Popular Front for the Liberation of Palestine, originally were doctors. From 1918 to 1919, Mao Zedong served as a library assistant at Peking University. Later he worked as principal of a primary school in his native Hunan province.[21] Obviously, most individuals from middle-class occupations do not become revolutionaries; yet intellectuals and other professionals do lead revolutionary movements. Despite the ideological rhetoric, the struggle for political dominance takes place not between the "capitalists" and the "proletariat" but among individuals fulfilling professional, bureaucratic, and landowning roles. From these occupations come both the old and the new political elite.

Although Marx assumed that the factory working class would play the dominant role in the forthcoming socialist revolution, during the twentieth century the peasantry has more enthusiastically supported revolutionary movements in China, Vietnam, Angola, and Guinea-Bissau. Although the Russian urban proletariat in Moscow and Petrograd did vote for leftist parties in 1917, the seizure of land by the peasants and the defection of peasant soldiers from the army also helped topple the provisional government. As Theda Skocpol and Ellen Kay Trimberger point out:

> Contrary to Marx's argument that the struggles of the bourgeoisie or proletariat would have the most impact, it has actually been the peasantry struggling against formerly dominant landed classes (and/or colonial or neo-colonial regimes) that has done the most—specifically in social revolutions from below—to undermine the class and political structures of old regimes and clear the way for the consolidation of revolutionary states on a new socioeconomic and political basis.[22]

What variables explain the different roles workers and peasants perform in movements for social change? Basic explanatory factors include the level of economic development, the degree of political repression, the economic group's beliefs, and its access to organizations that struggle to realize the group's goals.

In the industrialized, democratic states of West Europe, small farmers generally play a more conservative political role than either factory workers or such middle-class personnel as professionals, civil servants, and clerks. Compared with these other two economic groups, farmers are more likely to identify with traditional parental values, attend church, vote for conservative parties, oppose student protests, and support the struggle against communism. They seek from government lower taxes, lower interest rates, and higher guaranteed prices for their farm products.

In contrast, the factory working class gives the greatest support to Socialist and Communist parties. Less likely to attend church regularly and to believe in traditional religious beliefs such as the existence of God, the divinity of Christ, and life after death, workers want the church to play an active role in securing economic and political reforms. They seek concrete economic benefits from government policies, including full employment, a shorter work week, wage hikes that exceed price rises, expanded fringe benefits such as health care, greater income equality, and the preservation of union autonomy in the collective bargaining process. Programs to establish greater working-class control over job conditions take priority over extending public ownership of industries. In their attitudes toward civil liberties, particularly student protests, workers give greater support than farmers but show weaker enthusiasm than middle-class occupational groups.[23] In short, throughout contemporary West Europe, workers, compared with small farmers, adopt a more reformist posture toward social change.

Like their colleagues in the industrial societies, factory workers in less economically developed countries support reformist organizations and voice reformist demands. Concentrated in the urban areas, they are more exposed than peasants to the mass media, schools, and government officials. As a result, they develop more national orientations and stronger attachments to the existing state institutions. Employed largely in government enterprises, domestic private firms, or foreign private corporations, the working class becomes dependent on the efficient functioning of these economic institutions. Most often, their unions formulate an accommodating strategy, seeking higher wages, more extensive fringe benefits, perhaps greater worker autonomy in the plant, and better working conditions. All these preferences reflect reformist beliefs. For example, in Chile, over 60 percent of a Santiago sample of factory workers affirmed in 1968 that Chile needed "progressive reforms"; only 13 percent wanted a "real" revolution, a violent one if necessary. Rather than favoring state ownership of all industries, most workers supported either the maintenance of a private enterprise economy or nationalization of only heavy industry and transportation. Nearly all workers desired greater access to consumer goods and to private property for their personal use.[24]

In contrast to workers, peasants in underdeveloped societies may under certain conditions adopt a more revolutionary stance toward the existing stratification system. Unlike workers, they function in greater isolation from the urban elite. Relatively autonomous as producers, peasants in the Hunan province of China and in the Mekong

Delta region of Vietnam functioned within a decentralized sharecropping system. An alliance of state bureaucrats and landlords subjected the peasants to high taxes, high rents, high interest rates, and forced labor. These economies were linked to the world market. As the world prices for exported rice fell, the landless tenant farmers suffered a devastating loss. Their antagonism toward the national and international capitalist system thus heightened.

Many Chinese and Vietnamese peasants aligned themselves with the revolutionary socialist movements to secure a society free of centralized bureaucratic control, landlord exploitation, international capitalism, and status differences between the urban and rural populations. Particularly when foreign economic pressures, wars, and such natural disasters as floods, famines, and earthquakes destroyed the existing social order and caused the disintegration of the state, the peasants became a leading economic group allied behind the revolutionary socialist movement. By incorporating within the party the peasants' informal organizations—kin groups, age grades, peasant leagues, mutual aid societies, and local marketing associations—and by advocating concrete, local demands—low taxes, low rents, abolition of debts, easier access to land—Communist party leaders rallied major segments of the peasantry to their revolutionary cause.[25] After gaining political power, the Chinese and Vietnamese revolutionaries brought about fundamental changes in the social stratification system.

Notes

1. See Midge Mackenzie, *Shoulder to Shoulder: A Documentary* (New York: Knopf, 1975), p. 296.
2. Ibid., p. 33.
3. Ibid., pp. 269–270, 283–284; Keith Curry Lance, "Strategy Choices of the British Women's Social and Political Union, 1903–18," *Social Science Quarterly* 60 (June 1979): 51–61.
4. See Marion J. Levy, Jr., *Modernization and the Structure of Societies*, vol. 1 (Princeton, N.J.: Princeton University Press, 1966), pp. 19–26; David B. Truman, *The Governmental Process* (New York: Knopf, 1951), pp. 23–24; Seymour Martin Lipset, *Revolution and Counterrevolution: Change and Persistence in Social Structures* (New York: Basic Books, 1968), p. 153.
5. Lipset, *Revolution and Counterrevolution*, pp. 121–158.
6. Frederic and Mary Ann Brussat, *The Long Search: Feedforward Discussion Guide* (New York: Cultural Information Service, 1978), p. 12.
7. Quoted in Daniel Chirot, *Social Change in the Twentieth Century* (New York: Harcourt Brace Jovanovich, 1977), p. 201.
8. Leonard Thompson and Andrew Prior, *South African Politics* (New Haven, Conn.: Yale University Press, 1982), pp. 35, 66, 166–167; *Southern Africa Perspectives: South Africa Fact Sheet* (New York: Africa Fund, 1977).
9. See the analysis of political power in Charles F. Andrain, *Political Life and Social Change*, 2nd ed. (Belmont, Calif.: Wadsworth, 1975), pp. 96–112.
10. See Wsevolod W. Isajiw, "Definitions of Ethnicity," *Ethnicity* 1 (July 1974): 111–124; Ivo D. Duchacek, "Antagonistic Cooperation: Territorial and Ethnic Communities," *Publius* 7 (Fall 1977): 3–29; Donald L. Horowitz, "Cultural Movements and Ethnic Change," *Annals of the American Academy of Political and Social Science* 433 (September 1977): 6–18; Nathan Glazer, "The Universalisation of Ethnicity," *Encounter* 44 (February 1975): 8–17; Nathan

Glazer and Daniel P. Moynihan, "Why Ethnicity?" *Commentary* 58 (October 1974): 33–39; Harold R. Isaacs, "Basic Group Identity: The Idols of the Tribe," in *Ethnicity: Theory and Experience,* ed. Nathan Glazer and Daniel P. Moynihan (Cambridge, Mass.: Harvard University Press, 1975), pp. 29–52.

11. Crane Brinton, *The New Jacobins* (New York: Macmillan, 1931), p. 189. For general analyses of the interactions between politics and religion, see Andrain, *Political Life and Social Change,* pp. 53–89; David E. Apter, *The Politics of Modernization* (Chicago: University of Chicago Press, 1965), pp. 292–312; Reinhard Bendix, *Kings or People: Power and the Mandate to Rule* (Berkeley: University of California Press, 1978), pp. 21–60, 93–106.

12. George L. Mosse, *Nazi Culture* (New York: Grosset and Dunlap, 1968), pp. 235, 341–345.

13. See Crane Brinton, *The Shaping of the Modern Mind* (New York: Mentor Books, 1953), pp. 203–211; Christel Lane, "Ritual and Ceremony in Contemporary Soviet Society," *Sociological Review* 27 (May 1979): 253–278.

14. L. C. Young and S. R. Ford, "God Is Society: The Religious Dimension of Maoism," *Sociological Inquiry* 47, no. 2 (1977): 89–97.

15. For this interpretation of economic class, see Erik Olin Wright, *Class Structure and Income Determination* (New York: Academic Press, 1979), pp. 3–55; Lipset, *Revolution and Counterrevolution,* pp. 125–129.

16. See Donald J. Treiman, *Occupational Prestige in Comparative Perspective* (New York: Academic Press, 1977), pp. 235–259.

17. Daniel Bell, *The Coming of Post-Industrial Society* (New York: Basic Books, 1973), pp. 12–33, 126–128, 487.

18. See Robert D. Putnam, *The Comparative Study of Political Elites* (Englewood Cliffs, N.J.: Prentice-Hall, 1975), pp. 22–27; Robert D. Putnam, "The Political Attitudes of Senior Career Civil Servants in Western Europe: A Preliminary Report," *British Journal of Political Science* 3 (July 1973): 266–267; Joel D. Aberbach, Robert D. Putnam, and Bert A. Rockman, *Bureaucrats and Politicians in Western Democracies* (Cambridge, Mass.: Harvard University Press, 1981), pp. 47–58; M. Donald Hancock, *Sweden: The Politics of Postindustrial Change* (Hinsdale, Ill.: Dryden Press, 1972), p. 183; *Congressional Quarterly Almanac 1975,* vol. 31 (Washington, D.C.: Congressional Quarterly, 1976), pp. 44–45.

19. See David Butler and Dennis Kavanagh, *The British General Election of February 1974* (New York: St. Martin's Press, 1974), p. 215; David Butler and Anne Sloman, *British Political Facts 1900–1975,* 4th ed. (New York: St. Martin's Press, 1975), p. 155; R. W. Johnson, "The British Political Elite, 1955–1972," *Archives Européennes de Sociologie* 14, no. 1 (1973): 35–77; R. W. Johnson, "The Political Elite," *New Society* 27 (January 24, 1974): 188–191; W. L. Guttsman, "The British Political Elite and the Class Structure," in *Elites and Power in British Society,* ed. Philip Stanworth and Anthony Giddens (London: Cambridge University Press, 1974), pp. 22–44; *New Society* 51 (March 13, 1980): iv; Jean Charlot, "Les élites politiques en France de la IIIe à la Ve République," *Archives Européennes de Sociologie* 14, no. 1 (1973) 79–84; *Congressional Quarterly Almanac 1975,* pp. 44–45.

20. Mary McAuley, *Politics and the Soviet Union* (New York: Penguin Books, 1977), pp. 268–271, 296; David Lane, *The End of Inequality? Stratification under State Socialism* (Baltimore, Md.: Penguin Books, 1971), pp. 120–128; David Lane, *The Socialist Industrial State: Towards a Political Sociology of State Socialism* (London: George Allen and Unwin, 1976), pp. 124–129; T. Anthony Jones, "Modernization and Education in the U.S.S.R.," *Social Forces* 57 (December 1978): 528–529; Jeffrey W. Hahn, "Stability and Change in the Soviet Union: A Developmental Perspective," *Polity* 10 (Summer 1978): 554–562.

21. Thomas H. Greene, *Comparative Revolutionary Movements* (Englewood Cliffs, N.J.: Prentice-Hall, 1974), pp. 22–32; Putnam, *The Comparative Study of Political Elites,* pp. 191–196; Chirot, *Social Change in the Twentieth Century,* pp. 132–145.

22. Theda Skocpol and Ellen Kay Trimberger, "Revolutions and the World-Historical Development of Capitalism," in *Social Change in the Capitalist World Economy,* ed. Barbara Hockey Kaplan (Beverly Hills, Calif.: Sage, 1978), p. 126.

23. See Michael S. Lewis-Beck, "Explaining Peasant Conservatism: The Western European Case," *British Journal of Political Science* 7 (October 1977): 447–464; Ronald Inglehart, *The Silent Revolution: Changing Values and Political Styles among Western Publics* (Princeton, N.J.: Princeton University Press, 1977), pp. 213, 280; John R. Low-Beer, *Protest and Participation: The New Working Class in Italy* (New York: Cambridge University Press, 1978), pp.

51–52; Rodney Stark, "Class, Radicalism, and Religious Involvement in Great Britain," *American Sociological Review* 29 (October 1964): 698–706; François Isambert, "Les ouvriers et l'Église catholique," *Revue française de sociologie* 15 (Octobre–Décembre 1974): 529–551; Duncan Gallie, "Social Radicalism in the French and British Working Classes: Some Points of Comparison," *British Journal of Sociology* 30 (December 1979): 500–524; Duncan Gallie, "Trade Union Ideology and Workers' Conceptions of Class Inequality in France," *West European Politics* 3 (January 1980): 10–32.

24. Christian Lalive d'Epinay and Jacques Zylberberg, "Une variable oubliée de la problématique agraire: Le prolétariat urbain (Le cas du Chili)," *Civilisations* 23–24, no. 1–2 (1973–1974): 51–64; Peter Winn, "Loosing the Chains: Labor and the Chilean Revolutionary Process, 1970–1973," *Latin American Perspectives* 3 (Winter 1976): 70–84.

25. James Scott, "Hegemony and the Peasantry," *Politics and Society* 7, no. 3 (1977): 267–296; Jeffery M. Paige, *Agrarian Revolution: Social Movements and Export Agriculture in the Underdeveloped World* (New York: Free Press, 1975), pp. 27–28, 63, 318–319, 330–333, 369–376; Theda Skocpol, "Review Article: What Makes Peasants Revolutionary?" *Comparative Politics* 14 (April 1982): 351–375.

CHAPTER

3

Social Stratification

The law in its majestic equality forbids rich and poor alike to sleep under bridges, to beg in the streets, and to steal bread.
—ANATOLE FRANCE

Whatever the claims of political leaders ruling a country, all systems reveal *social stratification*—that is, political, economic, and cultural inequalities. From the most general perspective, social stratification refers to the rankings of individuals and groups in terms of their differential political power, wealth, and status. These dimensions of social stratification—political power, wealth, and prestige—correspond to three analytical sectors of society: the polity (political system), economy, and culture.[1]

Dimensions of Social Stratification

POLITICAL POWER

The political sector revolves around the formulation and implementation of public policies. As Sheldon Wolin points out:

> At some point within the system, certain institutions are recognized as having the authority to make decisions applicable to the whole community. The exercise of this function naturally attracts the attention of groups and individuals who feel that their interests and purposes will be affected by the decisions taken. When this awareness takes the form of action directed towards political institutions, the activities become "political" and a part of political nature.[2]

This interpretation of politics stresses the public consequences of individual and group activities. Political struggles focus on the production and distribution of power that has impacts on a wide segment of society.

Political power refers to the use of resources to secure public consequences. To exercise effective power, groups and individuals must first possess certain resources. Key resources include weapons, wealth (goods and services), political authority, moral virtue, personal attractiveness, knowledge, and group approval such as status, prestige, respect, and honor.

Second, a power wielder must have the will or motivation to transform these resources into actions that influence the conduct of public affairs. Rather than touring the Caribbean on a pleasure jaunt, a politically motivated individual channels his wealth into efforts to influence tax and expenditure policies passed by the legislature.

Third, an effective power wielder demonstrates effective political skills in using resources. The ability to exercise both coercive and consensual power is important for securing compliance. Especially in a democratic society, leaders rely on consensual power. If a group has mastered the ability to bargain, negotiate, compromise, cooperate with others, and form alliances, then the transformation of its resources into effective political power becomes more likely. In a dictatorial society, political leaders place a premium on mastering those skills needed to exercise effective coercive power. Those who control the military and police usually manage to gain power or retain government office. But whether in a democracy or a dictatorship, individuals, groups, and organizations exercise the greatest political power when they can most effectively use their resources to attain desired public consequences.[3]

Max Weber defined power as "the chances which a man or group of men have to realize their will in a communal activity, even against the opposition of others taking part in it."[4] However, the exercise of political power involves more than overcoming others' resistance; the mobilization of apathetic individuals and the coordination of formerly isolated activities also form a vital part of the political power struggle. Especially during times of social disintegration, the overcoming of resistance becomes crucial. When war, famine, and foreign economic pressures bring social collapse, revolutionaries have the greatest opportunities to seize political power. At these times, organizations that wield the effective consensual and coercive power needed to overcome opposition groups will exercise decisive political power. Yet even during a revolutionary era, let alone in more quiescent times, not all groups will mount resistance to ambitious political leaders. Some groups will remain isolated from interpersonal contacts and apathetic toward political involvement.

Particularly if an organization wants to secure a fundamental transformation of the existing social stratification system, it must rouse the apathetic from their political slumber and coordinate the scattered activities of formerly isolated individuals. During the 1930s and 1940s, Mao Zedong and the Chinese Communist party succeeded in these tasks; they not only overcame the opposition of Chiang Kai-shek and the Nationalist regime but also mobilized the peasantry behind the revolutionary cause and coordinated peasant efforts around the socialist transformation of China.

As the Chinese case illustrates, the effective exercise of political power involves both the distribution and the production of resources for public ends. Through encouraging industrialization and mass education, political leaders can expand the resource base—that is, produce more resources such as weapons, wealth, and information. By controlling access to these scarce resources, they can secure greater obedience to their policies.

From the perspective of social stratification, the gap between the powerful and the powerless reveals the basic political inequalities within a society. The powerful possess scarce resources, have the motivation to become politically involved, and demonstrate effective skills in their use of resources. The political elite has the greatest access to the public policy process. Its members control the means of producing resources: the industries and the schools. As a result, they possess the resources and the skills needed to translate their preferences into public programs. In making and carrying out public decisions, the political participants exert decisive influence.

In contrast, the politically powerless, the nonparticipants, play only a passive role in the political struggle. Even if they have the will to participate, they possess neither the resources nor the skills to shape public outcomes. The political elite in the civilian government institutions, military, police, dominant political parties, and political interest groups either refuses to listen to the nonparticipants' demands or else disregards their policy preferences. With only limited access to the governing institutions, the powerless are passive spectators watching others participate in the political dramas of our age.

WEALTH

Social stratification also involves differential access to scarce economic resources. At the most general level, the economic sector of society concentrates on the production and distribution of one type of resource—wealth or goods and services. Economic resources include the classical trilogy: *land* (natural assets—that is, land, water, air, oil, minerals), *labor* (human skills, knowledge, expertise, entrepreneurial abilities), and *capital* (physical machines, equipment, tools, and so forth). From the use of these resources derive various types of monetary income, such as wages, salaries, rent, interest, and dividends. Especially within the industrialized economies, both "capitalist" and "communist," fringe benefits available to the politico-economic elite include free cars, vacations at luxurious resorts, free travel, apartment houses, homes, health care, and special access to prestigious educational institutions. Particularly outside the communist states of East Europe, Asia, and Cuba, property constitutes an important basis of economic stratification. Compared with the poor, the wealthy own capital goods (plants, equipment, machinery), corporate stocks and bonds, life insurance, land, real estate, homes, automobiles, and consumer durable goods. All these properties give the wealthy the potential economic power to shape the conduct of political affairs.

A group's relationship to the production and distribution of economic resources determines its position within the economic stratification system. The economic elite dominates production. Whether or not its members legally own the means of production, they determine investment and the allocation of economic resources. They control the use of physical capital, such as equipment, machinery, and technological innovations. They also supervise the labor force. From the distributional standpoint, they obtain privileged access to scarce economic resources, including property, cash income, and fringe benefits. In contrast, those groups and individuals at the bottom of the economic totem pole exert virtually no influence over the investment process, the use of capital equipment, and the employment of human labor. As a result, they gain only limited access to property, cash, and noncash benefits.[5] From these different relationships to the production and distribution of economic resources derives the fundamental cleavage within the economic stratification system: the gap between the rich and poor.

Both the production and the distribution of economic resources shape the public policy process. Comprehensive social service programs—health care, mass education, family allowances, income maintenance, old-age pensions—are found most often in a wealthy, industrialized economy that can supply the resources needed to finance them. Furthermore, the distribution of wealth partly determines relative access to the political system. Those groups possessing the most economic assets have the greatest opportunities to translate their preferences to public policies. For example, the American government spends a lower percentage of the gross national product (GNP) on health care than do most democratic European governments. The low priority accorded to government expenditures for medical care stems from the dominant position of private insurance company executives, private physicians, and private hospital administrators within the American economic stratification system. In Europe, however, these private groups generally possess less economic influence to press their claims on government health policy.

In turn, political structures influence the production and distribution of economic resources. After World War II, the West Germans instituted certain structural arrangements, the "social market" economy, that helped attain a high economic growth rate. The English, however, failed to develop the proper balance among government, private businesses, and trade unions needed for maximizing productivity. Political structures also affect the distribution of resources, both among competing public programs and among social groups. The centralization of government, the power of government agencies relative to social groups, and the organizational role performed by political parties affect the priorities for political action. For instance, most Communist party officials in the Soviet Union and other East European countries have given highest priority to heavy industry. Maximizing agricultural productivity and producing more consumer goods such as private cars and homes assume a lower governmental priority.

In contrast, in the market economies of West Europe and North America, the political elite places higher importance on manufacturing consumer goods and producing a food surplus. Compared with the Soviet regimes, these societies have less centralized government structures. Social groups exert greater power vis-a-vis government agencies. Greater competition occurs among diverse political parties. As a result, consumers have more freedom to register their preferences on the economic and political market. Along with this consumer freedom go greater economic inequalities than are found in most East European countries. Although managerial, professional, and administrative groups still retain economic dominance within East Europe, government and party leaders there have managed to narrow the income gap between managers and skilled factory workers.[6] In short, the political power exercised by such structures as government institutions, political parties, and political interest groups influences the specific types of social groups gaining the most benefits from public policies.

STATUS

The status dimension of social stratification corresponds to the cultural sector of a society, just as political power is linked to the polity and wealth to the economy. From an analytical perspective, the cultural system focuses on the creation and transmission of values, norms, expressive symbols, and cognitive knowledge. Moral values prescribe general directions of action; they evaluate certain options as ethically desirable. As one type of evaluative standard, religious values affirm conceptions of ultimate ends—that is, notions of faith, grace, and salvation. Derived largely from moral–religious values, legal norms lay down more specific rules of behavior in concrete situations. Expressive symbols, including artistic objects, rituals, and myths, not only embody basic societal values and norms but also provide a basis for solidarity. Cognitive culture consists of the general knowledge and specialized information needed to operate a society. Although primarily nonevaluative, this knowledge may assume moral value, particularly in an industrialized economy. Those groups and individuals who display high cognitive rationality—technocrats, scientists, computer programmers, professionals in general—may achieve a high status for their skills at translating resources into public policies. In sum, all these forms of culture—moral values, religion, legal norms, expressive symbols, and cognitive knowledge—provide meaning and information about desirable states of affairs.[7]

The cultural values, norms, and expressive symbols of a society specify the social status of particular groups and individuals. Status means honor, prestige, and group approval. From a society's culture stem notions about the essence of honor. Throughout the world, status depends on both ascription and achievement. Some ethnic or caste groups (the South African Whites and the Brahmins in India) gain higher honor for their inherited qualities. Other groups (the black South Africans and the Indian untouchables) rank lower in status. Whatever their accomplishments, men generally receive higher honor than women. Similarly, older persons are accorded greater respect than youth.

However important the ascriptive bases of cultural stratification, achievement criteria also separate "superior" groups from their "inferiors." A society's cultural values prescribe those achievements regarded as most worthy of respect. For instance, in a theocracy, groups whose members display religious knowledge and virtue earn high status. Countries divided by religious cleavages usually accord high prestige to only some religious groups. In Northern Ireland, the Protestant political elite made sure that Roman Catholics secured lower respect than Protestants. In feudal societies, those men demonstrating warrior skills and military prowess won high prestige. Later in history, capitalist societies reserved special status for those groups that accumulated wealth through hard work, perseverance, and individual initiative. The socialist regimes gaining power in East Europe stressed knowledge of Marxist-Leninist ideology and effective work within the Communist party as the prime bases for high status. Although party officials wanted to industrialize their economies rapidly, technical expertise and managerial efficiency generally assumed a subordinate place to professional party work.

Whatever the basis of social prestige, whether ascriptive or achievement criteria, the dominant cultural values categorize people into the pure and the defiled, the honorable and the dishonorable, the respectable and the disrespectable. Those groups with high honor receive special deference from their "inferiors."

Although cultural values specify the bases of social honor, what groups articulate the dominant interpretations of these general values? Do a few elite groups determine social status, or do the prestige rankings stem from mass sentiments? Studies carried out in North America, West Europe, East Europe, Africa, Asia, and Latin America suggest that people make divergent evaluations of ethnoreligious groups, on the one hand, and occupations, on the other. Throughout the world, people usually perceive that their own ethnic or religious group deserves a higher status than other ethnoreligious groups. In countries plagued by ethnic divisions, such as South Africa, the dominant political elite accords a higher status to members of its own ethnic group. Yet the group regarded as "inferior," such as college-educated black South Africans, interprets this prestige ranking as unfair, unjust, and illegitimate. Through educational activities, its members work to convince the mass of Africans to overcome any feelings of cultural inferiority.

In contrast to evaluations of ethnic groups, the rankings of occupations show greater agreement. Throughout the world, people view administrators, managers, professionals, and technicians as occupations with the highest social status. Clerks, sales personnel, and skilled factory workers receive less prestige. Groups receiving the least honor include those performing unskilled labor and service jobs. Regardless of a nation's economic or political system, nearly all countries reveal similar prestige rankings of occupations. The two exceptions are a few preindustrial societies and the socialist states of East Europe. Residents of the rural villages in India accord higher status to farmers than to nonfarming occupations. Compared with people in the rest of the world, East Europeans rank skilled manual occupations, such as mining, high in social status and perceive that white-collar clerical and office personnel have lower prestige.[8] The East European stress on upgrading the social status of manual occupations partly stems from the ideological values found within Marxism-Leninism.

CONGRUENCE OF POLITICAL POWER, WEALTH, AND STATUS

To what extent do societies express a congruence among political power, wealth, and status? Do those groups ranking high on wealth also receive high status and exercise the dominant political power? Or do the three dimensions of social stratification reveal an incongruent relationship? Under the latter situation, wealthy groups, especially the *nouveaux riches*, may not gain deference or easy access to political power. Whereas most Marxists perceive that a group's relation to the means of production determines social status and political power, the Weberians place more emphasis on the incongruent linkages among political power, social honor, and wealth. For Max Weber, the tensions between high wealth and low status motivated groups to press for social changes that would close the gap between these two aspects of stratification.[9] How do we reconcile these conflicting perspectives? The empirical evidence suggests that the degree of congruence among political power, wealth, and status depends on the following variables:

1. The unit under analysis, whether an individual or a group
2. The rapidity of social change taking place in a society
3. The rigidity of the stratification system

First, groups, rather than individuals, reflect greater congruence among the three dimensions of social stratification. After examining over fifty countries, Donald J. Treiman concluded that those occupational groups with high education and high earnings also enjoy high social prestige. An occupational group that controls scarce, valued resources generally holds high political power and status.[10] As we have seen, most government offices throughout the world are filled by individuals from high-prestige occupations: managers, lawyers, educators, doctors, landlords, and so forth.

Similarly, not only occupational groups but also ethnic groups often reveal a congruence among power, wealth, and status. Particularly in societies conquered by a foreign power, ethnic groups ranking low on wealth usually lack political power and status. For example, European settlers conquered the indigenous peoples of South America, North America, and South Africa. Today in the Americas, the Indians are the poorest group, the most powerless, and the persons with the lowest status. Some rulers of the United States, Brazil, Paraguay, Argentina, and Chile have even attempted to exterminate all the Indians residing in these nations. Areas of Africa settled by Europeans, particularly the Republic of South Africa, have experienced the sharpest ethnic cleavages. In South Africa, the Whites dominate the political system, accumulate the most wealth, and demand the greatest deference from the subjugated black Africans. By contrast, the indigenous peoples, the black Africans, have virtually no voice in the public policy process, receive the lowest earnings, and suffer degrading status humiliations.

Unlike multiethnic societies dominated by conquering European settlers, societies undergoing voluntary ethnic migration feature greater incongruence among the three dimensions of social stratification. For example, the Chinese have emigrated throughout Southeast Asia. In Malaysia, although they lack political power, they do enjoy greater wealth than the Malay people. In the United States, ethnic groups voluntarily migrating to America—Irish, Italians, southern Europeans, Mexican Americans, Chinese, Japanese—have enjoyed greater opportunities for social mobility than have the indigenous Indians or the African slaves brought to the states by force.[11] For these immigrants, the freedom to gain wealth or political power represented ways to increase their status.

Societies remaining free of foreign conquest or labor immigration have experienced the least ethnic polarization. Until recently, Switzerland represented the best example. Here each ethnic group contains members with divergent incomes; rich and poor are found among both the French-speaking and the German-speaking peoples. Both these ethnic groups have the freedom to influence cantonal and federal governments. In recent years, however, the entrance of migrant workers from Italy, Spain, Yugoslavia, and Turkey into Switzerland has threatened ethnic unity. These emigrants are generally poorer, less politically powerful, and lower in prestige than the native Swiss.

Although occupational groups everywhere and ethnic groups under foreign conquest usually secure congruent rankings on their power, wealth, and status, the same congruence does not characterize individuals. Even in a rigid social stratification system, individuals at the bottom of the totem pole have some opportunities to improve their positions. For instance, under feudalism, a few children of serfs could experience upward social mobility by becoming priests in the Roman Catholic church, joining the army, or moving to the city and working as merchants. Although today most black South Africans are poor, some have gained wealth and education. These individuals will lead the movements for political change to transform the conditions of their ethnic group.

A second factor affecting the degree of congruence among political power, wealth, and status involves the pace of social change in a society. Relatively tranquil societies experience the greatest congruence among the three dimensions of social stratification. However, in societies wracked by social change, this equilibrium becomes upset. War, foreign economic pressures, domestic economic strains (depressions, incipient industrialization, strikes), and such natural calamities as earthquakes, floods, and famines disturb the social equilibrium. The legitimacy of the existing stratification system declines. Individuals become less fatalistic about their future prospects. Rather than uncritically accept the existing structural arrangements, people challenge the right of the elite to wield dominant political power, accumulate wealth, and flaunt superior status. Under these conditions, the normative glue holding a society together dissolves. Disadvantaged groups gain the freedom to upgrade their political, economic, and cultural standings.

Third, the congruence among power, wealth, and status depends on the rigidity of the social stratification system, a variable closely related to the rapidity of social change. In the least flexible societies (those where opportunities for social mobility are least prevalent), groups ranking high on political power also enjoy superior status and income. For instance, during the feudal period, the landlords exercised dominant political power, accumulated the most wealth, and received the greatest deference. In contrast, the serfs were powerless, poor, and judged a "defiled" group. The beginnings of industrialization and capitalism opened up the social stratification system. Men of formerly low status now gained the chance to accumulate wealth. Although the landed aristocrats continued to dominate government agencies and enjoy social honor, they began to lose their wealth at the expense of the emerging capitalists. This incongruence among political power, wealth, and status explains many of the political conflicts plaguing West Europe between 1450 and the early twentieth century.

Social Stratification under Feudalism, Capitalism, and State Socialism

The three dimensions of social stratification—political power, wealth, and status—can be used to compare three significant models of societies: feudalism, capitalism, and state socialism. The feudal pattern remained the dominant form until the late nineteenth and early twentieth centuries in parts of East Europe, Asia, and Latin America. The capitalist society began to emerge around 1450 in northern Italy, Holland, Britain, and France. Today, as international markets unite the world, it represents the most pervasive economic form. During the mid nineteenth century, when capitalism dominated the economies of Britain, France, Germany, and the United States, socialist movements began to organize a challenge to the existing capitalist system. At the close of World War I, the socialist movement split into two separate wings. The democratic socialists of West Europe, seeking reforms in the capitalist economy, sought greater economic equality and civil liberties for the working class. In Russia, however, Lenin and the Communist party gained government power and imposed a state socialist regime. Civil liberties became subordinate to the tasks of industrializing the agrarian society and increasing equal opportunities for urban factory workers. After World War II, state socialist societies emerged in East Europe, China, North Korea, Vietnam, and Cuba.

Feudalism, capitalism, and state socialism are *models* of societies, not photographic reproductions of any one concrete society. In an analytical model, the features are fully integrated and logically related; the inconsistencies, ambiguities, and nuances of empirical situations are eliminated. Rather than offer a complete view of empirical reality, the analytical model presents a simplified picture of the world. By simplifying complex situations and providing abstract dimensions by which they can be compared, these models enable us to understand better the functioning of actual societies.

From three general categories—wealth, political power, and status—we can derive more specific dimensions for comparing feudalism, capitalism, and state socialism. Key features of wealth include the level of economic development, the coordination of economic resources (the organization of production), property relations, the link between work and ownership, and the degree of economic specialization. Under political power come such important variables as the scope of state control, the fusion of economic and political power, and the degree of political equality. The status variable consists of such dimensions as the bases of respect, the degree of equality, and the extent of freedom for social mobility. Finally, for each type of society, we want to know the relative congruence of political power, wealth, and status. Table 3-1 summarizes these four aspects of social stratification.[12]

FEUDALISM

All feudal societies had agricultural economies where land constituted the main source of property. Although towns existed for traders to supply the landed aristocracy with luxury goods, the rural areas and villages remained the dominant center of economic activity. The organization of production revolved around making enough goods to satisfy the luxury needs of landlords and the subsistence needs of serfs. Work and ownership over the means of production were separated. Whereas the landed aristocrats regarded their land holdings as their own private property, the serfs performed a wide range of general economic activities. For example, they planted crops, irrigated land, harvested produce, collected firewood, and constructed roads, canals, and dams. Despite their investments of labor in the land, the serfs consumed only a share of the agricultural goods; a sizable portion went to the landlords. Economic production and consumption occurred within a family setting; producer and consumer roles were largely integrated, rather than separated between household and factory. Because of the low economic specialization and primitive farming tools, agricultural productivity remained limited.

Compared with the capitalist pattern, feudalism represented a

TABLE 3-1 Social stratification in feudal, capitalist, and state socialist societies

Dimension of social stratification	Feudalism	Capitalism	State socialism
1. Wealth			
a. level of economic development	nonindustrial economy, rural areas dominant	industrializing, industrial economy with surplus, towns develop	industrializing, industrial economy with gap between urban & rural areas
b. coordination of economic resources	production for direct use	production for exchange: market and price system	state planning
c. property ownership	private (landlords)	private (capitalists)	public (state)
d. relations between work & ownership/control of means of production	separated: landlords vs. serfs	separated: capitalists vs. workers	separated: party-state elite vs. workers
e. degree of economic specialization	low	high	high
2. Political power			
a. scope of state control	limited	expanded	very comprehensive
b. fusion of economic & political power	high (fusion in landowning aristocracy)	low (differentiation of economic and political power)	high (party elite does not own capital but controls access to wealth)
c. degree of political equality	low	higher	low (rule by party-state elite)
3. Status			
a. bases of respect	personalized ties to overlord	impersonal ties to means of production (capital)	impersonal ties to party ideology and to professional expertise
b. degree of equality	most unequal	more equal	more equal
c. degree of freedom for social mobility	very limited	higher social & geographical mobility than under feudalism	higher social & geographic mobility than under feudalism
4. Congruence of political power, wealth, and status	highest (landlords enjoy the greatest power, wealth, and status)	lower (new rich may lack political power and status)	high (party-state elite enjoys the greatest political power and access to wealth but may have lower status)

more decentralized political system. At least during the early feudal period, local landlords exercised the dominant political power. Regional landed families maintained their own armies; the king did not have the military force to control rural life throughout the territory. Indeed, the "state" consisted mainly of the king, a few civil servants personally attached to him, and, in England and France, representative estates composed of landed aristocrats who advised the king. Even in the more centralized czarist Russia, where the czar had long gained political dominance over the landowners, the central government lacked the bureaucratic structure to implement the czar's directives. During the mid nineteenth century, Russia had one-fifth the civil servants per thousand persons found in France and one-fourth the British rate. Yet the latter two societies had already passed through the feudal framework to enter the capitalist phase of development. Thus, in Russia, autocratic feudal central government had only rudimentary means to implement public policies at the local village level.[13]

Particularly in the early, more decentralized feudal societies, economic and political power were fused in the landowning aristocracy. The landlords not only controlled the dominant means of production but also exerted the dominant power over the local fief. Under this feudal system, sharp political inequalities separated the different estates. Each rigid estate—landlords, their vassals, and the serfs—operated under a different legal framework. The rules applicable to the lords gave them far more political rights than the rules regulating interactions among the serfs.

Like political power and wealth, the status system in feudal societies revealed marked inequalities. The bases of respect largely rested on ascriptive grounds. A man born into a noble family received high respect; women and persons of humble birth did not. Personalized ties united superiors and inferiors. Just as the landed gentry owed personal loyalty to the king, so the vassal and the lord were united by patron–client relationships. Vassals gained some rights to land in exchange for rendering some military services to their lords. Under this feudal system, the lords held all the rights and the peasants enjoyed few privileges. Freedom for peasant social mobility was extremely limited. Although especially during wars, famines, plagues, and other calamities a few peasants did gain the opportunities for geographical movement that would possibly lead to higher social status, most people born serfs remained serfs for life.

In summary, of all three societies, the feudal type demonstrated the highest congruence among the dimensions of social stratification. A sharp division separated the landlords from the serfs. The landlords monopolized access to wealth, political power, and social status. The serfs endured the greatest economic, political, and cultural inequalities. Only with the occurrence of wars, natural disasters, and emerging capitalist industrialization did this rigid feudal system begin to break down.

CAPITALISM

Although remnants of feudalism still survive in parts of Latin America, Asia, the Near East, and Africa, capitalism has become the prevalent system throughout the world during the twentieth century. Most nations are organized on capitalist lines. At the world system level, more and more states have been incorporated into the international capitalist market dominated by corporations in the United States, West Europe, and Japan. Capital has become more mobile than ever before; investments by multinational corporations take place not only in the most industrialized states but also in the "nonaligned" underdeveloped areas and even within the communist camp itself. Indeed, the anticapitalist leaders of East Europe, China, Vietnam, and Cuba organize their societies on some principles traditionally associated with the capitalist system. Given the dominant importance of capitalism, how can we best compare its basic features? Although actually existing capitalist economies reveal important differences, the following model of its social stratification system highlights the crucial ways this type of society departs from feudalism.

Unlike feudalism, which existed in agricultural societies, capitalism thrives under industrializing and industrial economic conditions. First towns and then large cities develop as the centers of industrial activity. Production exists for exchange, not just for direct use. Through the market and price system, the capitalists—merchants, financiers, manufacturers—trade goods on both the national and international markets.

To gain a surplus of revenues over costs, these capitalists stress the need for technological efficiency and capital accumulation. Investment in new stocks of capital, such as equipment and machinery, becomes the primary requirement for raising economic productivity. In the model of capitalism, most means of production are privately owned. At least in the later stages of capitalist development, a basic separation occurs between those who own the productive forces and those who carry out the basic labor. Whereas under feudalism production and consumption were integrated and people performed general economic roles, a high specialization of labor pervades capitalist economies. People work in factories, stores, and offices, rather than at home. Their economic tasks are specialized. Through this division of labor, the capitalists expect to raise labor productivity and efficiency.

Despite the association of a laissez-faire ideology with capitalist development, the power of the state actually expands under capitalism; it carries out a more comprehensive scope of activities than in most feudal societies. The economic role of the state varies according to the level of economic development and the cultural heritage of a particular society. During the early stages of capitalist formation, the state generally performed more limited activities, especially in the United States, England, and Holland. Here the central government mainly established "law and order," guaranteed contracts, promoted trade, encouraged manufacturing, provided transportation and communication facilities, upheld a national stable currency, and ensured widespread geographical labor mobility, particularly from the rural areas to the cities. Through all these functions, the central government facilitated the creation of a larger economic market.

Beyond these three nations, the state carried out even more comprehensive activities. For example, in Prussian Germany, France, czarist Russia, Japan, and parts of Latin America, the state took the lead in creating an industrialized structure. The Prussian government established factories and mines. Before World War I, the Japanese government created diverse industries, including iron foundries, machine shops, coal mines, and shipyards. The state supervised and subsidized private entrepreneurs. State expenditures provided social overhead capital (railways, communications) as well as financial assistance to iron and steel industries. By low taxes on business firms and high government expenditures for the capitalists, the Japanese government stimulated rapid industrialization.

During the later stages of capitalist development, the central government has come to exercise even more comprehensive power over economic decision making. In the emerging corporate economy, where the state, giant corporations, and strong trade unions share power, the national governmental policies encourage investment and guarantee high profits for the private capitalist class. Government now regulates the business cycle, increasing aggregate demand during slack periods and restraining total spending when a boom ensues. Through raising productivity and lowering business costs, public economic policies try to increase profit rates. These fiscal decisions involve low taxes on corporations and high expenditures for research, economic development, communication facilities, technical education, and retraining. Vis-a-vis the world market, national governments implement policies intended to ensure international financial stability; these policies stress free trade, expanded exports, and efficient international currency exchanges.[14]

Despite the growing interpenetration between government and business in an "advanced" capitalist economy, from a comparative perspective, capitalism still features a greater differentiation of economic and political power than found under feudal conditions. The early laissez-faire theorists, especially Adam Smith, made a sharp distinction between the "state" and the "society." According to him, whereas the state rules through coercive force, society exemplifies the voluntary contractual arrangements of a "free market" where cooperation, not coercion, regulates personal interactions. Although this interpretation exaggerates the differences between the political and economic sectors of a capitalist society, the state and the private business firms did gain greater autonomy than had existed under feudalism, where the landlord monopolized both political and economic power.

Capitalism has also brought greater political equality to people than they experienced under feudal rule. Capitalist thinkers stress the need for equality before the law to replace the old system of different legal norms for each estate. Now all people, regardless of their economic station, are subject to the same legal principles. Of course, as Anatole France cynically pointed out, political equality exists alongside economic inequalities. In its "majestic equality," the law "forbids rich and poor alike to sleep under bridges, to beg in the streets, and to steal bread."[15]

Regardless of these continuing economic inequalities, the new capitalist order brings more status equality than prevailed in the feudal system. At least in theory, if not always in practice, every individual, whatever his or her original status at birth, has more equal opportunities to rise in the social stratification system. Individuals gain the freedom to move from the rural areas to find work in the industrial cities. Along with this freedom of geographical mobility goes the freedom to pursue social mobility.

Achievement, rather than inherited personal qualities, becomes the primary basis of respect. A person's performance, especially contributions to economic production, determines social status. Compared with the old personal ties to the feudal lord, now impersonal ties to the means of production regulate social intercourse. People are valued for their economic skills. Capitalist economic theorists view concrete human beings as impersonal factors of production; their labor and talents are seen as "human capital" analogous to the physical capital of plants, equipment, and machinery. Within this capitalist framework, a meritocracy dominates the society. Those individuals who demonstrate the most efficient economic and political performance gain special respect. Technicians, managers, and skilled administrators govern both political and economic sectors.

Even in a highly industrialized capitalist society, more incongruence characterizes political power, wealth, and status than under feudalism. Greater role specialization prevails. Individuals who have talents for accumulating wealth do not necessarily have the required skills for governing political organizations. Besides economic performance, other more ascriptive bases of social honor—sex, family background, ethnic origin—still remain in a capitalist society.

STATE SOCIALISM

During the twentieth century, the main challenge to the capitalist system has come from the state socialists governing the Soviet Union, East Europe, China, Vietnam, Cambodia, Laos, North Korea, and Cuba. First in Russia in late 1917 and later in East Europe and Asia, leaders of Communist parties seized political power and established state socialist regimes. In certain fundamental respects, the stratification systems within the Union of Soviet Socialist Republics and the Socialist Republic of Vietnam diverge from democratic socialist countries such as Sweden, Norway, Denmark, West Germany, and Britain.[16] On the one hand, these social democracies operate modified market, highly industrialized, capitalist economies. Especially in Sweden and West Germany, a large segment of economic activities remains under private ownership. The government mainly regulates private economic firms, tries to prevent booms and busts, provides public health services, supplies old-age pensions to the elderly and family allowances to young parents, and encourages public educational opportunities. Political leaders attain parliamentary power through competitive elections. A dedication to civil liberties enables opposition groups to challenge government policy and incumbent leaders. Few social democrats assert that Marxist thinking guides their governmental decisions.

On the other hand, the socialist states dominated by ruling Communist parties administer a centrally planned economy. State and party officials control access to the means of production; they have used political means to industrialize their agrarian countries. Bargaining and coercion within the Communist party, rather than competitive elections, determine recruitment to top political offices. Although there is some freedom to criticize public policies within party circles, the dominant elite denies most opposition groups the civil liberties to challenge party–state authorities.

Distribution of wealth. State socialist regimes have implemented policies to lessen the economic inequalities prevailing under the pre-revolutionary regime. Through execution, imprisonment, deportation, and socialist "reeducation," Communist party leaders abolished the economic power formerly exercised by the landlords and large-scale capitalists. The state took over the major means of production, particularly heavy industry, transportation, and communications. Individuals could no longer amass huge fortunes through their ownership of land and capital.

Other public policies enacted by the Communist party and the government have contributed to greater economic equality than had existed under the prerevolutionary regime. Most workers earn a "social wage" that comprises not only cash income but also such important fringe benefits as free health care, free education, and subsidized public transportation, housing, and day-care centers. By raising the minimum wage and freezing the salaries of the highest-paid managers and professionals, communist governments have taken steps to reduce the income differences among workers with different skills. All these policies have reduced the economic inequalities associated with a rigid stratification system.[17]

Despite these trends toward more income equality, class distinctions still remain. A "new class" of party officials has arisen to direct these societies. Although the major means of production have come under "public" control, the state and Communist party, not the working class, control access to land and capital. The political elite does not legally own the capital; yet its members determine the allocation of economic resources (the investment of money and capital), the use of physical capital, and the daily activities of the workers—all functions performed by the capitalist class in Western market economies.

As in most Western societies, the managerial and professional intelligentsia occupy the top positions in the social stratification system of the Soviet Union. Party cadres, managers, professionals, scientists, and engineers secure the highest salaries, the greatest access to political power, and the most prestige. As members of the "new class," they obtain special bonuses for overtime work, receive the highest pensions, secure free monthly food allowances, buy luxury goods in special shops, use chauffeured automobiles, enjoy vacations at fancy resorts, and reside in spacious houses. Their children also gain special access to higher education, making it possible for members of the current political elite to transmit their advantages from one generation to the next.

Occupations at lower ranks on the stratification totem pole gain fewer of these scarce resources. In the USSR, unskilled manual workers, state farmers, and especially collective farmers enjoy less favored treatment than the managers and professionals. As a result, those at the bottom of the social stratification system—the ones with the least education, the fewest skills, and the lowest prestige—feel the most alienation toward the existing Soviet system. Although unhappy with their position, they take a fatalistic attitude, feeling powerless to change the current policies or incumbent political leaders.

Even in less industrialized China and Vietnam, where the leaders have treated the peasantry more favorably than in the Soviet Union, the gap between the rural and urban areas still lingers on. Few urban

Chinese youth want to spend time working on the rural communes. The urban residents hold pleasanter jobs, inhabit superior housing, lead healthier lives, and gain more opportunities for education. Similarly, in Vietnam, compared with the rural folk, the city people gain more social services (sickness insurance, maternal benefits, old-age pensions), secure greater access to higher education, and perform less public labor, such as building dikes and other irrigation facilities. As in East Europe, the dominant political elite governs from an urban base. Partly for this reason, economic inequalities coincide with political inequalities.[18]

Political power. Although Marx envisioned the withering away of a repressive state in the forthcoming communist society, during the last thirty years none of these countries has experienced any weakened power of the state. Indeed, as a result of these socialist revolutions, the political power of the government bureaucrats, military, and police has increased, not lessened. Government has grown more centralized as it has gained more control over life in the rural villages. The degree of coercion new revolutionary states exert has expanded and the scope of power has broadened. More and more activities fall under government control. State stores, rather than private shops, sell consumer goods. The Party and government manage schools, health facilities, and heavy industrial firms (steel and petrochemical plants, for example).[19] Under these socialist regimes, political and economic power have become fused; yet unlike the feudal case, the political structures—the dominant party and the state—determine the allocation of economic rewards.

Social status. The status inequalities found in these state socialist countries contradict the Marxian ideals of cultural equality. Two bases of respect influence an individual's social prestige: *ideological awareness* and *expertise*. Communist party members who demonstrate a higher consciousness as manifested by service to the collectivity, hard work, and public honesty supposedly deserve highest status. These people embody the ideals of the new socialist man and woman. Because Communist party leaders aim to industrialize their societies rapidly, managers, professionals, technocrats, scientists, and engineers also rank high on social prestige. Together these two groups—the "reds" and the "experts"—exercise dominant political power, receive the highest salaries, and enjoy the greatest prestige; they occupy the top positions in the social stratification system.

Despite this stress on ideological awareness and expertise as the primary bases of social status, not all individuals have an equal opportunity to move upward through the social stratification system. In the Soviet Union, other East European states, China, Vietnam, and

Cuba, men enjoy higher esteem than women. For instance, in the Soviet Union, few women hold high positions in the most powerful organs of the Communist party, such as the Central Committee and the Politburo. Soviet women receive around two-thirds the average salaries men earn, a figure slightly higher than in Canada or the United States but lower than in Scandinavian social democracies (Sweden, Denmark, and Norway). As in most Western capitalist states, women are overrepresented in low-paying clerical positions but underrepresented in managerial–professional jobs. Women have fewer opportunities to gain employment as skilled industrial workers, who earn higher wages than office and clerical personnel.

Different ethnic groups in the USSR also live under unequal conditions. The Russians, with about 53 percent of the population, receive the highest status. They dominate the national all-Union party and government organs. Central Asian nationalities—ethnic minority groups such as the Uzbeks, Tatars, Kazakhs, Turkmenians, Chuvashis, Kirghiz, Tadjiks, and Bashkirs—rank lower in prestige; yet they do exercise some political power in the eastern republics of the USSR.

Even all economic groups do not have the same opportunities to rise in the social stratification system. True, sons of manual workers can study to become engineers and thereby improve their positions. Children on the collective farms, however, enjoy fewer advantages. Not until 1975 did the Soviet authorities give collective farmers the internal passport needed for free geographical mobility. Today most farmers' sons can expect to rise no higher than a manual industrial worker.

Policy intentions versus outcomes. Although Marx believed that postcapitalist societies would witness a greater concern for the whole community, these communist regimes have so far failed in their efforts to realize new socialist men and women. The self-interested behavior associated with a capitalist economy has resurfaced. Communist party leaders bemoan the corruption, bribery, absenteeism, and laziness plaguing their societies. In China after the death of Mao and in Cuba after Che Guevara left the island to fight in Bolivia, material incentives began to replace moral incentives; workers who made the greatest contributions to economic production received the highest salaries and certain other economic rewards, such as access to a television set and washing machine. Although Communist party leaders have tried to abolish the market system, it went underground only to reappear as a "black market." For example, in southern Vietnam, entrepreneurs have gained considerable wealth by selling scarce rice on the black market; their incomes even outdistance the earnings made by civil servants in the Socialist Republic of Vietnam.[20]

In sum, although private ownership of the means of production has largely disappeared in most socialist states dominated by a strong Communist party, the capitalist bases of social stratification have reappeared. The various conflicts Marx associated with a class society still remain: the gaps between urban and rural areas, a repressive state and society, individual self-interest and an altruistic concern for the whole community, and the general human being and the specialized worker. As in capitalist societies, the central state has grown more centralized and bureaucratic. Similar to the situation in West Europe and the United States during the nineteenth century, a political elite in communist states today suppresses independent trade unions. Rather than representing workers' interests, the unions function mainly to stimulate higher labor productivity. By stressing specialized economic roles, party leaders also aim to attain higher growth rates. All these features bear a close resemblance to the stratification systems found in capitalist economies.

As a prophet of the nineteenth century and heir to the Enlightenment tradition, Marx took a more optimistic attitude than Western intellectuals today take about the possibilities of changing the existing social stratification systems. In his view, through the application of science and reason, the proletariat would overcome the deficiencies of the capitalist system. Contemporary Western social theorists remain more pessimistic. Given the gap between Marxist ideals and the actual performance of state socialist regimes, they doubt the feasibility of ever attaining the ideal society Marx sketched. Efforts to stage socialist revolutions have now spread to the less industrialized areas of the Third World. Whereas Marx foresaw anticapitalist revolutions emerging first in the most industrialized economies of West Europe, during the twentieth century socialist revolutionaries have instead come to power in Asia, Africa, and Latin America—particularly in agrarian societies governed by a state bureaucracy that disintegrated because of war, foreign economic pressures, and internal politico-economic crises. Under these destabilizing conditions, revolutionary intellectuals and middle-class politicians, not the factory working class, have led the movements to change the social stratification systems of their underdeveloped societies.

Changes in the Social Stratification System

TYPES OF SOCIAL CHANGES

Changes in the social stratification system may encompass an *expansion of opportunities* for individual and group mobility. Through obtaining more education or taking a new job with increased skills and greater responsibilities, an individual may gain the chance to move upward in the social stratification system. Opportunities for group mobility also decrease the rigidity of a social system. Trade union members have engaged in collective bargaining to raise the economic position of the whole working class. Ethnic group leaders in the United States, India, and elsewhere have pressured their governments to grant more educational, housing, and employment benefits to members of their disadvantaged group; affirmative action programs represent one example.

Social change may mean the *exchange of group positions;* those groups now at the bottom of the social stratification totem pole will ascend to the top positions under transformed conditions. Movements struggling for national independence from colonial rule demanded that indigenous Africans and Asians replace the dominant white Europeans in government posts. After the attainment of political independence, African civil servants fill the positions formerly occupied by British and French bureaucrats.

Christian movements representing oppressed groups claim that in the future ideal society—the Kingdom of God—"the last shall be first." Jesus compared the fate of the rich man and the poor man, Lazarus:

> The poor man died and was carried by the angels to sit beside Abraham at the feast in Heaven. The rich man died and was buried, and in Hades, where he was in great pain, he looked up and saw Abraham, far away, with Lazarus at his side. . . . Abraham said, "Remember my son, that in your lifetime you were given all the good things, while Lazarus got all the bad things. But now he is enjoying himself here, while you are in pain."[21]

Orthodox religious groups and radical secular political movements often compete for the same oppressed people. For example, in the poorer regions of northern Sweden, the Communist party and the fundamentalist Pentecostal sects try to win support from the same alienated, poverty-stricken groups.[22] In other cases, radical movements try to synthesize the appeals of orthodox religion and secular revolution. Today in Latin America, radical Catholic priests blend aspects of Marxism with Christianity in a "liberation theology." During the Allende regime in Chile (1970–1973), the Christians for Socialism identified themselves with the cause of the poor and oppressed. For them, Christ embodied the "new man" sent to liberate the oppressed. They perceived the destruction of capitalism and the construction of an equalitarian, fraternal society as a step toward the Kingdom of God. Through the revolutionary struggle, they saw the working class creating a "new man."[23]

More secular revolutionary movements opposed to orthodox religion also claim that a socialist revolution will upset the existing group positions. During the mid nineteenth century, the Marxist

Socialists in Europe expected that in the new order the oppressed proletariat would replace the exploiting capitalist class. A century later Mao Zedong promised to abolish the landlord class and bring the peasantry to economic and political power.

A change in the social stratification system may bring greater *leveling*. Whereas in the prerevolutionary society a vast gap separated the rich from the poor, under revolutionary conditions all persons, regardless of sex, age, or ethnic affiliation, will supposedly enjoy more equal resources. They will have similar wealth, status, and influence over the exercise of political power.

One of the most fundamental transformations in the social stratification system revolves around changes in the *value bases* of ranking people. As we have seen, the transition from feudalism to capitalism involved a change from valuing people according to their inherited personal qualities (noble birth, sex, age) to judging people by their accumulated wealth. During the 1920s in the Soviet Union, ideological awareness of the tenets of Marxism-Leninism replaced landed wealth and private possession of capital as the bases for a high ranking in the system. From the beginnings of the People's Republic of China in 1949, ideological orthodoxy has competed with technical expertise as the foundation for ranking individuals. The "reds," led by Mao Zedong, struggled against the "experts." A spokesman for the latter group, Deng Xiaoping, claims that it does not matter if a cat is black or white but whether it catches mice. In his view, pragmatic accomplishments should take precedence over ideological consciousness in the Chinese stratification system.

Revolutionaries, reformists, conservatives, and reactionaries have adopted different positions toward these four types of changes in the social stratification system. Revolutionaries support the most wide-ranging, comprehensive changes. They seek greater leveling, expanded opportunities for group mobility, an exchange of group positions to ensure more benefits for the disadvantaged, and a change in the value bases for ranking people so that political achievements and ideological awareness replace inherited personal qualities.

Pledging to narrow the gap between rich and poor, reformists desire greater opportunities for individuals to gain social mobility. From their perspective, every individual, whatever his or her social origin, should be evaluated according to personal achievements.

Conservatives seek limited modifications in the social stratification system. Only minor adjustments should be made in the process by which persons gain political power, wealth, and status. According to them, spiritual equality before God is more important than secular attempts to upset the present rankings. Efforts to secure fundamental changes in the social stratification will produce too much disorder, anarchy, and chaos.

Reactionaries want to restore a rigid, elitist stratification system that has disintegrated. They aim to ensure that the old displaced elite returns to its top position.[24] For instance, the restoration of European colonial rule to Asia and Africa would represent a reactionary change, as would the return to power by the landowning aristocracy in modern capitalist France.

POLITICAL MOBILIZATION FOR SOCIAL CHANGE

How do changes in the social stratification system occur? What specific processes are involved? The following analysis assumes that the most effective mobilization for change occurs among groups experiencing the greatest objective segregation from other groups and the highest degree of subjective group consciousness. People who have a weakly developed group awareness and who live among other diverse groups show the least likelihood of mobilizing for a changed social stratification system. Successful political mobilization to change the social stratification system depends on favorable objective and subjective conditions.

Objective conditions. From the objective standpoint, members of a disadvantaged group have a high degree of interaction among their own group but remain isolated from other groups, especially the dominant elite. Pervasive interactions within the group, combined with segregation from opposing groups, produce high objective solidarity. If the subordinate group is large and homogeneous, if low occupational and ethnoreligious status reinforce each other, if exit from the subordinate group is difficult, and if the ruling elite lacks the power to prevent members of the subordinate group from organizing a political movement, then mobilization becomes most likely. Moreover, when individuals of a group all work at the same occupation, live in the same area, and participate in the same associations, then all these within-group interactions increase the favorable prospects for political mobilization.[25]

Group consciousness. Regardless of these objective conditions, a subordinate group will fail to achieve effective mobilization if it lacks subjective group consciousness. Five dimensions appear crucial to group consciousness:

1. Members of a group strongly identify with that group, which exerts a powerful attraction on them.
2. Group members perceive that they share similar interests. Common grievances are needed to mobilize groups at the bottom of the social stratification system. Shared deprivations, both absolute and relative, often channel discontent into political mobilization.

3. Individuals within a group believe that their interests are opposed to the interests of the dominant elite. Because they consider reconciliation of interests to be impossible, the subordinate group mobilizes for struggle against opposing groups. Individuals become willing to work for group goals.

4. Political mobilization assumes the dominance of public or common concerns; political activities revolve around public policy. Effective mobilizers must convince individuals to link their fate with the fate of the larger political system. People must come to view their self-interests from the perspective of the whole society.

5. Both the leaders and at least some members of the subordinate group should share a vision of an alternative society structured differently from the existing system.

Successful political mobilization thus requires not only resentment toward the status quo, but a shared vision of a new society that motivates people to undergo hardships for a future public good.[26]

Social change in the western industrial world. These objective and subjective conditions suggest some reasons for the failure of working-class revolutions to erupt in the industrialized world, as Marx expected. Marx's own definition of social class explains the weakness of class solidarity. Focusing on the peasantry of nineteenth-century France, he wrote:

> In so far as millions of families live under conditions of existence that separate their mode of life, their interests, and their cultural formation from those of the other classes and bring them into conflict with those classes, they form a class. In so far as these small peasant proprietors are merely connected on a local basis, and the identity of their interests fails to produce a feeling of community, national links, or a political organization, they do not form a class.[27]

This passage just as accurately describes the industrial working class today. The feelings of subjective class solidarity are relatively weak. Class consciousness is underdeveloped.

Most workers in the Western world do not strongly identify with the working class. Other community attachments based on ethnicity, religion, age, and geographic region compete with economic identification. Nationalism as a general sentiment transcending class divisions has exerted stronger ties than commitment to worldwide proletarian solidarity. Survey studies taken in such places as France, Italy, Canada, Sweden, and the United States show an incongruence between individuals' objective occupation and their subjective class identification; many manual workers identify with the middle class, and many nonmanual employees identify with the working class.

Many persons do not wish to align themselves with any class.[28] Under these conditions, political mobilizers cannot easily unite all members of the "working class."

Individuals within the same occupational group often do not share similar interests. Not only in the United States but also in other parts of the industrial world, ethnic, linguistic, religious, and regional cleavages divide the working class. Even within the occupational sphere, diverse interests based on different skill levels arise; unskilled workers often voice different demands from skilled workers. Many occupations do not fit into the two homogeneous classes Marx predicted in the advanced stages of capitalist development. Office clerks and skilled factory workers may hold divergent views about the best ways to secure greater wealth and status. Among the bourgeoisie, multinational corporation executives, mom-and-pop grocers, and university professors organizing independent research projects obviously do not share all the same interests.[29]

Within the industrial world, powerful social institutions discourage class struggles. Churches, schools, the mass media, and ethnic associations play a key role in socializing individuals; all these institutions stress the need for greater harmony among members of different economic classes. National political institutions reinforce ties to the nation-state. Before a radical political party has the opportunity to reach individuals, these individuals have probably been taught from childhood the importance of transclass values.[30]

Rather than taking a general view of the whole society, most members of the working class stress their immediate, concrete, material interests: higher pay, expanded fringe benefits, job security, healthier working conditions, and mechanisms for handling the individual worker's grievances. Highly skilled workers, such as electronics technicians, are the most likely to demand greater control over their jobs.[31] All these demands, whether for greater material benefits or increased worker control in the factories, exemplify what Lenin called "trade union consciousness." In his view, only the professional revolutionaries, the bourgeois radicals, can comprehend the general political direction of a society. Possessed of a socialist political consciousness, they view daily concrete experiences from a long-term societal perspective. Lenin wanted these revolutionary intellectuals to direct the working class toward a socialist society—that is, toward a change in the whole social system, not just some part, such as a single factory.[32]

Finally, most industrial working-class individuals lack a vision of an alternative society, especially the socialist vision Marx and Lenin sketched. Although not all deprived workers enjoy their current life situations, few perceive alternative possibilities of organizing society. Some fatalistically resign themselves to the status quo. Others take individualistic steps to improve their economic positions; migration, education, and self-help schemes represent a few examples. Particularly in England, Germany, and the Scandinavian countries, workers are organized into unions that have improved the collective welfare of the working class. Yet whatever the response to economic deprivation—fatalism, individual self-help, or trade union participation—most workers pragmatically accept the existing social order. They perceive few possibilities of establishing an alternative society.[33]

Despite these similarities in workers' class consciousness throughout the industrial world, the European working class has developed a slightly stronger group awareness than have American workers. Particularly in northwestern Europe—Scandinavia, Britain, and West Germany—trade unions organize a fairly high proportion of the factory workers, over 80 percent in Sweden and about 40 to 50 percent in Britain and Germany. Strong socialist parties have occupied government positions. Competing with several political parties in a multiparty system, they have scored electoral victories approaching 50 percent. Either alone or in coalition with other democratic parties, socialists gain control of the executive. Although they work within the capitalist system and downplay the class struggle, these socialist parties and the trade unions aligned with them give the workers some degree of group awareness, even if only trade union consciousness.

In the United States, however, the working class has never developed a strong class consciousness; its participation in the electoral process remains lower than in Europe, where socialist parties and unions mobilize the workers to participate in politics. In America, neither socialist parties nor trade unions have played such a powerful political role. Most socialists lost their local offices at the end of World War I. Since the end of the Second World War, the proportion of the total work force enrolled in labor unions has declined to about 20 percent. The middle class controls the major institutions of society: schools, churches, the mass media, ethnic associations, both major political parties, and government agencies. All these organizations integrate the working class into the existing society. The absence of powerful working-class organizations means that few workers develop strong working-class consciousness. Even during the 1930s, when the unemployment rate surged to 25 percent of the work force, more wage earners and unemployed persons identified with the middle than with the working class. Fewer than one-half the members of these two groups perceived any conflict between management and workers. During the depression, most Americans, including the poorest, took an optimistic view about future economic prospects for themselves and their children. For the majority, individual hard work, rather than government policies, constituted the best way to improve one's economic position.[34] Under these conditions of weak subjective group consciousness and high objective integration with the rest of society, the American working class has not mobilized for active participation in the electoral process and for fundamental changes in the social stratification system.

Social change in the Third World. During the twentieth century, the greatest successes in political mobilization have occurred throughout the nonindustrial world, rather than in the industrialized West, although in most parts of Asia, Africa, and Latin America, the poorest segments of the population never get mobilized. Segregated from wealthier groups yet lacking a strong group consciousness, they resemble the "lumpenproletariat" Marx described.[35] Unemployed or part-time workers, they beg in the streets, commit petty crimes, and often ally with the police to gain a few material benefits. Occasional spontaneous riots alternate with general political passivity. As expected, they are difficult to mobilize behind a revolutionary movement.

In contrast to these deprived but immobilized groups, the Chinese peasants during the 1930s and 1940s did mobilize around revolutionary leaders for a basic transformation of the existing system. Mao Zedong, the Communist party, and the People's Liberation Army largely succeeded because of favorable objective and subjective conditions. Objectively, the peasant class was large and fairly homogeneous. Neither ethnic nor religious divisions split the peasants. Few opportunities existed for social mobility. At a time when the Japanese were establishing dominance throughout Southeast Asia, migration to another country seemed futile. Most important, the Communist party and the People's Liberation Army managed to isolate the peasants in the interior regions from extensive supervision by the landowners, Nationalist government bureaucrats, and Chiang Kai-shek's army. Particularly after 1937, the Chinese Communists established a separate alternative regime in northern China free of Kuomintang control.

Subjectively, the peasants developed a fairly strong class political consciousness. They identified with the peasantry rather than with the landowning aristocracy. They held common grievances and perceived shared interests: lower rents, reduced interest rates, decreased taxes on grain, lower salt prices, land redistribution, improved health care, and greater security against bandits and the ruling Kuomintang officials. The peasants came to believe that the landlords and their supporters in the Nationalist government would never grant these demands. When the invading Japanese armies allied with the landowners against the poor peasants, the national struggle reinforced the class struggle.

Because Chiang Kai-shek showed less enthusiasm about fighting the Japanese than about destroying his enemies in the Chinese Communist party (CCP), many poor peasants rallied to support the Communists. Mao Zedong, Zhou Enlai, and other CCP leaders linked abstract socialist goals with the peasants' concrete material needs. The CCP leadership convinced the peasants that their individual and family fate depended on the success of the revolutionary struggle. Mao also sketched a vision of an alternative society based on an equalitarian interpretation of Chinese peasant traditions, such as common ownership of land, fraternal cooperation, and opposition to the agrarian state bureaucracy. In the northern regions of China, he instituted an alternative political system that gave the peasants lower taxes, greater access to land, protection against warlords, and the opportunity to trade their produce at temple fairs.[36] In short, Mao's political mobilization succeeded because favorable objective and subjective conditions prevailed.

Through the Chinese Communist party, the People's Liberation Army, and other organizations, Mao carried out his mobilizing activities. Organizational mobilization strengthened peasants' political consciousness. Mobilization involved explaining political objectives—that is, the reasons for collective political action. Activities directed by the CCP related general, abstract objectives to the peasants' concrete needs. Maoist mobilization also specified the public policies needed to attain the shared goals; these policies encompassed the educational, economic, health, and political–military sectors. The Communists employed several diverse tactics to implement the mobilization effort. Communist leaders talked to the peasants. For the literate people, leaflets, bulletins, newspapers, pamphlets, and books carried the political message. Plays and ballets conveyed basic political values. Through mass organizations—unions, peasant leagues, students' associations, women's groups, and schools—the Communist party taught new values. By building on such traditional structures as family, village, and mutual aid groups, party leaders secured cooperation among the peasants. Often these traditional agencies became transformed into party auxiliaries.[37] All these organizational activities helped mobilize segments of the Chinese peasantry behind the defeat of the Kuomintang government.

After coming to governmental power throughout China in 1949, the Communist party mobilized the population to work for fundamental social changes. Especially at the local level, the peasants gained increased opportunities to participate in political affairs, primarily through party organizations. Their subsistence needs were largely met. Peasants enjoyed higher status than under the *ancien régime*. All these changes involved basic modifications in the social stratification system. The landlord class lost its political and economic power to government and party bureaucrats. By joining the army or the Party, peasants secured upward social mobility. As the gap between the few rich and the many poor narrowed, greater economic leveling took place. Ideological awareness and expertise replaced inherited birth and property accumulation as the bases of social prestige. In short, the Chinese Communist party secured basic changes in the social stratification system by forging a link between powerful mass organizations and a comprehensive political ideology.

Notes

1. For analyses of these three dimensions of social stratification, see W. G. Runciman, ed., *Max Weber: Selections in Translation*, trans. E. Matthews (Cambridge, England: Cambridge University Press, 1978), pp. 43–61; Reinhard Bendix and Seymour Martin Lipset, eds., *Class, Status, and Power: Social Stratification in Comparative Perspective*, 2d ed. (New York: Free Press, 1966), esp. pts. I and III; W. G. Runciman, "Towards a Theory of Social Stratification," in *The Social Analysis of Class Structure*, ed. Frank Parkin (London: Tavistock, 1974), pp. 55–101.
2. Sheldon S. Wolin, *Politics and Vision: Continuity and Innovation in Western Political Thought* (Boston: Little, Brown, 1960), pp. 6–7.
3. For a discussion of the exercise of political power, see Charles F. Andrain, *Political Life and Social Change*, 2d ed. (Belmont, Calif.: Wadsworth, 1975), pp. 96–113.
4. Runciman, *Max Weber*, p. 43.
5. See Gavin Mackenzie, "Class," *New Society* 22 (October 19, 1972): 142–144; Erik Olin Wright, *Class, Crisis and the State* (London: New Left Books, 1978), pp. 74–97.
6. Gerhard Lenski, "Marxist Experiments in Destratification: An Appraisal," *Social Forces* 57 (December 1978): 369–371; Walter D. Connor, *Socialism, Politics, and Equality: Hierarchy and Change in Eastern Europe and the USSR* (New York: Columbia University Press, 1979), pp. 217–223, 231.
7. Talcott Parsons, "Culture and the Social System Revisited," *Social Science Quarterly* 53 (September 1972): 253–266.
8. Donald J. Treiman, *Occupational Prestige in Comparative Perspective* (New York: Academic Press, 1977), esp. pp. 59–157, 223–234; Connor, *Socialism, Politics, and Equality*, p. 93.
9. Runciman, *Max Weber*, pp. 43–61; Seymour Martin Lipset, *Revolution and Counterrevolution: Change and Persistence in Social Structures* (New York: Basic Books, 1968), pp. 125–138.
10. Treiman, *Occupational Prestige in Comparative Perspective*, pp. 96–97, 113–116.
11. Pierre L. van den Berghe, "Ethnic Pluralism in Industrial Societies: A Special Case?" *Ethnicity* 3 (September 1976): 242–255.
12. For comparative analyses of feudalism, capitalism, and socialism, see Anthony Giddens, *The Class Structure of the Advanced Societies* (New York: Harper & Row, 1975), pp. 82–91; John E. Elliott, "Marx's Socialism in the Context of His Typology of Economic Systems," *Journal of Comparative Economics* 2 (March 1978): 25–41; Göran Therborn, *What Does the Ruling Class Do When It Rules?* (London: New Left Books, 1978).
13. See Reinhard Bendix, *Kings or People: Power and the Mandate to Rule* (Berkeley: University of California Press, 1978), pp. 201, 225–227, 528–529; Immanuel Wallerstein, *The Modern World-System* (New York: Academic Press, 1974), pp. 31–32; Joshua Prawer and S. N. Eisenstadt, "Feudalism," in *International Encyclopedia of the Social Sciences*, vol. 5 (New York: Free Press, 1968), pp. 393–403; Robert J. Holton, "Marxist Theories of Social Change and the Transition from Feudalism to Capitalism," *Theory and Society* 10 (November 1981): 833–867; Frederic L. Pryor, "Review Article: Feudalism as an Economic System," *Journal of Comparative Economics* 4 (March 1980): 58–60.
14. See A. F. K. Organski, *The Stages of Political Development* (New York: Knopf, 1965), pp. 56–93; Robert O. Keohane, "Economics, Inflation, and the Role of the State: Political Implications of the McCracken Report," *World Politics* 31 (October 1978): 108–128; Andrew Gamble and Paul Wal-

ton, *Capitalism in Crisis: Inflation and the State* (Atlantic Highlands, N.J.: Humanities Press, 1977), pp. 162–170; James O'Connor, *The Fiscal Crisis of the State* (New York: St. Martin's Press, 1973), pp. 6–9, 97–174.
15. Quoted in Philip Green, "Decentralization, Community Control, and Revolution: Reflections on Ocean Hill–Brownsville," in *Power and Community: Dissenting Essays in Political Science*, ed. Philip Green and Sanford Levinson (New York: Vintage Books, 1970), p. 247.
16. Gregory Grossman, *Economic Systems*, 2d ed. (Englewood Cliffs, N.J.: Prentice-Hall, 1974), pp. 45–54, 72–149.
17. Lenski, "Marxist Experiments in Destratification," pp. 369–371; Janet G. Chapman, "Are Earnings More Equal under Socialism: The Soviet Case, with Some United States Comparisons," in *Income Inequality: Trends and International Comparisons*, ed. John R. Moroney (Lexington, Mass.: Heath, 1979), pp. 43–59; Ivan Szelenyi, "Social Inequalities in State Socialist Redistributive Economies," *International Journal of Comparative Sociology* 19 (March–June 1978): 63–87.
18. Lenski, "Marxist Experiments in Destratification," pp. 364–383; Seymour Martin Lipset and Richard B. Dobson, "Social Stratification and Sociology in the Soviet Union," *Survey* 19 (Summer 1973): 114–185; Jeffrey W. Hahn, "Stability and Change in the Soviet Union: A Developmental Perspective," *Polity* 10 (Summer 1980): 546–562; Connor, *Socialism, Politics, and Equality*, pp. 248–259; Tran Nhu Trang, *The Transformation of the Peasantry in North Viet Nam* (Ph. D. dissertation, Department of Political Science, University of Pittsburgh, 1972), pp. 389–392.
19. Theda Skocpol and Ellen Kay Trimberger, "Revolutions and the World-Historical Development of Capitalism," in *Social Change in the Capitalist World Economy*, ed. Barbara Hockey Kaplan (Beverly Hills, Calif.: Sage, 1978), pp. 126–130.
20. Hahn, "Stability and Change in the Soviet Union," pp. 546–557; David Lane, *Politics and Society in the USSR*, 2d ed. (New York: New York University Press, 1978), pp. 382–457; Klaus von Beyme, "Soviet Social Policy in Comparative Perspective," *International Political Science Review* 2, no. 1 (1981): 73–94; Lenski, "Marxist Experiments in Destratification," pp. 373–379; Connor, *Socialism, Politics, and Equality*, pp. 262–266; Michael Swafford, "Sex Differences in Soviet Earnings," *American Sociological Review* 43 (October 1978): 657–673; Sharon L. Wolchik, "Ideology and Equality: The Status of Women in Eastern and Western Europe," *Comparative Political Studies* 13 (January 1981): 445–476; John R. Moroney, "Do Women Earn Less under Capitalism?" in *Income Inequality*, pp. 141–157; *OECD Observer* no. 104 (May 1980): 7. In two essays, John M. Echols III shows that state socialist societies, compared with capitalist societies, have greater economic equality but not more ethnic or sexual equality. See his "Does Socialism Mean Greater Equality? Comparison of East and West along Several Major Dimensions," *American Journal of Political Science* 25 (February 1981): 1–31; "Racial and Ethnic Inequality: The Comparative Impact of Socialism," *Comparative Political Studies* 13 (January 1981): 403–444.
21. Luke 16: 22–23, 25 (American Bible Society translation).
22. Seymour Martin Lipset, *Political Man: The Social Bases of Politics* (Garden City, N.Y.: Doubleday, 1960), pp. 106–108.
23. See John Eagleson, ed., *Christians and Socialism: Documentation of the Christians for Socialism Movement in Latin America*, trans. John Drury (Maryknoll, N.Y.: Orbis Books, 1975), pp. 117–118.
24. See Andrain, *Political Life and Social Change*, pp. 30–34; David E. Apter, *Some Conceptual Approaches to the Study of Modernization* (Englewood Cliffs, N.J.: Prentice-Hall, 1968), pp. 39–40.
25. Mayer N. Zald and Michael A. Berger, "Social Movements in Organizations: Coup d'Etat, Insurgency, and Mass Movements," *American Journal of Sociology* 83 (January 1978): 841–847; Charles Tilly, *From Mobilization to Revolution* (Reading, Mass.: Addison-Wesley, 1978), pp. 69–84.
26. See Michael Mann, *Consciousness and Action among the Western Working Class* (London: Macmillan, 1973), esp. p. 13.
27. Karl Marx, *Political Writings, Vol. II: Surveys from Exile*, ed. David Fernbach (New York: Vintage Books, 1974), p. 239.
28. See Joseph Lopreato and Lawrence E. Hazelrigg, *Class, Conflict, and Mobility: Theories and Studies of Class Structure* (San Francisco: Chandler, 1972), p. 204; Guy Michelat and Michel Simon, "Classe sociale objective, classe sociale subjective et comportement électoral," *Revue française de sociologie* 12 (Octobre–Décembre 1971): 512; Jean-Claude Rabier, "Review Article: On the Political Behaviour of French Workers," *Acta Sociologica* 21, no.

4 (1978): 365–367; James W. Rinehart and Ishmael O. Okraku, "A Study of Class Consciousness," *Canadian Review of Sociology and Anthropology* 11 (August 1974): 206; Göran Ahrne, Ulf Himmelstrand, and Leif Lundberg, "'Middle Way' Sweden at a Cross-Road: Problems, Actors, and Outcomes," *Acta Sociologica* 21, no. 4 (1978): 323; Kay Lehman Schlozman and Sidney Verba, *Injury to Insult: Unemployment, Class, and Political Response* (Cambridge, Mass.: Harvard University Press, 1979), pp. 115–117; Marvin E. Olsen, "Social Classes in Contemporary Sweden," *Sociological Quarterly* 15 (Summer 1974): 337; E. M. Schreiber and G. T. Nygreen, "Subjective Social Class in America: 1945–68," *Social Forces* 48 (March 1970): 351–352; John C. Goyder, "A Note on the Declining Relation between Subjective and Objective Class Measures," *British Journal of Sociology* 26 (March 1975): 103–104; Mary R. Jackman and Robert W. Jackman, "An Interpretation of the Relation between Objective and Subjective Social Status," *American Sociological Review* 38 (October 1973): 569–582; Mary R. Jackman, "The Subjective Meaning of Social Class Identification in the United States," *Public Opinion Quarterly* 43 (Winter 1979): 443–476.

29. Wright, *Class Crisis and the State*, pp. 61–97; Mann, *Consciousness and Action among the Western Working Class*, p. 70.

30. See Lipset, *Revolution and Counterrevolution*, pp. 159–176; Frank Parkin, *Class Inequality and Political Order* (New York: Praeger, 1971), pp. 48–102.

31. Ronald Inglehart, *The Silent Revolution: Changing Values and Political Styles among Western Publics* (Princeton, N.J.: Princeton University Press, 1977), p. 280; John R. Low-Beer, *Protest and Participation: The New Working Class in Italy* (New York: Cambridge University Press, 1978), pp. 1, 45–62; 200–240; Thomas A. Kochan, "How American Workers View Labor Unions," *Monthly Labor Review* 102 (April 1979): 29.

32. V. I. Lenin, *What Is To Be Done?* (Peking: Foreign Languages Press, 1975), pp. 37, 57, 199.

33. Michael Mann, "The Social Cohesion of Liberal Democracy," *American Sociological Review* 35 (June 1970): 423–439.

34. Sidney Verba and Norman H. Nie, *Participation in America: Political Democracy and Social Equality* (New York: Harper & Row, 1972), pp. 267–298, 340–341; Sidney Verba, Norman H. Nie, and Jae-on Kim, *Participation and Political Equality: A Seven-Nation Comparison* (New York: Cambridge University Press, 1978), pp. 63–75; Sidney Verba and Kay Lehman Schlozman, "Unemployment, Class Consciousness, and Radical Politics: What Didn't Happen in the Thirties," *Journal of Politics* 39 (May 1977): 291–323; Giuseppe di Palma, *Apathy and Participation: Mass Politics in Western Societies* (New York: Free Press, 1970), pp. 146, 193.

35. Karl Marx, *Political Writings, Vol. I: The Revolutions of 1848*, ed. David Fernbach (New York: Vintage Books, 1974), p. 77. Marx and Engels described the "lumpenproletariat" of casual workers and unemployed persons as the "social scum," the "bribed tool of reactionary intrigue."

36. See L. Bianco, "Peasants and Revolution: The Case of China," *Journal of Peasant Studies* 2 (April 1975): 313–335; Ralph Thaxton, "Peasants, Capitalism and Revolution: On Capitalism as a Force for Liberation in Revolutionary China," *Comparative Political Studies* 12 (October 1979): 289–334; Ralph Thaxton, "On Peasant Revolution and National Resistance: Toward a Theory of Peasant Mobilization and Revolutionary War with Special Reference to Modern China," *World Politics* 30 (October 1977): 24–57; Theda Skocpol, "France, Russia, China: A Structural Analysis of Social Revolutions," *Comparative Studies in Society and History* 18 (April 1976): 175–210; Theda Skocpol, "Old Regime Legacies and Communist Revolutions in Russia and China," *Social Forces* 55 (December 1976): 284–315.

37. Charles Tilly, "Revolutions and Collective Violence," in *Handbook of Political Science*, vol. 3, ed. Fred I. Greenstein and Nelson W. Polsby (Reading, Mass.: Addison-Wesley, 1975), p. 504.

PART

Political Beliefs

Political beliefs interact with social structures to shape the policy process. Not only the political power of social groups but also the interpretations and priorities given to certain beliefs influence political decision making. As a basic cultural foundation of political systems, beliefs serve several functions in the policy process. First, they define the problems policymakers want resolved through government actions. For example, compared with a politician who seeks to maximize the private business executive's economic freedom, a political leader who gives a higher priority to socioeconomic equality will more likely perceive widespread poverty as a serious social problem. Therefore, the latter policymaker will demonstrate stronger support for income redistribution measures.

Second, political beliefs specify alternative decisions for resolving a problem such as severe inflation. In the United States, the value of business freedom discourages reliance on wage and price controls as an effective strategy for curtailing rapid price increases. Lacking this strong commitment to freedom for economic decision makers, Soviet government officials show no reluctance to impose wage and price controls to curb rapid price increases.

Third, political beliefs influence the criteria for choosing the best policy option. Such values as freedom and equality designate the most desirable policy. Policymakers' conceptions of efficiency lead them to select the option regarded as the most feasible to implement.

Fourth, policymakers use certain policies to justify their rule by claiming that these public policies have maximized moral–spiritual values—justice, civic virtue, moral righteousness—and such material outcomes as economic equality or freedom from foreign attack.

Based on these four functions, the analysis of political ideology in part II examines the meanings and priorities placed on freedom and equality. Chapter 4 compares classical conservatism, classical liberalism, democratic socialism, communism, and fascism. Chapter 5 analyzes the effect of these ideologies on the public policies implemented in different political systems.

CHAPTER
4

Political Ideology
The Meaning of Freedom and Equality

> *Unequal distribution of income is inherently an unequal distribution of freedom. Thus a redistribution of income, to the extent that it reduces the freedom of the rich, equally increases that of the poor. Their control of their lives is increased.*
> —KENNETH J. ARROW

> *Two world wars and a major depression have advanced bureaucracy and its inherent regimentations to a point where the ideology of equality becomes more and more a means of rationalizing these regimentations and less and less a force serving individual life or liberty.*
> —ROBERT A. NISBET

Since the French Revolution of 1789, when cries for "Liberté, Egalité, Fraternité" sounded throughout France, freedom and equality have constituted the central ideological values in political life. Both the vertical and horizontal images of the political system have focused on different degrees of freedom and equality.

Until the French Revolution, most intellectuals viewed the political world through vertical metaphors—that is, in terms of "up" and "down." They conceived of society, the individual, and polity as organisms. Just as the mind dominated the body, so the government dominated the governed. The political, religious, economic, and family sectors of society all revealed vertical, hierarchical relationships. Within the family, the father, the elders, and the men had authority over the children and women. The landlords dominated the serfs. The pope ruled as head of the Roman Catholic church with the laity at the bottom of the hierarchy. Similarly in the political system, the king acted as head; his subjects remained at his feet. According to these elitist, conservative metaphors, "up" conveyed a positive image; rulers at the top enjoyed freedom to control others at the bottom, who lacked both freedom and equality. Ascent implied a movement toward greater power; descent meant a change to an inferior position. According to the Apostles' Creed, Jesus Christ "descended into hell; then he ascended into heaven and sits at the right hand of God the father."

With the coming of the French Revolution, ideologues began to perceive politics in terms of horizontal, not vertical, images. They viewed liberty and equality from a left-right perspective. At the first meeting of the French National Assembly in 1789, the opponents of King Louis XVI sat on the left of the rostrum and members supporting the king took their seats on the right. According to the revolutionary intellectuals, political relationships must be based on equalitarian fraternal friendship ties, not those of father and son. Freedom and equality should replace subordination and elitism. Hence, "left" came to mean the following:

1. Equality among the many
2. Freedom from established authority of the Catholic church, landed elite, and court nobility
3. Secularism—that is, freedom from the established church
4. A fundamental change in the stratification system involving the overthrow of the church, the monarchy, and feudal landlords

In contrast, "right" signified

1. Elitism or dominance by the few
2. Subordination to the established authorities
3. Loyalty to the sacred order, where Jesus Christ sits at the *right* hand of God
4. Continuity with the *ancien régime* dominated by monarchy, church, and landowners[1]

These new horizontal metaphors thus implied greater equality and freedom than the vertical images of the political system.

Today the concepts of freedom and equality continue to form the focal point of ideological discourse. After analyzing the political writings of four ideologies—capitalism, democratic socialism, the Leninist interpretation of communism, and fascism as espoused by Adolf Hitler—Milton Rokeach concluded that freedom and equality are the two most distinctively political values.[2] Whatever their priorities, ideologists have made more references to freedom and equality than to any other values. Hence, this chapter concentrates on the interpretations of freedom and equality found in five ideologies: classical conservatism, classical liberalism, democratic socialism, communism, and fascism.

Dimensions of Political Ideology

Over the last 200 years, the term *ideology* has changed meaning. The concept originated in France during the late eighteenth century. At this time, the French revolutionaries attacked the divine right of the king to rule. They also questioned orthodox religious traditions associated with the established Roman Catholic church. A French philosopher, Destutt de Tracy, coined the term *ideology* to denote a science of ideas based not on the discredited principles of faith and authority but rather on more objective impressions gained from the physical senses. For de Tracy, ideology was essentially an empirical method for observing the world.

During the next century, however, Karl Marx took a somewhat different position. He contrasted scientific socialism with unscientific ideologies based on false consciousness. In his view, ideology constituted both a rationalization for actions taken on nonideological grounds—the search for political power, wealth, and status—and a subjective blinder that distorts an understanding of the social situation.

Social scientists today view ideology in more detached terms. For them, it represents a systematic set of principles linking perceptions of the world to explicit moral values. An ideology not only interprets the meaning of events but also posits the need to change or maintain the existing situation.[3] According to Carl J. Friedrich, "Ideologies are action-related systems of ideas . . . related to the existing political and social order and intended either to change it or to defend it. . . . [They] designate a reasonably coherent body of ideas concerning practical means of how to change, reform (or maintain) a political order."[4] From this conception derive three dimensions of ideology: its structure (style of reasoning), functions, and content.

STYLE OF REASONING

The structure of an ideology—its style of reasoning—involves abstract, deductive thought patterns. Ideology refers to a general, abstract, systematic set of principles, rather than to specific, concrete, and random beliefs. Ideologues link particular details to general principles. They perceive concrete events in light of abstract ideas. Stylistically, ideologues also engage in deductive thinking; they deduce specific conclusions from general theoretical principles. For example, how do ideological politicians interpret poverty? An activist member of the Italian Communist party locates the sources of poverty in general economic conditions; it springs from the "retarded capitalism" experienced by Italy. The cleavage between the industrialized north and the underdeveloped, poverty-stricken south reflects the linkage of Italy into the world capitalist system. In contrast, a nonideological member of the British Conservative party denies that much poverty remains in England. Reasoning from personal experience, he argues inductively that most working-class residences in his constituency have television aerials on their roofs. Whatever poverty that does exist derives from the wage freeze enacted by the Labour party.[5]

Education, political activism, and preferences for social change all affect the extent to which people engage in an ideological—abstract, deductive—style of reasoning. Less formally educated individuals, political inactives, and ones not seeking fundamental changes in the status quo are least likely to think ideologically. For them, the esoteric ideological "isms" remain incomprehensible and meaningless. The abstract interpretations of freedom and equality appear less important to them than such personalized, concrete, and immediate liberties as the equal rights to own a car, obtain a job, watch football games on television, and bowl on Wednesday night.

By contrast, formally educated persons, political activists, and people preferring fundamental changes in the existing social stratification system, especially a radical creation of a new social order, tend to think more abstractly, deductively, and systematically about political issues. In particular, ideology has the greatest functional importance for Marxist-Leninists, who take abstract principles the most seriously. The principles of Marxism-Leninism encourage individuals to abandon their reliance on habit and routine as guides to behavior and instead live according to a vision of a changed social order. In the USSR, China, Vietnam, and Cuba, Marxist-Leninist revolutionaries have viewed ideology as a comprehensive, systematic program for political action to reconstruct the society. These leaders use abstract theoretical principles—dialectical change, economic contradictions, the relations and forces of production—to justify their struggle to liberate the industrial workers and peasants from exploitation and to establish a more economically egalitarian society.

FUNCTIONS

Ideology serves both an interpretative and a policy-related purpose.[6] An ideology's philosophical principles explain the key problems facing a society and also interpret key events; they provide meaning behind life and history. Particularly when traditional beliefs seem to have little relevance in explaining events, a new ideology becomes a primary means to perceive and understand the world. During these periods, the old patterns of legitimacy have largely disintegrated. Conceptual confusion prevails. People hence seek an explanation of rapid change, an interpretation of experience that gives purpose, meaning, and significance to human behavior. To fulfill this need for meaning, ideology may provide a "world image" that simplifies reality and offers an explanation for complex behavior.

The policy-related dimensions of ideology—its program for action—perform several functions:

1. They shape the purposes and priorities for political action. What particular problems should be resolved through political means? For what specific projects—national defense, health care, education—should the government allocate resources?

2. Once political leaders have decided that they should try to resolve certain social problems, such as unemployment and inflation, through the public policy route, political ideology influences the selection of the most desirable and feasible policies. For example, should government officials cope with inflation by cutting state expenditures, raising taxes, increasing the interest rates, or decreasing the money supply? In this regard, ideologies operate as perceptual screens that filter out some options.

3. By justifying actions, leaders who hold political power try to gain acceptance for their policies. If they do not hold government offices, ideologues challenge established authority, criticize existing policies, and offer proposals for change. Hence, ideologies may serve either to legitimate the existing regime or to delegitimize the incumbent officeholders and the established political systems.

4. Ideologies can mobilize human efforts behind a cause. By rallying people behind shared policy objectives, they strive to strengthen shared identity and social solidarity.

CONTENT

The content of political ideology focuses on both fundamental philosophical principles and the bases of political power. These two aspects relate to its interpretative and policy-related functions.

Philosophical principles. Ideologies such as conservatism, liberalism, democratic socialism, communism, and fascism all deal with the following philosophical issues:

1. The nature of the self—Is one good or evil, active or passive, changeable or unchangeable?

2. The interaction between the self and the society—What relationship should exist between the individual and the collectivity?
3. The relation of the self to the physical environment—Should the individual submit to nature, achieve harmony with it, or master the environment?
4. The view of history—What is the relative focus placed on the past, present, and future? Does history reveal a trend toward progress or decay? Is history viewed as cyclical or linear?[7]

As table 4-1 indicates, ideologies offer diverse answers to these philosophical questions. For example, democratic socialism as interpreted by the English historian R. H. Tawney and the Nazi beliefs voiced by Adolf Hitler are sharply opposed. The socialist Tawney perceived human nature as good, active, and changeable. Viewing society as a fellowship, he assumed that individuals would realize their highest potentialities only in a socialist society governed through democratic procedures. Tawney took a fairly optimistic view of history. He saw societies progressing toward greater enlightenment; through their present labors, democratic socialists would realize the good society in the future.

Hitler assumed a more pessimistic view toward individuals, society, and the future. For Hitler, people were basically evil and unchangeable. Some races were biologically unequal; most people lacked the active will to determine their destinies. According to Hitler, individuals thus need a strong state and leader to curb their passions. He perceived history as decay; decadent doctrines—individualism, liberalism, Marxist socialism, and communism—threatened to corrupt German society. Therefore, the German people, under his guidance, had to renounce these false doctrines and restore the past glories embodied in the First Reich—the medieval Teutonic empires—and in the Second Reich of the powerful, united German state under Bismarck.

In their attitudes toward changes in the social stratification system, the classical conservatives and the communists take divergent positions. The conservatives historically have viewed people as basically evil, passive, and unchangeable; they expect individuals to accept their station in life without struggling to gain upward personal mobility or to advance the status of a dispossessed class. Societies rise and fall. Any hope of future progress seems doomed; hence, people should concentrate on the past heritage and present conditions, rather than on any illusory future glories.

On most of these issues, the communists, especially Lenin, have assumed the opposite perspective toward social change. Stressing the human ability to change social conditions, they expect a transforma-

TABLE 4-1 The philosophical principles of ideologies

	Conservatism	Liberalism	Socialism	Communism	Fascism
Ideologue	Burke, Disraeli, Churchill, Bismarck, de Maistre, de Bonald, Maurras	Locke, Smith, Ricardo, Malthus, Bastiat, Woodrow Wilson, Herbert Hoover, Franklin D. Roosevelt, Daniel Bell, Friedrich A. Hayek, Robert Nozick	R. H. Tawney, Norman Thomas, Willy Brandt	Marx, Lenin, Trotsky, Bukharin, Gramsci, Mao	Hitler, Mussolini
Issues: (1) nature of person	evil, original sin: dominance of passions	good or mixture of good & evil: self-interest vs. power of reason	good	good under new economic system: socialism and full communism	evil: need for strong state and leader to curb passions
	passive	active	active	active: stress on will	active/passive: active leader but passive followers
	unchangeable	changeable	changeable	changeable through exposure to new environmental stimuli	unchangeable: biological inequality
(2) relation of self to others	collectivism (society) over individual	individualism	balanced concern for individual & collective: society as fellowship	collectivism of class over individual	collectivism of race and nation over individual
(3) relation of self to physical environment	harmony with nature	mastery over nature	balance between mastery over nature & harmony with nature: concern for ecology	mastery over nature: industrialize and electrify the country	mastery over nature
(4) view of history	cyclical: rise and fall	linear—but also awareness of pain and scarcity	linear—a view of history as progress	linear—a view of history as progress	decay
(5) time orientation	past and present	future: need to delay gratifications and to save	future	future: ideal society of full communism lies in future	past: restore past glories (Rome, II Reich)

tion of human behavior under the new economic system of first socialism and then full communism. Through exposure to new environmental stimuli, individuals will become more altruistic, public-regarding, and willing to serve the public welfare. Lenin viewed history as movement toward greater progress; the ideal society of full communism, where economic abundance coexists with social equality, lies in the future, not the past.

The classical liberals and the democratic socialists show the greatest agreement on basic philosophical issues. Both ideologies affirm the need for reformist changes. From their view, people are good, active, and changeable. They have the ability to bring the physical environment under human control. Through the exercise of will, individuals can make historical progress. Education and industrialization will create a better life for all.

Although agreeing on these issues, liberals and socialists differ somewhat in their expectations of a beneficent future. Socialists take a more optimistic position; liberals express greater pessimism about realizing an ideal society. Closely linked with the rise of capitalism, liberalism assumes that individual self-interest—the desire for greater wealth and status—motivates human behavior. Because individual interests can never be satisfied, economic scarcity will always remain, even in a fully industrialized society. As more and more individuals strive to enrich themselves, class struggle threatens the social order. Thus, liberals remain skeptical about realizing an abundant future society where people live in fellowship.[8]

Programs for political action. A political ideology contains not only a set of philosophical doctrines but also a program for action.[9] In this regard, the bases of political power and the interpretation of freedom and equality become especially important. Who now rules? Who ought to govern a society? How should the political leaders be selected? How will the rulers justify their exercise of power? What public policies will they pursue; that is, how will the priority and interpretations given to freedom and equality influence their preferences for certain public policies?

More than any other values, freedom and equality highlight actual and preferred conditions in the social stratification system. Politics deals partly with the struggle for scarce resources that can be converted into binding public policies. Freedom and equality become especially important in this political struggle. *Freedom* refers to the expansion of choices in the use of scarce resources. Individuals and groups with the greatest freedom can maximize their alternatives, mainly because they have access to a wide range of resources and have the right to use them for shaping public decisions. *Equality* means a general similarity in the distribution of resources, such as political authority, wealth, knowledge, rectitude, and human respect. Those who gain access to crucial resources and secure the freedom to use the resources in the policy process can exert the political power to change or maintain the social stratification system. The priorities given to freedom and equality, as well as the interpretations of these general values, influence the specific policy goals sought through government decision making.[10]

Despite their central place in political ideologies, the concepts of freedom and equality remain highly general, abstract, and vague; only by clarifying their meanings can we make valid comparisons among conservatism, liberalism, democratic socialism, communism, and fascism. As the following discussion of five ideological "isms" indicates, the types of freedom and equality correspond to the three sectors of society—the political, economic, and cultural systems.

At the most general level, freedom means the expansion of choices. More specifically, political freedoms (civil liberties) include the rights to participate in politics, articulate views about public decisions, challenge the government, organize nonviolent opposition to government leaders and policy, and gain access to political decision making.

Economic freedoms involve a wide range of options open to producers, distributors, and consumers. As producers, farmers can own land and till the soil. Owners and managers can operate their businesses without outside interference. Workers can form a union, bargain collectively with the employer, and move to a new job. As distributors, entrepreneurs enjoy the rights to engage in free exchange of goods and services. Consumers have available a wide choice of goods for purchase.

Cultural freedoms comprise the right to pursue both rectitude and status (honor, respect, prestige). Individuals have the opportunity to worship in the church of their choice. They also enjoy the right to social mobility—that is, freedom to rise in the social status network and to attain higher prestige.

Ideologies differ according to the stress placed on freedom for the individual or the collectivity. For instance, whereas liberals emphasize individual liberties or self-determination, fascists focus on the need for national independence, and communists advocate the liberation of the proletarian class from capitalist exploitation.

Like freedom, equality refers to conditions within the three sectors of society. In general, equality means similar access to scarce resources. Political equality signifies a variety of different situations: one vote for each person, similar treatment before the law, similar access to political leaders to press demands for public policies, and a similar weight in political decision making. If every person or group wields the same power in the formulation of public policies, then political equality will be maximized.

Traditionally, economic equality has meant two different types: equal opportunity to gain wealth (equality at the start of the economic race) and the possession of the same level of economic rewards at the end of the race. The latter condition implies equal access to goods and services.

Cultural equality involves both rectitude and status. If every person, regardless of power, wealth, or status, receives the same dignity as a human being, then moral–spiritual equality of human worth prevails in that society. When no elite gains special deference for its "superior" position and all people are treated the same in social interactions, equality of status ranks high. Under these conditions, women, youth, ethnic and religious minorities, and poorer classes gain the same respect as do men, older people, majority ethno-religious groups, and the wealthy.

Ideologues often express different attitudes about the unit that deserves equality. Whereas liberals and democratic socialists stress individual equality, fascists focus on the collectivity. When Hitler became chancellor of Germany in 1933, he advocated equality between the German nation and other West European nations. Later during the 1930s, he asserted the need for Germany to dominate other states.

Milton Rokeach compares ideologies by the priorities they give to freedom and equality; yet the specific interpretations of these two values seem just as important as the rankings. According to Rokeach, fascism and democratic socialism show the greatest divergence. Whereas Hitler gave a low priority to freedom and equality, democratic socialists have judged both values as highly desirable. Classical liberalism (capitalism) and communism also demonstrate different priorities. Liberalism ranks freedom high but equality low. In contrast, Leninism evaluates equality more favorably than freedom.[11] To what extent are these rankings valid? How does classical conservatism interpret freedom and equality? Answers to these questions depend on the specific meaning each ideology attributes to freedom and equality. Although different proponents of the same ideology have formulated somewhat diverse interpretations of these twin concepts, I shall focus on the general, basic themes common to each ideological perspective.

Classical Conservatism

During the last 200 years, classical conservatives have articulated ideas associated with the dominant social groups of their time. Before and immediately after the French Revolution, conservatives identified with the orthodox church, the monarchy, and the landed aristocracy. As the industrialization process gained momentum in late nineteenth-century Europe, entrepreneurs and industrialists came to voice some conservative notions. During the present industrial era, managers and technocrats in Europe, Latin America, and Asia have sympathized with conservative principles. Classical conservatism has thus attracted a following all over the world during many different periods, including agrarian, industrializing, and industrial eras.

Who are the major articulators of the conservative ideology? A recent survey carried out among Conservative party members of Parliament in England revealed that Winston Churchill, Benjamin Disraeli, and Edmund Burke exercised the greatest influence on these parliamentarians' thinking.[12] In France, the conservative movement includes more reactionary figures, such as de Maistre, de Bonald, and Maurras, on the one hand, and more flexible, pluralistic writers such as Benjamin Constant and Alexis de Tocqueville, on the other. Compared with British conservatives, German conservatives, including Adam Müller and Otto von Bismarck, placed greater stress on the need for a strong state authority.

MONIST AND PLURALIST INTERPRETATIONS

Classical conservatives have historically separated into two philosophical camps: the monists and the pluralists. The monists—de Bonald, de Maistre, Maurras—wanted the state and the orthodox church to exercise dominant authority. The pluralists—Burke, Disraeli, Churchill, de Tocqueville, and Constant—perceived the desirability of shared power. From their perspective, a variety of social groups—voluntary associations, local communities, regional organizations—bring needed diversity to the society. Within the political system, local governments, autonomous courts, and a balance of power at the national government level provide checks on central state authority. According to these conservative pluralists, a constitutional government limited by legal restraints effectively guarantees freedom against the leveling, conformist, equalitarian tendencies of contemporary mass society.[13]

Freedom. Classical conservatives, especially the monist camp, assert the primacy of social authority over individual freedom. Individuals are basically evil. Ruled by their emotions and passions, they fall victim to self-indulgence. Excessive liberty leads to anarchy, which in turn sets the foundations for eventual tyranny. Because self-imposed restraints cannot check individuals' deleterious conduct, social institutions such as the state, church, and family must restrain the evil tendencies of human nature. Thus, political liberty is not an absolute value. Instead, freedom must coexist with the authority exercised by social institutions. From this conservative viewpoint, duty should supersede individual rights. Order must triumph over self-indulgence.

Compared with the monistic conservatives, the pluralistic conservative thinkers found in Canada and England have placed greater stress on the need for legal restraints on individual freedoms. According to this view, the law originates from above; originally the king declared the law. It protects freedom in an orderly way. Because true freedom can thrive only under political order, freedom and legal authority enjoy a complementary, not a contradictory, relationship. In its attitude toward the individual, the law specifies the need for individual responsibility to the community; yet it also protects the individual from the conformist pressures of the majority.[14]

Despite this focus on order, authority, and duty, the classical conservatives have also promoted political freedom by justifying the need for diversity. In particular, such conservatives as Alexis de Tocqueville wanted modern society to retain some pluralistic features of the feudal order. With the advance of industrialization, mass education, and the mass media, contemporary societies fall prey to uniformity. For this reason, they must try to recapture some of the variety, gradation, and diversity characteristic of preindustrial societies. Only by strengthening small, autonomous structures—local governments, neighborhood communities, regional organizations, churches, and other voluntary associations—can people check the dangers from a powerful, bureaucratic central state that threatens political freedom.

Unlike the classical liberals associated with the rise of capitalism, few classical conservatives enthusiastically campaigned for widespread economic freedom from the state. In the Western world, conservatism arose under feudal conditions. Although the landlord enjoyed considerable freedom to use his land as he saw fit, the serf lacked that freedom. During the industrial era, conservatives associated themselves with mercantilist, statist, and corporatist doctrines. All these concepts posited a powerful role for the state in regulating economic affairs and planning economic welfare for the common good.

Although most pluralistic English conservatives stressed freedom of private property rights, they also asserted the need for state control over the use of private wealth. With the rise of the welfare state during the mid twentieth century, some conservatives want the national government to play a paternalistic role in protecting the poor. For instance, Harold Macmillan, Conservative prime minister of England from 1957 through 1963, saw state planning as a way to increase economic production, raise the standard of living for all citizens, and thereby avoid class conflict and fundamental income redistribution measures. According to Macmillan, by promoting the welfare state and a planned economy, an activist conservative government would cement the loyalties of the working classes to the established political system.[15]

Historically, classical conservatives have not supported a wide degree of religious freedom. Originally identified with the established church—the Anglican church in England and Canada, the Roman Catholic church in West Europe and Latin America, the Islamic faith throughout Africa, the Near East, and Asia—conservatives opposed the separation of the church from the state. They perceived an established church as necessary to restrict self-indulgence. A diversity of independent churches would bring anarchy, disorder, and chaos to society. During the late twentieth century, most classical conservatives in the Western world have come to accept religious pluralism. Yet some, such as Plinio Corrêa de Oliveira, the founder of the Brazilian Society for the Defense of Tradition, Family, and Property, still assert that the orthodox beliefs derived from God, revelation, and the church should dominate government decision making. He has denounced the French socialist government for practicing "state secularism," adhering to "laicism," and implementing an "atheistic" program.[16]

Classical conservatives, especially the monists, have also downplayed freedom for individuals to rise through the social stratification system and thereby gain higher status. The monists affirm the need for each person to keep in his or her own "place." According to them, the insatiable striving for status will lead to frustration, political discontent, and social disorder. Therefore, individuals must lower their expectations and remain content with their station in life. As the famous Anglican church hymn intones: "The rich man in his castle, the poor man at his gate, God made them high or lowly and ordered their estate." Such pluralist conservatives as Disraeli, although upholding a graded, differentiated stratification system, favored a more flexible social structure. He viewed England as a "nation of classes but not of castes," a society where individuals enjoy some freedom to move between social classes.[17]

Equality. Although classical conservatives take an ambivalent view toward freedom, nearly all agree that equality deserves a low priority. Whereas the monists regard both freedom and equality as undesirable, the pluralists assert the primacy of freedom over equality. Both conservative camps believe that hierarchy should take precedence over equality. In the political sphere, the superior classes ought to rule. Feudalism saw the landed aristocracy exercising political dominance; those of noble birth acted as the elite. With the emergence of industrialization during the nineteenth century, commercial businessmen gained greater political authority. In the twentieth century, the corporate state has witnessed the rise to power of managers, technocrats, professionals, and experts.

Whatever the social classes dominating a society, they, rather than the "capricious, passionate multitudes," should govern the political system in an elitist manner. Conservatives justify the need for a governing class by formulating an analogy between the political system and the human organism. Just as the head dominates the body, so the political elite must rule the rest of society. If the feet were ever to become equal with the head, the society would disintegrate. Therefore, attempts to attain full political equality ultimately lead to disaster.[18]

From the conservative perspective, equality of economic rewards violates the natural hierarchy that regulates the universe. Demands for economic leveling and uniformity encourage people to raise their expectations so as to satisfy their appetites. The pursuit of self-indulgence produces economic disorder. By establishing the authority of private property and rights to inherit property, society guarantees greater order, stability, and continuity with the past.

In their attitudes toward cultural equality, conservatives accord higher priority to spiritual than to status equality. Yet the conservative view of spiritual equality reveals some ambivalence. On the one hand, religious conservatives affirm the existence of a spiritual hierarchy. According to Roman Catholic thinkers, God the Father and Jesus Christ occupy the top of the hierarchy. Below them come the Virgin Mary and the angels, followed by the saints. Within the Church of God on earth, the pope exercises dominant authority as the vicar of Christ. Below him stand the cardinals, archbishops, bishops, and priests, with the laity at the bottom of the ecclesiastical hierarchy. On the other hand, classical conservatives stress the equality of all people before God. Whatever his or her status on earth, every individual is a child of God. Yet because every person has inherited original sin, efforts to change society fundamentally in a more equalitarian direction are impossible.

Although people may enjoy spiritual equality before God, they certainly should not be equal in status on earth. Conservatives perceive class differences as natural, not artificial. Because differences among people are inborn and unchangeable, status distinctions should remain. Those at the bottom of the social stratification system need to show deference toward their "superiors." In this functional social hierarchy, individuals outside the "natural aristocracy" occupy a subordinate role.[19]

CONTEMPORARY CONSERVATIVE IDEOLOGIES

Most classical conservative ideas originated in a feudal, agrarian context; during the late twentieth-century industrial era, many conservatives have modified their views to reflect a more secular, voluntarist ethos. Within Western nations today, self-styled contemporary "conservatives" divide into two diverse schools. The corporatists want to recapture the pluralistic features of the feudal order. In place of the medieval estates composed of the landed aristocracy, court nobility, Catholic clergy, and urban businessmen, new organized groups, especially large-scale private corporations, govern the society in cooperation with state bureaucrats. The corporatist ethos advocates paternalistic rule by administrators from the government and business sectors. Professionals and experts move freely from one sector to another, justifying the need for rule by a meritorious managerial elite. Government plays an activist role; it manages, plans, supervises, and regulates economic oligopolies and trade unions. National unity, order, and economic cooperation take priority over the individual interest seeking, disorder, and economic conflict associated with the market model of pure competition.

Reacting to the bureaucratic corporatist tendencies of modern industrial societies, other conservatives have advocated more laissez-faire ideas. Originally associated with classical liberalism, these notions of the "free market" assume an individualistic orientation. Rather than becoming organized into bureaucratic groups, individuals pursue their self-interests. Government plays a limited role; it lays down and enforces the rules of the political game. Just as political parties compete for government power, so economic firms compete on the market to satisfy consumer preferences. Particularly in the United States and Britain, conservative party leaders have adopted these principles upholding the free market. For example, in the United States, Barry Goldwater and Ronald Reagan have most enthusiastically embraced this interpretation of "conservatism." English Tory leaders Margaret Thatcher and Keith Joseph want to restore the market system to England's corporatist economy. From the perspective of all these laissez-faire conservatives, only a capitalist system can preserve liberty and avert the deleterious equalitarian tendencies facing the twentieth-century welfare state.[20]

Classical Liberalism

Classical liberalism originated in England along with the emergence of capitalism. Liberal merchants, manufacturers, financiers, and intellectuals articulated ideas that diverged from classical conservative support for the monarchy, the established church, the mercantilist state, and feudal status distinctions. Politically, they demanded either the abolition of the monarchy or the establishment of a parliamentary government where the parliament made crucial decisions and a constitutional monarch reigned but did not rule. According to the classical liberals, impersonal law, rather than a monarch, should undergird political authority.

Economically, the liberals supported greater freedom for the private entrepreneur. Under the mercantilist system, the powerful nation-state regulated foreign trade, internal commerce, and manufacturing; the state existed to promote national security and industrialization. In place of the mercantilist state, liberals sought to establish a more laissez-faire policy. Government interference in private economic affairs should largely end; individuals operating small-scale private firms should have the opportunity to pursue their self-interests free from tight state controls.

Culturally, the classical liberals supported the separation of the church from the state. Only through this disestablishment policy could individuals secure true religious freedom. Within the social stratification system, liberals strove for greater freedom of social mobility. Each individual, regardless of inherited status at birth, should have the right to improve his or her position. In short, the classical liberals stressed the primacy of individual freedom over the hierarchical order associated with conservatism.

Classical liberalism has attracted the greatest following in England and America, two nations where capitalism historically gained the strongest foothold. In the United States, no other ideology has rivaled liberalism in its effect on public policymaking. Neither classical conservatism nor socialism ever secured a powerful institutional base. John Locke (1632-1704) profoundly influenced the founders of the American nation, including the writers of the Constitution. As a classical liberal, Locke believed in government by popular consent, the rule of the majority, a balance of power between a representative legislature and the executive, the dominance of the popularly elected legislative branch, legal restraints on government power, impartial justice administered by independent courts, and the need for government to protect private property.[21] Three hundred years after Locke outlined these beliefs, American politicians still adhere to them. Despite the differences between Democrats and Republicans over the proper scope of government activity, both parties agree on the tenets of "Lockean liberalism."

Particularly since the end of World War II, many West German political leaders have embraced liberal views about the relations between government and the economy. Influenced by the triumphant American occupying forces, the German Federal Republic's first two chancellors, Konrad Adenauer and Ludwig Erhard, allowed private business executives considerable economic autonomy and influence over the framing of government economic policy. Today the Christian Democrats, Free Democrats (liberals), and the Social Democrats have accepted the principles of the "social market" economy, under which the federal government promotes an efficient market.

CLASSICAL LIBERAL VIEW OF FREEDOM

Classical liberals affirm the primacy of freedom over equality of economic rewards. From their viewpoint, government constitutes the basic threat to individual liberty. They oppose government tendencies to exercise coercive, monopolistic, and arbitrary power. Individuals should remain free to organize against government oppression and against the personal, arbitrary, discretionary authority of government bureaucrats. Hence, individuals and voluntary associations must enjoy the rights to exercise their civil liberties, including free speech, free press, and free association. All these political freedoms can be best maintained if the laws strictly limit government power. A constitutional government implies that general, abstract, impersonal, known, and certain rules applicable to all persons regulate government decision making. Under this constitutional system, individuals retain considerable freedom to act within their private sphere. If social problems arise, individuals, voluntary associations, and local governments should first try to resolve them. Only when these agencies fail should people turn to the national government. According to the liberal perspective, government should function mainly to prevent the coercion and violence of private groups and to provide certain noncoercive services that private enterprises do not supply, including informational, educational, health, and cultural services enriching the freedom of each individual to make his or her own decisions.[22]

Committed to a capitalist economic system, classical liberals contrast the coercive state with the voluntary, free market. According to them, state officials tend to govern coercively and arbitrarily; however benign their goals, centralized, bureaucratic power usually results. By contrast, the free market is based on voluntary exchanges. When "pure competition" exists, economic decisions derive from impersonal laws of supply and demand, not from the arbitrary will of a single person. Because the market decentralizes decision making, it guarantees economic freedom to producers, sellers, and consumers. In a purely competitive economy, all have the freedom to accumulate property. Consumers have a free choice of goods and services. Each business firm controls only a small part of the market. Because no concentrated industries restrict the entry of new firms into profitable markets, an enterprise has the freedom to move to areas of the market where product demand is high and supplies are low.

From the classical liberal perspective, the market is self-regulating; it needs no government interference to ensure its smooth operation. Government-owned firms, especially state monopolies, reinforce the power of state bureaucrats, who tend to function inefficiently under guidelines granting administrative discretion. Government control over income distribution also strengthens the state bureaucracy because expert planners are needed to allocate resources. Government regulation of private businesses should occur only when they restrain competition, deny equal opportunities to other firms, and engage in unfair, unsafe practices.[23] Yet even these regulatory powers have alarmed most classical liberals. In their opinion, government attempts to lessen economic grievances through regulatory devices have usually created more problems than they have solved.

Friedrich A. Hayek associates the present economic malaise not with oppressive concentrated industries but rather with government and its trade union allies. True, he regards corporate monopolies as an evil, especially when they bar the entry of other firms into a product market. However, under most conditions, monopolies represent a minor problem, exerting only a transitory and temporary effect. Unless a monopolist owns a spring in an oasis and thus controls the water supply, Hayek does not view monopolistic enterprises as truly "coercive." Instead, in contemporary industrial societies, labor unions, along with government, wield the real coercive power. Under the closed or union shop, labor organizations control the labor supply and raise the real wages of workers in that enterprise. By protecting their status, government gives greater coercive power to unions and thus restricts market freedom.[24] Within the welfare state supported by socialists and trade unionists, the chief dangers

> come from inflation, paralyzing taxation, coercive labor unions, an ever increasing dominance of government in education, and a social service bureaucracy with far-reaching arbitrary powers—dangers from which the individual cannot escape by his own efforts and which the momentum of the overextended machinery of government is likely to increase rather than mitigate.[25]

Thus, only a return to the free competitive market can ensure real economic freedom.

Basing their ideas on free market principles, classical liberals have strongly supported religious freedom. During the precapitalist periods, most societies functioned under an established church. People drew no sharp distinction between the sacred and secular realms. Like the religious system, the economic and political systems were supposed to pursue moral–spiritual values: justice, virtue, civic welfare, the public good. Throughout the West European feudal era, Catholic clergy usually served as government bureaucrats. The emergence of capitalism during the fifteenth and sixteenth centuries, however, led to demands for a separation of the church from the state.

Classical liberals argue that the secular and sacred orders comprise distinct, separate spheres. For them, religious freedom means the separation of church from state as well as tolerance for all religious denominations. Just as one has the freedom to choose competing products on the market, so one should retain the freedom to choose one's own church. Just as liberals favor competition among economic firms, so they advocate competition among diverse churches. Liberals have viewed both conscience and interest from an individualistic, subjective perspective. The separation of church from state makes religion a private, subjective concern. No single religious institution has the power to tell a person what to think. Similarly, in the market economy, no government institution should dictate the individual's self-interest.[26]

Not only religious freedom but also status freedom becomes a liberal objective, for capitalism depends on both capital and labor mobility. In a market economy, prestige should stem mainly from one's achievements. Regardless of birth, age, sex, ethnic group membership, religious affiliation, or original economic position, each individual must have the freedom to achieve upward mobility. Individuals who make the greatest contributions to economic productivity will secure the highest prestige.

CLASSICAL LIBERAL VIEW OF EQUALITY

Classical liberals have historically asserted the priority of liberty over equality, especially equal economic rewards. Yet during the twentieth century, liberals have supported certain types of noneconomic equality. Politically, they have campaigned for equality before the law—that is, the equal right to public liberties. Under this notion, the laws should apply equally to all persons. Although before the twentieth century English liberals sought to restrict the suffrage to the propertied, tax-paying, and well-educated citizens, today's liberals want all adults to enjoy the right to vote and to run for public office.[27]

From the liberal perspective, equal opportunity takes precedence over equality of economic condition. People are motivated largely by self-interest. If everyone receives the same economic rewards, such as equal income, then few will have the incentive to work harder and to increase production. Government attempts to promote economic equality will lead to a regimented economy. Instead of pursuing equal rewards, liberals have sought greater equality of economic opportunities. Regardless of inherited status, every individual should secure opportunities to gain an education and hold a job that matches his or her qualifications. Monetary rewards should derive from performance and abilities. Because not every person in the same job performs equally well, equal opportunities will lead to unequal economic outcomes.[28]

Compared with the classical conservatives, the classical liberals have supported greater cultural equality. Not only in heaven, but also on earth, all individuals should enjoy equal respect as human beings. Regardless of their social position or biological inheritance, all persons deserve mutual respect as moral persons. Most liberals believe that social inequalities are artificial, not natural, and can be overcome through educational and environmental improvements. From the liberal viewpoint, a rigid social stratification system based on inherited privileges violates the equal right for all persons to improve their social conditions.[29]

CONTEMPORARY LIBERAL IDEOLOGIES

Classical liberalism arose when the individual and small-scale firm made crucial decisions. Today bureaucratized governments, private corporations, and labor unions dominate political and economic life. Faced with the growing importance of these institutions, contemporary liberals have divided into three camps: libertarianism, corporate liberalism, and reformist liberalism. Although all three seek to preserve the market economy and affirm the priority of freedom over equality, they disagree about the proper responsibilities for government.

Libertarianism. Adopting a laissez-faire position, libertarians want to resurrect the "minimal state." Government should play a passive role; it needs only to protect individuals against force, fraud, and theft; secure law and order; and enforce contracts. Under this laissez-faire situation, small-scale entrepreneurs compete in the market. Self-interest, the desire to enrich one's own wealth and status, motivates behavior. Unions play only a limited role in economic decision making. Libertarians assume that their system maximizes individual freedom because each person retains the right to choose his or her own welfare.[30] Given the high priority accorded to individual liberty, equal economic rewards and even equal opportunity are neither desirable nor feasible.

Corporate liberalism. Although agreeing with the libertarians in their ranking of freedom over equality, the corporate liberals depart from them by stressing not the individual but large-scale institutions—government, private business corporations, and trade unions—as the primary centers of decision making. To a large extent, economic decisions no longer are made on the competitive market; instead, bureaucrats within the state, domestic corporate firms, multinational corporations, and labor unions plan for the common welfare. The collective interests of these corporate structures assume primacy over individual self-interests. Rather than competing, government, corporations, and unions should cooperate for the national good.

Under these corporate arrangements, government officials assume expanded responsibilities. Although opposing excessive government regulation, corporate liberals believe that the state needs to regulate business cycles, stimulate economic growth, encourage investment, inspire business confidence, restrain inflationary pressures, and guarantee international financial stability through policies that promote free trade, efficient currency exchanges, and expanded exports. According to corporate liberals, particularly when severe inflation strikes the economy, the government must "discipline" the workers by setting lower wages, raising unemployment, and opposing greater equality of income distribution.[31]

To a great extent, all these corporate liberal policies resemble the stands taken by the corporate conservatives, even though the conservatives show less enthusiasm about involving trade union officials in the planning structures. Freedom of the large-scale corporation takes priority over income equality of the working class. Government regulation of private enterprises serves primarily to promote the economic well-being of the corporation.

Reformist liberalism. Of the three contemporary liberal camps, reformist liberalism places the greatest stress on the need for government to encourage both freedom and equality. Reformist liberals want voluntary associations to play the leading role in political decision making. From their perspective, the government must represent the interests of the disadvantaged: migrant farmers, ethnic minorities, consumers, youth, low-income senior citizens, and people on public assistance. By organizing the currently powerless, such interest groups as unions, ethnic associations, consumer federations, welfare rights organizations, and retirement associations will expand the liberty of these groups and bring them greater equality in the decision process.

Compared with the classical liberal position, the reformist liberals perceive government playing an activist role. Government agencies should allocate resources to economically depressed areas, redistribute wealth, stabilize business cycle booms and busts, and promote economic growth. In a complex industrial society, the state also must promote scientific advances, technical research, and higher education. Through such policies as public education, income maintenance, family allowances, old-age pensions, and environmental conservation, government can expand services available to individuals, thus giving them more equal resources and greater equality of opportunities. All these programs occur mainly through expanded government regulation of the economy, not through public ownership.[32]

Since the New Deal era of the 1930s, reformist liberalism has attracted a powerful following within the American Democratic party, as chapter 8 will show. President Franklin Roosevelt wanted to save the capitalist system through reformist policies that involved a more equal distribution of wealth. In his view, the steeply progressive income tax and a federal inheritance tax, not government ownership, represented the best strategies to realize greater income equality.[33] Contemporary reformist liberals articulate similar views. For them, liberalism means both individual freedom and socioeconomic equality. The government ought to stimulate economic equality by expanding comprehensive services: unemployment compensation, social security, health care, education, and public housing. By opening up opportunities for ethnic minorities and women, the government can also promote ethnic and sexual equality. Reformist liberalism also values individual liberty. Unpopular groups, such as the Nazis, Ku Klux Klan, Communist party, and atheists, should have the civil liberties to express their views.

Reformist liberals take divergent stands on government regulation of cultural lifestyles and private business activities. On the one hand, they seek fewer government restrictions over such individual activities as marijuana smoking, divorce, birth control, abortion, and homosexuality. On the other hand, reformist liberals favor greater government restrictions on private business firms. Antitrust actions, antipollution measures, and laws promoting healthier, safer working conditions are three examples. Although such policies may limit the freedom of the private business owner, reformist liberals claim that these regulatory programs will expand the citizen's freedom.[34] Reformist liberals assume that all these policies should function within a modified market economy. For them, government reforms of the market's operation, rather than a socialist economy, represent the best ways to promote freedom and equality.

Democratic Socialism

Just as the classical liberals have articulated ideas opposed to classical conservative principles, so the democratic socialist movement arose to challenge certain liberal beliefs. Socialist political parties emerged during the mid nineteenth century, when the industrialization process under capitalism began to gain momentum in most West

European societies. Representing an uneasy alliance of industrial factory workers and reformist intellectuals (teachers, writers, and journalists), the democratic socialist movement sought to expand civil liberties and to secure greater economic equality without a violent overthrow of the capitalist system. Before World War I, socialists concentrated on winning the right to vote for all persons and on establishing the right of trade unions to bargain collectively with management. Political democracy and civil liberties constituted the primary goals.

During the period from the depression years of the 1930s through the early 1970s, socialists struggled to obtain greater economic equality for all citizens. Holding government power either alone or in coalition with other parties, the socialists enacted comprehensive social service programs: old-age pensions, income maintenance, family allowances, health care, and unemployment compensation. They also strove for economic growth, largely through government stimulation of investment in a modified market economy. Beginning in the 1970s, some socialists, especially in France and Sweden, attempted to bring economic democracy to the workplace. One Swedish plan proposes the gradual transference of company profits to a capital fund controlled by the workers. Through their trade unions, the workers would decide ways to accumulate capital and allocate resources.[35] By such programs, democratic socialists work toward peacefully transforming the capitalist economies in West Europe into a more socialist mode of production.

Today socialist parties attract the greatest support in Western democratic nations. Centers of socialist strength include Britain, West Germany, Scandinavia, Austria, Belgium, Holland, France, New Zealand, and Australia. Except in countries where a powerful Communist party challenges the socialists, industrial factory workers continue to provide the main electoral base behind Social Democratic parties. Especially since the end of World War II, democratic socialists have also won some white-collar workers and middle-class professionals to their side.

Because socialists uphold democratic values, no single orthodoxy has ever brought complete agreement to the socialist movement. A variety of diverse interpretations of socialism compete for support. Observers sometimes perceive as many socialisms as socialists.

TAWNEY'S INTERPRETATION

R. H. Tawney is perhaps the best exemplar of democratic socialist principles. An economic historian and college professor, Tawney (1880–1962) played an active role in the British Labour party. In 1975, Labour members of Parliament cited Tawney and Marx as the two authors who had most influenced their thinking.[36]

Freedom. According to Tawney, all three sectors of society—the polity, economy, and culture—should express a commitment to freedom. For him, freedom means an expanded range of alternatives open to ordinary persons, the opportunity for them to control the moral and material conditions of their lives. Within the political sphere, people should have the right to participate in the decision-making process; decentralized government becomes important for maximizing widespread popular participation. Opposing the concentration of political power, he also rejects the arbitrary exercise of power. The rule of law should provide known, explicit standards for restraining political officials' actions. Tawney assumes that the rights to free speech, study, teaching, writing, organization, and movement will make possible a democratic transition to socialism:

> It is not certain, though it is probable, that Socialism can in England be achieved by the methods proper to democracy. It is certain that it cannot be achieved by any other; nor, even if it could, should the supreme goods of civil and political liberty, in whose absence no Socialism worthy of the name can breathe, be part of the price.[37]

Tawney not only consistently supports political freedom but also economic freedoms, especially for workers and consumers. Examining the economic role of government, private business corporations, unions, and consumers, he challenges assumptions made by defenders of capitalism. Private business monopolies exert public consequences; they function as bureaucratic tyrannies, remaining unaccountable to the public. In the workplace, the capitalist class operates a factory dictatorship. Workers become enslaved to capital and managers.

Just as socialists oppose concentrations of political power, so they should work toward lessening the concentration of wealth. Nationalization of basic industries—banking, transportation, electric power, coal, armaments, minerals—constitutes one method for averting capitalist economic tyranny. Yet public ownership represents only one means to enlarge the workers' economic freedom, not an end in itself. If nationally owned firms fail to encourage workers' participation in economic decision making, do not serve the public, and remain unaccountable to the public, then they too, like private monopolies, will resemble bureaucratic dictatorships. From Tawney's perspective, all economic structures, whether publicly or privately owned, should promote workers' control. Just as doctors control their professions, so factory workers should enjoy the economic freedom to help manage their industries.

Tawney interprets economic freedom as the opportunity of the economically weak to check the oppression exercised by the powerful. According to him, freedom implies the economic security of workers and consumers. Thus, he supports the rights of trade unions to represent workers' interests, to negotiate a wide range of issues with management, and to engage in collective bargaining. Yet no single class, even the proletariat, should exercise constraint over other classes. For this reason, he rejects trade union syndicalism, under which the unions dominate both government and industries.

Tawney wants government to represent not only workers' needs but also consumers' interests. Government planning departments should encourage private firms to protect consumer and worker interests. Under ideal socialist arrangements, every individual will enjoy the fundamental freedom to choose his or her occupation. The freedoms to acquire property, invest capital, and gain a profit will assume secondary importance. Tawney assumes that socialism will expand the economic freedom of wage earners and people receiving small salaries, even if it restricts the freedom of the wealthy to acquire huge incomes.[38]

Within the cultural sphere, Tawney also upholds the need for individual freedom. His interpretation of socialism rests on an individualistic, not a collectivistic, foundation. The individual, rather than the group, class, or collective, remains the fundamental unit. Each individual should have the freedom to realize his or her potentialities. Freedom means individual self-determination. Although in a socialist society individuals must have freedom to move upward in the social stratification system, social mobility should not be the primary goal. The desire to acquire more property, possessions, wealth, and status marks the capitalist society. Under ideal socialist arrangements, individuals will show a primary concern for service, active citizenship, and fellowship. Although the individual must not become subordinate to the collective, he or she will not live in an atomized, isolated condition, as under capitalism. The individual in a socialist order will retain diverse interests and ideas, yet show a spirit of fellowship toward others.

Rather than becoming subservient to a mystical collective, the individual should remain free to practice religious liberty. Rejecting the secular political religion found in the Soviet Union, Tawney refuses to subordinate religious values to political ends. Politics cannot provide spiritual salvation; the Kingdom of God lies beyond history. Thus, democratic socialists must struggle to realize a more just, equalitarian social order, not heaven on earth.[39]

Equality. Unlike the classical liberals, who see a basic contradiction between freedom and equality, Tawney perceives the two values as compatible. In his view, inequality endangers liberty. Equalitarian measures should expand ordinary persons' alternatives. Equality of social conditions in the polity, economy, and culture will help individuals develop their highest potentialities. Yet if liberty for self-realization conflicts with equality, Tawney assumes that freedom should take priority. Because individuals differ in their inherited traits and environmental circumstances, full social equality remains difficult to achieve. For Tawney, the pursuit of equal opportunity and condition becomes more important than the attainment of complete equality.[40]

Tawney interprets political equality as the opportunity for the average individual to play an active part in political decision making. Rather than the state or large-scale private corporations dominating the individual's life, citizens participate in political affairs and educate themselves about complex political issues. Even though under socialism not everyone will ever exercise the same degree of power, all will secure equality under the law, which will protect everybody from the abuse of power.[41]

Like the classical liberals, Tawney gives greater support to equal opportunities than to equality of economic rewards. Although opposing a class-based society where only a few people enjoy special privileges of wealth, he also rejects equal incomes for all persons. In his view, economic rewards, whether equally or unequally distributed, should not form the main goal of life. Rather, all individuals should gain the equal opportunities to develop their abilities through education. Members of different classes ought to obtain equal access to health services, education, and economic security. Regardless of inherited social position, everyone should have the same right to pursue a career; entry to occupations should be based on individual abilities, not class origin.

Whereas Tawney accepts the notion of equal opportunities to develop one's abilities, he rejects equal opportunities enabling some persons to gain the inordinate wealth that sharply separates them from the poorest segments of society. Tawney wants to base the distribution of economic rewards on the contributions and services rendered the whole community, not just a single class. Under his ideal socialism, individuals will receive only those rewards that they need to perform their social functions.[42]

Tawney's commitment to cultural equality flows from his democratic, humanistic orientation. Even though all people do not have the same wealth, moral character, intelligence, and abilities, they deserve equal respect. Because all persons are supremely important to God, they must be treated as equal in value, human worth, and human dignity. No privileged elite should receive special deference. According to Tawney, capitalist values, unlike socialist principles, treat human beings not as ends in themselves but as instruments of production. Under ideal socialism, Tawney hopes class distinctions will disappear. People will be judged on their character and service to others, not on their wealth or class background. Only when social inequalities diminish will individual freedom flourish.[43]

Since the end of World War II, democratic socialists have sketched various interpretations of socialism based on different relationships between freedom and equality. Three important interpretations include state planning or corporate socialism, welfare state socialism, and market socialism under workers' control.

CORPORATE SOCIALISM

The state planning brand of corporate socialism assumes that experts and professionals—economists, managers, scientists, and engineers—can best plan the economy so that it serves the public welfare. According to this version, three large-scale bureaucratic institutions—government, private corporations (concentrated industries), and labor unions—dominate the contemporary economic scene. Acting in cooperation with professionals from the business and union sectors, government bureaucrats can best attain economic growth, full employment, low inflation, and provision of services to the disadvantaged. Centralization of economic decision making will lead to greater equality because everyone will receive uniform treatment. Rather than stressing the need for private enterprisers or workers to exercise economic freedom, corporate socialists uphold the need for managers of nationalized firms, public corporations, and state-holding companies to retain their autonomy over economic decisions. Even if the government assumes formal ownership of a firm, its board of directors should manage the nationalized company free from interference by legislators, cabinet ministers, or appointed civil servants.[44]

WELFARE STATE SOCIALISM

Especially in Sweden and West Germany, nations where social democratic parties exercise considerable political power, government economic policies reflect a commitment to welfare state socialism. Compared with the corporate, state planning brand of socialism, government plays a less active role in economic life. Particularly in Sweden, labor unions participate in economic decision making. Over 90 percent of Swedish companies remain under private ownership. Government-owned firms operate the postal service, telephones, radio stations, television networks, railroads, and alcohol and tobacco industries. Other parts of the economy contain either privately owned firms or a mixture of public and private enterprises; the mixed sector prevails in such industries as steel, iron ore, electricity production, and shipbuilding.

From the welfare state perspective, government basically functions to mitigate market deficiencies. Through tax and expenditure policies, government officials stimulate investment, prevent severe booms and busts, and, especially in Sweden, secure greater income equality. In both Sweden and West Germany, government provides extensive social services: old-age pensions, health care, family allowances, and unemployment compensation.[45] By enacting these policies, social democrats try to maintain the freedom of the private firm while equalizing benefits among the whole population.

MARKET SOCIALISM

Market socialism under workers' control favors a system under which the government owns the means of production yet yields control over productive resources to decentralized workers' cooperatives. Within these cooperatives, workers make the crucial decisions about investment, use of physical capital, and daily workplace activities. Workers have freedom to choose their occupation. Managers of the different cooperatives freely exchange raw materials, fuel, machinery parts, financial services, and finished products. Consumers remain free to buy goods on the market. Operating through this market system, consumers, workers, and managers of cooperatives thus engage in voluntary exchanges; they secure mutual benefits.

Under these arrangements, government tax and expenditures policies partially rectify the inequalitarian tendencies of capitalist markets. Progressive income taxes, combined with high expenditures for income maintenance, health care, education, and family allowances, help equalize resources among all classes. Steeply graduated taxes on high profits and laws against monopolies restrain the capitalistic tendencies for private concentrated industries to dominate the market. According to market socialists, decentralized control exercised by workers' cooperatives also averts the dangers of centralized state bureaucratism.[46] In sum, they believe that market socialism will combine market freedom with socialist equalitarian values. By establishing workers' cooperatives, they hope to realize the vision of freedom and equality sketched not only by Tawney but by Karl Marx as well.

Communism

Karl Marx and Vladimir Lenin have served as the authoritative figures behind communist ideology. Their ideas solidify communist movements in different parts of the world. Despite the post–World War II emergence of different national roads to communism, as shown by the split between the Soviet Union and China, most communist ideologues accept Marx and Lenin as their intellectual forefathers. Regardless of their differences, Soviet, Chinese, Vietnamese, and Cuban political leaders all use Marxism-Leninism to justify their public policies. This analysis of communist ideology hence equates "communism" with "Marxism-Leninism." I will note the similarities and the differences in the ways Marx and Lenin interpreted freedom and equality.

MARX'S VIEWS

Freedom. Marx perceived freedom to mean liberation from the capitalist system. For him, this task of proletarian emancipation involved revolutionary changes in the political, economic, and cultural sectors of society. Yet in struggling for the abolition of capitalism and the establishment of a communist society, Marx demonstrated an ambivalence toward political freedom. On the one hand, especially during the 1840s, he actively campaigned for the extension of civil liberties in Germany, particularly for the end of censorship. Political freedom meant liberation from state bureaucratic control over mind and body. He equated dictatorship with state domination of society, particularly with rule by the bureaucracy and the military. Political democracy involved popular control from below—that is, from the proletariat. Immediately after the proletariat seized political power, the government would become the servant, not remain the master, of society.

On the other hand, Marx occasionally referred to the need for a proletarian dictatorship during the transition from capitalism to communism: "Between capitalist and communist society lies a period of revolutionary transformation from one to the other. There is a corresponding period of transition in the political sphere and in this period the state can only take the form of a *revolutionary dictatorship of the proletariat.*"[47] According to Marx, during this transition period the proletariat will use force, even terror, to achieve the communist revolution, which involves the abolition of classes, the abolition of private property, and workers' ownership of the means of production, especially transportation, railways, and factories. With the disappearance of antagonistic class interests, the state as an agent of class rule will also disappear. In the highest stage of communism, society will regain its freedom from the state.[48] In short, Marx interpreted political freedom to mean liberation from state oppression and class rule. Yet the means to secure the classless society involved political coercion.

Unlike the "bourgeois democrats," who sought expanded civil liberties but the maintenance of capitalist ownership of the means of production, Marx always linked political freedom to working-class attainment of economic freedom from capitalism. According to Marx, capitalism had enlarged economic freedoms. Whereas the feudal system had restricted freedom under the guild system, capitalism had brought freer trade and competition. The liberation of the workers from feudal serfdom meant that they acquired greater freedom of labor mobility. Yet, despite these enlarged freedoms, capitalism still had not freed workers from the dominance of grinding labor, commerce, trade, money, egotism, material self-interest, and private property. For Marx, the basic contradiction of capitalism was that it secured a greater economic abundance than had ever been realized, but workers still had not gained mastery over this wealth so that they could use these economic resources to satisfy basic human needs.[49]

Marx also supported liberation from the cultural oppression he associated with capitalism and classical liberalism. He welcomed the separation of church and state advocated by capitalist thinkers; certainly, this separation allowed more religious freedom than did the established state religion linked to the medieval feudal order. Yet as an atheist and a historical materialist, Marx campaigned for freedom from religious mysticism, illusions, and false consciousness. According to him, only when individuals become liberated from religion will they attain human emancipation, a freedom transcending political and religious liberties.

Unlike classical liberal thinkers, Marx did not view status mobility as the highest form of cultural freedom. From his perspective, the individual's urge to move upward in the social stratification system pervades capitalist society; self-interest—the desire to improve one's wealth and status—reflects the domination of envy. With the disappearance of class distinctions in the forthcoming communist society, Marx assumed that the individual would gain liberation from an obsession with higher status.[50]

Equality. Just as Marx linked human freedom to the advent of a classless society, he associated equality with the abolition of class distinctions. During the nineteenth century, he realized that several Western capitalist states, such as the United States, Britain, and France, had established formal political equality; that is, compared with feudal arrangements, the suffrage had expanded and more people gained equal rights under the law. Although the British had instituted representative government, a gap between the rulers and ruled still remained. The propertied classes dominated the government; the mass of workers retained only a passive role. For Marx, true political equality would come when the proletariat actively participated as equals in the decision-making process. This situation would exist only in a communist society. According to Marx, to overthrow the capitalist political order and establish communism, the working class must become organized in political parties and unions that remain independent from the propertied classes.

Marx wanted the proletariat to play a spontaneous, egalitarian role in political parties. In 1879, Marx and his colleague, Frederick Engels, wrote to leaders of the German Social-Democratic Workers' party: "The emancipation of the working class must be the work of the working class itself. We cannot ally ourselves, therefore, with people who openly declare that the workers are too uneducated to free themselves"[51] Rather than bourgeois intellectuals dominating the socialist political party, philosophers and workers should collaborate to put socialist theory into political practice. Whereas the proletariat supplies the numbers and the material weapons needed to conquer political power, intellectuals provide the theoretical weapons and knowledge to foment revolution. According to Marx, when intellectuals from the bourgeoisie operate within such political organizations as the International Working Men's Association, they must adopt the proletarian outlook. Only by cooperating in a political party can the philosophers and workers stage the socialist revolution and thereby abolish classes.[52]

Just as full political equality will emerge only in a classless society, Marx also assumed that true economic equality depends on the elimination of class privileges. In his view, the demands for equal economic rewards, equality among classes, and equal opportunities to secure scarce resources all reflect the conditions of a class-ridden society. Marx identified equality of wages with "crude communism." Under these conditions, people work to subsist, rather than to develop their full potentialities. Scarcity, not economic abundance, prevails. Attempts to level incomes express envy and greed. From Marx's perspective, the call for an equalization of classes and for harmony between labor and capital explicitly accepts the basic framework of a capitalist society. Instead, he wanted the communist political movement to assert the need for a class struggle and the abolition of classes. Marx also associated equal opportunities to secure scarce economic resources with capitalism. Under the highest stage of communism, however, the productive forces will be fully developed and the propertied classes will have disappeared. With the attainment of economic abundance, distribution will occur according to human needs.[53]

Marx believed that the highest stage of communism will bring full cultural equality to all people. The status distinctions of previous class-ridden societies will disappear. Rather than being judged on their property, inherited social position, nationality, ethnic origin, or religious creed, individuals will be treated as human beings who enjoy basic human dignity. Under communism, the individual will no longer be regarded as a commodity or a factor of production. Instead, everyone will live together in a "positive humanism" and receive equal human respect.[54]

LENIN'S VIEWS

Lenin, the most influential communist thinker during the twentieth century, did not stress the humanistic orientation of the early Marx. Rather, he downgraded political freedom and upheld political elitism. His most important contribution was his stress on a professionally organized vanguard political party that would first conquer political power and then work to implement a socialist economy.

Communist political parties began to organize after the Soviet revolution of late 1917. Before that time, democratic socialists and communists generally worked together in a single political movement. For example, in Russia, the Bolshevik faction, organized by Lenin in 1903, formed a section within the Russian Social Democratic Labor party. After overthrowing the provisional government, the Bolsheviks in 1918 established themselves as the only political party in the Soviet Union. During the early 1920s, the communists in Europe broke away from the social democrats to form independent parties. Whereas the democratic socialists rejected Lenin's political strategy and economic policies, the Communist parties supported the new Soviet regime. Today West European Communist parties receive the greatest electoral backing in Italy, France, Finland, Iceland, Spain, and Portugal, where they have drawn main voter support from manual workers and some leftist intellectuals. In East Europe and in some Asian nations—China, Mongolia, North Korea, Vietnam, Laos, and Cambodia—Communist parties govern the state. Particularly in China, peasants form the backbone of the Communist party. Despite their different orientations, most communist leaders in these countries claim to follow Leninist principles.

Freedom. Leader of the Soviet state between late 1917 and 1923, Lenin promised eventual freedom from exploitation, but his regard for freedom was relativistic, not absolute. The priority placed on freedom depended on a society's stage of development. Generally, he supported more political freedom before the Soviet revolution than after 1917. Basing his ideas of historical development partly on Marx's writings, Lenin distinguished five stages. First, under the feudal economy, which prevailed in Russia until the abolition of serfdom during the early 1860s, Lenin strongly supported civil liberties, especially the rights of the urban intelligentsia, peasantry, and incipient factory working class to agitate against the feudal czarist state.

Second, Lenin held that, in the capitalist stage, the proletariat should have the political freedom to prepare for the socialist revolution by organizing political parties, forming trade unions, and printing newspapers. According to him, capitalism never developed such a powerful base in Russia as in the more industrialized Western countries. Between 1890 and 1914, the czarist state, rather than an independent bourgeoisie, spearheaded the capitalist drive for industrialization. After the overthrow of the czar in February 1917, the "bourgeois republic" lasted only until October of that year. From Lenin's perspective, capitalism everywhere, whether in the industrialized states of West Europe or the underdeveloped Russian nation, allowed only "bourgeois freedom." He perceived that the propertied classes of so-called democratic states suppressed the revolutionary proletariat. According to him, the revolutionary working class had to struggle to gain real political freedom—not just the right to criticize the capitalist status quo but also the liberty to organize a socialist movement.

Third, although Marx made only occasional references to a revolutionary dictatorship of the proletariat, Lenin made this concept the cornerstone of the new Soviet regime. According to him, the proletarian dictatorship represented a transition stage between the overthrow of capitalism and the advent of socialism. Particularly between 1918 and 1921, when the Soviet government fought a civil war against the "counterrevolutionaries," he stressed the need for the state to exercise ruthless coercion and iron discipline. In April 1918, he mentioned some democratic features of the new Soviet state— rule by the majority, popular elections to soviets (councils), recall of elected officials, control from below, and criticism of state bureaucratism and the Communist party's shortcomings. But after the civil war began in May 1918, he downplayed the democratic features while stressing the need for dictatorial rule.

For Lenin, both the Party and the state had to govern with a single will. The state must use "barbarous methods in fighting barbarism." Lenin saw the need for ruthless coercion to suppress the former exploiters, to win the civil war, and to destroy all the symptoms of disintegration that accompany the breakdown of the old order— crime, corruption, profiteering, and anarchy. In May 1918, he wrote:

> We still have too little of that ruthlessness which is indispensable for the success of socialism. . . . Another thing is that the courts are not sufficiently firm. Instead of sentencing people who take bribes to be shot, they sentence them to six months' imprisonment. These two defects [short prison sentences and inability to stamp out corruption] have the same social root: the influence of the petty-bourgeois element, its flabbiness.[55]

Reflecting this ruthless, coercive orientation, Lenin made an analogy between the Party and an army. Revolution meant war. The

Communist party had to function like an army. No other political parties should challenge the Communist party's supremacy. Even within the Party, no organized factions must disturb the need for iron discipline and a single will. Lenin held that during these wartime conditions, when the Soviet state faced powerful enemies from inside and outside the nation, the people had to demonstrate their "unquestioning obedience to the will of a single person, the Soviet leader."[56] Hence, communism became militarized.

Fourth, whereas Marx had referred to a "first phase" and a "more advanced phase of community society," Lenin equated the first phase with socialism and linked the higher stage to full communism. In his view, classes still exist in the socialist stage; therefore, a state is needed to suppress the bourgeoisie and to construct the socialist economy. According to him, during this phase, the majority—the proletariat and the peasantry—has political freedom; however, the minority—the bourgeoisie—lacks freedom. Only with the emergence of full communism will genuine political freedom for all people become possible. Because no antagonistic classes will remain, the state as an agency of class repression withers away. Exploitation by police, military, and the state bureaucracy ceases because it is no longer functionally necessary.[57] For Lenin, these two stages lay in the future. He concentrated on building socialism through the establishment of a workers' state; the dictatorship of the proletariat prepared the way for the socialist stage.

Lenin's interpretation of economic freedom rested on a class basis. From his standpoint, "real" economic freedom meant emancipation from landowner and capitalist exploitation. The proletariat and the peasantry must gain freedom from hunger, starvation, wage slavery, and economic exploitation. Under this conception, neither the landlords nor the capitalists should exercise any freedom. Beginning in 1921, Lenin's New Economic Plan advocated state ownership of large-scale means of production, along with state supervision of cooperatives managed by small farmers. Lenin thus intended for state control of trade and state planning to coexist with some private ownership of small farms.

Lenin's attitude toward religious freedom changed over time. In 1902, he strongly criticized czarist persecution of religious sects, especially the Jews. However, after the Bolsheviks gained political power, he stressed the freedom to criticize religion more than the liberty to practice it. As an atheist, he equated religion with ignorance and superstition. Attacking the Russian Orthodox clergy who preached "reactionary" ideas and defended the "exploiters," Lenin demanded freedom from religious oppression.

In contrast to his interpretation of religious freedom, Lenin throughout his career consistently upheld freedom for ascriptive groups to transcend their inherited personal status. For him, all ethnic groups in the Soviet Union, especially the non-Russian nationalities, should enjoy cultural freedom. Similarly, women should become emancipated from "domestic slavery" and have the freedom to participate in economic and political life. According to Lenin's conception of Marxism, the class rather than the individual should enjoy status freedom. The desire of the individual to rise in the social stratification reflected a petty-bourgeois capitalist mentality. Because no individual can ever become really free from society, only collective freedom for women, ethnic groups, the proletariat, and the peasantry are real possibilities.[58]

Equality. Lenin's greatest departure from Marx's ideas centered on his advocacy of political elitism. Whereas Marx stressed the need for an egalitarian relation between intellectuals and the masses, Lenin asserted the primacy of the party elite over the masses. In 1902, fifteen years before the successful Soviet revolution, Lenin sketched the notion of a vanguard party composed of full-time professional revolutionaries. He never abandoned this elitist orientation.

Although Marx took a fairly optimistic view of the proletariat's spontaneous ability to direct the socialist revolution, Lenin assumed a more pessimistic attitude toward the masses' will and ability to stage a revolution. Against those socialists who believed that a socialist society would not arrive until all the proletariat had realized a fully developed socialist consciousness, Lenin wanted to conquer political power *before* the working masses were ready for socialism. In his view, most people are apathetic, inert, dormant, convention-ridden, and guided by habit; they readily accept the need for subordination and control. Therefore, the Communist party, as the vanguard of the working class, must raise the workers' political consciousness. Party leaders, primarily intellectuals, must educate the masses to establish a new socialist order. By coordinating activities, articulating general goals, and specifying the means to achieve these objectives, the Party will bring the socialist society into being. Through organization, education, and general leadership, the Party arouses the masses from their political slumber, enlightens them, and prepares them for socialism.

Even though Lenin stressed the vanguard role for the Party, he also wanted to expand the opportunities for the masses to participate in political affairs. Rather than becoming isolated from the masses, the Party must lead them and remain closely attached to them. To accomplish this leadership role, the Party should guide several mass organizations, including trade unions, study circles, women's associations, and youth groups. With a broad membership and a decentralized structure, these mass organizations will enable everyone to participate in decision making. By contrast, the Party must comprise a narrower membership of professional revolutionaries who operate within a more centralized, secret organization. In short, Lenin expected that a vanguard political party would provide the elitist direction needed to guide the society toward socialism. Led by the Party, mass organizations would allow some political equality to occur. Only after the disappearance of classes and the establishment of full communism would complete political equality be achieved. With the abolition of the state, the need for political subordination would also vanish.[59]

Lenin's interpretation of economic equality derived from the distinctions he drew between the socialist and full communist stages of development. Before the Soviet revolution, he held that in the proletarian state, a government official should receive the same salary as the average worker's wage; that is, all workers must obtain the same pay. After 1917, however, Lenin stressed the inequalitarian aspects of socialist society. The civil war brought about declining production. Therefore, experts, engineers, agronomists, technicians, and all those with specialized skills must receive higher salaries during the transition toward full communism. These material incentives are needed to increase productivity and to reward people for harder work and higher production. Not until the era of full communism will wage equality exist. Only then will Marx's vision of "from each according to his abilities, to each according to his needs" be realized. In the meantime, the labor performed and the amount of goods produced should determine the distribution of economic rewards.

Although Lenin expected that economic inequalities would remain under socialism, he wanted the new Soviet government to play an active role in equalizing resources among the population. By redistributing land to the poor peasants and by allocating bread, milk, other food, housing, and clothing to the poor, the government ensures that the proletariat and peasantry live under more equal conditions than during the czarist regime.[60]

However strong his support for extending economic equality, Lenin failed to advocate more cultural equality. True, he did want to end the status distinctions that pervaded the czarist bureaucratic government. According to him, everyone should be regarded as a worker. Regardless of position, sex, or nationality, all people should treat each other as equals. In particular, government bureaucrats should no longer receive special deference or privileges. Yet during the transition period to full communism, complete cultural equality was impossible. Rather than viewing all persons as possessing equal human worth, Lenin dichotomized people into "good" and "bad" groups. He labeled as bad the landowners, capitalists, parasites, exploiters, and anti-Party people. The good people were the poor peasants, the proletariat, the productive classes, the exploited, and party personnel. Not until the abolition of classes and the establishment of full communism would all people live in cultural equality.[61]

Although Leninism remains today the dominant expression of communist ideology, two other interpretations—anarcho-communism and structural pluralism—also attract a following in parts of West Europe and Latin America.[62] Generally, communist leaders who hold government office, especially in East Europe, Asia, and Cuba, adhere to Leninist principles. Anarcho-communist and structural reformists form opposition groups challenging more conservative government leaders. Particularly in Italy, Spain, and Chile, the anarcho-communist movement has developed some support on the Left. Opposed both to Soviet Leninists and to anarcho-communists, the structural pluralists who lead the Communist parties in Spain and especially Italy have voiced a democratic interpretation of communism. Their brand of communism upholds political freedom yet hopes to attain more fundamental changes in society than so far secured by the social democrats.

ANARCHO-COMMUNISM

Rejecting the bureaucratic emphasis of Leninism, the anarcho-communists place a higher value on freedom and especially on political equality. Like the Leninists, they oppose capitalism, particularly its stress on the rule of money, individual self-interest, private ownership of property, and bureaucratic private business corporations. As communists, they assert a collectivist ethos and the need for public, not private, ownership of the means of production. Unlike the Leninists, however, anarcho-communists want to see communism attained through widespread popular participation, not through bureaucratic control by either a centralized state or a dictatorial party. From the anarchists' perspective, politics means egalitarian spontaneity, not elitist organization. Opposing hierarchical authority relations, they seek more egalitarian ties between leaders and masses. The masses must assume direct initiative for bringing about socialism and communism. Functioning through workers' councils (soviets), popular assemblies, neighborhood associations, peasant committees, and so forth, the workers themselves can take direct action to realize their goal. Under an anarcho-communist society, the party will not represent itself as the vanguard of the proletariat; rather than mobilizing from above, it will mobilize the masses from below and coordinate the activities of the mass associations.

Along with a belief in political equality goes a commitment to political freedom. Anarcho-communists seek liberty from all forms of bureaucratic oppression, including the centralized state, a professional military, a bureaucratized church, gigantic private corporations, and even professional party organizations that rule society as the dictatorship of the proletariat. In short, from the anarchist perspective, politics means spontaneous popular participation in public decision making. Society becomes dominant over the state.[63]

STRUCTURAL PLURALISM

Another challenge to the Leninist position comes from the structural pluralists. Particularly in Italy, the beliefs of those who lead the *Partito Comunista Italiano* (PCI) derive less from Leninist ideas than from principles held by Antonio Gramsci. A founder of the PCI in 1921 and general secretary of the Party between 1924 and his imprisonment by Mussolini's Fascist government in 1926, Gramsci modified Lenin's principles to adapt communist ideology to the more democratic, industrialized conditions of Western Europe. Before 1926, Gramsci did retain a verbal commitment to such Leninist concepts as the dictatorship of the proletariat, the vanguard role of the Party, and the need for strong political organization and mass discipline. Like Lenin, he also opposed reformism, parliamentary democracy, constitutionalism, anarchism, and syndicalism. Making an analogy between the Party and a professional army, he rejected organized factional groups within the PCI.[64]

Despite this adherence to Leninist principles of political organization, Gramsci placed greater emphasis than did Lenin on civil liberties and political equality. Focusing more attention on cultural liberation, Gramsci saw widespread socialization in new cultural values as a prerequisite for realizing a socialist society.[65] By gaining popular consent, the Party can best realize the cultural liberation of the working masses. According to Gramsci:

> The Communist Party is the instrument and historical form of the process of inner liberation through which the worker is transformed from *executor* to *initiator*, from *mass* to *leader* and *guide*, from brawn to brain and purpose. As the Communist Party is formed, a seed of liberty is planted that will sprout and grow to its full height only after the workers' State has organized the requisite material conditions.[66]

Compared with Lenin, Gramsci also demonstrated a stronger commitment to political equality, especially in his attitude toward relations between party intellectuals and the masses. He saw the Communist party as the "Modern Prince," the collective will of the working class. Departing from Machiavelli's and Lenin's focus on tactics and rational calculation as the primary ways to gain political power, Gramsci strove to transcend the old distinctions between elitist organization and mass spontaneity. The party intellectuals have the responsibility to organize, educate, guide, inspire, and persuade the masses—that is, to raise their political consciousness. In turn, the masses supply the energy, popular enthusiasm, and spontaneity needed to build a new society. Yet in working closely with the masses, party intellectuals should renounce elitist, autocratic pretenses. The Party must gain the consent of factory workers as well as poor peasants so that it becomes a mass-based organization.[67]

During the post–World War II era, PCI leaders have selected the more egalitarian, civil libertarian themes from Gramsci's writings to articulate a distinctive Italian way to socialism, a path different from the one pursued in the Soviet Union under Lenin and especially Stalin. Even though Gramsci rejected reformism and alliances with bourgeois parties, PCI leaders today voice a commitment to freedom and equality that expresses a pluralist view. Rejecting Lenin's notions about the dictatorship of the proletariat, they advocate a pluralistic interpretation of political freedom. According to them, all political structures must achieve a broader, more representative social base. Rather than be dominated by the middle and upper classes, the state should rest on a multiclass foundation so that representatives from the working classes and poor peasantry gain a chance to share in political decision making. The Communist party must lead the mass struggle; yet it can best implement public policies through alliances with other democratic parties—that is, with all parties except the fascist *Movimento Sociale Italiano*.

Political life for contemporary PCI leaders revolves around electoral activities and struggles to secure a more representative, modernized government. Instead of seizing power through violence, PCI officials prefer to win control of the government through peaceful, evolutionary means. After gaining political power, they want the state to modernize the economy—a task involving increased productivity, industrialization, agrarian reform, and the provision of more egalitarian social services.

Consistent with Gramsci's orientation, the PCI also seeks greater political equality. They strive for expanded mass participation by factory workers, small farmers, and small-scale business people. In the PCI view, when these less-advantaged groups take a more active role in political and economic decision making, the balance of power will come to favor the working classes. By gaining opportunities for self-government and control over their own lives, the masses will feel less alienated. Thus, they will show less tendency to support either a violent anarchistic movement on the Left or a neofascist movement on the Right.[68]

Fascism

Although contemporary Italians identify fascism as a rightist movement, historically, fascist beliefs have demonstrated a more ambiguous relationship to left-right categories than have other political ideologies.[69] In terms of their orientation toward the status quo, classical conservatives clearly want to maintain continuity with the past order; classical liberals seek gradual reforms; democratic socialists support greater changes, especially a lessening of class privileges; and communists advocate the most fundamental transformation of the existing society. Fascists have sought dramatic changes in the present social order as well as maintenance of the status quo, even a reversion to a preexisting society, such as the Roman Empire or the medieval Teutonic empires. Benito Mussolini, the Fascist leader who ruled Italy from 1922 through 1943, stressed the need for fascists to borrow freely from all ideologies, whether revolutionary or reactionary: "We do not believe in dogmatic programs ... We permit ourselves the luxury of being aristocratic and democratic, conservative and progressive, reactionary and revolutionary, legalists and illegalists, according to the circumstances of the moment, the place and the environment."[70]

As Mussolini indicated, fascists have accepted and rejected aspects of the other four ideologies. First, from classical conservatism, they borrow notions about the cult of the personal leader, the subordination of women, and the organic state and society, with its stress on functional interdependence and harmony. Yet fascists reject the conservative support for a limited state and especially for a powerful established church with control over public education and moral behavior.

Second, like classical liberals, fascist ideologues also support private property, private ownership of capital, economic efficiency, maximization of production, and the unequal distribution of income according to productive achievements, not human needs. Yet fascists oppose such liberal political principles as majority rule, minority rights, individual self-expression, parliamentary democracy, and constitutional restraints on the state. Unlike economic liberals, fascists reject free trade but support extensive state regulation of private economic firms.

Third, although Mussolini was originally a Socialist party leader between 1908 and 1914 and Adolf Hitler led the National Socialist German Workers' party, both strongly rejected democratic socialist ideas. Indeed, in their attitudes toward freedom and equality, fascists and democratic socialists take the most divergent positions. As Hitler once said: "Why need we trouble to socialize banks and factories? We socialize human beings."[71] For him and Mussolini, socialism thus meant political indoctrination and education, rather than public ownership of the means of production.

Fourth, fascism shows a closer resemblance to the Leninist interpretation of communism than to democratic socialism. Lenin, Hitler, and Mussolini all stressed the supremacy of the collective over the individual, the need to organize the political party like an army, and rule through the exercise of a strong will. Collectivism, militarism, and voluntarism took precedence over individualism, pacifism, and social determinism. Yet in other respects, fascism departed from basic communist principles. For instance, Leninists have advocated party domination of the state, collective leadership, an atheistic society, and a society based on the working class. For them, Marxist theory should serve as a guide to political action. In contrast, fascists assign greater decision-making powers to the state vis-a-vis the party, stress personal leadership, reject atheism, and identify collectivism with the nation or the race, not with an economic class. According to such fascists as Mussolini, political action takes primacy over abstract theoretical doctrines; political leaders should make their decisions on pragmatic grounds—that is, practical results—rather than on theoretical considerations.[72]

Fascism is a twentieth-century phenomenon. It emerged in Italy and Germany after the end of World War I as a response to the war and the establishment of a Soviet state in Russia. Later the fascist movement spread to East Europe, Spain, Portugal, South Africa, and parts of Latin America.

Particularly in Italy and Germany during the 1920s, the fascist parties gained greatest support from those groups that suffered from the war and feared the rise of communism in their countries. These groups included a broad class composition: the lower middle class (small craftsmen, small shopkeepers, minor white-collar employees); small farmers; young, upwardly mobile workers who rejected unions, Socialists, and Communists; some landowners and large-scale industrialists; male unemployed youth; war orphans; and especially war veterans who believed that left-wingers in government power had betrayed their nation after the war. For all these people, the ideological themes articulated by Hitler and Mussolini seemed relevant to their needs.

BELIEFS OF HITLER AND MUSSOLINI

Freedom. Rejecting political freedom, both Hitler and Mussolini justified their autocratic rule on monistic grounds. As we have seen, freedom implies diversity of views, expansion of choices, and conflict among ideas—all pluralist concepts. In contrast, fascism opposes conflict, diversity, and free choice; instead, it believes in one strong state, one leader, one nation, one people, and one party. Indeed, the Italian word *fasces* refers to the Roman symbol of power—a bundle of rods bound together by thongs, with an axe head at one end. For Mussolini, this symbol implied that a single will had to govern fascist Italy; no class conflicts provoked by either Socialists or Communists should disturb the unity of state and society.[73]

Hitler took a similar view about the need for one leader, one strong state, and one party to govern a homogeneous people. According to him, the great personality—the Aryan leader—must exercise supreme power through his assertion of a single, unchallenged will. As head of the organic state, he also rules as head of the German fatherland. Government must exercise dominant control over art, literature, theater, and the mass media. Rather than allow a free press, Hitler demanded that the newspapers become the instruments of national self-education. Attacking the parliamentary democracy and multiparty system associated with the Weimar Republic, he abolished other parties after he came to political power in 1933 and made the Nazi party the only party in the government. In July 1933, Hitler announced: "The Party has now become the State."[74] Later he equated the Nazi party with himself as supreme leader. Consistent with his monistic orientation, he also perceived the German nation as one homogeneous people—a *volkic* organism. Hitler determined to eliminate from the societal organism all those individuals whom he regarded as "racially impure," especially the Jews. Under these monistic ideological conditions, freedom held little value. According to Hitler, freedom meant anarchy and disorder. For him, "real freedom" involved liberating the German nation from those who never deserved freedom—Jews, atheists, Marxists, parties governing the Weimar Republic, and "carping" newspapers.[75]

In accordance with these collectivist beliefs, the rights of the nation-state took precedence over individual rights of political self-expression. Hitler called on individuals to sacrifice their own will to preserve national freedom. Mussolini asserted that the Fascist state would determine those liberties that individuals should enjoy; to him, the freedom of the state held priority over individual liberties.[76]

Rejecting capitalism, socialism, and communism, fascists have opposed economic freedom for industrialists and especially for factory workers. True, Hitler and Mussolini did favor the freedom to accumulate private property, to engage in economic competition, to maximize economic efficiency, and to work hard. Rather than advocating state ownership of business enterprises, they demanded state regulation of privately owned firms. Hitler wanted to nationalize only the property owned by the Jews, Socialists, and Communists. Yet he never supported a laissez-faire economic policy. From his viewpoint, industrialists should serve the state. Economic autarky must replace international free trade. Labor unions should be controlled by the Nazi party; they had no rights to strike or act independently of the German fatherland. Even though Hitler opposed freedom of economic production, he favored free consumption. During the 1930s, he tried to increase his popular legitimacy by promising Germans the right to own a cheap "people's car," a Volkswagen.[77]

Compared with Mussolini, Hitler took more active steps to curtail religious freedom. Although during the 1920s Mussolini voiced a few anti-Semitic remarks, linking Jews with Bolshevism, in general nationalism and statism took priority over racism and anti-Semitism. Hostility toward Jews was far weaker in Italy than in Central Europe, especially Germany, Austria, and Poland. The Roman Catholic church operated a powerful established institution in Italy. Therefore, despite Mussolini's hope that the Italian people would adopt fascism as their faith and religion, the need to make compromises with the Catholic church, especially the pope and other high clergy, deterred Mussolini from instituting fascism as a new political religion. Only after he became allied with Hitler in foreign policy did anti-Semitism become a cornerstone of his domestic policy. In 1938, the state issued a Manifesto of Fascist Racism, which denied Jews religious, political, and economic freedoms. As a result, several Italian Jews lost their academic and government posts.[78]

In Germany, however, Jews lost not only their religious, political, and economic freedoms but also their lives. From the beginning of Hitler's political career in the early 1920s until his death in 1945, anti-Semitism formed the basic foundation of his political ideology. In *Mein Kampf*, Hitler wrote:

> As National Socialists we see our program in our flag. In the *red* we see the social idea of the movement, in the *white* the nationalistic idea, and in the *swastika* the fight for the victory of the idea of creative work, which in itself always was and always will be anti-Semitic.[79]

Hitler determined to deprive Jews of their freedom and life because he identified them with all the "evils" of twentieth-century society: capitalism, Marxism, communism, parliamentary democracy, universalism, and pacifism. Although Jews had long lived in Germany as national citizens, he regarded them as anti-German. For him, racism and nationalism meant the abolition of the Jewish population.

Although a Catholic, Hitler never granted extensive religious freedom to Christian churches. He did consider Christianity the foundation for German national morality; Article 24 of the Nazi party platform advocated "the freedom of all religious confessions in the state," but with this important qualification: "in so far as they do not imperil its stability or offend against the ethical and moral senses of the German race." As early as 1923, he declared the German nation as the supreme god: "We do not have any other God—only Germany." After gaining political power in the early 1930s, Hitler denied Christian clergy the right to criticize the state and challenge his policies. In his view, churches should not have the freedom to participate in politics or pursue political objectives. Instead, Hitler wanted churches to concentrate on the "inner freedom of the religious life," which he defined as matters of faith and doctrine.[80]

Hitler gave a restricted definition to status freedom as well as religious freedom. According to him, neither Jews nor women should enjoy any freedom to rise in the social stratification system. However, he did support the rights of German male youths, regardless of social origins, to improve their educational and economic positions in life.[81]

Equality. Neither Hitler nor Mussolini advocated political equality; rather, they boasted of their elitist tendencies. Both leaders asserted that the best men should rule their societies free of mass pressures from below. Leaders exercise authority; followers have the right to obey. Mussolini proclaimed:

> Fascism denies that numbers, by the mere fact of being numbers, can direct human society; it denies that these numbers can govern by means of periodical consultations; it affirms also the fertilising, beneficient and unassailable inequality of men, who cannot be leveled through an extrinsic and mechanical process such as universal suffrage. . . . Fascism rejects the absurd conventional falsehood of political equality.[82]

Similarly, Hitler told young Nazis in 1934: "We do not seek equality but mastery. We shall not waste time over minority rights and other such ideological abortions of sterile democracy."[83]

Hitler's attitudes toward the German *Volk*, the organic state, and the Nazi party all exemplified his political elitism. Appealing to some Germans' feelings of national humiliation after their defeat in World War I, Hitler initially asserted the need for equality between the German nation and other European nations. In reality, however, he wanted the German *Volk*, the Aryan race, and the German nation to dominate the world. Hitler sought to organize both the state and the Nazi party like elitist military organizations. As in a professional army, the rulers must exercise unconditional authority; the troops at the bottom must demonstrate their absolute obedience to the supreme leader or commander-in-chief. Accordingly, in 1934, he demanded that all army officers swear their personal loyalty to *der Führer*. He organized the Nazi party like a military apparatus, complete with army uniforms, salutes, and precision marching. Rather than actively participating in political affairs, the masses demonstrated their political equality before Hitler by ritualistic political marches and demonstrations.[84]

Hitler expressed stronger support for equality of economic opportunity than for political equality. As an elitist, he opposed equality of economic rewards and identified "economic leveling" with communism. From his perspective, those who produced the most goods should receive the highest income. Yet he rejected "excessive" differentiation of wages and promised young German males, if not women and Jews, equal opportunities for employment and education. In *Mein Kampf,* Hitler advocated using the school system to ensure equal opportunity for the most talented male youth from all social classes. After gaining political power in 1933, he attacked the educated aristocrats who dominated the universities and the government bureaucracy. Hitler lowered educational requirements for university admission and tried to purge the civil service of highly educated personnel. He urged that racial purity, loyalty to the Nazi party, and athletic prowess, not academic performance on tests, become the main bases for judging students. Because most Nazis were young men who lacked a formal university education, these policies expanded economic opportunities for those groups who had been relatively disadvantaged in the Weimar Republic.[85]

Hitler found no place in his political beliefs for cultural equality. Compared with other ideologies, Nazism placed the greatest stress on biological elitism. According to him, Jews were born an inferior race; Aryans were born the superior race. A person's skin color indicated superiority. Because the Aryans have the lightest pigmentation, Hitler asserted that they must rule the world. Annihilation of European Jews became his program for guaranteeing racial purity. For Hitler, biological inferiority denied not only spiritual equality but also status equality. Because individuals are unequal, the inferior should defer to their superiors. Rather than showing equal respect to all people, Germans must defer to those men with superior capabilities. According to Hitler, equal duties to the nation-state and its leader, not equal rights for all people, should form the basis of German solidarity.[86]

MILITARY FASCISM IN LATIN AMERICA

Although Hitler and Mussolini died at the end of World War II, their ideological influence remains alive today. Except in Italy, no fascist political party has attracted more than 5 percent of the popular vote in any West European nation during the postwar period; yet in South Africa, parts of the Arab Middle East, and especially Argentina, Chile, and Uruguay, leaders with fascist orientation control the government. Gino Germani has described the military regimes that emerged in Argentina, Chile, and Uruguay during the 1970s as "functional substitutes of fascism."[87] An appropriate label for these Latin American regimes is "military fascism."

What are the similarities among the ideologies of Hitler, Mussolini, and contemporary military leaders in Chile, Uruguay, and Argentina? All these regimes replaced a government based on civil liberties and parliamentary democracy. The prefascist governments allowed electoral competition, a free press, and opportunities for all movements, including leftist unions and political parties, to mobilize popular support. Competition between rightist and leftist organizations polarized the nation. In Italy, Germany, and Chile, communist and socialist parties posed a threat to the conservative middle classes. In Argentina, the People's Revolutionary Army, a pro-Trotsky organization, and the Montoneros, a left-wing Peronista group, staged guerrilla attacks, as did the Tupamaros in Uruguay. Internal struggles between private armed bands, along with the deteriorating economic conditions, weakened the legitimacy shown toward the parliamentary government.

The fascist leaders came to political power determined to abolish parliamentary democracy, suppress leftist parties, crush the unions, and demobilize the factory workers, small farmers, and farm laborers. Seeking to defend the interests of upper- and middle-class people who felt threatened by socialist and communist movements, the fascist leaders imposed restraints on political freedom and economic equality. They attacked the principles of liberal, parliamentary democracy under which leftist organizations had the freedom to compete for electoral support and to express their civil liberties. Demanding strong, powerful, orderly government, they identified multiparty coalition governments with political anarchy.

In control of government, the fascists subordinated legislative power to dominance by the executive branch. State and society became organized along military lines. Military values of duty, hierarchy, orderly authority, discipline, and obedience to the leader became the paramount virtues. The classical liberal values of negotiation, compromise, bargaining, and coalition formation in parliament were downgraded as antithetical to orderly development.

These fascist regimes adopted an ultranationalist position; defense of the nation-state took precedence over protection of individual freedoms. Particularly in Argentina and Germany, nationalism implied anti-Semitism. Attacks on leftist organizations—trade unions, democratic socialist parties, communist parties—carried nationalist overtones, for the fascist leaders claimed that these Marxist organizations were serving the interests of the Soviet Union or Cuba, not the will of the fatherland.

Although the fascists opposed Marxism, they did not support a fully laissez-faire economic policy. Instead, they strengthened state regulation of the economy. Pursuing a technocratic orientation, they brought technical experts, economists, engineers, and managers into government power to plan the economy free from union, socialist, or communist pressures. The goal was to expand productivity by curtailing income equality. Public policies to implement this objective included strict control over wages, tax laws that favored the wealthy, and the reduction of government-provided social services assisting the poor.

Despite these resemblances between European fascism and Latin American military regimes, in other respects the ideologies expressed by Hitler, on the one hand, and military officers in Argentina, Chile, and Uruguay, on the other, diverge. Latin American military fascism has been more deeply influenced by classical conservative beliefs and represents a less sharp break with the status quo. Compared with German Nazism, it allows greater institutional freedom, especially for the Roman Catholic church, private economic corporations, and the family. For example, military fascism aims to secure less totalistic control over the population than did Hitler. The military officers oppose establishing a single political party with a mass base; instead, they want the professional military, civilian bureaucracy, and technical experts to rule the society. They desire passive, apathetic obedience, not active mass support.

Rather than instituting a cult of the leader, the military fascists govern through more collegial, collective leadership. The top military leader does not become an object of mass veneration.

Social institutions outside the military and civilian bureaucracy—especially the Roman Catholic church and domestic as well as foreign private corporations—retain greater autonomy than in Nazi Germany. Linking Christian beliefs with national values, military leaders in Argentina and Chile have allowed some high Catholic clergy the freedom to criticize the regime. Indeed, the Catholic church now remains the most powerful institution opposing the punitive fascist policies toward factory workers, poor farmers, the unemployed, and leftist intellectual dissidents.

In short, although Hitler, Mussolini, and Latin American military officers all have opposed political, economic, and cultural equality, contemporary military fascists have shown a greater acceptance of social pluralism. In this regard, they more closely resemble Spanish general Francisco Franco (1936–1975) than Hitler.

Summary

The five ideologies—classical conservatism, classical liberalism, democratic socialism, communism, and fascism—express diverse interpretations of freedom and equality; they also rank these twin values differently. (See tables 4-2 and 4-3 for a summary.) Fascism and democratic socialism show the most divergent rankings of freedom and equality. Whereas fascist leaders give the lowest priority to freedom and equality, democratic socialists place the highest value on the two beliefs. For the classical liberals, freedom assumes greater value than equality of economic rewards. Compared with classical conservatives, liberal thinkers show greater support for both these beliefs, especially civil liberties, free competition, free trade, equality

TABLE 4-2 Ideological interpretations of freedom

Ideology	Political freedom	Economic freedom	Spiritual freedom	Status freedom
Classical Conservatism	opposes political freedom: Authority, duty, and order take precedence over freedom, individual rights, and self-indulgence. Supports political freedom: Society needs diversity & pluralism, not uniformity.	opposes economic freedom: State regulates private business.	opposes religious freedom: Society needs a union of church and state.	opposes status freedom: Individuals must maintain their inherited station in life.
Classical Liberalism	supports civil liberties; rejects coercive, monopolistic, and arbitrary power exercised by the state. Laws must regulate government power.	supports freedom for private entrepreneurs & consumers on the free market. Liberals place less stress on freedom for trade unions and factory workers.	supports separation of church and state	supports freedom for individuals to rise through social stratification system
Democratic Socialism	supports civil liberties, including rights for all to participate in political decision making	supports freedom for workers and consumers; opposes both concentration of private wealth and bureaucratic state dictatorship	supports religious liberty & separation of church & state; opposes secular political religion	supports freedom for individuals to realize their potentialities, mainly through education
Communism (Leninism)	supports political freedoms for socialists in the feudal & capitalist stages of development; opposes civil liberties for "counterrevolutionaries" during stages of dictatorship of the proletariat & socialism; supports freedom in full communism era, when no state, no classes, & no exploitation exist	supports economic freedom for proletariat and poor peasantry; opposes freedom for landlords and capitalists	supports separation of church & state; greater stress on freedom to criticize religion than on freedom of worship	supports freedom for proletariat, poor peasants, women, all nationalities, and ethnic groups to gain upward mobility
Fascism	opposes civil liberties and political diversity; supports political rule by one leader, one state, one homogeneous people (*Volk*), and one party	opposes economic freedom for industrialists and especially factory workers; supports freedom of economic consumption	opposes religious freedom, particularly church criticism of government leaders & policies	opposes freedom for women & Jews to rise in social stratification system; supports freedom for young Aryan males to gain upward mobility

TABLE 4-3 Ideological interpretations of equality

Ideology	Political equality	Economic equality	Spiritual equality	Status equality
Classical Conservatism	opposes political equality; stresses hierarchy over equality: The best, most responsible, & educated classes must rule.	opposes economic leveling	supports spiritual equality of all people before God; favors ecclesiastical hierarchy on earth	opposes equal status on earth; supports deference to the elite
Classical Liberalism	supports equality before the law	opposes equality of economic rewards; supports equality of economic opportunity	supports equality of human beings: All deserve equal respect as moral persons.	supports equality of social interactions; rejects deference to elite
Democratic Socialism	supports equality of everyone to participate in political decision making as active citizens; favors political equality before the law	supports equal economic opportunities to realize one's abilities; opposes both equal incomes for all persons and large differences in wealth	supports notion that all people are equal in human worth	supports equality of social interactions; rejects deference to privileged elites
Communism (Leninism)	opposes political equality; favors rule by vanguard party that functions like an army; party controls mass associations, which provide opportunities for mass political participation. Real political equality will emerge only under full communism.	supports government policies to secure greater income equality; favors wage inequalities as incentives to stimulate production during socialist stage; real economic equality will not occur until stage of full communism	opposes spiritual equality between "good" people (proletariat, poor peasants, exploited classes, party cadres) and "bad" people (capitalists, landlords, exploiters, antiparty groups)	supports status equality, especially for proletariat, poor peasants, women, and ethnic groups; stresses notion that all people should be treated as workers
Fascism	opposes political equality: Society is an organism ruled by an elite & great leader (*il Duce, der Führer*). Party & state function like an army.	rejects equal economic rewards but favors equal opportunity to expand production	opposes spiritual equality between "superior" Aryans and "inferior" Jews	opposes status equality between Aryan males & other "inferior" groups; supports deference to the great leader

before the law, and equal opportunities for the individual to rise in the social stratification system.

The communist interpretation diverges from liberal views. According to Lenin, "real" freedom and "true" equality will be attained only during the future stage of full communism when class conflict, class domination, and state repression have ceased. Until that stage arrives, a strong party-state needs to dominate political life, restricting the civil liberties of dissidents who challenge the Communist party dictatorship. In Lenin's view, during the transition to full communism, the government has the egalitarian responsibility to help the poor and exploited secure basic social services, including health care, public education, full employment, and inexpensive housing. From the Leninist perspective, these public policies will enable the proletariat and poor peasantry to attain economic liberation.

Notes

1. See three articles by Jean Laponce: "In Search of the Stable Elements of the Left-Right Landscape," *Comparative Politics* 4 (July 1972): 455–475; "Spatial Archetypes and Political Perceptions," *American Political Science Review* 69 (March 1975): 11–20; "Relating Biological, Physical, and Political Phenomena: The Case of Up and Down," *Social Science Information* 17, no. 3 (1978): 385–397. See also S. E. Finer, "Left, Right, and Rhetoric," *New Society* 36 (June 10, 1976): 587–588.
2. Milton Rokeach, *The Nature of Human Values* (New York: Free Press, 1973), pp. 165–188.
3. Daniel Bell, *The End of Ideology*, new rev. ed. (New York: Collier Books, 1962), pp. 393–407.
4. Carl J. Friedrich, *Man and His Government: An Empirical Theory of Politics*, (New York: McGraw-Hill, 1963), pp. 89–90. See also Bernard Barber, "Function, Variability, and Change in Ideological Systems," in *Stability and Social Change*, ed. Bernard Barber and Alex Inkeles (Boston: Little, Brown, 1971), p. 248.
5. For an analysis of the style or structure of an ideology, see Robert D. Putnam, *The Beliefs of Politicians: Ideology, Conflict, and Democracy in Britain and Italy* (New Haven, Conn.: Yale University Press, 1973), esp. pp. 34–48.
6. For analyses of the functions of political ideology, see Clifford Geertz, "Ideology as a Cultural System," in *Ideology and Discontent*, ed. David E. Apter (New York: Free Press, 1964), pp. 47–76; Charles F. Andrain, "The Political Thought of Sékou Touré" in *African Political Thought: Lumumba, Nkrumah, and Touré*, ed. W. A. E. Skurnik (Denver: University of Denver Monograph Series in World Affairs, 1968), pp. 129–135.
7. See Florence Kluckhohn and Fred Strodtbeck, "Variations in Value Orientations: Dominant and Variant Value Orientations," in *Contemporary Analytical Theory*, ed. David E. Apter and Charles F. Andrain (Englewood Cliffs, N.J.: Prentice-Hall, 1972), pp. 160–187, esp. p. 164.
8. For analyses of classical liberalism, see Sheldon S. Wolin, *Politics and Vision* (Boston: Little, Brown, 1960), pp. 314–331; Albert O. Hirschman, *The Passions and the Interests* (Princeton, N.J.: Princeton University Press, 1977).
9. Zbigniew Brzezinski and Samuel P. Huntington, *Political Power: USA/USSR* (New York: Viking Press, 1965), p. 21.
10. Rokeach, *The Nature of Human Values*, pp. 168–169.
11. Ibid., pp. 170–186.
12. John Hall, Joan Higgins, and Tony Rees, "What Influences Tory MPs?" *New Society* 38 (December 9, 1976): 505–507.
13. N. K. O'Sullivan, *Conservatism* (New York: St. Martin's Press, 1976).
14. Rod Preece, "The Anglo-Saxon Conservative Tradition," *Canadian Journal of Political Science* 13 (March 1980): 3–32; H. A. Morton, "The American Revolution: A View from the North," *Journal of Cana-*

dian Studies 7 (May 1972): 43–54; Gad Horowitz, "Notes on 'Conservatism, Liberalism, and Socialism in Canada,'" *Canadian Journal of Political Science* 11 (June 1978): 393; Klaus Epstein, *The Genesis of German Conservatism* (Princeton, N.J.: Princeton University Press, 1966), pp. 5–22.
15. Robert Eccleshall, "English Conservatism as Ideology," *Political Studies* 25 (March 1977): 78; Philip W. Buck, ed., *How Conservatives Think* (Baltimore: Penguin Books, 1975), pp. 150–152.
16. Plinio Corrêa de Oliveira, "What Does Self-Managing Socialism Mean for Communism: A Barrier? Or a Bridgehead?" *Los Angeles Times*, December 13, 1981, pt. I-A, p. 6.
17. Buck, p. 27; Robert Lindsay Schuettinger, ed., *The Conservative Tradition in European Thought* (New York: Putnam's, 1970), p. 226; Glen Petrie, "Saints and Functionaries," *New Society* 51 (March 20, 1980): 595.
18. Buck, *How Conservatives Think*, p. 70; Eccleshall, "English Conservatism as Ideology"; Horowitz, "Notes on 'Conservatism, Liberalism, and Socialism in Canada,'" pp. 389–393; Robert Nisbet, "Preface," *Journal of Contemporary History* 13 (October 1978): 629–634.
19. Raymond Plant, "Community: Concept, Conception, and Ideology," *Politics and Society* 8, no. 1 (1978): 94–98.
20. O'Sullivan, *Conservatism*, pp. 119–153; R. E. Pahl and J. T. Winkler, "The Coming Corporatism," *Challenge* 18 (March–April 1975): 28–35.
21. Louis Hartz, *The Liberal Tradition in America* (New York: Harcourt Brace and World, 1955); George H. Sabine, *A History of Political Theory*, rev. ed. (New York: Henry Holt, 1950), pp. 523–540; Richard Ashcraft, "Political Theory and Political Reform: John Locke's Essay on Virginia," *Western Political Quarterly* 22 (December 1969): 742–758.
22. See Friedrich A. Hayek, *The Constitution of Liberty* (Chicago: University of Chicago Press, 1960), esp. pp. 208–209, 222–225, 262–267.
23. Herbert Hoover, *American Individualism* (Garden City, N.Y.: Doubleday, 1922), pp. 54–55; Herbert Hoover, *The Challenge to Liberty* (New York: Scribner's, 1934), pp. 2, 58–76, 114–115.
24. Hayek, *The Constitution of Liberty*, pp. 136, 265–284.
25. Ibid., p. 305.
26. Wolin, *Politics and Vision*, pp. 331–342.
27. Hayek, *The Constitution of Liberty*, p. 155; Martin Diamond, "The Declaration and the Constitution: Liberty, Democracy, and the Founders," *The Public Interest* no. 41 (Fall 1975): 39–55; Martin Diamond, "The American Idea of Equality: The View from the Founding," *Review of Politics* 38 (July 1976): 313–331; David Miller, "Democracy and Social Justice," *British Journal of Political Science* 8 (January 1978): 1–19.
28. Hoover, *The Challenge to Liberty*, pp. 57–59; Daniel Bell, *The Cultural Contradictions of Capitalism* (New York: Basic Books, 1976), p. 263.
29. John Rawls, *A Theory of Justice* (Cambridge, Mass.: Harvard University Press, 1971), pp. 60–62, 440–441, 510–511.
30. Robert Nozick, *Anarchy, State, and Utopia* (New York: Basic Books, 1974).
31. Koulas Mellos, "Developments in Advanced Capitalist Ideology," *Canadian Journal of Political Science* 11 (December 1978): 850–861; Robert O. Keohane, "Economics, Inflation, and the Role of the State: Political Implications of the McCracken Report," *World Politics* 31 (October 1978): 108–128.
32. Gad Horowitz, "Conservatism, Liberalism, and Socialism in Canada: An Interpretation," *Canadian Journal of Economics and Political Science* 32 (May 1966): 161–166; Bell, *The Cultural Contradictions of Capitalism*, pp. 223–226.
33. Arthur M. Schlesinger, Jr., *The Age of Roosevelt: The Politics of Upheaval* (Boston: Houghton Mifflin, 1960), pp. 325–326.
34. See Alden S. Raine, *Change in the Political Agenda: Social and Cultural Conflict in the American Electorate*, Sage Professional Papers in American Politics, vol. 3, series no. 04-035 (Beverly Hills, Calif.: Sage, 1977); Aage R. Clausen, *How Congressmen Decide: A Policy Focus* (New York: St. Martin's Press, 1973).
35. Ulf Himmelstrand, "Sweden: Paradise in Trouble," *Dissent* 26 (Winter 1979): 125.
36. John Hall and Joan Higgins, "What Influences Today's Labour MPs?" *New Society* 38 (December 2, 1976): 457.
37. Ross Terrill, *R. H. Tawney and His Times: Socialism as Fellowship* (Cambridge, Mass.: Harvard University Press, 1973), pp. 151–152; see also pp. 146–150; R. H. Tawney, *Equality* (London: George Allen and Unwin, 1952), pp. 182–183, 258–260; J. M. Winter and D. M. Joslin, eds., *R. H. Tawney's Commonplace Book* (London: Cambridge University Press, 1972), pp. 22, 34, 60.

38. Terrill, *R. H. Tawney and His Times*, pp. 166–168, 250–279; Tawney, *Equality*, pp. 186–209, 258–267.
39. Terrill, *R. H. Tawney and His Times*, pp. 128, 157, 178–218; Tawney, *Equality*, pp. 258–265.
40. Tawney, *Equality*, pp. 47, 182–187, 260.
41. Terrill, *R. H. Tawney and His Times*, p. 261; Tawney, *Equality*, p. 186.
42. Terrill, *R. H. Tawney and His Times*, pp. 121–130; Tawney, *Equality*, pp. 13–15, 42, 105–113; Alan Ryan, "R. H. Tawney: A Socialist Saint," *New Society* 54 (November 27, 1980): 408–410.
43. Terrill, *R. H. Tawney and His Times*, pp. 121–136, 155, 207, 267; Tawney, *Equality*, pp. 12–16, 36–50, 194, 222; Winter and Joslin, *R. H. Tawney's Commonplace Book*, pp. 5–13, 67–68.
44. Norman Birnbaum, "The French Left: Squabbling toward the Election," *Nation* 225 (October 29, 1977): 424–428; Lawrence C. Mayer and John H. Burnett, *Politics in Industrial Societies: A Comparative Perspective* (New York: Wiley, 1977), pp. 366–369.
45. Norman Furniss and Timothy Tilton, *The Case for the Welfare State* (Bloomington: Indiana University Press, 1977), pp. 122–152; Guido Goldman, "The German Political System," in *Patterns of Government: The Major Political Systems of Europe*, 3d ed., ed. Samuel H. Beer and Adam B. Ulam (New York: Random House, 1973), pp. 569–573.
46. David Miller, "Socialism and the Market," *Political Theory* 5 (November 1977): 473–490; Arthur DiQuattro, "Alienation and Justice in the Market," *American Political Science Review* 72 (September 1978): 871–887; Charles E. Lindblom, *Politics and Markets* (New York: Basic Books, 1977), pp. 33–49, 330–343; Charles E. Lindblom, "Capitalism, Socialism, and Democracy," *Commentary* 65 (April 1978): 57–58.
47. Karl Marx, *Political Writings, vol. III: The First International and After*, ed. David Fernbach (New York: Vintage Books, 1974), p. 355.
48. Ibid., pp. 250, 333–335; Karl Marx, *Political Writings, vol. I: The Revolutions of 1848*, ed. David Fernbach (New York: Vintage Books, 1974), pp. 86–87, 325–326; Karl Marx, *Political Writings, vol. II: Surveys from Exile*, ed. David Fernbach (New York: Vintage Books, 1974), pp. 243–244.
49. Marx, *The First International*, p. 144; Karl Marx, *Early Writings*, trans. Rodney Livingstone and Gregor Benton (New York: Vintage Books, 1975), pp. 229–234, 346. See also G. A. Cohen, *Karl Marx's Theory of History: A Defence* (Princeton, N.J.: Princeton University Press, 1978), pp. 187, 306–307.
50. Marx, *Early Writings*, pp. 211–245.
51. Marx, *The First International*, p. 375.
52. Ibid., pp. 81, 91–92, 145, 270, 373–374; Marx, *Early Writings*, p. 257.
53. Marx, *Early Writings*, pp. 332–333, 346–347; Marx, *Surveys from Exile*, pp. 280, 347–353; Bell, *The Cultural Contradictions of Capitalism*, p. 262.
54. Marx, *Early Writings*, pp. 395, 419; Marx, *The First International*, p. 83.
55. V. I. Lenin, *V. I. Lenin: Selected Works* (New York: International Publishers, 1971), p. 447; see also pp. 35, 51, 124–132, 343, 418–429, 444, 463.
56. Ibid., p. 427; see also pp. 421–426, 518–535, 560, 575, 627–631. For analyses of the militarization of communism, see Sheldon S. Wolin, "The Politics of the Study of Revolution," *Comparative Politics* 5 (April 1973): 352–355; Irving Louis Horowitz, *Foundations of Political Sociology* (New York: Harper & Row, 1972), pp. 205–229.
57. Lenin, *Selected Works*, p. 328; Alfred B. Evans, Jr., "Developed Socialism in Soviet Ideology," *Soviet Studies* 29 (July 1977): 410–411, 414.
58. V. I. Lenin, *What Is To Be Done?* (Peking: Foreign Languages Press, 1973), p. 72; Lenin, *Selected Works*, pp. 151, 443, 492–493, 501, 534, 657, 662–664, 690.
59. Lenin, *What Is To Be Done?*, pp. 37, 98, 136–138, 154, 199–202; Lenin, *Selected Works*, pp. 281, 298, 323, 374, 465, 488, 537–546, 572–573, 624–626, 660.
60. Lenin, *Selected Works*, pp. 294, 331–336, 379, 417, 501–505.
61. Ibid., pp. 305, 343, 347, 382, 393, 492–493, 646–647.
62. For this classification of communist ideologies, see Carl Boggs, Jr., "Revolutionary Process, Political Strategy, and the Dilemma of Power," *Theory and Society* 4 (Fall 1977): 359–393.
63. Stefan Morawski, "The Ideology of Anarchism—a Tentative Analysis," *Polish Sociological Bulletin* no. 37 (no. 1, 1977): 31–47; William Chadwick, "The Mailed Fist vs. the Invisible Hand," *Reason* 10 (September 1978): 18–23.
64. See Antonio Gramsci, *Selections from Political Writings, 1910–1920*, ed. Quintin Hoare, trans. John Mathews (New York: International Publishers, 1977), pp. 65–67, 87, 128, 139–149, 155, 192–194; Antonio Gramsci, *Selections from Political Writings, 1921–1926*, trans. and ed. Quin-

tin Hoare (New York: International Publishers, 1978), pp. 26, 32, 36, 82, 121, 166, 195, 215, 228, 232–237, 358, 365, 368, 375.
65. For analyses of Gramsci's political ideology, see Carl Boggs, *Gramsci's Marxism* (London: Pluto Press, 1976); James Joll, *Antonio Gramsci* (New York: Penguin Books, 1978); Paul Piccone, "Gramsci's Marxism: Beyond Lenin and Togliatti," *Theory and Society* 3 (Winter 1976): 485–512; Walter L. Adamson, "Towards the Prison Notebooks: The Evolution of Gramsci's Thinking on Political Organizations 1918–1926," *Polity* 12 (Fall 1979): 38–64; Mark E. Kann, "Antonio Gramsci and Modern Marxism," *Studies in Comparative Communism* 13 (Summer–Autumn 1980): 250–266; Joseph V. Femia, "The Gramsci Phenomenon: Some Reflections," *Political Studies* 27 (September 1979): 472–483.
66. Gramsci, *Writings, 1910–1920*, p. 333. See also Gramsci, *Writings, 1921–1926*, pp. 212, 364, 432; Antonio Gramsci, *Selections from the Prison Notebooks*, trans. and ed. Quintin Hoare and Geoffrey Nowell Smith (New York: International Publishers, 1971), pp. 34, 341–367; Antonio Gramsci, *Letters from Prison*, trans. and ed. Lynne Lawner (New York: Harper & Row, 1973), pp. 46–49, 238.
67. Gramsci, *Writings, 1910–1920*, pp. 100, 140–146, 306–309; Gramsci, *Writings, 1921–1926*, pp. 198, 315–316, 418–419; Gramsci, *Prison Notebooks*, pp. 10, 129, 199–205, 332–335, 392–397, 418–423.
68. See Boggs, "Revolutionary Process, Political Strategy, and the Dilemma of Power," pp. 372–381; Enrico Berlinguer, "One Year after June 20th," *The Italian Communist: Foreign Bulletin of the PCI* no. 2 (April–June 1977): 84–97; Max Gordon, "The Theoretical Outlook of the Italian Communists," *Socialist Revolution* 7 (May–June 1977): 29–58; Eric Shaw, "The Italian Historical Compromise: A New Pathway to Power?" *Political Quarterly* 49 (October–December 1978): 411–424.
69. Samuel H. Barnes, *Representation in Italy: Institutionalized Tradition and Electoral Choice* (Chicago: University of Chicago Press, 1977), pp. 103–107.
70. Quoted in S. J. Woolf, "Italy," in *European Fascism*, ed. S. J. Woolf (New York: Vintage Books, 1969), pp. 43–44.
71. Quoted in A. J. Nicholls, "Germany," in Woolf, *European Fascism*, p. 63. See also Rokeach, *The Nature of Human Values*, p. 175.
72. A. James Gregor, "Fascism and the 'Countermodernization' of Consciousness," *Comparative Political Studies* 10 (July 1977): 242.
73. Piero Melograni, "The Cult of the Duce in Mussolini's Italy," *Journal of Contemporary History* 11 (October 1976): 229.
74. Adolf Hitler, *The Speeches of Adolf Hitler, April 1922–August 1939*, vol. 1, ed. Norman H. Baynes (London: Oxford University Press, 1942), p. 265.
75. Ibid., pp. 66, 85–96, 242–256, 339, 447–458, 500; Adolf Hitler, *My New Order*, ed. Raoul de Roussy de Sales (New York: Reynal and Hitchcock, 1941), pp. 21–30.
76. Hitler, *Speeches*, p. 872; Benito Mussolini, "The Doctrine of Fascism," trans. I. S. Munro, in *Readings on Fascism and National Socialism*, ed. members of the Department of Philosophy, University of Colorado (Chicago: Swallow Press, 1952), pp. 10, 21, 23.
77. Hitler, *Speeches*, pp. 93, 105, 504–505, 848, 892–936, 943, 949, 980; Adolf Hitler, *Mein Kampf*, trans. Ralph Mannheim (Boston: Houghton Mifflin, 1943), pp. 599–602.
78. Edward R. Tannenbaum, *The Fascist Experience: Italian Society and Culture, 1922–1945* (New York: Basic Books, 1972), pp. 78–79; Ernst Nolte, *Three Faces of Fascism* (New York: Holt, Rinehart and Winston, 1966), pp. 224–232; P. Vita-Finzi, "Italian Fascism and the Intellectuals," in *The Nature of Fascism*, ed. S. J. Woolf (New York: Vintage Books, 1969), p. 242.
79. Quoted in *Readings on Fascism and National Socialism*, p. 87.
80. Hitler, *Speeches*, pp. 51–61, 367, 370, 399, 449; George L. Mosse, *Nazi Culture* (New York: Grosset and Dunlap, 1968), pp. 235, 341–345.
81. Hitler, *Speeches*, p. 731; Hitler, *Mein Kampf*, p. 431.
82. Mussolini, "The Doctrine of Fascism," pp. 17–18.
83. Quoted in Paul Hayes, *Fascism* (New York: Free Press, 1973), p. 112.
84. Hitler, *My New Order*, pp. 21, 101–102, 218, 370–374, 409; Hitler, *Mein Kampf*, pp. 384, 443, 457; Tannenbaum, *The Fascist Experience*, p. 79.
85. Hitler, *My New Order*, pp. 79–100; Hitler, *Speeches*, p. 860; Hitler, *Mein Kampf*, pp. 431, 436, 443; William Jannen, Jr., "National Socialists and Social Mobility," *Journal of Social History* 9 (Spring 1976): 339–366.
86. Hitler, *Mein Kampf*, pp. 292–308, 383–384, 403, 435, 442; Hitler, *Speeches*, pp. 255, 731, 740–741.
87. Gino Germani, *Authoritarianism, Fascism, and National Populism* (New Brunswick,

N.J.: Transaction Books, 1978), pp. 43–79. See also Herbert S. Levine, "The Culture of Fascism," *Nation* 219 (August 17, 1974): 103–107; Christopher Seton-Watson, "Fascism in Contemporary Europe," in Woolf, *European Fascism*, pp. 342–353; Christopher Hitchens, "Two Dictatorships," *New Statesman* 95 (January 13, 1978): 38–41; David Rock, "Revolt and Repression in Argentina," *World Today* 33 (June 1977): 215–222; Brian Loveman and Thomas M. Davies, Jr., eds., *The Politics of Antipolitics: The Military in Latin America* (Lincoln: University of Nebraska Press, 1978), pp. 3–12, 176–180, 198–207.

CHAPTER
5

Political Ideology and Public Policy

> *Each step in the process of decision making depends on the initial stipulation of values to be served. . . . The better metaphor for policy analysis may not be the mathematical equation but the legal brief—it is a reasoned case for a preferred course of public action.*
>
> —CHARLES W. ANDERSON

What is the effect of political ideology on public policy? As Charles W. Anderson suggests, the policy process partly reflects political leaders' value preferences; beliefs both guide political actions and justify policymakers' decisions. Yet several variables other than ideological beliefs about freedom and equality shape the content of public policies. The *personal* variables affecting policymakers include their motivation (will) to act on their beliefs, the perceived salience of freedom and equality, the importance of other values (justice, national defense, peace, progress), the expected consequences of public policy actions, and the information available about popular attitudes, interest-group demands, and the technical feasibility of implementing a specific program. *Situational* variables include the political leader's organizational control over the environment, the strength of rival power centers, the economic resources available to implement a policy, the content of constitutional regulations and specific laws that authorize particular policies, and the past policies shaping present actions.

These personal and situational factors condition the policies a government formulates, thereby restraining leaders' ability to translate their political beliefs into public policies. For example, even if conceptions of equality motivate officials to increase income equality, all the other factors may prevent them from acting on their beliefs.[1] For these reasons, social scientists cannot easily estimate the effects of political ideology on specific policies concerning freedom and equality. Despite these qualifications, the empirical evidence gathered since World War II suggests that political beliefs about freedom and equality have shaped public policies toward civil liberties and the distribution of wealth.

Commitment to Civil Liberties

Societies governed by democratic socialist and liberal political parties have shown the highest degree of civil liberties, which comprise electoral competition, universal suffrage, lack of press censorship, a nondictatorial police and military, and rights for the opposition to organize. These nations include Norway, Sweden, Denmark, Finland, Iceland, the Netherlands, Belgium, Luxembourg, Austria, Switzerland, the United Kingdom, Ireland, New Zealand, Australia, Canada, the United States, Costa Rica, and Barbados.

Even within this relatively democratic camp, ideological interpretations of freedom and equality influence the degree of civil liberties extended to specific organizations. As we have seen, liberalism is the ideological antithesis of communism; socialism most sharply diverges from fascism. During the post–World War II era, British and Scandinavian government leaders, influenced by democratic socialism, granted political freedoms to Communist party members and trade union officials. Yet British officials showed less willingness to support civil liberties for fascists, such as the neo-Nazis, white racists, and Black Muslims.

By contrast, American government officials attempted to deny left-wing organizations, particularly Communists, their rights to free expression. During the Truman, Eisenhower, Kennedy, Johnson, and Nixon administrations, left-wingers became the major target of government harassment. The Federal Bureau of Investigation resorted to illegal tactics, such as wiretapping, burglary, and forged communications, against not only the Communists but also the Socialist Workers party, which maintained no organizational connections with any communist-dominated foreign government and which carried out its activities in a nonviolent way. Although the Justice Department and the FBI also kept watch over white racist organizations, those groups retained greater freedom to pursue their operations without government interference.[2]

Countries governed by conservative leaders show a weaker commitment to civil liberties than do nations where socialists and liberals exercise predominant influence. Between 1950 and 1980, these included Italy, France, Spain, and Greece, besides several regimes in Latin America, Asia, and the Near East.

Fascist and communist regimes generally score at the bottom of most civil liberties scales. Historically, of the two main fascist regimes of the 1930s, Fascist Italy, more deeply influenced by the classical conservatism of the Roman Catholic church, allowed greater freedoms than did Nazi Germany. Political coercion in Italy remained limited until 1943. For instance, between 1926 and 1943, only twenty-five persons were condemned to death. Antonio Gramsci wrote his most famous works while in prison. Within the Fascist corporate state, the party never gained control over the state or all the society. As supreme leader, Mussolini mediated among several groups: the monarchy, army, state bureaucracy, Roman Catholic church, large private business corporations, banks, landowners, and the fascist syndicates. In particular, the church, bureaucracy, armed forces, and police retained considerable independence from the Fascist party and even Mussolini himself.[3] In Nazi Germany, however, Hitler attained stronger coercive power over the state and society. No rival competing institutions, such as an established church or monarchy, remained to challenge his policies, which reflected his dogmatic, racist ideology.

In communist-dominated states, especially the Soviet Union, the single party has gained the greatest control over government and social groups. Leninist political beliefs, combined with the autocratic czarist heritage, have motivated Soviet officials to crush organized opposition. Although contemporary Soviet leaders rule less repressively than did Stalin, they have curbed the activities of dissidents, including ethnic groups (Ukrainians, Latvians, Estonians), religious opposition (Jews, Baptists, Jehovah's Witnesses), and intellectuals (writers, artists). Leninist ideology justifies the dominant role played by the Communist party and the Party's refusal to allow any organized opposition that challenges the Soviet system. Other East European states, especially Hungary and Yugoslavia, permit somewhat greater freedom. Except Czechoslovakia, few East European nations experienced a democratic heritage before the Communists came to political power after World War II; their autocratic history has conditioned the contemporary dictatorships. Yet Leninist beliefs reinforced these states' autocratic historical tendencies; so the contemporary dictatorships probably grant slightly less political freedom than their precommunist predecessors. Particularly in Czechoslovakia, the pre–World War II regime operated a comparatively democratic society, with rival groups enjoying some civil liberties. Today, however, the Czech people enjoy far fewer political liberties than before the war. Indeed, the Czechoslovakian Communist party directs one of the most repressive governments in East Europe.[4]

Commitment to Economic Equality

COMMUNISM

Even if communist states in East Europe have placed greater restrictions on political freedom than did the precommunist leadership, they have increased income equality. The government and Communist party have possessed the power and the willingness to implement egalitarian public policies. Public expenditures for education, housing, health care, and social services (old-age pensions, family allowances, work injury pensions, maternity benefits) constitute a high share of the government budget; most individuals can obtain these items at a low price or at no cost to themselves. Generally, the inexpensive nature of these necessities benefits poorer citizens.

Like the expenditure programs, government policies toward wages and public ownership of industries also have an egalitarian effect. Under capitalism, managers of private firms assume the primary responsibility for determining employees' wage rates. The wealthiest people obtain their income from entrepreneurial and investment income: interest, rents, capital gains, dividends, and so forth. Under state socialism, however, government wage boards have the power to equalize wages throughout the country. The state nationalizes the means of production; public officials, not private stockholders, handle capital investment. The Soviet government has abolished capital gains (except on art objects, jewelry, and stamp collections), dividends, most interest (except on personal savings accounts), and rents on private property such as land. Profits earned by state enterprises return to the state, rather than to wealthy private investors. By eliminating these sources of income, communist governments have thereby lessened economic inequalities.

Despite the egalitarian claims made by Communist party officials, state socialist societies have hardly abolished all income inequalities. As in the industrialized capitalist nations, women, rural folk, and the nonunionized work force still receive fewer economic benefits than men, urban residents, and union members. For instance, in the Soviet Union today, women secure about two-thirds the earnings of men, a percentage similar to West European figures. While encouraging boys to train for high-paying, skilled factory occupations, Soviet education policies channel girls into lower-paid service jobs, such as clerical work, sales, typing, teaching, and health care. Rural residents on the collective farms receive the fewest economic advantages. State farmers, skilled manual workers, intellectuals, and party–government officials all gain higher incomes and more fringe benefits, such as medical care, old-age pensions, and access to vacation resorts. Compared with the nonunionized work force, union members secure more generous cash and noncash benefits.

Regardless of these contradictions to economic equality, most observers assume that East European communist nations reveal greater economic equality than do many Western capitalist societies. The Soviet Union, which is less egalitarian than Hungary, Czechoslovakia, Bulgaria, and Rumania, attains greater income equality than the United States, Italy, France, or West Germany.[5] Certainly, the tenets of Leninist ideology had some effect on these economic results.

FASCISM

In contrast, fascist ideology motivated Hitler and Mussolini to decrease income equality in their nations. Hitler implemented few policies to reduce economic inequalities. The privileged classes—landlords, civil servants, and businessmen in the iron, steel, and chemical industries—retained their economic privileges; only the marked decline in unemployment from the 1932 levels improved the economic conditions of poorer Germans. Similarly, in Italy, Fascist economic policies benefited mainly large landowners and large industrialists. Mussolini's government abolished government regulation of life insurance companies, discontinued wage and price controls, ended the land redistribution program, lowered inheritance taxes, decreased personal income taxes paid by the wealthy, and exempted business firms from paying income taxes. By reinforcing the economic privileges of the wealthy, all these policies brought greater economic inequality, a condition that reflected Mussolini's ideological preferences.[6]

DEMOCRATIC SOCIALISM

In the Western capitalist world, countries where democratic socialist parties exercise dominant influence show the greatest income equality. A study of ten nations' posttax income distributions during the 1960s and early 1970s showed that Sweden, Norway, the Netherlands, and the United Kingdom were the most equal. Canada, Australia, the United States, and West Germany ranked lower on the equality scale. The three most inequalitarian countries were Spain, Italy, and France.[7] These three groups of nations correspond to three different ideological positions: democratic socialism, classical liberalism, and classical conservatism.

Particularly in Sweden and Norway, democratic socialists have wielded the government power needed to translate their egalitarian beliefs into public policies. First, for the most of the post–World War II period, they controlled the executive branch of government. During all elections, they won the largest share of votes to the national legislature, usually between 40 and 50 percent. Therefore, they gained the government power to implement egalitarian fiscal policies. High progressive income taxes redistributed income from the wealthier citizens to poorer citizens. The poor also benefited from high social service expenditures for job training, unemployment insurance, health care benefits, and old-age pensions.

Second, because Swedish and Norwegian public officials manage a centralized, unitary government structure, they have the power to implement uniform, egalitarian public policies. By contrast, political leaders in the United States, Canada, West Germany, and Switzerland—all federal systems with less income equality—must contend with decentralized structures that give veto powers to those groups opposing greater income equality. Faced with powerful state or provincial governments, constitutional courts, and second legislative chambers representing regional interests, federal government leaders can exercise only limited powers. Even if they favor economic equality, they cannot easily enact and then implement equalitarian public policies.

Third, the Swedish and Norwegian social democratic parties have stimulated widespread voting turnouts, especially among the working class. Cultural cleavages based on religion, ethnicity, language, and regional sentiments are relatively weak; instead, primordial politics become subordinate to the politics of class interests. These socialist parties provide some channels of participation for groups other than prosperous, well-educated, middle-class businessmen, who remain most opposed to income redistribution policies. In Sweden and Norway, socialist ideologies proclaim the need for government to pay some attention to working-class needs and to enact economic policies benefiting lower-income citizens.

Fourth, compared with other Western capitalist countries, Sweden and Norway have powerful labor movements. These Scandinavian unions are relatively centralized; collective bargaining occurs at the national level, rather than within a specific industry or enterprise. Thus, the central union organization can press for wage equality across several sectors of the economy. Because a high proportion (over 70 percent) of the labor force belongs to a union, the central trade union leaders can rally money and votes behind the social democratic parties' electoral campaigns. When the socialist parties hold government office, union officials gain direct access to the cabinet ministers who formulate economic policies. Both Sweden and Norway need to sell their exports on the world market; thus, labor costs must remain low so that export prices will be competitive. Union leaders often agree to accept lower wage increases in exchange for egalitarian income maintenance policies that raise their disposable incomes.[8]

Compared with the Swedish Social Democratic party, the British Labour party has exerted a less egalitarian impact. Despite the political power wielded by the Labour party since World War II, neither its expenditures policies nor its tax programs have equalized income distribution. Although rich people's share of wealth declined a bit between 1959 and 1977, posttax income shares remained about the same. For instance, in 1959, the wealthiest 10 percent of the population held 25 percent of total income; nearly twenty years later, they still possessed 23 percent.

Regardless of Britain's reputation in the United States as a profligate welfare state, British income transfer programs are really not that beneficent. Government expenditures have actually transferred a slightly larger share of national income from rich to poor in the United States than in Britain. British expenditures for health, education, and housing may benefit middle-class individuals more than low-income people. Furthermore, British taxes have not substantially reduced income inequalities.

Like the situation in the United States and Canada, the actual rates for all taxes are roughly proportional. National income taxes are more progressive than local property taxes; wealthy persons pay relatively low tax rates on their homes and land. Social security contributions to the National Insurance Fund are regressive, although less so than the value-added (sales) tax. Because the regressive value-added, property, and social security taxes offset the more progressive national personal income tax, the overall tax system tends to exert a proportional effect on income distribution.[9]

Both income and wealth are more equally distributed in Sweden than in Britain. Four reasons explain the more egalitarian thrust of Swedish social democratic policies. First, as we have seen, success in attaining income equality depends partly on the government strength of socialist parties. Between 1933 and 1976, the Swedish Social Democrats controlled the executive, usually in a coalition with other smaller parties. Thus, they had the time to implement egalitarian policies. By contrast, the British Labourites won control of Parliament and the executive for only about half the time between 1946 and 1980. Even when in power, they expressed a weaker commitment to enacting egalitarian policies than did the Swedish Social Democrats.

Second, Swedish public officials operate a more centralized government; civil servants and top party leaders can make decisions without fearing that other groups will veto their policies. Although Britain, like Sweden, is a unitary state, local government officials, court justices, and senior civil servants enjoy more autonomy from leaders of the dominant party in the House of Commons. This more decentralized British structure enables groups opposing greater income equality to block the central government's policies.

Third, the Swedish Social Democratic party has attracted wider electoral support; it regularly wins a larger share of both manual and white-collar votes than does the Labour party. In Sweden, members of all social classes—not only the working class but also a majority of the middle class—believe that the government should ensure that business owners, salaried employees, and factory workers enjoy more equal treatment, incomes, working hours, and vacation opportunities. In contrast, British workers express less enthusiasm about economic equality; rather than interpreting socialism as the extension of equality, they equate socialist principles with higher pay and improved working conditions.

Fourth, the union movement is less powerful in Britain than in Sweden. Swedish unions, especially the LO (Swedish Trade Union Federation) that represents manual workers, are stronger, more united, and more centralized. Based on industrial unions, the trade union federation works closely with the Social Democratic party in support of wage equality. By contrast, a lower percentage of the British labor force belongs to a union. The central organization—the Trades Union Congress—is weaker, more decentralized, and less united. Craft unions have historically been more important in Britain than in Sweden; generally, they have supported less egalitarian policies than have industrial unions. Today local union officials, shop stewards, and committees of stewards exert decisive power over collective bargaining. Because these local unions remain independent of national Trades Union Congress leaders, the TUC can wield only limited control over local affiliates. Given this decentralized union structure, the national TUC exercises only limited influence over the parliamentary Labour party and the prime minister. Similarly, under these decentralized conditions, British unions, compared with their Swedish counterparts, maintain greater autonomy from the socialist parties. In Britain, the unions show less willingness than in Sweden to rally behind egalitarian policies preferred by left-wing socialists.[10]

The Netherlands seemingly represents an exception to the tendency for powerful socialist parties and strong union movements to produce income equality. In Holland, the socialist party is electorally weaker than in Norway, Sweden, or Britain; yet Dutch posttax income equality is higher. What explains this apparent contradiction? Compared with other countries where income inequality is greater—for example, France, Spain, Italy, and West Germany—the Netherlands lacks strong right-wing parties ideologically committed to classical conservative or laissez-faire beliefs. Three types of parties compete for support: the Christian Democratic federation composed of two Protestant factions and one Catholic segment, the Labor party, and the Liberal party, which wins the fewest votes. All parties encourage high political participation; the working class and middle class have about the same rates of voting turnout and campaign activities. Both the Christian Democrats and socialists attract widespread support from manual workers; for instance, in 1977 the Christian Democrats secured 30 percent and the Labor party 43 percent of working-class votes. Although only 40 percent of the Dutch labor force is unionized and decentralized unions predominate, the national union headquarters has some power to shape collective bargaining agreements, including the size of wage increases. Since World War II, Dutch union leaders have supported greater wage equality. Thus, the important role played by national unions in collective bargaining, along with the need for the religious party to maintain working-class support, have encouraged the governing Christian Democrats to enact egalitarian public policies, such as progressive income taxes and high expenditures for social services.[11]

CLASSICAL LIBERALISM

Leaders who articulate classical liberal beliefs command the greatest government power in Canada, West Germany, and especially the United States; these nations have secured lower income equality than societies where democratic socialists play a powerful role. American political leaders have stressed equality of economic opportunity over equal economic rewards. According to classical liberal principles, unequal earnings provide an incentive for the individual to work hard and to increase production. Under the ideal liberal society, individuals' economic rewards should be based on their abilities and achievements, not on cash transfers granted by the government. In accordance with these liberal interpretations of equality, American national government leaders have not placed income equality at the top of the political agenda. Measures to curb inflation take precedence over programs to curtail unemployment. Interest groups representing private corporations successfully discourage national legislators from passing tax laws that would secure more equalitarian outcomes. Expenditures for social services—pensions, health care, unemployment compensation, child allowances—as a percentage of the GNP are comparatively low.[12]

CONSERVATISM

Conservative politicians usually dominated the national governments in France, Italy, and Spain between 1950 and 1980. As a result, these governments implement less egalitarian fiscal policies. Compared with Sweden, Norway, and Holland, the Latin Catholic nations feature a lower level of public expenditures as a proportion of the gross domestic product. Especially in Spain, spending on social services and transfer payments is also lower. The tax systems are generally regressive, with income taxes amounting to less than 7 percent of the gross domestic product. Extensive tax avoidance and illegal evasion plague all three countries; wealthy persons escape paying taxes or else gain special deductions, exemptions, and abatements. Hence, neither the tax nor the expenditures policies have lessened economic inequalities in France, Italy, and Spain to the extent that has occurred in Sweden, Norway, and Holland, where the central government budget has redistributed a sizable share of the total national income from the wealthier citizens to the poor.[13] Thus, in all these nations, the economic policies that government officials enact partly reflect their ideological priorities.

Notes

1. For an analysis of the relationship between attitudes (ideological beliefs) and actions (policies), see Charles W. Anderson, "The Place of Principles in Policy Analysis," *American Political Science Review* 73 (September 1979): 711–723; Herbert C. Kelman, "Attitudes Are Alive and Well and Gainfully Employed in the Sphere of Action," *American Psychologist* 29 (May 1974): 310–324.

2. See Ivo K. Feierabend, Betty Nesvold, and Rosalind L. Feierabend, "Political Coerciveness and Turmoil: A Cross-National Inquiry," *Law and Society Review* 5 (August 1970): 93–118; Raymond D. Gastil, "The Comparative Survey of Freedom—IX," *Freedom at Issue* no. 49 (January–February 1979): 3–14; George Thomas Miles, *Interpretation of Civil Liberty in Great Britain and the United States* (Ph.D. dissertation, Department of Political Science, University of Massachusetts, 1973), pp. 109–147; Robert J. Goldstein, *Political Repression in Modern America* (Cambridge, Mass.: Schenkman, 1978).

3. Piero Melograni, "The Cult of the Duce in Mussolini's Italy," *Journal of Contemporary History* 11 (October 1976): 221–237; Edward R. Tannenbaum, *The Fascist Experience: Italian Society and Culture, 1922–1945* (New York: Basic Books, 1972), pp. 79–81; Stanley G. Payne, *Fascism: Comparison and Definition* (Madison: University of Wisconsin Press, 1980), pp. 42–104.

4. Alec Nove, "How Repressive Is the Soviet Union?" *New Society* 26 (November 15, 1973): 391–392; Walter D. Connor, *Socialism, Politics, and Equality: Hierarchy and Change in Eastern Europe and the USSR* (New York: Columbia University Press, 1979), p. 338.

5. P. J. D. Wiles, *Economic Institutions Compared* (New York: Wiley, 1977), pp. 367–381, 436–445; Connor, *Socialism, Politics, and Equality*, pp. 215–266, 307–321, 335–337; Steven Stack, "Direct Government Involvement in the Economy: Theoretical and Empirical Extensions," *American Sociological Review* 45 (February 1980): 146–154; John M. Echols III, "Does Socialism Mean Greater Equality? A Comparison of East and West along Several Major Dimensions," *American Journal of Political Science* 25 (February 1981): 1–31; Ivan Szelenyi, "Social Inequalities in State Socialist Redistributive Economies," *International Journal of Comparative Sociology* 19 (March–June 1978): 63–87; Martin C. Schnitzer and James W. Nordyke, *Comparative Economic Systems*, 2d ed. (Cincinnati, Ohio: South-Western, 1977), pp. 362–387; Michael Swafford, "Sex Differences in Soviet Earnings," *American Sociological Review* 43 (October 1978): 657–671; Alastair McAuley, "Earnings and Incomes in the Soviet Union," *Soviet Studies* 29 (April 1977): 234; Gerhard Lenski, "Marxist Experiments in Destratification: An Appraisal," *Social Forces* 57 (December 1978): 364–383; Steven Lukes, "Socialism and Equality," *Dissent* 22 (Spring 1975): 154–168; and three essays in John R. Moroney, ed., *Income Inequality: Trends and International Comparisons* (Lexington, Mass.: Heath, 1979): John R. Moroney, "Introduction," pp. 4–7, 16–17; Harold F. Lydall, "Some Problems in

Making International Comparisons of Inequality," pp. 30–34; Janet G. Chapman, "Are Earnings More Equal under Socialism: The Soviet Case, with Some United States Comparisons," pp. 43–59.
6. Alexander J. Groth, "The 'Isms' in Totalitarianism," *American Political Science Review* 58 (December 1964): 888–901; Roland Sarti, *Fascism and the Industrial Leadership in Italy, 1919–1940: A Study in the Expansion of Private Power under Fascism* (Berkeley: University of California Press, 1971); S. J. Woolf, "Italy," in *European Fascism*, ed. S. J. Woolf (New York: Vintage Books, 1969), pp. 39–60; S. Lombardini, "Italian Fascism and the Economy," in *The Nature of Fascism*, ed. S. J. Woolf (New York: Vintage Books, 1969), pp. 152–164; William Jannen, Jr., "National Socialists and Social Mobility," *Journal of Social History* 9 (Spring 1976): 352.
7. Malcolm Sawyer, "Income Distribution in OECD Countries," *OECD Economic Outlook: Occasional Studies*, July 1976, pp. 17–19.
8. See David R. Cameron, "The Expansion of the Public Economy: A Comparative Analysis," *American Political Science Review* 72 (December 1979): 1243–1261; Christopher Hewitt, "The Effect of Political Democracy and Social Democracy on Equality in Industrial Societies: A Cross-National Comparison," *American Sociological Review* 42 (June 1977): 450–462; Steven Stack and Christopher Hewitt, "The Effects of Political Participation and Socialist Party Strength on the Degree of Income Inequality," *American Sociological Review* 44 (February 1979): 168–172; John Dryzek, "Politics, Economics, and Inequality: A Cross-National Analysis," *European Journal of Political Research* 6 (December 1978): 399–410; Francis G. Castles and R. D. McKinlay, "Public Welfare Provision, Scandinavia, and the Sheer Futility of the Sociological Approach to Politics," *British Journal of Political Science* 9 (April 1979): 157–171; Frank Castles and Robert D. McKinlay, "Does Politics Matter: An Analysis of the Public Welfare Commitment in Advanced Democratic States," *European Journal of Political Research* 7 (June 1979): 169–186; Sten G. Borg and Francis G. Castles, "The Influence of the Political Right on Public Income Maintenance Expenditure and Equality," *Political Studies* 29 (December 1981): 604–621; Walter Korpi and Michael Shalev, "Strikes, Industrial Relations, and Class Conflict in Capitalist Societies," *British Journal of Sociology* 30 (June 1979): 178; Conrad A. Blyth, "The Interaction between Collective Bargaining and Government Policies in Selected Member Countries," in *Collective Bargaining and Government Policies* (Paris: Organisation for Economic Cooperation and Development, 1979), pp. 59–93, esp. pp. 92–93.
9. See Charles F. Andrain, *Politics and Economic Policy in Western Democracies* (North Scituate, Mass.: Duxbury Press, 1980), pp. 179–202; Martin Schnitzer, *Income Distribution: A Comparative Study of the United States, Sweden, West Germany, East Germany, the United Kingdom, and Japan* (New York: Praeger, 1974), pp. 60–93, 165–199; Thomas Franzén, Kerstin Lövgren, and Irma Rosenberg, "Redistributional Effects of Taxes and Public Expenditures in Sweden," *Swedish Journal of Economics* 77, no. 1 (1975): 31–55; Richard Scase, *Social Democracy in Capitalist Society: Working-Class Politics in Britain and Sweden* (London: Croom, Held, 1977), pp. 58–61; A. B. Atkinson, "Inequality under Labour," *New Society* 48 (April 26, 1979): 194–195; Stewart Lansley, "Changes in Inequality and Poverty in the UK, 1971–1976," *Oxford Economic Papers* 32 (March 1980): 134–150; Chris Pond, "Inequalities Widen," *New Society* 54 (November 6, 1980): 279–280; "Tax System Hurts the Poor," *New Society* 51 (February 21, 1980): 896.
10. See John D. Stephens, "Class Formation and Class Consciousness: A Theoretical and Empirical Analysis with Reference to Britain and Sweden," *British Journal of Sociology* 30 (December 1979): 389–414; Korpi and Shalev, "Strikes, Industrial Relations, and Class Conflict in Capitalist Societies," pp. 164–187; Scase, *Social Democracy in Capitalist Society*; Richard M. Coughlin, *Ideology and Social Policy: A Comparative Study of the Structure of Public Opinion in Eight Rich Nations* (Ph.D. dissertation, Department of Sociology, University of California, Berkeley, 1977), pp. 153–174.
11. Cameron, "The Expansion of the Public Economy," pp. 1257–1259; Castles and McKinlay, "Public Welfare Provision," p. 171; Colin S. Rallings amd Rudy B. Andeweg, "The Changing Class Structure and Political Behaviour—A Comparative Analysis of Lower Middle-Class Politics in Britain and the Netherlands," *European Journal of Political Research* 7 (March 1979): 37; Sidney Verba, Norman H. Nie,

and Jae-on Kim, *Participation and Political Equality: A Seven-Nation Comparison* (London: Cambridge University Press, 1978), p. 287; Jan Pen, "A Clear Case of Income Leveling: Income Equalization in the Netherlands," *Social Research* 46 (Winter 1979): 682–694.
12. See Andrain, *Politics and Economic Policy*, esp. pp. 10–59, 173–230.
13. Sawyer, "Income Distribution in OECD Countries," pp. 14–20; Hewitt, "The Effect of Political Democracy and Social Democracy," p. 545; *Revenue Statistics of OECD Member Countries 1965–1979* (Paris: Organisation for Economic Cooperation and Development, 1980), pp. 45–46, 55; *National Accounts of OECD Countries, 1962–1979*, vol. 2 (Paris: Organisation for Economic Cooperation and Development, 1981), table 9 for each nation; *OECD Observer* no. 109 (March 1981): 20–21; "The Rise in Public Expenditure: How Much Further Can It Go?" *OECD Observer* no. 92 (May 1978): 8; Olivier Lorsignol, "Counting the Cost of Welfare's Growing Burden," *Vision* no. 66 (May 1976): 33.

PART

Political Structures

A third foundation of political systems is the power of government institutions and political parties in the public policy process. The structural dimensions of government involve the interactions among central government organizations, lower government agencies, and social groups. When comparing political systems, the political scientist pays particular attention to five dimensions of government power:

1. The balance between coercive and consensual power in formulating and implementing public policies
2. The degree of centralized government power
3. The extent to which a single political organization, either a government agency or a political party, coordinates the policy process
4. The degree of social pluralism—that is, the relative independence of social groups from the government
5. The scope of government power—the range of activities falling under government control

Chapter 6 uses these five structural dimensions to compare modern government systems in North America, West Europe, East Europe, Africa, and Latin America.

Chapter 7 analyzes the impact of government on the economic sector, especially the power of private corporations and labor unions. Four models—capitalism, corporatism, state socialism, and market socialism—illustrate the structural relationships between the political and economic systems.

Chapter 8 examines the power of political parties in the decision-making processes of constitutional governments. Whereas the dominant party in state socialist societies and other bureaucratic dictatorships claims to represent the whole system, political parties in constitutional systems form one part of the governing institutions. Rather than a monistic power relationship, pluralistic arrangements characterize the interactions among party activists, government officials, heads of social groups, and voters. A single party does not permanently guide the government; instead, several parties, government agencies, social groups, and the electorate share political power in constitutional systems.

CHAPTER
6

Governments

What is government itself but the greatest of all reflections on human nature?

—JAMES MADISON

Why is government necessary? Focusing on the relations between government and social groups, political theorists since the time of the ancient Greeks have suggested two different answers. One interpretation takes a positive view of government. Because social groups have neither the will nor the resources to attain common goals, government exists to direct the populace toward moral ends. The Greek philosopher Plato (427–347 B.C.) and his student, Aristotle (384–322 B.C.), assumed that government was necessary for people to realize their highest potentialities. They made no distinction between government and society, between the political and the social. Having no term for "society," they perceived that the *polis*, the organized political community, performed general activities.

In effect, the Athenian *polis* functioned as a moral, religious, educational, and economic community, as well as a political association. For Plato, the *polis* should reconstitute the existing order according to a set of ideal principles or eternal Forms. Because only philosophers have true knowledge of these unchanging Forms, they have the responsibility to reshape the existing corrupt world in light of ideal values. According to Aristotle, only the *polis*, the "final and perfect association," realized the self-sufficient life. Because the *polis* exists for the sake of attaining moral goodness, it must perform comprehensive, rather than specialized, activities. Therefore, it should regulate property relations, cultivate the soul, and educate the citizens toward mental pursuits.[1]

Since the time of Plato and Aristotle, other political philosophers, such as Hegel (1770–1831), have sketched similar visions of the positive role government plays in social life. Unlike the Greeks, Hegel recognized the pluralistic nature of modern society. Writing during the early nineteenth century in Prussian Germany, he upheld the distinction between private and public activities. Yet like Plato and Aristotle, he posited a superior role for the government. Amid the individualism, group diversity, and widespread pursuit of particular interests characterizing modern civil society, the state exists to provide solidarity and to integrate the conflicting interests. Hegel contrasted the comprehensive activities of the state with the more particular functions of other associations. For example, the family does seek the general welfare, but for only a limited kinship group. Commercial and professional groups in the market society focus on the pursuit of their own segmental interests. Only the state shows a general altruism; thus, individuals and social groups need the state to transcend their limited self-interests and to realize the general, comprehensive, solidary purposes of the whole community.[2]

The classical liberal theorists, such as James Madison, one author of *The Federalist Papers*, disputed this positive interpretation of the modern state. Writing at the end of the eighteenth century, at a time when state conventions were debating the adoption of the new American federal constitution, Madison stressed the negative and limited functions of modern government. Like Hegel, Madison recognized that economic interest groups, or what he called "factions," operated primarily to pursue their own interests—that is, greater wealth, power, and status for themselves. According to him, however, government exists neither to destroy nor to transcend these self-interested factions but rather to regulate the group struggle. As he wrote in *The Federalist Papers*, nos. 10 and 51, individuals and groups are naturally self-interested. "If men were angels, no government would be necessary." Because human beings are not angels, we cannot rely, as did Plato, on enlightened statesmen or on moral, religious motives to attain justice. Instead, freedom involves incorporating different interest groups in government operations. When interest and ambition check each other, an enlightened political conscience becomes unnecessary.

A system of countervailing powers secures the desirable balance between anarchy and tyranny. For Madison, anarchy results when several powerful self-interested social groups oppress the weaker factions. Tyranny operates if all government power becomes concentrated in the same individuals. Madison believed that the republican system drawn up by the 1787 constitutional convention would avert both tyranny and anarchy, because the system provided for the representation of diverse interests. Within society, the multiplicity of interests would secure freedom. Within the central government, the division of powers among legislative, executive, and judicial branches would check the dangers of tyranny. Competition between the federal and state governments would also guarantee freedom. By regulating the inevitable group conflicts inherent in a market society, government would secure order. Hence, the family, church, and private business firms would have the liberty to pursue their own interests free from both group and government oppression.[3] In sum, Madison perceived government as a concrete structure needed to regulate the group struggle so that diverse groups could pursue their own interests.

The Concept of Government

Political theorists have interpreted government in terms of its distinctive goals, means, and consequences. Not only the ancient Greeks but also some contemporary social scientists view government as a goal-seeking structure. From the Platonic perspective, even if political leaders never fully attain civic virtue, their behavior must be judged according to whether they have followed their own private interests or the common good.[4] Similarly, contemporary social scientists often define government from a normative viewpoint. Some conceive that government exists to provide order for the whole society. Others believe that government has the primary responsibility for a society's maintenance and adaptation to change.[5]

As these definitions suggest, the main problem of interpreting government from a normative, goal-seeking orientation lies in the difficulty of distinguishing the purposes unique to government. Historically, government leaders have pursued a wide variety of goals. Some have tried to attain civic virtue, order, and societal maintenance. Others have seemingly aimed at civil vice, disorder, and societal disintegration. Furthermore, which goals ought to take priority as uniquely governmental ends? Civic virtue and moral perfection may come into conflict with order and system maintenance. Finally, other social organizations, such as the church, also have responsibility for pursuing the general welfare and moral goodness. Therefore, as Max Weber reminds us, the conception of government in terms of its moral ends remains inadequate for understanding political life:

> There is scarcely any task that some political association has not taken in hand, and there is no task that one could say has always been exclusive and peculiar to those associations which are designated as political ones. ... Ultimately, one can define the modern state sociologically only in terms of the specific *means* peculiar to it, as to every political association, namely, the use of physical force.[6]

Like most modern social scientists, Weber interprets the state, one form of government, in terms of the distinctive means (physical force) used to enforce obedience:

> A state is a human community that (successfully) claims the *monopoly of the legitimate use of physical force* within a given territory.... The state is considered the sole source of the "right" to use violence. Hence, "politics" for us means striving to share power or striving to influence the distribution of power, either among states or among groups within a state.[7]

From this perspective, government appears as the organization of violence and coercion; the army and the police constitute the distinctive units of the modern state. Even if such democratic processes as electioneering and coalition building do not involve outright exercise of physical force, they do reveal coercive threats.[8]

Unfortunately, this "realistic" conception of government contains as many limitations as the normative perspective. Historically, few governments have held a monopoly of weapons. In fact, not until around 1700 did even a few central governments in West Europe gain control over most coercive forces; only at that time did the army come under central government domination. Central police forces emerged a century later. Before then, physical coercion was largely decentralized. At the local level, peer group pressures and other informal sanctions, rather than a specialized military or centralized police force, regulated "deviant" behavior. Even if the central government did exercise a monopoly over physical coercion, the exercise of that coercion was rarely considered "legitimate," as indicated by the widespread local resistance to growing state control. Between 1400 and 1800, West Europe experienced numerous food riots, anti-tax rebellions, violent struggles against central government attempts to control local churches, and revolts against military conscription. Presumably, all these forms of resistance indicated a popular disregard for the state's legitimacy or "right" to use violence.[9]

Another difficulty with defining the state in terms of physical force stems from a faulty conception about the nature of political power. As chapter 3 suggests, coercive power refers mainly to a *way* of using resources, not to the resources themselves. Physical coercion means more than the mere possession of extensive weapons. Instead, we can best conceive of coercive power as the use of resources so that punishment actually results or that someone feels threatened by possible future punishments. Under this interpretation, all social organizations, not just the central government, can use resources in a coercive way, a consensual manner, or most often a combination of coercion and consensus.

Faced with the limitations of viewing government in terms of the goals its leaders should seek or the methods they use to rule, other social scientists focus on the *consequences* of government activities. According to this conception, government is a steering instrument, a concrete structure that actually steers society or the social groups within it. The word *government* derives from the Latin *gubernare*—to steer, to pilot, to navigate—which comes from the Greek *kubernan*. For Plato, politics or governing involves steering; government leaders act as navigators. Just as the navigator uses the steering mechanism (the helm) to guide ships to port, so the government leader uses government to guide social groups toward certain goals.[10] From this perspective, government leaders seek a variety of goals, not just moral perfection, civic virtue, public order, or system maintenance. When exercising power, they use a variety of resources in both a coercive and consensual manner.

The consequences that result from the exercise of political power may not necessarily correspond with the leaders' stated intentions. As George Bernard Shaw commented in *Man and Superman*, although the government official wants to reach his destination safely, he may in fact land on the rocks. Poking fun at Plato's analogy between the political philosopher and the navigator, Shaw constructs the following exchange between Don Juan and the Devil:

> Don Juan: Does a ship sail to its destination no better than a log drifts nowhither? The philosopher is Nature's pilot. And there you have our difference: to be in Hell is to drift: to be in Heaven is to steer.
> The Devil: On the rocks, most likely.[11]

The interpretation of government as a steering instrument does not confuse formal authority with the actual power to make crucial decisions for society. Whatever its formal authority, government is the concrete structure that actually steers society; its policies have a widespread public impact on the society. As Robert Vaison points out:

> A policy is public, then, not because of the legal status of the particular organization (or individual) formulating it but rather because of the nature and effect of the policy itself. It is public if it directly or indirectly affects members of the society outside the organization initiating the policy.[12]

The comparative political scientist must ascertain the extent to which the family, church, and economic firms, as well as the formal institutions labeled "government," actually steer the society. Before the rise of the modern nation-state, these other social organizations acted like governments. Within the stateless societies of precolonial Africa, the councils of elders, composed of the heads of various families, made binding policies affecting the whole village; in effect, they steered the society.

During the European Middle Ages, the Roman Catholic church exercised power over a wide variety of activities—taxation, defense, education, health, provision of social welfare, and coordination of economic goods. When it made and carried out decisions linked to these comprehensive activities, the church acted like a government or steering instrument for society; it exerted a general impact on social groups.

Between 1750 and 1900, economic corporations, such as the British East India Company, the United Dutch East India Company, the British South Africa Company, and the Royal Niger Company, made binding policies over the inhabitants of Asian and African territories. Through their own courts and police forces, they administered justice and provided order, two activities associated with government.

In the United States between 1870 and 1950, some corporation executives controlled the political processes within a company town. They formulated local regulations, controlled access to the town, censored the mails, handled credit, provided housing for the workers, owned churches and schools, and recruited ministers, teachers, and police. By performing these comprehensive activities, corporation executives effectively steered social life within the company town.[13]

Today some observers believe that multinational corporations, with budgets larger than those of most nation-states, actually exercise greater impact on non-Western societies than does the formal central government. If they do indeed steer these societies, we may regard them as "governments," even if they do not have formal governmental authority.

By focusing on the consequences of structural activities, we broaden the conception of government. Not all concrete structures bearing the label "government" really steer a society. To understand the actual power relations within a society, we need to examine the interaction between families, churches, economic firms, and formal government institutions. What impact does each organization have on the society, especially on the other associations? Answers to this question will help the investigator uncover the effective steering mechanisms.

Emergence of the Nation-State

As the dominant governmental form today, the nation-state represents a type of government arising in a specific historical context — that is, fifteenth-century West Europe, especially England, Spain, France, and Holland. State officials attempted to secure dominance over both the local feudal lords and the more universal Roman Catholic church. In the beginning, the centralizing monarch embodied state sovereignty; he ruled through a dynastic state, a government type where the same family dominates for several generations. Later, at the time of the French Revolution of 1789, when King Louis XVI lost his head, the dynastic state transformed into the nation-state. Rather than belonging just to the king, the state supposedly now belonged to all the people. During the next 150 years, similar transformations took place in most other West European societies. Although the king rarely lost his head, he did lose his supreme political power. Parliament, actually the cabinet and civil service, came to exercise the decisive power. Instead of ruling, the monarch reigned as a ceremonial figure.

Originally, the state also consolidated its power against not only local feudal lords and their families but also against the Roman Catholic church. The state stood forth as a specialized administrative structure separate from the church. Although secular, it was regarded, like the church, as eternal and transcendental. State officials gained the power to regulate ecclesiastical affairs.

Especially between 1450 and 1800, the state asserted its supremacy over economic affairs. At this time, the capitalists allied with the monarch to pursue an economic policy of mercantilism. Under the mercantilist system, the nation-state closely supervised economic enterprises. Because states were engaged in bitter conflicts with each other, foreign policy took precedence over domestic matters. Each state tried to import as much gold and silver bullion as possible so that it had the wealth to carry out an aggressive foreign policy. To strengthen the political power of the state, government officials regulated foreign trade, monetary affairs, domestic investment, prices, and wages. Domestic economic monopolies became common. Overseas, governments founded colonies to provide raw materials to the home country. Assuming that manufacturing and industrial development would reinforce state power, government officials encouraged these economic activities. Unlike laissez-faire theorists, such as Adam Smith, mercantilists believed that the public interest coincided with the will of the state, not with the desires of private entrepreneurs. Hence, state officials dictated economic policy to the emerging capitalist class.[14]

Despite their later support for a laissez-faire economic policy, the capitalists in England, France, and even the United States originally supported the rise of a strong state. Compared with feudal systems and the commercial city-states, the nation-state expanded the geographic scope of political power. By establishing "law and order," guaranteeing contracts, promoting trade, encouraging manufacturing, upholding a stable currency, and ensuring widespread geographic labor mobility, a strong national government facilitated the creation of larger economic markets. For this reason, the emerging European businessmen usually allied with the monarch to strengthen the power of the state.

Even in the United States, such diverse leaders as Tom Paine and Alexander Hamilton supported the establishment of a stronger national government than existed under the confederal system.

Hamilton, a mercantilist, wanted the national government to subsidize the American manufacturers. A more populist, democratic thinker than Hamilton, Tom Paine represented the interests of small business owners and artisans. They wanted a more powerful national government that would establish the conditions, such as a national bank, for an extensive economic market. Only after the emergence of giant economic corporations following the Civil War did American business leaders come to articulate laissez-faire notions about the proper structural relationship between government and private economic firms.

Similarly, in Europe, especially England, the nineteenth century represented the greatest popularity of laissez-faire doctrines. Reflecting the views of Adam Smith and David Ricardo, business leaders sought to remove the government restrictions on private economic activity that had been erected during the mercantilist era.[15] Outside the United States, Canada, and Britain, however, the tradition of a strong state regulating private firms persisted throughout the nineteenth and twentieth centuries.

During the twentieth century, the nation-state has become the dominant government form throughout the world. With the breakup of European colonial empires in the post–World War II era, African and Asian colonies gained their political independence. Seizing control of the bureaucratic structures from colonial civil servants, Afro-Asian nationalist leaders tried to strengthen state power vis-a-vis local families, religious organizations, and economic groups. In the more industrialized parts of Europe and Latin America as well, the state strengthened its power. Both in West and East Europe, the social service state expanded its functions in such areas as health, education, economic planning, and housing. During the 1960s and 1970s, most Latin American countries experienced military coups. After the military gained control of the state, it ruled more coercively than had the more democratic regimes.

The following sections analyze three aspects of the growing powers of the contemporary nation-state. First, I examine several structural dimensions of state power. Then I compare three specific types of nation-states: personal autocracies, bureaucratic dictatorships, and constitutional governments. Next I explain the reasons for the greater strength of state power in some countries (the Soviet Union and France) than in other nations (the United States and Britain).

Structural Dimensions of State Power

Rather than compare nation-states according to their formal government institutions (for example, presidency, cabinet, parliament, courts of law), many political scientists have based their comparisons on general structural dimensions that reflect interactions among the central state organs, lower government agencies, and social groups.[16] Five structural dimensions characterize a powerful nation-state: monopoly of coercive force, centralization of power, coordination of government activities, specialization and autonomy from social groups, and comprehensive scope of power. I shall use these five components of state power to compare different types of nation-states.

MONOPOLY OF COERCIVE FORCE

First, a powerful state monopolizes the means of coercion, denying lower government agencies and social groups the right to hold weapons. As agents of physical coercion, the military and police wield crucial control. The modern nation-state early became involved in numerous foreign wars. As a result, the power of the professionalized army increased. In turn, the military strove for greater government centralization, territorial integrity, and political specialization—all structural aspects of the state. A specialized police force also accompanied the consolidation of strong state power.

CENTRALIZATION OF POWER

Second, a powerful state features a high centralization of political power. The national or central government gains dominance over local political units, such as village assemblies, town councils, municipal governments, and provincial administrations. This centralized power enables the state to maintain the territorial integrity of the nation. Because central state structures govern clearly defined territorial boundaries, local organizations lack the power to secede from the state to join a neighboring state or to establish another independent nation-state.

COORDINATION OF GOVERNMENT ACTIVITIES

Third, under a powerful nation-state, a single agency formally coordinates the functional activities of government. Originally, the monarch claimed to exercise "sovereignty," the absolute legal right to make final decisions binding on the society. He and the royal bureaucracy coordinated central government activities. When the king lost his power, the president, parliament, or dominant political party assumed the sovereign authority formerly exercised by the monarch.

SPECIALIZATION AND AUTONOMY FROM SOCIAL GROUPS

Fourth, in its relationship with social groups, a powerful state becomes both differentiated (specialized) and independent. Ancient government forms, like those in precolonial segmentary African societies or in the Athenian city-state, made no clear distinction between public and private spheres. Government activities were neither differentiated nor independent from other social groups, such as leading families, the church, or economic associations. With the emergence of the nation-state, political activities came to be performed by more specialized government institutions: legislatures, executives, administrations, and courts. These state institutions also attempted to gain a functional autonomy from powerful primordial, religious, and economic groups.

COMPREHENSIVE SCOPE OF POWER

Fifth, particularly in industrialized societies, a strong nation-state exercises a wide scope of power; that is, it performs a comprehensive variety of activities: system maintenance, construction of an economic infrastructure, and provision of social services to individuals. When the modern nation-state system first came into existence during the fifteenth century, the central government concentrated on system maintenance—the preservation of the territorial integrity of the fragile nation-state. Most public policies involved defense, foreign affairs, internal order, and the raising of revenues through levying taxes and printing a national currency.

At the beginning of the nineteenth century, the construction of an economic infrastructure assumed greater importance as a distinctive state activity. Government policies stimulated the construction of public works, such as roads, railways, and canals. Postal and telegraph services spread throughout the national territory. State subsidies promoted industry, commerce, and agriculture.

During the twentieth century, particularly after World War I, the growing popularity of democratic values, the rising strength of socialist movements, the industrializing process, and the severe effects of world wars led state officials to design public policies that allocated social services to individuals.[17] As industrialization advanced, individuals have become less self-sufficient. The growing specialization of labor, interdependence, and societal impersonality stimulate popular demands for government to enact public policies that will meet individual needs. Since World War II, central governments have thus spent an increasing share of public revenues on such programs as health, education, social security (old-age pensions), unemployment compensation, family allowances, and recreational facilities. All these services have increased the state's scope of power.

Types of Nation-States

PERSONAL AUTOCRACIES

Personal autocracies have prevailed at the early stage of a state's development. In Europe between 1600 and 1800, so-called "absolute monarchs" ruled such states as France, Prussian Germany, Spain, and Russia. In France, for example, Louis XIV (1643–1715) governed the French nation as the "Sun King," the radiating center of all political authority. Claiming to embody the state, he declared: "L'État, c'est Moi" (I am the state). Similarly, after African territories secured political independence during the late 1950s and early 1960s, personal autocratic rule became widespread. Although the traditional monarchies had long since decayed under colonial rule, new presidential monarchies emerged, led by military officials or nationalist politicians. Kwame Nkrumah of Ghana, Sékou Touré of Guinea, Félix Houphouët-Boigny of the Ivory Coast, Idi Amin of Uganda, and Mobutu Sese Soko of Zaire are examples of personal autocrats on the African continent.[18]

Absolutist monarchies in pre-twentieth-century Europe. European traditional monarchs claimed to exercise absolute rule; however, their control over society was limited. Compared with the more bureaucratic twentieth-century dictatorial military or party state, their absolutist state was weak rather than strong. True, the monarch tried to monopolize the means of coercion. Gradually gaining control over regional armies controlled by feudal nobles, the king instituted a more professionalized standing army and war fleet. Yet the continuous involvement in foreign wars led to military defeats as often as to victories. State debts increased as the army floundered through a succession of abortive military maneuvers. As a result, the monarch maintained only limited control over the instruments of coercion within the nation.

The monarch's power over local governments was also less centralized than the absolutist label would suggest. Even under Louis XIV, who concentrated political power in the royal court, the central state bureaucracy lacked the resources to implement all the detailed royal edicts. Thus, the monarch had to delegate authority to various local agencies such as royal *intendants* (provincial administrators), *parlements* (judicial corporations or courts of appeal), municipal corporations, and local communities of privileged nobles. Although supervised by these royal officials, the villages largely retained independent power over local decision making. Even in Russia, where personal autocratic rule reached a high level and where the czar allowed little autonomous power to the landed aristocracy, the central state lacked the resources to control village life. Nominally supervised by the czarist bureaucracy, the village communes and assemblies made crucial decisions at the local level. Because the provincial administration was understaffed and often poorly qualified, the heads of local families operating through these local organizations exercised effective decentralized power.

Although the European monarch claimed to embody sovereign authority—the legal right to exercise supreme, absolute, unified, indivisible, ultimate, and perpetual power—in reality, he lacked the staff to coordinate all government activities effectively. The need to delegate authority meant that the king had to rely on others for accurate information about policy implementation. Yet the failure to receive accurate information or to process it intelligently often led to ineffective coordination of policymaking activities.

Under the monarchical system of personal rule, the central state also never gained complete independence from social groups, including aristocratic families, the church, and economic enterprises. Even though the king moved to curtail the power of the feudal nobility, aristocratic lords still retained some privileges, such as exemption from certain taxes, military service, and legal regulations. Particularly in Russia and Sweden, the monarch secured control over churches. The Orthodox church in Russia and the Lutheran church in Sweden became state churches. Yet the churches did not lose all their autonomy. In exchange for the king's powers to appoint high clergy and to seize church property for the Crown's domain, church officials secured a monopoly over religious worship and the right to advise the ruler on political matters.

Through a mercantilist policy, the monarch tried to consolidate his control over private business firms and to strengthen the power of the nation-state. Under mercantilism, the state controlled prices, regulated competition, directed production toward specific projects, and supervised the training of laborers. By expanding exports and accumulating the nation's bullion reserves, the monarch sought to raise the revenues needed for waging international war and for operating a lavish court. Despite these statist attempts to regulate the economy, many economic activities operated beyond state control. Feudal aristocrats retained private ownership of their land. Peasants raised their crops free from bureaucratic supervision. Economic entrepreneurs freely carried on an active smuggling trade. Without an industrial infrastructure and an efficient state bureaucracy, monarchical power over the economy remained limited.

As the preceding discussion suggests, the autocratic ruler also wielded a limited scope of power. Major government activities revolved around maintaining the nation-state's territorial integrity. Actively involved in international wars, the monarch concentrated on recruiting troops for the armed forces and on raising taxes to finance the war effort; most taxes were levied on land, trade, and people. Besides defeating foreign powers, securing internal order preoccupied the emerging state bureaucracy. By 1800, central police forces had begun to emerge in several European nations. Pursuing a mercantilist economic policy, the central state also started to construct an economic infrastructure. The state subsidized the building of railroads, highways, and canals. It established a uniform national currency and a national tax system. As means to wage war, weapons and armed fleets took high priority in the manufacturing sector. However, the central government devoted little attention to providing social services for individuals. The church, family, and individual still assumed major responsibility for health, education, employment, and old-age security.[19]

In sum, the autocratic ruler in Europe between 1400 and 1800 failed to secure extensive control over the society. Although monarchs governed as dictators at the central government level, they wielded only limited power over local government officials, village life, and social groups. Not until the nineteenth and twentieth centuries did the top state leaders gain the industrial resources and the bureaucratic staff needed to shape life throughout the society. The weak power that personal rulers wielded thus contradicted their claims to absolute sovereign authority.

Autocratic rule in twentieth-century Africa. In some contemporary African nations, although the personal ruler may want to strengthen the new state's power, the presidential monarch actually undermines the establishment of effective political institutions. An institution is a stable collection of roles with three primary dimensions:

1. Role *expectations*—the rules specifying the rights and duties associated with a position such as bureaucrat, president, or legislator
2. Role *sanctions*—the rewards and punishments that result from obeying or disobeying the role expectations
3. The *perceptions* and *behavior* of an individual who occupies a particular role[20]

Compared with contemporary Africa, more industrialized societies, whether democracies or dictatorships, have clearer role expectations.

The sanctions operate independently of the central ruler; other agencies outside the main leader's control have the power to prescribe penalties for violations of the rules. For example, in the United States, congressional and Supreme Court actions motivated Richard Nixon to resign the presidency. The power of political institutions hence seems to overweigh the power of a single individual ruler.

In Africa, however, the institutional basis of rule remains fragile. Role expectations are ambiguous; because of the recent origin of state institutions, modern bureaucratic expectations come into conflict with more traditional informal expectations associated with ethnic group and family life. The personal ruler has the power to prescribe role sanctions; obedience brings personal favors, including access to the state treasury. Disobedience means exile, torture, or death, as happened under General Amin in Uganda. For these reasons, the presidential monarch's role perceptions and behavior play a crucial part in political decision making. Like Machiavelli's prince, the African president has the opportunity to create new institutions that mirror his perceptions of appropriate role behavior. More often than not, however, personal intentions clash with the outcomes. By killing the educated Africans, smashing the bureaucracy, wasting the public treasury on lavish personal displays, and allowing widespread corruption, the African ruler may actually destroy the state institutions. Rather than guiding the ship safely to port, the absolute ruler can steer the ship so badly that it lands on the rocks, as happened in Uganda under Idi Amin. Instead of maintaining the political system, he helped undermine the Ugandan nation-state.[21]

As an examination of the five structural components of the state indicates, most contemporary African states, particularly the personal autocracies, are weak, fragmented, and noninstitutionalized. First, like the autocratic monarchs of seventeenth-century Europe, African leaders today try to monopolize the means of coercion in the state. They concentrate on strengthening the coercive power of the military and police. Yet neither they nor their army officers have secured extensive control over the use of armed force. Guerrilla bands in the hinterlands try to seize political power. Foreign armies intervene in military struggles. Whatever their pretensions to imperial grandeur, contemporary African rulers thus appear militarily impotent.

Second, decentralization of political power remains common. True, at the central government level, the personal ruler tries to consolidate power around his person; neither the legislature nor the courts retains autonomous power. At the regional and local levels, however, traditional leaders still exercise considerable decision-making power, at least the power to veto central government orders. Since the colonial power drew territorial boundaries independent of ethnic group locations, an ethnic group in one national territory often strongly identifies with the same group living in a neighboring nation-state. Thus, boundary disputes and demands for secession plague several African states. Under these irredentist conditions, many African leaders have difficulty governing territories where the boundaries of the state are not accepted.

Third, although some African rulers try to play the role of a presidential monarch, few have gained effective coordination of government activities. Most rulers lack the resources to exercise full sovereignty—that is, supreme authority within their territory and independence from external control. Rather than wielding absolute, unified, and perpetual authority, they demonstrate partial, fragmented, and short-lived authority.

Fourth, most African states are neither differentiated nor independent from social groups. Nearly all leaders govern culturally pluralistic societies, where family ties, ethnic loyalties, and religious identifications remain strong. The distinction between the private and the public spheres seems murky. Political life—the struggle to influence public policy—revolves around ethnic group conflicts, family rivalries, regional disputes, and patron–client connections. All these private groups become intimately involved in the policy process. Individuals seek political office to gain personal favors for themselves and their relatives; hence, corruption abounds. Public policies exist for private group gain. Instead of an independent, differentiated relationship linking the state with social groups, both show a functional interdependence.

Fifth, the autocratic rulers wield a limited scope of power in contemporary Africa. Under their neomercantilist strategy of economic development, the state concentrates on increasing the power of the new nation-state, which tries to defend the territory against external attack, to maintain internal security, to expand exports, to raise financial revenues, and to protect the national interest at international conferences. Defense, diplomacy, and external trade hence constitute the major state activities. The construction of an economic infrastructure also assumes some importance.

Although some state enterprises have been established, most African leaders strive for state direction and regulation of the economy, not widespread government ownership or comprehensive economic planning. Lacking a large, professionally trained state bureaucracy, the autocratic regimes stress the need for the state to construct communication and transportation facilities, subsidize foreign private investment, regulate imports and exports, and establish a unified national market. Even if they call themselves "African socialists," most African rulers give low priority to providing social services to individuals. Without an industrialized economic base, these new states cannot easily finance government expenditures on health care, education, old-age pensions, employment opportunities, leisure facilities, and public housing.[22] In sum, the activities of personal autocracies in Africa revolve around strengthening the territorial power of the state and on expanding national wealth, not on providing comprehensive social services. The state thus exercises a limited scope of power.

BUREAUCRATIC DICTATORSHIPS

Bureaucratic dictatorships control a stronger state than do personal autocracies. According to Max Weber, bureaucracy as an "ideal type" reveals several features:

1. Centralized, hierarchical relations prevail. Superiors at the top of the hierarchy strictly supervise the operations of personnel who work at the bottom of the hierarchy. Authority flows downward from the central bureaucrats, not upward from the lower-ranking civil servants.

2. The office and the person holding a bureaucratic position are separated. The role, not the individual role incumbent, assumes key importance. Individual bureaucrats make decisions according to the impersonal rights and duties associated with their position, rather than according to their personal discretion.

3. Appointment to an office takes place on the basis of individuals' professional qualifications and expertise, not their personal connections with a superior. Individuals spend a lifetime career in the bureaucracy; promotions are based on seniority and professional competence.[23]

During the twentieth century, two types of bureaucratic dictatorships—military bureaucracies in Latin America and party–state bureaucracies in communist regimes—have wielded extensive state power. In Argentina, Brazil, Chile, and Uruguay, when military dictatorships replace constitutional governments, the state's coercive, centralized power expands. A professionalized military bureaucracy makes the key decisions. Governed by technocrats, the civil service becomes more bureaucratized. A third powerful bureaucratic institution—the multinational corporation—also shares in politico-economic decision making. Although communist party-states pursue different ideological objectives and economic policies than the Latin American military dictatorships, they also follow bureaucratic rule. In the Soviet Union, other East European states, China, Vietnam, and North Korea, a powerful party bureaucracy checks the state bureaucracy. A professionalized military is tightly integrated into the party–state apparatus. Rather than "withering away," the state became more powerful (coercive, centralized, coordinated, autonomous, and comprehensive in scope) after the Communist party gained control of the government.

Communist party-states. In the communist party-states, the military and police play a dominant role. By keeping a vigilant watch over "dissident" activities, the police help maintain order and state control. Besides defending the nation-state against foreign aggression, the armed forces perform internal security functions.

Unlike the constitutional regimes, which retain a sharp distinction between military and civilian roles, the party-state integrates the military with the civilian sector. The armed forces are civilianized and the party is militarized. In all communist states, the civilian party controls the military and police. In the Soviet Union, the Bolshevik party engineered the revolution. As we saw in chapter 4, Lenin perceived an analogy beween the Party and an army. For him, revolution was civil war; only through military organization could the Communist party crush its counterrevolutionary opponents. Stalin strengthened the militarization process of party operations. According to him, "No army at war can dispense with an experienced General Staff if it does not want to court certain defeat. . . . The working class without a revolutionary party is an army without a General Staff. The Party is the General Staff of the proletariat."[24]

In China, Vietnam, and Cuba, party and army roles have historically been less differentiated than in the Soviet Union. Although subordinate to the Chinese Communist party, the People's Liberation Army has performed both military and civilian functions, such as waging war against Chiang Kai-shek, educating the populace, mobilizing the peasants for economic development projects, and maintaining order among contesting groups. In China, more so than in the USSR, top party leaders have also been military strategists. Just as the army plays a dominant role in civilian society, so the Party operates as a military instrument. This militarization of communism has reinforced the state's coercive power.

Communist party-states also feature a high centralization and coordination of political power. Organized hierarchically, the central government exercises the dominant power over regional and local governments, whose officials must submit to the orders handed down by top party–state leaders. In the Soviet Union, the centralized, hierarchical, bureaucratic trends are particularly pronounced. China under Mao Zedong and contemporary Yugoslavia have experienced greater regional decentralization.

Whatever the degree of centralized power, the Communist party in all communist societies coordinates government activities; it exercises "sovereign" authority. The Party dominates the policy process. From government ministers, technical specialists, trade union officials, and other organizations, it collects the information needed for political decision making. After weighing alternatives, the top party leaders, who are also the leading government officials, formulate basic policies, such as the priorities given to heavy industry, agricultural production, defense, and social services. Local party organizations then supervise the implementation of these public policies by government agencies and state enterprises. Local party activists also encourage citizens to report any deficiencies in policy administration to party organizations. In this way, the centralized party hierarchy assumes responsibility for coordinating the policy process.

Just as the Party dominates government decision making, it limits the independent power of social groups. Power relations in the party-state are monistic, not pluralistic. Besides differentiating itself from social groups—primordial, religious, and economic—the party-state achieves extensive autonomy from these groups. Unlike the situation in pluralistic constitutional regimes, where groups operate independent of state control, in communist states the Party incorporates nearly all groups within its fold. The Party organizes trade unionists, peasants, writers, artists, veterans, women, old people, youth, and students.

The organizations that mobilize social groups operate as "transmission belts" between Party and individual; they function both as instruments of popular participation and state control. Through these mass organizations, individuals articulate political demands; in turn, the central party–state leaders use these associations to transmit orders down through the hierarchy. The bureaucratization of social groups accompanies the bureaucratization of government. In short, no autonomous social group dominates the state structures; instead, a "ruling class" of party–state managers operates formal government institutions; with an engineering mentality, they try to produce changes in the society.

Of all the different types of nation-states, the communist party-states have exercised the widest scope of political power. The government performs a comprehensive range of activities, including the maintenance of territorial integrity, the construction of an economic infrastructure, and the provision of social services to individuals. Whereas in most other government systems a variety of groups—families, churches, private entrepreneurs, independent trade unions, foreign private investors—help stimulate economic development and provide basic services, in the communist party-states, government agencies carry out these tasks. Rather than subsidizing private enterprises, the state establishes public enterprises to promote rapid industrialization. The government also assumes responsibility for allocating social services, including health care, education, recreational facilities, cultural enrichment, family allowances for children, and pensions for the elderly. All these comprehensive activities expand the power of the state over individuals' lives.[25]

Latin American military dictatorships. Although the military dictatorships of Argentina, Brazil, Chile, and Uruguay pursue different ideological objectives and public policies than does the communist party-state, they too follow a bureaucratic mode of political rule. The military officers who staged coups in these four Latin American societies replaced relatively constitutional governments that exercised consensual, decentralized, and pluralistic power. Before the coups, various organizations—trade unions, peasant associations, newspapers, universities, political parties—had the civil liberties to express their demands to government officials. Popular competitive elections offered a mechanism for registering discontent and supporting certain policy positions.

After the military seized political power, however, it quashed civil liberties. Political repression increased, especially against left-wing movements. As the state centralized its power, local governments lost their autonomy. Military officers and civilian technocrats who coordinated the policy process exercised "sovereign authority." If allowed to function, the legislature merely ratified the executive orders of military officials. The state asserted its independence from social groups, especially trade unions, peasant associations, and small business owners. All these groups lost their access to state bureaucrats; in particular, unions lost the right to strike and to engage in free collective bargaining. The state assumed the right to represent worker and peasant interests. Finally, the military dictators, especially in Brazil, expanded the state's role in stimulating industrial investment and capital accumulation.

In short, like the communist party-states, the Latin American military bureaucracies have used coercive means, wielded centralized government power, achieved a higher coordination of state activities than their constitutional predecessors, and reduced the independent power of social groups, especially trade unions and peasant associations.[26]

Despite this similar mode of bureaucratic rule, crucial differences also separate the Latin American military dictatorships from the communist party-states. After all, the military officers came to power vowing to crush the Socialist and Communist parties, trade unions, peasant rebellions, and left-wing terrorists. Once in control of government, the armed forces govern on a different base of class rule and implement divergent public policies than do the Communist parties in East Europe, Asia, and Cuba.

The military dictatorships rule a weaker state and a more pluralistic society. For example, they have gained less extensive control over the means of coercion than have communist party-states. In both types of nation-states, the central government uses coercion to repress political opponents; indeed, compared with contemporary communist states, the four Latin American military-dominated states engage in more widespread, systematic torture of political opponents. Torture—the infliction of acute pain—operates as a routine administrative practice, rather than as an occasional way to suppress dissent. Not only the state but also paramilitary groups somewhat independent of government supervision engage in terror, torture, and assassination. Especially in Argentina, the top military leaders have failed to gain complete control over such groups as the Argentine Anti-Communist Alliance that torture and assassinate left-wing opponents.[27] In the communist states, however, the Party strictly supervises military and police activities. Although a higher rate of political dissidents per 100,000 population are imprisoned in communist states than in Latin American military dictatorships, organizations independent of Communist party control have fewer opportunities to use coercive force.

Compared with communist party-states, the Latin American bureaucratic states wield less centralized and coordinated power. Regional and local governments retain slightly greater autonomy. More important, no bureaucratically organized, dominant political party operates to coordinate the policy process. Either the military officers ban all political parties or else they allow parties few decisive powers over decision making. A professionalized military and a technocratic civil service coordinate government activities. They, not party leaders, formulate, implement, and supervise public policies.

In contrast to the Communist party elite, Latin American military dictators govern more pluralistic societies. Although the militarists crush the independent power of trade unions, peasant associations, and organizations representing small entrepreneurs (traders, merchants, and artisans), the state does allow multinational corporations and large-scale domestic private business firms to retain some economic autonomy. Indeed, it encourages extensive foreign private investment, loans from the International Monetary Fund and World Bank, and domestic private capital accumulation. Unlike trade union and peasant leaders, national and international capitalists have access to military officers and civilian technocrats who grant them special incentives to expand industrial investment. Through a bargaining process, military officers, civilian technocrats, domestic corporate executives, and international capitalists decide public policies free from popular interference.

Whereas in communist states the dominant party mobilizes workers and peasants in mass associations, Latin American military dictatorships demobilize these two groups. By banning leftist parties and suppressing independent trade unions, the state prevents lower-income people from organizing demands for higher pay, better working conditions, and increased consumer goods.

Finally, the Latin American military state exercises a less comprehensive scope of power than does the communist party-state. The military–civilian government bureaucrats concentrate on strengthening the state's territorial integrity and on constructing a more powerful economic infrastructure. The maintenance of internal order and the defense against communist "subversion" take precedence. After staging the coup d'etat, military leaders raise taxes, expand other financial revenues, and try to achieve a favorable balance of payments. Government economic activities revolve around expanding industrial investment, increasing exports, encouraging rapid economic growth rates, curtailing inflation, reducing wages, and eliminating inefficient private national business firms. Concerned with maximizing industrial investment, the state gives low priority to expanding consumer goods for the poor, increasing economic equality, or providing comprehensive social services. Families, private enterprises, and especially Roman Catholic churches assume primary responsibility for helping low-income individuals with their health, employment, nutritional, and educational needs. Thus, as the state tries to become an engine of capital accumulation, it plays a less active role in allocating basic social services to the poor.

CONSTITUTIONAL GOVERNMENTS

Unlike personal autocracies and bureaucratic dictatorships, constitutional regimes establish more effective mechanisms for ensuring representative government. Political representation means that government officials display accountability to some agency beyond themselves. In North America, West Europe, Australia, New Zealand, India, Japan, Costa Rica, and Venezuela, key government leaders owe some accountability to the voters. In parliamentary regimes such as Britain and Sweden, the voters elect legislators; the political party or parties gaining the most seats in parliament then choose the prime minister, who in turn selects a cabinet. The prime minister, cabinet, and appointed civil servants govern as an executive. In presidential regimes, such as the United States, France, and Venezuela, the electorate chooses both the president and the legislators. A greater division of powers occurs between the executive and legislative branches, although the legislature is far weaker in France than in the United States. Whether in a parliamentary or a presidential system, elected leaders remain accountable to the voters. If government officials fail to formulate and implement public policies preferred by a majority of the voters or if most voters dislike the personal characteristics of their elected leaders, then citizens have the authority to vote them out of office. Under this conception, representation implies a responsiveness to voters' views.[28]

The authors of *The Federalist Papers* foresaw the need to ensure a proper balance between the exercise of government power and the maintenance of effective representation. To secure justice, order, and stability, Alexander Hamilton and James Madison advocated a stronger national government than had existed under the Articles of Confederation. Yet they also stressed the need to make the legislative and executive branches of the federal government accountable to the citizens. According to Madison: "In framing a government which is to be administered by men over men, the great difficulty lies in this: you must first enable the government to control the governed; and in the next place oblige it to control itself."[29]

This issue of securing the best form of representative, constitutional government still faces democratic leaders today. How can a society best secure a government that will effectively use its power to resolve social problems yet avoid a lapse into tyranny? Arbitrary, tyrannical government results when officials who exercise political power concentrate all power in themselves, remaining unaccountable to any other group. Under immobilist systems, governments possess crucial responsibilities but lack the power to carry them out; government can neither initiate new policies nor implement established policies designed to meet pressing social crises. The following analysis of the five structural dimensions of state power explores how constitutional governments in North America and West Europe have dealt with the dilemma between power and responsibility.[30]

Restraints on coercive power. Constitutional governments establish civilian restraints on the wielders of coercion, especially the military and police. Consensual government power prevails over coercive force. Neither the military nor the police exercises independent political power.

Historically, France, Britain, and the United States have demonstrated divergent patterns of government coercion. In France, the military and police have formed key bases of state power. Early in its modern history, during the sixteenth and seventeenth centuries, the French central state established a regular standing army and a specialized police force. The police had general responsibilities to maintain public order, prevent fires, ensure a sanitary environment, regulate aliens, and register baptisms and burials. Military officers often intervened directly in civilian political institutions. Not until the 1970s did civilian officials solidify their control over the military and police. Today the elected president of the republic controls the armed forces; the Ministry of Interior, along with administrative courts, supervises police operations.

By contrast, in Britain neither the national military nor the central police gained the independent political power that they wielded in France. Local English aristocrats resisted the establishment of a strong army and central police until the nineteenth century. Even today the British police remain under more decentralized control than do French police. Only recently has the central government's Home Secretary, the national cabinet office responsible for internal security, won the authority to formulate regulations about the recruitment, promotion, termination, and discipline of local chief constables. Yet they still retain considerable autonomy from civilian officials such as the Home Secretary, elected local councillors, court judges, and local police committees.

In the United States, compared with Britain and particularly France, a professional military and a centralized police organization have wielded less extensive government power. Professional armed forces remained weak until World War II. State, county, city, and town police, not national police agencies, dominate the criminal justice system. Local police officers are often formally accountable to an elected mayor and appointed police commissioners; however, they exert minimal control over police activities. The major supervision originates inside the police organization from the police chief and police review boards. The lack of central government supervision over local police reflects the comparatively weak power of the American nation-state.[31]

Decentralization of power. Nearly all constitutional governments to some extent decentralize decision-making authority. The old distinction between "unitary" and "federal" states obscures the crucial powers local governments wield. For instance, France, Italy, Britain, and Sweden all function as unitary states; the central government supposedly has sovereignty—the supreme authority to make and enforce laws within a specified geographic area. Yet most unitary states, especially Italy, Sweden, and Britain, delegate important responsibilities to regional governments.

The French central bureaucracy most fully embodies the strong state tradition. Relatively efficient, unified, and cohesive, it possesses the power to implement public policies effectively. Despite these centralized arrangements, urban mayors, councillors in the *départements*, and regional councillors share some policymaking authority with the prefects—the civil servants accountable to the central state in Paris. These local officials have recently pressed the national government for a greater "deconcentration" of political power throughout France. The Italian state bureaucracy is weaker, more corrupt, and less unified than the French civil service. As a result, it faces difficulties carrying out the policies approved by the central parliament. Discouraged about the limited power of the national government to resolve basic problems, regional government leaders have recently gained greater authority over the Italian policy process.

Both the Swedish and the British central governments delegate crucial responsibilities to local government agencies. In Sweden, county governments help implement public policies, especially in the health care field. Even though the United Kingdom lacks a federal constitution, the central government has devolved some power to the regions. For example, Scotland maintains a separate legal system, an independent educational system, and its own established church, the Presbyterian Church of Scotland.[32]

Although federal systems feature greater decentralization, their constitutions give the national government significant decision-making authority. According to the formalistic definition, in a federal system, compared with a unitary state, the central government shares greater sovereignty with regional (provincial, state) governments that intervene between the national government and local (city, town) agencies.[33]

Yet in the actual operations of such federal systems as West Germany, Canada, and the United States, the national government retains significant authority over regional and local governments. In the Federal Republic of Germany, the national bureaucracy specifies uniform administrative and judicial standards for all the *Länder* (states); it supervises local administrative practices and regulates the training of *Länder* civil servants.

The distinctive political heritage of French-speaking Quebec has encouraged other Canadian provinces to demand political autonomy from the federal government in Ottawa. Recently, the provincial governments have increased their political influence, especially over health policy, education, and legal matters. Despite these decentralizing pressures, the federal civil service still wields extensive authority, particularly in the economic policy domain. The Canadian federal government owns and operates railroads, airlines, a television network, and radio stations. To administer these public corporations and implement other government programs requires a large federal civil service; over 40 percent of all Canadian public employees, compared with only 20 percent of American civil servants, work for the federal government.

Like the Canadian federal system, the U.S. federal structures disperse government responsibilities among the national, regional, city, and town governments. During the American Revolutionary War, the colonists rebelled against imperial authority and centralized rule. Since then, the "state" has referred to Massachusetts and Virginia, not to a sovereign central government. True, the central government bureaucracy achieved greater power during the 1930s. Yet even today leaders in the states retain extensive influence over domestic decisions, particularly those affecting education, health, highway construction, welfare services, and environment regulations. Although around 20 percent of state government revenues come from the central government, state leaders play a key role in deciding the specific ways to allocate these funds. However great the political decentralization in the United States, all state governments follow a uniform common law; the national Supreme Court has the authority to invalidate state court decisions.[34]

Coordination by elected officials. Most constitutional governments, except the United States system, feature a fairly high coordination of government activities by elected officials. Among contemporary democracies, three types of government coordination commonly occur:

1. In most states, parliament formally exercises sovereignty; actually, the prime minister, cabinet, and civil servants coordinate activities.
2. In France, the president of the republic assumes primary responsibility for making political decisions; under his direction, the cabinet of ministers and civil servants implement public policies.
3. In the United States, a division of powers occurs; the executive, Congress, and the courts all share decision-making authority. No single formal institution exercises sovereignty or coordinates the operations of diverse government operations.

In Britain, Canada, West Germany, the Scandinavian countries, the Netherlands, and Italy, the parliamentary system fuses legislative and executive powers. The elected parliament, not a ceremonial president or monarch, plays the key decision-making role. The party or parties securing the most seats in the parliament form the government. Chosen from the legislature, the prime minister appoints a cabinet of ministers, composed mainly of other legislators. Together, the prime minister, cabinet, and senior civil servants wield executive power. Whereas the prime minister directs the government, the monarch or president serves as head of state, primarily a ceremonial role. After a prescribed period of time (three, four, or five years) or after the government loses a vote of confidence in the parliament, the government resigns and new elections for the legislature are held.

In the parliamentary system, political parties perform important coordinating activities. Parliamentary government is basically party government. Usually, several political parties, not just two, hold seats in the lower house of parliament. Because one party rarely secures 51 percent of the seats, the leading parties must select a coalition government. Through bargaining with each other, political party leaders eventually reach a decision about the specific party leaders who become prime minister and cabinet ministers. Alternatively, if the other legislators concur, a minority government may take office with less than 51 percent of the seats. It remains in power so long as a majority of parliamentarians agree to give it a vote of confidence on major political issues. When that agreement no longer holds, then the government must resign. In short, the retention of government power in a multiparty parliamentary system depends on maintaining high party cohesion and securing coalitions with other political parties.

Under the multiparty parliamentary system, legislators from several parties directly select the governing officials. Therefore, the electorate can exert only limited influence over the particular parties that form the government. Voters cannot easily hold one party accountable for public policies, their social impacts, and the problems facing society.

In a two-party system, such as the United States, political representation appears more direct; yet coordination of government activities remains more fragmented. If a majority of voters dislikes the leadership or policies of the party holding legislative office, they can vote the rascals out and choose the opposition party as the majority party in Congress. The voters, not the legislators, select the president. Yet if different parties control the executive and legislative branches, the electorate cannot hold only one party responsible for the perceived policy failures.

In contrast to parliamentary systems, the United States presidential–congressional system divides political powers between the executive and legislative branches; political parties play a less powerful coordinating role. In both the presidency and Congress, no powerful coordinating mechanism integrates government activities. The American cabinet and civil service are weaker than in Britain, where the cabinet and senior civil servants decide basic policy. Moreover, political party leaders exert less effective influence in the American Congress than in the British House of Commons, where high party cohesion is needed to keep the government in power. Within the American legislative branch, no single institution, such as a political party, can coordinate the activities of the powerful committees, subcommittees, and legislative staffs.

In the American political system, despite the pretensions of the "imperial president," no government agency exercises sovereignty or ultimate authority. Here government powers are dispersed among several branches. Whereas the president dominates foreign policy, Congress checks the presidential role over domestic policies and even over several foreign policy issues. Conflict and bargaining occur between the president and members of Congress, especially committee chairs. When the president and the majority of legislators hold divergent party affiliations, policy conflicts become particularly severe. Even when the same party dominates both Congress and the presidency, political harmony seems difficult to secure. Professional civil servants, policy specialists, experts, and technocrats in the executive branch often owe no personal or party loyalty to the president; thus they often act counter to his directives.

The three branches of American government not only divide political powers but also share activities. For example, the president, Congress, and Supreme Court all participate in making laws: the president proposes; Congress disposes; and the Court, by interpreting the law, decides such policy issues as school desegregation, reapportionment, abortion, and rights of criminal defendants. Congress also performs both judicial and legislative activities. Members of Congress receive petitions and have the right to take actions that may resolve individual grievances.

Because no single agency coordinates these diverse activities, the problems arising from overlapping jurisdictions fragment the U.S. policy process. For instance, in the House of Representatives, over fifteen different committees handle health care bills; the Interstate and Foreign Commerce, Ways and Means, and Government Operations committees assume main responsibility. Other government institutions dealing with health policies include the Senate, Social Security Administration, Veterans Administration, and the Public Health Service. Given these overlapping jurisdictions and specialized orientations of different government agencies, no general policy leadership exerts the power necessary to unify the policy process.[35]

Unlike the American presidential–congressional system, the contemporary French system locates sovereign authority in a single government institution—the presidency, which governs with the assistance of the central state bureaucracy. Elected by all the voters, the French president claims to embody the national will. Certainly, he plays the dominant role in formulating public policies and supervising their implementation. Under the constitutional arrangements of the Fifth Republic, the president appoints the prime minister, dismisses him, selects the cabinet ministers, and removes them from office. Whereas in England members of Parliament hold cabinet posts, in France legislators who want to serve in the cabinet must give up their parliamentary seats. Many cabinet ministers are civil servants and technocrats; they, along with the French bureaucracy, formulate basic policies that adhere to the president's directives.

In contrast to the U.S. Congress, the French legislature—the National Assembly and Senate—exercises limited authority over executive administration, the budget, public enterprises, and national economic planning. Rather than making policy, the prime minister executes presidential decisions. He and cabinet ministers also help steer bills formulated by the president, the cabinet, and civil servants through the National Assembly. National Assembly members now concentrate on securing a few favors for constituents, amending a few bills, and questioning cabinet ministers about the operations of their departments.

Only if the National Assembly comes under control of political parties opposed to the president can it wield crucial veto power over policy formulation. Under these rare conditions, the National Assembly may veto bills presented by the president and prime minister, persuade the president to appoint a new prime minister who enjoys the assembly's confidence, or even force the president to resign.[36]

Pluralism. Although the model of a powerful nation-state specifies that the state becomes both differentiated and independent from social groups, today all constitutional governments are relatively pluralistic. No sharp distinction separates the private from the public sphere. In West Europe, Britain, Canada, and the United States, private agencies, such as business firms, labor unions, and even churches, help administer public policies. Instead of an independent relationship characterizing government and social groups, both show a functional interdependence. Rather than the central government dictating to private social organizations, government officials and heads of these groups bargain, negotiate, and compromise with each other. Various social groups participate in government decision making, thus strengthening the pluralist policy process. Because these groups have the independent power to criticize government leaders, denounce their policies, and organize an opposition, the right to express civil liberties becomes institutionalized. Social pluralism thus reinforces the government decentralization and legal guarantees of political freedom.

In the United States and Britain, social group pluralism seems stronger than in France, where the central government exerts greater control over social groups. The Anglo-American policy process disperses political power among a variety of social groups: private business corporations, labor unions, farmer organizations, ecology groups, consumer organizations, and so forth. Several different groups articulate their preferences for public policies to government ministers, cabinet officials, civil servants, and legislators; by so doing, they play a crucial part in policy formulation. After policies are formulated, business firms, trade unions, and agricultural groups often help implement these policies. Especially in the United States, private businesses exercise considerable influence in the policy process at all government levels. Even if not united on all policy issues, business executives have historically shaped the broad outlines of most American public policies.

In Britain, unions carry more political weight than in America. Aligned with the Labour party, they can veto government income policies (wage and price control decisions). Together with government officials and corporation representatives, union heads share decision-making authority.

Not only in America but also in Britain, the extensive involvement of social groups in the policy process gives them the power to veto activist government policies designed to meet the severe social crises caused by inflation, unemployment, low productivity, and economic stagnation. Rather than government tyranny, political *immobilisme* seems a more common outcome of fragmented policymaking.

In France, the central government exercises greater power over social groups. Political power is concentrated in Paris among the state bureaucrats and technocrats. Particularly under the three Gaullist presidents who governed France from 1958 through 1981, the state administrators seemed more receptive to industrialists' demands than to pressures exerted by trade unions and other social groups. Confronted by fewer powerful private veto groups, the central government has thus played a more directive, activist role in dealing with contemporary social problems.[37]

Extensive scope of power. Nearly all constitutional governments, especially those in Scandinavia, the Netherlands, France, and Italy, wield an extensive scope of power; the government performs more comprehensive activities than all other types of states except the communist party-state. Before the twentieth century, these constitutional states concentrated on maintaining their territorial integrity and constructing an economic infrastructure. They gave priority to external defense, internal order, foreign affairs, the institution of efficient mechanisms for raising financial revenues, the construction of a public communication–transportation system, and the promotion of rapid economic development through both public enterprises and government subsidies to private business firms. In the twentieth century, particularly in the post–World War II era, the allocation of government services to individuals has vastly expanded. Now almost all constitutional governments have instituted comprehensive policies that provide income, education, and health care to the citizenry.

Today the Scandinavian, Dutch, and French governments wield the greatest scope of power; the British government performs fewer functions; and the United States central government engages in the least comprehensive range of activities. Let us consider the operation of government-owned industries and the provision of social services (education, health care, income maintenance) as two important activities of the modern constitutional state.

The French state operates the largest number and variety of publicly owned enterprises. Most transportation, communication, and power industries, as well as banks, have come under government ownership. Britain and especially Sweden manage somewhat fewer public enterprises. The United States features the lowest degree of government ownership. Here privately owned firms dominate most economic sectors; a few industries, such as railroads, the postal service, and electricity, have a mixed blend of public and private ownership.

Government allocation of social services resembles the crossnational pattern shown for government ownership of industries. The Swedish, Dutch, and French governments spend the highest proportion of the gross domestic product (GDP) on total social services, including education, health, and income maintenance (old-age pensions, unemployment compensation, family allowances, and so forth). In Britain, the government allocates slightly fewer public funds as a percentage of the GDP for all these social services. American citizens obtain from the government the least comprehensive and generous services, especially health care and income maintenance benefits. A lower proportion of the American population than citizens in other Western industrial democracies receives government social services. For example, unlike most European countries, the United States lacks a comprehensive public health system enrolling all citizens and a child allowance system under which all families, not just poor mothers with dependent children, receive cash benefits.[38] In short, despite their advanced industrial development and affluence, Americans today live under a relatively weak state that performs fewer types of activities than do most European constitutional governments.

SUMMARY

Table 6-1 summarizes information about the strength of the nation-state in personal autocracies, bureaucratic dictatorships, and constitutional governments. A powerful state monopolizes coercive force, centralizes political power, coordinates government activities, operates independent of social groups, and exercises a comprehensive scope of activities. According to these five criteria, the communist party-states, especially the Soviet Union, manage the strongest state. The military bureaucracies of Latin America, particularly Brazil, wield greater power than African personal autocracies. Among the constitutional regimes, France has the most powerful state, the British central government is somewhat less strong, and the American

TABLE 6-1 Strength of the nation-state

Structural aspect of the state	Personal autocracies		Bureaucratic dictatorships			Constitutional governments	
	Europe (1700s)	Africa (1970s)	Latin America	Soviet Union	France	Britain	United States
1. monopoly over coercive force power of military & police	limited / strong	limited / strong	medium / strongest	very extensive / strongest	extensive / strong	extensive / weak	limited / weak
2. centralization of power	low	low	high	highest	high	lower	lowest
3. degree of government coordination agencies of coordination	limited / monarch	limited / presidential monarch	high / military officers, civilian technocrats	highest / Communist party	high / president and civil servants	high / prime minister and cabinet	lowest / none (power divided among presidency, Congress, Supreme Court)
4. degree of social pluralism powerful groups	medium / aristocratic families, church, economic firms	medium / ethnic groups, families	weak / multinational corporations, large-scale domestic business	weakest / Party	medium / industrial firms	strong / unions, civic action associations, business	strong / voluntary associations, especially business
5. scope of government power							
(a) extent of government-owned industries	low	medium	medium	highest	high	high	lowest
(b) extent of government social services	low	low	medium	highest	high	high	medium

CHAPTER 6 GOVERNMENTS 201

central government exercises the weakest power. What variables explain the divergent strengths of the contemporary nation-state?

Reasons for the Power of Nation-States

Of the factors explaining the power of the nation-state in the United States, Britain, France, Russia, Latin America, and Africa, three variables seem especially important. Table 6-2 summarizes these three general reasons.

1. The geopolitical situation stimulated the rise of a powerful state. As a society became actively involved in international wars, the state became stronger.

2. A rigid stratification system barring extensive social mobility established the conditions for a powerful state. In those societies where a rigid feudal system originally existed, the state exercised greater power, especially in the later stages of feudalism; however, a flexible capitalist system limited state power.

3. Political beliefs both motivate and justify the state's role in social life. The dominance of classical liberalism in the political culture minimized the importance of a strong state. In contrast, classical conservatism, communism, and fascism placed greater emphasis on an active, not a passive, state.

INVOLVEMENT IN WAR

A nation's active involvement in international war necessitated the rise of a professionalized army and thus a strong state structure. As Charles Tilly observed, "War made the state, and the state made war."[39] The geopolitical situation of a country affected a state's recourse to war. Before the twentieth century, island nations experienced less military danger than did a continental power; thus, they relied on a navy, rather than a standing army, for defense and expansion.

From the seventeenth through the nineteenth centuries, the United States remained geographically isolated from European warfare. Neither Canada nor Mexico represented a powerful military threat. During the 1800s, wars with the Indians preoccupied the American military. The bloodiest, most costly armed struggle occurred between Northern and Southern states, rather than between the U.S. government and a foreign power. Although the central government became stronger during the Civil War, after the war ended the country demobilized. Not until the twentieth century did the United States become actively involved in foreign wars, which strengthened the central government's power.

As an island nation, Britain relied on its navy to defend itself from

TABLE 6-2 Reasons for the power of nation-states

Reason	United States	Britain	France	Russia	Latin America	Africa
1. Involvement in land wars 1600–1900	limited	limited	extensive	very extensive	extensive in 1800s	limited
2. Historical rigidity of social structure: power of						
a. landlords	flexible	flexible	rigid	very rigid	rigid	flexible
	weak: Southern slaveowners in 19th century; agribusiness in 20th century	powerful landed gentry 1500–1900	strong but retained some independence from monarchical state before 1789	landlords dependent on czarist state for power (1700–1917)	powerful: feudal landowners in 19th century and export agribusiness in late 20th century	limited power in sub-Saharan Africa
b. peasants	weak in 19th century: dominance of small cash-crop farmers in North	weak: dominance of yeoman farmers and tenant farmers	exploited under monarchical regime before 1789	exploited under czar (1600–1917)	exploited by landowners 1800–1980s	high political independence from state control
c. capitalists	powerful	powerful	strong in 19th and 20th centuries	weak before and after 1917 Revolution	strong multinational corporations and large-scale private business	weak African control of large-scale industries; strong small-scale traders and handicraft producers
d. workers	weak unions	strongly organized in trade unions	exploited before World War II	exploited	exploited: weak unions	weak unions: low level of industrialization
3. Importance of political ideologies	classical liberalism	pluralist classical conservatism, classical liberalism, democratic socialism	classical conservatism (Gaullism), fascism (Vichy regime), communism, democratic socialism (Mitterrand presidency)	monistic classical conservatism (czarism), communism (Marxism-Leninism)	monistic classical conservatism, fascism	neotraditionalism, African populism

foreign attack and to pursue its aims on the European continent. The absence of landed warfare decreased any need for a professionalized standing army. The priority given to sea power enabled the British to expand international trade.

France and Russia, as land powers, became involved in numerous continental wars. Between 1500 and 1780, French monarchs needed a powerful state to finance a professional army that fought the English, Germans, Dutch, Austrians, Italians, and Spanish. From the sixteenth through the twentieth centuries, Russians engaged in more warfare than even the French. Wars with central Asians (Mongols), Crimean Tartars, Swedes, Germans, French, Dutch, Poles, Hungarians, and Turks created a militarized state in Russia. Facing these international threats, czarist officials instituted a strong state structure with powerful, professionalized armed forces recruited from the landed nobility.[40]

RIGID SOCIAL STRUCTURE

A rigid social stratification system facilitated the rise of a strong state. The established elite relied on a powerful state structure to maintain the rigid social system. Opposition leaders who sought a more flexible system wanted a strong state that would break down the rigid, inequalitarian social structures barring upward social mobility. Especially where a feudal landed nobility monopolized land and government offices, the state seemed more powerful, as in France and Russia both before and after the revolutions. Where private capitalists exercised greater influence, as in the United States, Britain, and Holland, social mobility was more prevalent. A weaker state thus emerged.

United States. In the United States, the absence of a rigid feudal system, combined with the considerable power exerted by private capitalists, decreased pressures for a strong central government. No large peasantry or landed nobility ever existed here. In the South, the slaveholders acted not as a feudal elite but as agrarian capitalists producing cotton for sale on the world market. Elsewhere in the western part of the American nation, small-scale independent cash-crop farmers, rather than a landless peasantry, raised crops, such as grain, partly for sale overseas, especially in Britain. Like the southern slaveholders, these western farmers resisted the growth of a strong state in Washington, D.C.

Besides these agrarian capitalists, other economic groups, including merchants, manufacturers, and even skilled workers, supported no movement for a powerful central government in the European statist tradition. The absence of a feudal heritage, with its rigid class distinctions, discouraged efforts to establish a socialist party that would campaign for active state intervention in the economy. Because most white males had gained the right to vote by the 1840s, before the rise of industrialization, they could exert some pressure on local government officials, such as urban mayors, to redress some economic grievances. Trade union movements that began organizing after the Civil War concentrated on economic, not political, objectives; they sought rights to collective bargaining, higher wages, and healthier, safer working conditions. Because the white working class had already won the suffrage, most union leaders saw no reason for organizing a labor party, as in Scandinavia or England, to demand the vote and comprehensive government-administered social service programs. Particularly before the depression days of the 1930s, the dominance of private business at all government levels—national, state, local—weakened support for the central government playing an activist role in economic affairs.

Compared with most nineteenth-century European societies, the United States had more inexpensive land available to low-income persons; a more flexible class structure enabled some people at the bottom of the social stratification system to gain upward social mobility. Thus, few economic groups felt the need to press for a strong central government that would institute a more flexible social system.

Of all groups, American Blacks have most enthusiastically supported a powerful central government to crush local oppression. Southern black slaves possessed fewer rights than did even European peasants. During the 1860s, federal government troops abolished the slave system and smashed the slaveholders' political power. One hundred years later, federal government intervention secured desegregated public accommodations and voting rights for the black population. Hence, in the United States, rigid racial interactions led to a stronger state presence that tried to create a more open, flexible system for the Blacks.

Britain. Britain has experienced a more flexible class system than France or Russia. In England, political leaders did not confront the large peasant class that existed on the European continent; the English agrarian class structure was more pluralistic. As early as the sixteenth century, an independent yeoman farming group began to emerge. Oriented to commercialized, capitalist agriculture, a few yeomen farmers became wealthy freeholders. Other poor farmers left the land to work in the new factories manufacturing wool and textiles. Many members of the old landed elite operated urban businesses.

The absence of a large peasant class, the growing political power of the yeoman farmers, and the alliance between landlords and new capitalists all checked the emergence of a strong state in London. During the mid seventeenth century, Charles I tried to establish the absolute sovereignty of the monarch; however, the landed gentry, along with Puritan intellectuals and common law judges, resisted. After a brief civil war in which the king was executed and Cromwell ruled as supreme leader, the monarchy was restored in 1660. Nevertheless, Parliament succeeded in checking the monarch's political power. Thus, in London, the monarch and legislators, mainly landed gentry, agreed to share decision-making authority. In the local areas outside London, aristocratic nobles, such as justices of the peace, played the dominant administrative role. Only after 1850 did pressures arise from creating a centralized professional civil service.

The English capitalists exercised more independent political power than European business owners. Experiencing greater social mobility, the new entrepreneurs often became part of the old aristocracy; in turn, some members of the landed gentry class assumed new economic roles as merchants or manufacturers. These groups resisted any trends toward bureaucratic state centralization.

Compared with the European socialist parties, the English Labour party more strongly opposed state action to redress working-class grievances. Wedded to a strong cooperative movement and an influential trade union organization, the Labourites between 1880 and 1940 opposed most government efforts to establish more generous unemployment insurance and old-age pensions; they wanted the unions and the cooperatives, not the state, to administer these policies.

France. Unlike England or the United States, France retained a rigid social stratification system for a longer historical period. Before the French Revolution of 1789, the feudal landed nobility adopted a rigid posture toward both the middle class and the peasantry. The landed aristocracy dominated the major institutions of the *ancien régime:* the state bureaucracy, local *parlements* (courts of appeal), army, and Catholic church. Even though during the eighteenth century segments of the emerging middle class—bankers, merchants, manufacturers, lawyers, journalists—began to acquire considerable economic power, the titled aristocrats prevented middle-class commoners from holding high office in these institutions. The feudal nobility also maintained a sharp distance from the peasants, who had to pay high rents to the landlords. Through their control over the state bureaucracy and the *parlements,* the landed nobility gained exemptions from paying taxes. Lacking the power to tax the nobles, the monarch had to levy high taxes on the peasantry; these tax rates exceeded those imposed on the English poor farmers. As a result, unlike England, France faced numerous peasant revolts against high taxes during the seventeenth and eighteenth centuries. To crush these domestic revolts and to wage war abroad, the state grew stronger.

Although the feudal landlords occupied the dominant position in prerevolutionary French political institutions, they never gained the autonomous power the English aristocrats won against their monarch. True, the French king lacked the power to tax the landed aristocracy; yet the feudal nobles were unable to control royal absolutism.

By the 1780s, the French faced a revolutionary situation that further strengthened state power. The monarchy encountered opposition from nearly all social classes: the feudal nobility, middle-class commoners, and the peasantry. Under these brittle social conditions, a revolutionary civil war erupted in 1789. First the nobles and peasants allied against the monarch. Later the peasants turned on the feudal aristocracy. During the early 1790s, representatives of the middle class—lawyers, intellectuals, merchants, lower-ranking civil servants—came to dominate the government. Opposed to the social chaos of the 1790s, the military officer Napoleon Bonaparte seized control of the state in 1799. As a consequence of revolutionary pressures and military rule, the French state increased its power. The new republican state was even more centralized and bureaucratic than the prerevolutionary absolutist regime.

Historically, French capitalists have exercised weaker power over the state than have English or especially American capitalists. Bureaucrats, military officers, and real estate speculators, not industrialists or merchants, controlled the state. Government bureaucrats assumed greater responsibility in France than in England for promoting rapid industrial development. During the nineteenth century, the state built roads, dug canals, constructed factories, and established technical schools. Until 1884, the government forbade workers to strike or organize labor unions. In short, even though the capitalists did not directly control the French state, government policies created a national market, instituted a uniform legal system, diminished feudal provincialism, and repressed factory workers' economic freedom; all these public policies helped further capitalist interests, thereby making private business firms dependent on the state for their economic prosperity.

Until the post–World War II era, the French working class experienced rigid economic conditions. Although all males gained the right to vote in 1848, they lacked basic economic rights. For a long time, French industrialists and entrepreneurs resisted worker efforts to form strong labor unions. The socialist parties that emerged during the late nineteenth and early twentieth centuries wanted the state to guarantee workers certain equalitarian rights in the economy that they already possessed in the political system. These demands revolved around greater freedom for the unions and improved working conditions. When the Communist party established a separate organization from the Socialists, it also demanded a stronger state that would equalize economic conditions and hence extend the French revolutionary ideals to the economic sphere.

Russia. Compared with Americans, English, and French, the Russians have historically confronted the most rigid social system, especially before 1917. In the czarist regime, the peasants lived under particularly wretched conditions. The serf system remained in operation until 1861. Between 1649 and 1861, a period when English peasants gained some social mobility, many Russian serfs lived like slaves on feudal estates. Repressed and bound to the land, the peasants lacked social mobility. Czarist regulations banned the sale and purchase of extensive lands; however, serfs could be sold to new lords. Taxes on the serfs were higher than in England or even France. After the abolition of serfdom in 1861, the peasants' economic situations improved somewhat. Yet they still lacked extensive landholdings and had to pay high rents to the landlords or high redemption payments to the former landowners.

Dependent on the czarist state and resented by the peasants, the Russian landed aristocracy lacked autonomous political power. Most landowners were politically subordinate to the czar; they became army officers, court officials, or state bureaucrats. Oriented toward state service and residing in the urban areas, few hereditary nobles directly managed their own estates. As absentee landlords, they still levied high rents and redemption payments (compensation for the loss of serf ownership) on the peasants. Yet even the landlords failed to prosper after the emancipation of serfs because they borrowed money from the czarist treasury to buy land and thus incurred huge debts owed the state.

In this rigid czarist system, the urban industrialists and merchants also lacked independent political power. Foreign private investors, especially from France and Germany, played a key role in promoting industrial development. Particularly after 1890, the czarist state became deeply involved in creating an industrial infrastructure. It constructed railroads, operated mines, and subsidized iron and steel production. Between 1888 and 1913, the economic growth rate, stimulated by these state policies, rapidly accelerated. Large-scale, technologically modern factories emerged, especially in the western, urban regions of Russia. Trade unions and socialist political parties arose to protest the harsh working conditions facing the factory workers. Industrialists, both foreign and domestic, depended on the state police to repress working-class organizations.

Under these brittle, rigid social conditions, revolution seemed almost inevitable. When the czarist state disintegrated during the First World War, the Bolsheviks gained state power in late 1917. Leninist beliefs, czarist traditions, internal civil war, and threats of foreign invasions all strengthened the power of the new Soviet state. Under Lenin and Stalin, the central government became more centralized, hierarchical, bureaucratic, coercive, and expansive than even the old czarist state.[41]

POLITICAL BELIEFS

As a third factor affecting the strength of the state, political beliefs both reflect and condition the social stratification system. The relative importance of various ideologies—classical conservatism, classical liberalism, democratic socialism, communism, fascism—depends partly on the power of diverse social groups. In turn, the content of the beliefs—the notions of freedom, equality, individualism-collectivism, moral and material welfare—influence the struggle for state power. Where classical liberalism and, to a lesser extent, democratic socialism dominate the political culture, these beliefs help limit central government powers. In societies more influenced by classical conservatism, communism, and fascism, the incentives for a limited state appear weaker.

Classical liberalism has historically enjoyed the widest influence in the United States; here no other belief system has even gained such dominant importance in the policy process. Partly as a result, Americans have lived under a comparatively weak central government. As we saw in chapter 4, liberalism stresses individual freedom—personal freedom from state interference. The liberal conception of equality accords highest priority to equal rights before the law and equal opportunities to achieve. According to liberals, a strong government does not guarantee equal opportunities to achieve social mobility. Instead, it produces political elitism vested in a centralized bureaucracy. Thus, liberals have valued a limited, decentralized government; locally controlled public education, not the central state, should equalize opportunities for all citizens.

Liberalism also places a high value on individual rights. From this individualistic perspective, the government must promote those conditions that enable individuals to achieve upward mobility. Social mobility occurs mainly through free competition among individuals rather than through government assistance to collective groups.

Under these liberal conceptions, the state neither embodies moral virtue nor takes primary responsibility for promoting material welfare. Independent churches that compete on the religious market should articulate the moral values for a society. Private enterprises mainly handle the tasks of securing rapid economic development and material welfare for the citizens.⁴²

In Britain, not only classical liberalism but also classical conservatism and democratic socialism have shaped the power of the state in the policy process. According to the classical conservative ideas pervasive during the eighteenth, nineteenth, and twentieth centuries, freedom and legal authority are complementary, rather than contradictory. Freedom can thrive only under government-provided order. Today, Conservatives, along with Democratic Socialists, stress the need for widespread civil liberties. Unlike the populist American conceptions, however, all English belief systems place somewhat greater reliance on the government to preserve political freedoms. English Conservatives have also accepted the need for a political elite to govern the society. Although Socialists have given stronger support to political equality and to an active role for the rank and file to initiate policy recommendations, they too, like the Conservatives, favor a strong, activist government responsible for planning the economy.

Recently, some English Conservatives (Margaret Thatcher and Keith Joseph, for example) have emphasized the liberal values of individualism; however, before the 1970s, most Conservatives gave greater precedence than Americans to collective values. Although disagreeing on the specific nature of the public interest, Conservatives and Socialists both believed that government should promote the collective welfare—a good that transcends the sum of aggregated individual interests. Whereas Socialists wanted government to represent the interests of the working class, Conservatives supported a governing class that would make crucial public policies.

More so than American liberals, English conservatives and democratic socialists perceive the state performing moral and material functions. Conservatives uphold the legal union between the Anglican church and the state; for them, an established church provides an ethically based order for society. Influenced by the principles of Benjamin Disraeli and Randolph Churchill, two nineteenth-century Tory leaders, conservatives since then have stressed the need for a managed economy, the extension of social services, and even some state-operated firms. Although democratic socialists have historically supported decentralized administration of social services by trade unions and cooperatives, after World War II the Labour party in government brought several firms under government ownership and expanded the state's social service programs. During the last decade, in contrast to the Conservative party leaders, Labour party activists have shown greater enthusiasm for nationalizing more industries and providing more comprehensive, generous government-financed social services.⁴³

In contemporary France, statist beliefs influence the political culture. Compared with English conservative leaders, the French conservatives delegate a stronger role to the state in managing social life. As articulated by Gaullist officials operating the government, French conservatism wants the state to provide order, direct economic planning, and stimulate rapid economic growth.

Other statist ideologies, including fascism and communism, also have gained greater support in France than in England. During World War II, the profascist Vichy regime dominated French society. Under the Vichy administrators, the state curtailed political freedoms, denounced both social and political equality, stressed national collectivist values over individual rights, and upheld central government regulation of moral values and material welfare. Since World War II, the French Communist party has won about 20 percent of the votes to the National Assembly and now helps govern several city governments. These Communist party leaders want the central state to play an even more extensive role in French society, especially by nationalizing several hundred privately owned industries. The two ideologies—classical liberalism and democratic socialism—that stress decentralized state power have until recently attracted limited support among French political leaders.

Historically, the Russians have lived under government officials who voice a strong statist orientation. Neither classical liberalism nor democratic socialism has attracted widespread government support. The czarist version of conservatism upheld the need for a highly centralized state that allowed few powers for local government agencies or private social groups.

According to the Leninist interpretation of Marxism, the state would play a dominant role in society until the establishment of full communism. From the Leninist perspective, the state needed to control individual political freedom, the economic freedom of private enterprises, and the rights of trade unionists. Political elitism, as embodied in a strong state and dominant single party, took precedence over political equality. Similarly, individualism became subordinate to the collective interests of the Communist party, Soviet state, Russian nation, and proletarian class. In the communist view, a powerful party-state could best govern society and represent working-class interests. The party-state assumed major responsibilities for moral and material welfare. Suppressing the power of the Russian Orthodox church, Communist party leaders saw themselves as political educators teaching new socialist values and creating new Soviet citizens. Along with the Party, the state promoted rapid industrialization, planned comprehensive social service programs, and tried to equalize economic opportunities for citizens. Under these policies of state socialism, the central government played a far more dominant role than in the mixed socialist–capitalist economies of West Europe.

CONCLUSION

The same three reasons explaining the strength of the state in the United States, Britain, France, and Russia also account for the greater power of the state in Latin America than in contemporary Africa. First, most Latin American countries attained national independence from Spain and Portugal during the first quarter of the nineteenth century; in contrast to African colonies that won their independence 150 years later, Latin America experienced a more violent road to nationhood. Such military leaders as Simón Bolívar, Bernardo O'Higgins, José de San Martín, and Antonio José de Sucre commanded the battles for national independence. After independence, civil and international wars wracked several Latin American territories during the nineteenth century. These wars strengthened the power of the state and the army officers—*caudillos*—who dominated both the national and local governments.

Except in Algeria, Mozambique, Guinea-Bissau, Angola, and Zimbabwe, the struggle for African independence took place under relatively peaceful conditions. The constitutional states of Britain, France, and Belgium dominated most parts of Africa. Unlike the more dictatorial bureaucrats managing Spain and Portugal, French and English colonial officials placed few obstacles in the path of political independence. Nationalist politicians, rather than military officers, led the movements for liberation for colonial rule. Success at the ballot box, not armed struggle, largely determined which African leaders gained control of the government during the early 1960s. Although civil and international wars today plague several countries and the armed forces govern about half the nations, the brief time elapsing since political independence has made a really powerful state rather infeasible at present.

Second, throughout their histories, most Latin Americans have lived under a more rigid social stratification system than have Africans. In Latin America, both feudalism and capitalism barred extensive social mobility, especially for the large peasant class. During both the nineteenth and twentieth centuries, landowners, mine owners, merchants, and international capitalists, along with the military, dominated local and national governments. Until the mid twentieth century, most peasants worked on huge estates where the landlord tightly controlled rural laborers' lives. The landowner basically steered rural society, controlling the farmers' access to land, employment, and housing. Because the government and local landowner forbade the peasant from voting in secret elections, joining a rural union, or working for a leftist party, opportunities for rural mobility and improvement of agrarian working conditions were minimal.

Factory workers in Latin America also confronted a rigid social stratification system. Domestic and international capitalists have encouraged the government to repress labor unions and left-wing political parties that threatened "economic stability" and high profits. Some multinational corporations operated company towns where business executives controlled the workers' access to housing, recreation, and even consumer goods.

To maintain this rigid stratification system, the Latin American state played a dominant role in the economy. Government leaders pursued policies of mercantilism and state capitalism, rather than the more pluralist capitalist strategies of England, Holland, and the United States. Under state capitalism, the state repressed rural and urban labor organizations, subsidized private investment, enacted high tariffs on imported goods, and levied high taxes on the poor but low taxes on the business elite. Under these policies, a rigid class system became entrenched. Poverty and high unemployment meant that few peasants or urban workers could exert any influence on the market. Possessing neither economic nor political power, they could not easily press for redistributionist policies that would create a more flexible social system.

By contrast, contemporary Africans live in less rigid social stratification systems. Unlike Latin America, sub-Saharan Africa, at least outside southern Africa, features more equal land distribution. Except in northern Nigeria, Ethiopia, and Rwanda, feudalism was relatively weak. Often the village owned the land in common; village leaders allocated parcels of land for use by different families. Although most Africans still work as farmers, they have historically enjoyed the opportunity to enter business. African merchants carried goods between North Africa and regions below the Sahara. In such areas as Ghana, African cash-crop farmers have grown cocoa for over a hundred years. Today European multinational corporations exert a less-dominant position than in Latin America; some African business executives and factory workers have opportunities to benefit from foreign investment. Under these flexible social conditions, the pressures to establish a powerful state seem less acute in Africa than in Latin America.

Third, the most influential beliefs in Latin America also have given rise to a strong state. Classical liberalism and democratic socialism have exerted only a weak influence on the government elite. Most political leaders seem more attracted to classical conservatism and, to a lesser extent, fascism. According to the conservative "organic statist" ideas voiced by Thomas Aquinas, Francisco Suárez, and contemporary Latin American intellectuals, society forms an organic community. Just as some parts of the human organism, such as the brain, take priority over the lesser organs, so in society the political elite—the head—should dominate the rest. Whatever their functional importance, all parts of the body are interdependent. In a well-functioning organism, the individual parts must work in harmony. In society as well, interest group and class conflicts must give way to the unity expressed in a harmonious community. The expression of individual rights inevitably leads to anarchy; thus, social order will prevail only if individuals subordinate their rights to a collective moral cause such as goodness and justice. From this conservative perspective, a strong state becomes necessary to promote collective purposes. Rather than an artificial mechanism, the state is a natural agency that must ensure order among the parts of a society, including family, church, and private associations.

Fascist beliefs have also appealed to some Latin American leaders, especially those in Brazil, Argentina, Paraguay, Chile, and Bolivia. Like conservatism, fascism stresses the need for an organic community and an organic state, under which the lower classes—peasants and workers—show unquestioning obedience to their political leaders. In general, however, Latin American states have exercised less political power than the fascist states in Nazi Germany and Mussolini's Italy. Instead, Franco's Spain and Salazar's Portugal have represented a more attractive fascist model to Latin Americans. These two Iberian states allowed greater pluralism in political decision making than did Hitler.

Compared with Latin America, Africa has been less influenced by European ideologies that posit a powerful role for the central government. Whereas Latin American nations represent settler societies governed by descendants of the Spanish and Portuguese, indigenous black African leaders now hold government power outside South Africa. No comprehensive, rigid ideology operates as a guide to public policy; rather, African officials justify their actions by blending aspects of traditional African ideas with European beliefs learned during the colonial period. Neither classical liberalism nor democratic socialism attracts extensive support. Although several countries experience a cult of leadership, fascism holds limited appeal. Most leaders either voice a conservative position based on African traditionalism and Islam or else articulate more radical populist beliefs. Both these ideologies place greater emphasis on the ethnic group or the mass populace than on a powerful central state. Even those leaders calling themselves "scientific socialists" seem more populist than Leninist. These populist leaders, who stress the need for the African people to direct political institutions, rarely create a powerful political organization, either a strong state or dominant party, that transforms the class structure. In most African territories, both populism and traditionalism thus posit a more limited role for the state than that advocated by East European, Mongolian, and North Korean communist leaders, who use a powerful state as a tool for industrializing their societies.[44]

Notes

1. *The Politics of Aristotle*, trans. Ernest Barker (New York: Oxford University Press, 1958), pp. 4–5; Sheldon S. Wolin, *Politics and Vision: Continuity and Innovation in Western Political Thought* (Boston: Little, Brown, 1960), pp. 36–37; Terrence Ball, "Theory and Practice: An Examination of the Platonic and Aristotelian Conceptions of Political Theory," *Western Political Quarterly* 25 (September 1972): 534–545.
2. See Shlomo Avineri, *Hegel's Theory of the Modern State* (London: Cambridge University Press, 1972), pp. 99, 132–154.
3. The quote by Madison comes from Alexander Hamilton, James Madison, and John Jay, *The Federalist Papers*, ed. Clinton Rossiter (New York: New American Library, 1961), p. 322; see also pp. 77–84, 320–325. Robert Dahl, *A Preface to Democratic Theory* (Chicago: University of Chicago Press, 1956), pp. 4–33, and Wolin, *Politics and Vision*, pp. 322–324, analyze the political implications of Madison's theory of government.
4. Aristotle, *The Ethics*, trans. J. A. K. Thompson (Harmondsworth, Middlesex: Penguin Books, 1953), pp. 245–246.
5. See Marion J. Levy, Jr., *Modernization and the Structure of Societies* (Princeton, N.J.: Princeton University Press, 1966), p. 436; David E. Apter, *Choice and the Politics of Allocation* (New Haven, Conn.: Yale University Press, 1971), p. 132.
6. Max Weber, "Politics as a Vocation," in *From Max Weber*, ed. H. H. Gerth and C. Wright Mills (New York: Oxford University Press, 1946), pp. 77–78.
7. Ibid., p. 78.
8. Randall Collins, *Conflict Sociology: Toward an Explanatory Science* (New York: Academic Press, 1975), pp. 352–353.
9. Samuel E. Finer, "State-Building, State Boundaries, and Border Control," *Social Science Information* 13 (August–October 1974): 83; Charles Tilly, "Reflections on the History of European State-Making," in *The Formation of National States in Western Europe*, ed. Charles Tilly (Princeton, N.J.: Princeton University Press, 1975), p. 61.
10. See Karl W. Deutsch, *Politics and Government: How People Decide Their Fate*, 3d ed. (Boston: Houghton Mifflin, 1980), pp. 7–8; Richard Rose, "Models of Governing," *Comparative Politics* 5 (July 1973): 468–470.
11. George Bernard Shaw, *Man and Superman* (New York: Penguin Books, 1977), p. 169.
12. Robert Vaison, "A Note on 'Public Policy,'" *Canadian Journal of Political Science* 6 (December 1973): 661–662.
13. Robert J. Goldstein, *Political Repression in Modern America* (Cambridge, Mass.: Schenkman, 1978), pp. 10–11.
14. John Herman Randall, Jr., *The Making of the Modern Mind*, rev. ed. (Boston: Houghton Mifflin, 1940), pp. 192–194; Robert Gilpin, *U.S. Power and the Multinational Corporation* (New York: Basic Books, 1975), pp. 25–43.
15. See Immanuel Wallerstein, *The Modern World-System* (New York: Academic Press, 1974), pp. 133–162; Tilly, "Reflections on the History of European State-Making," pp. 44–45; Seymour Martin Lipset, *The First New Nation* (New York: Basic Books, 1963), pp. 45–60; Eric Foner, *Tom Paine and the American Revolution* (New York: Oxford University Press, 1975). Complex relationships of conflict and consensus characterized the interaction among state officials, landowners, and capitalists. Sometimes two of the three groups allied; at other times, the same groups came into opposition.
16. Charles Tilly, "Western State-Making and Theories of Political Transformation," in Tilly, *The Formation of National States in Western Europe*, p. 638.
17. Richard Rose, "On the Priorities of Government: A Developmental Analysis of Public Policies," *European Journal of Political Research* 4 (September 1976): 247–289.
18. For analyses of personal autocracies in Europe and Africa, see Gianfranco Poggi, *The Development of the Modern State* (Stanford, Calif.: Stanford University Press, 1978), pp. 60–85; Perry Anderson, *Lineages of the Absolutist State* (London: Verso Editions, 1979); Robert H. Jackson

and Carl G. Rosberg, *Personal Rule in Black Africa: Prince, Autocrat, Prophet, Tyrant* (Berkeley: University of California Press, 1982); Thomas M. Callaghy, "The Difficulties of Implementing Socialist Strategies of Development in Africa: The 'First Wave,'" in *Socialism in Sub-Saharan Africa: A New Assessment*, ed. Carl G. Rosberg and Thomas M. Callaghy (Berkeley: University of California Institute of International Studies, 1979), pp. 112–129. David E. Apter, *The Politics of Modernization* (Chicago: University of Chicago Press, 1965), pp. 408–416, coined the terms *neomercantilism* and *presidential monarchy*.

19. Poggi, *The Development of the Modern State*, p. 66; Reinhard Bendix, *Kings or People: Power and the Mandate to Rule* (Berkeley: University of California Press, 1978), pp. 337–338, 523–530; Anderson, *Lineages of the Absolutist State*; Theda Skocpol, *States and Social Revolutions* (London: Cambridge University Press, 1979), pp. 112–157; Folke Dovring, "Scandinavia: Denmark, Finland, Iceland, Norway, Sweden," in *Crises of Political Development in Europe and the United States*, ed. Raymond Grew (Princeton, N.J.: Princeton University Press, 1978), p. 147.

20. Carl J. Friedrich, *Man and His Government* (New York: McGraw-Hill, 1963), p. 71.

21. See Jackson and Rosberg, *Personal Rule in Black Africa*, esp. pp. 1–82, 252–265.

22. Callaghy, "The Difficulties of Implementing Socialist Strategies of Development in Africa," pp. 126–128.

23. Reinhard Bendix, *Max Weber: An Intellectual Portrait* (Garden City, N.Y.: Doubleday Anchor, 1962), pp. 424–430; Erik Olin Wright, *Class, Crisis and the State* (London: New Left Books, 1978), pp. 181–225.

24. Joseph Stalin, *Leninism* (London: George Allen and Unwin, 1940), p. 74. See also Amos Perlmutter, *The Military and Politics in Modern Times* (New Haven, Conn.: Yale University Press, 1977), pp. 75–85, 229–250.

25. For analyses of the communist party-state, see David Lane, *The Socialist Industrial State: Towards a Political Sociology of State Socialism* (London: George Allen and Unwin, 1976), pp. 73–78; Skocpol, *States and Social Revolutions*, pp. 206–293.

26. See the following works by Guillermo A. O'Donnell: *Modernization and Bureaucratic-Authoritarianism: Studies in South American Politics* (Berkeley: University of California Institute of International Studies, 1973); "Corporatism and the Question of the State," in *Authoritarianism and Corporatism in Latin America*, ed. James M. Malloy (Pittsburgh, Penn.: University of Pittsburgh Press, 1977), pp. 47–87; "Reflections on the Patterns of Change in the Bureaucratic-Authoritarian State," *Latin American Research Review* 13, no. 1 (1978): 3–38; "Tensions in the Bureaucratic-Authoritarian State and the Question of Democracy," in *The New Authoritarianism in Latin America*, ed. David Collier (Princeton, N.J.: Princeton University Press, 1979), pp. 285–318.

27. Jorge I. Domínguez, "Assessing Human Rights Conditions," in *Enhancing Global Human Rights: 1980s Project/Council on Foreign Relations* (New York: McGraw-Hill, 1979), pp. 93–102; David C. Jordan, "Argentina's Military Commonwealth," *Current History* 76 (February 1979): 89.

28. For interpretations of representation, see Hanna Fenichel Pitkin, *The Concept of Representation* (Berkeley: University of California Press, 1972), esp. pp. 8–9, 60–91, 209–240; Levy, *Modernization and the Structure of Societies*, pp. 290–295.

29. Hamilton, Madison, and Jay, *The Federalist Papers*, p. 322. See also the arguments made by Alexander Hamilton, pp. 190–195 (nos. 30–31).

30. For a general analysis of constitutional government, see Poggi, *The Development of the Modern State*, pp. 86–149.

31. Comparative analyses of the powers of the military and the police appear in Samuel E. Finer, "State- and Nation-Building in Europe: The Role of the Military," in Tilly, *The Formation of National States in Western Europe*, pp. 84–163; David H. Bayley, "The Police and Political Development in Europe," in Tilly, *The Formation of National States in Western Europe*, pp. 328–379; Samuel P. Huntington, *Political Order in Changing Societies* (New Haven, Conn.: Yale University Press, 1968), pp. 93–191; Albert J. Reiss, Jr., "Discretionary Justice in the United States," *International Journal of Criminology and Penology* 2 (May 1974): 181–205; Tom Bowden, "Guarding the State: The Police Response to Crisis Politics in Europe," *British Journal of Law and Society* 5 (Summer 1978): 69–88; Stuart Morris, "British Chief Constables: The Americanization of a Role?" *Political Studies* 29 (September 1981): 352–364.

32. Henry W. Ehrmann, *Politics in France*, 3d ed. (Boston: Little, Brown, 1976), pp. 290–297; Harry Lazer, "Devolution, Ethnic

Nationalism, Populism in the United Kingdom," *Publius* 7 (Fall 1977): 54; Ivo E. Duchacek, "Antagonistic Cooperation: Territorial and Ethnic Communities," *Publius* 7 (Fall 1977): 3–29, esp. 15; Ivo D. Duchacek, *Comparative Federalism: The Territorial Dimension of Politics* (New York: Holt, Rinehart and Winston, 1970); Anthony Fusaro, "Two Faces of British Nationalism: The Scottish National Party and Plaid Cymru Compared," *Polity* 11 (Spring 1979): 362–386; Paul Barker, "Italy on a New Tack?" *New Society* 41 (September 15, 1977): 539–543; Sidney Tarrow, *Between Center and Periphery: Grassroots Politicians in Italy and France* (New Haven, Conn.: Yale University Press, 1977), pp. 7, 167–202.

33. Duchacek, *Comparative Federalism*, pp. 188–275.
34. Alan C. Cairns, "The Governments and Societies of Canadian Federalism," *Canadian Journal of Political Science* 10 (December 1977): 695–725, esp. 702; U.S. Bureau of the Census, Department of Commerce, *The Statistical Abstract of the United States: 1977* (Washington, D.C.: Government Printing Office, 1977), p. 306; Douglas V. Verney, "Has There Been a Distinctive Canadian Political Tradition?" *Journal of Commonwealth and Comparative Politics* 16 (November 1978): 231–255; Leon D. Epstein, "The Old States in a New System," in *The New American Political System*, ed. Anthony King (Washington, D.C.: American Enterprise Institute, 1978), pp. 352–369.
35. For comparisons of the presidential and parliamentary systems, see Douglas V. Verney, "Analysis of Political Systems," in *Comparative Politics: A Reader*, ed. Harry Eckstein and David E. Apter (New York: Free Press, 1963), pp. 175–191; Seymour Martin Lipset's comments in Irving Louis Horowitz and Seymour Martin Lipset, *Dialogues on American Politics* (New York: Oxford University Press, 1978), pp. 100–101. For analyses of American political institutions, see Richard Rose, "Government against Sub-Governments: A European Perspective on Washington," in *Presidents and Prime Ministers*, ed. Richard Rose and Ezra N. Suleiman (Washington, D.C.: American Enterprise Institute, 1980), pp. 284–347; Huntington, *Political Order in Changing Societies*, pp. 93–139; and the following essays in King, *The New American Political System:* Fred I. Greenstein, "Change and Continuity in the Modern Presidency," pp. 45–85; Hugh Heclo, "Issue Networks and the Executive Establishment," pp. 87–124; Samuel C. Patterson, "The Semi-Sovereign Congress," pp. 125–177; Martin Shapiro, "The Supreme Court: From Warren to Burger," pp. 179–211.
36. Ehrmann, *Politics in France*, pp. 267–330; Pierre Birnbaum, "State, Centre and Bureaucracy," *Government and Opposition* 16 (Winter 1981): 58–77; Kenneth Dyson, *The State Tradition in Western Europe* (New York: Oxford University Press, 1980), esp. pp. 25–78; Kay Lawson, "The Impact of Party Reform on Party Systems: The Case of the RPR in France," *Comparative Politics* 13 (July 1981): 416.
37. Jack Hayward, "Institutional Inertia and Political Impetus in France and Britain," *European Journal of Political Research* 4 (December 1976): 341–359; "Pressure Groups," *New Society* 48 (April 26, 1979): i–iv.
38. See Charles F. Andrain, *Politics and Economic Policies in Western Democracies* (North Scituate, Mass.: Duxbury Press, 1980), pp. 10–27; "The Rise in Public Expenditure: How Much Further Can It Go?" *OECD Observer* no. 92 (May 1978): 10; Richard Rose and Guy Peters, *Can Government Go Bankrupt?* (New York: Basic Books, 1978), pp. 254–257; Susan Fainstein and Norman I. Fainstein, "National Policy and Urban Development," *Social Problems* 26 (December 1978): 125–146.
39. Tilly, "Reflections on the History of European State-Making," p. 42.
40. Bendix, *Kings or People*, pp. 111, 440; Anderson, *Lineages of the Absolutist State*, pp. 29–34.
41. See Tilly, "Reflections on the History of European State-Making," pp. 3–83; Wallerstein, *The Modern World-System*, pp. 107–162; Francis G. Castles, "Barrington Moore's Thesis and Swedish Political Development," *Government and Opposition* 8 (Summer 1973): 316–318;" Anderson, *Lineages of the Absolutist State;* Michael Hechter, "Review Essay: Lineages of the Capitalist State," *American Journal of Sociology* 82 (March 1977): 1057–1074; Skocpol, *States and Social Revolutions;* Robert Brenner, "Agrarian Class Structure and Economic Development in Pre-Industrial Europe," *Past and Present* no. 70 (February 1976): 30–75; Lipset, *The First New Nation*, pp. 225–232; A. F. K. Organski, *The Stages of Political Development* (New York: Knopf, 1965), pp. 56–93; Hugh Heclo, *Modern Social Politics in Britain and Sweden* (New Haven, Conn.: Yale

University Press, 1974), pp. 89–90, 293–297; Leon D. Epstein, *Political Parties in Western Democracies* (New York: Praeger, 1967), pp. 130–135; Bendix, *Kings or People;* Rudolf Braun, "Taxation, Sociopolitical Structure, and State-Building: Great Britain and Brandenburg-Prussia," in Tilly, *The Formation of National States in Western Europe,* pp. 243–327; Michael Hechter and William Brustein, "Regional Modes of Production and Patterns of State Formation in Western Europe," *American Journal of Sociology* 85 (March 1980): 1061–1094.

42. Louis Hartz, *The Liberal Tradition in America* (New York: Harcourt Brace and World, 1955).
43. Samuel H. Beer, *British Politics in the Collectivist Age* (New York: Knopf, 1965).
44. For analyses of Latin America, see Helio Jaguaribe, *Political Development: A General Theory and a Latin American Case Study* (New York: Harper & Row, 1973), pp. 393–456; Richard M. Morse, "The Heritage of Latin America," in *The Founding of New Societies,* ed. Louis Hartz (New York: Harcourt Brace and World, 1964), pp. 123–177; Glen Caudill Dealy, "The Tradition of Monistic Democracy in Latin America," *Journal of the History of Ideas* 35 (October–December 1974): 625–646; Alfred Stepan, *The State and Society: Peru in Comparative Perspective* (Princeton, N.J.: Princeton University Press, 1978), esp. pp. 26–45; Brian Loveman, *Chile: The Legacy of Hispanic Capitalism* (New York: Oxford University Press, 1979), pp. 26, 199. For analyses of political beliefs and social structures in Africa, see Charles F. Andrain, "Democracy and Socialism: Ideologies of African Leaders," in *Ideology and Discontent,* ed. David E. Apter (New York: Free Press, 1964), pp. 155–205; Kenneth Jowitt, "Scientific Socialist Regimes in Africa: Political Differentiation, Avoidance, and Unawareness," in Rosberg and Callaghy, *Socialism in Sub-Saharan Africa,* pp. 133–173; Irving Leonard Markovitz, *Power and Class in Africa* (Englewood Cliffs, N.J.: Prentice-Hall, 1977); Barbara Stallings, *Economic Dependency in Africa and Latin America,* Sage Professional Papers in Comparative Politics, vol. 3, series no. 01–031 (Beverly Hills, Calif.: Sage, 1972); Goran Hyden, *Beyond Ujamaa in Tanzania: Underdevelopment and an Uncaptured Peasantry* (Berkeley: University of California Press, 1980), esp. pp. 9–37; Crawford Young, *Ideology and Development in Africa* (New Haven, Conn.: Yale University Press, 1982).

CHAPTER 7

Government in the Economy

> *In all the political systems of the world, much of politics is economics, and most of economics is also politics. . . . Historically the alternative to governmentalization of a national politico-economic system has been the market.*
> —CHARLES E. LINDBLOM

In the industrialized societies of North America, Latin America, West Europe, and East Europe, governments have come to play an increasingly important role in the economy since World War II. Today most governments enact policies intended to promote industrial growth, stimulate higher productivity, provide social services to individuals, reduce unemployment, and control price increases. Whatever their success in attaining these policy objectives, most political leaders in the industrialized world assume that government officials will be involved in economic decision making. The major policy differences among various countries arise over the relative power wielded by governments, private corporations, and labor unions in the economic policy process.

Faced with the important activities governments perform in modern industrial economies, political scientists have constructed typologies of politico-economic systems based on the degrees of public ownership and government control. Four important types include capitalism, corporatism, state socialism, and market socialism. Capitalism features private ownership of economic firms and social group (business) control of economic decision making. Corporatism blends private ownership with government controls over business and labor. State socialism combines public (state) ownership and government control. Under market socialism, public (social) ownership coexists with social group (workers') control of most economic decisions.[1] The following analysis of these four types examines the function of government in the economic policy process, the role of interest groups, the manner of representing individual interests, and the relation between the public and private spheres. (See table 7-1 for a summary of the four types of systems.)

Capitalism

Of all four system types, capitalism best represents the dominance of the private over the public sphere. Capitalists make a sharp distinction between the public and private sectors of society—between state and society. In most capitalist economies, especially the United States, private ownership prevails. Private business executives make the key economic decisions about production, investment, prices, employment, and wages. In this economic policy process, government officials operate as referees; they specify the rules, procedures, and laws that regulate interactions among business firms, unions, and consumers. The executive officials and legislators formulate the rules for adjudicating interest group conflicts; courts and administrative agencies then enforce the procedures.

Under these pluralist conditions, a variety of independent voluntary associations—business groups, trade unions, farm associations, consumer organizations—compete on the political market. Representing particular group interests, each association comes into conflict with other groups for a share of the economic pie. The process of reaching political decisions resembles the collective bargaining arrangements between labor and management. Agreed on basic procedures for resolving differences, each side retains the autonomy to demand a settlement that partially satisfies the group's interest claims.

Representation of individual economic interests involves both territorial and functional strategies. Just as diverse interest groups compete in the economic market, so different political parties compete on the political market. During elections, individuals vote for party candidates; the winners become legislators who seek to satisfy individual interests for greater concrete benefits, such as higher wages, higher pensions, greater access to employment, expanded educational opportunities, and lower gas prices. Less important than territorial legislative representation, functional representation occurs when individuals participate in an interest group that lobbies the legislators and civil servants for the satisfaction of individual interests.[2]

The liberal pluralist version of capitalism assumes the existence of a market economy where many small firms compete with each other;

CHAPTER 7 GOVERNMENT IN THE ECONOMY 221

TABLE 7-1 Contemporary politico-economic systems

	Capitalism	Corporatism	State Socialism	Market Socialism
1. ownership of economic firms	private	private	public (state)	public (society)
2. control of economic activities	social group (business firms)	government	government	social group (workers)
3. role of government in economic decision making	Government is the referee that formulates and enforces the rules in the interest group game.	Government manages, plans, supervises, and regulates private group activities.	Government directs economic activities and mobilizes workers toward a modernized and industrialized society.	Government outlines a general economic plan, coordinates activities of self-managed enterprises, & regulates money supply.
4. role of interest groups in economic decision making	Groups represent members' interests and compete for share of economic pie.	Under government supervision, groups cooperate to expand production.	Groups stimulate higher production, teach the workers productive skills & labor discipline, & provide social services.	Groups (especially workers' councils & unions) administer self-managed enterprises.
5. manner of representing individual economic interests	Popularly elected legislatures, based on territorial districts, represent individual interests; to a lesser extent, so do functionally based interest groups.	State and nongovernment bureaucrats represent interests; in constitutional regimes, parliament has some representative functions.	Communist party and mass associations linked to party represent interests; elected Soviets play a less important representative role.	Workers' councils, unions, legislative assemblies at all government levels, and communist party share in representative functions.
6. relation between public & private sectors	distinct (Capitalists assume that pursuit of private gain will unintentionally lead to public good.)	merged (Public policies are delegated to private groups for implementation.)	merged (Communist party-state elites politicize private activities.)	distinct (Elite recognizes legitimacy of public and private interests and tries to reconcile the two.)
7. relative dominance of public and private sectors	Private sector dominates public sector.	Public sector (a government stressing nationalism, unity, order, cooperation) dominates private sector.	Public sector (strong state and single party) dominates all private activities.	Private sector (private farm & small-scale private firm) is subordinate to publicly owned, worker-managed enterprises.

however, in the modern industrialized world, oligopolies (concentrated industries) control the market. Often a few large corporations (four or fewer) control over 50 percent of a product market; they also dominate key sectors of the whole economy. Because these giant corporations have the economic power to restrict the entry of new firms into the market, only limited competition takes place. Under these oligopolistic conditions, individuals cannot easily find an organization to represent their interests before government officials. Economic policymaking comes under the control of large-scale bureaucratic institutions, such as administrative agencies, private corporations, and large-scale labor unions. Particularly in Austria, Sweden, Britain, and Norway, corporatism comes to replace the more pluralistic competitive capitalism.

Corporatism

Unlike capitalism, the corporate state merges the public with the private sphere. The government manages, plans, supervises, and regulates economic activities. It authorizes particular private organizations to represent group interests before government officials. In turn, these private organizations, especially labor unions and business corporations, gain some responsibilities for implementing public policies. The old system of territorial representation, under which each individual voter makes direct demands on a legislator to enact a preferred economic policy, no longer seems so operative. Instead, to exert decisive influence over the economic policy process, each individual must be an active member of some organized group that has access to government officials. State and nongovernment professional bureaucrats, rather than legislative amateurs, play the key role in representing individual interests. When deciding public policies, they stress the need for both government and private agencies to cooperate for the national good, not to engage in conflict associated with competitive capitalism. In short, corporatism blends private ownership of firms with active government control over economic decision making.

Although corporatism emphasizes the need to mix private ownership with government controls, the actual power government exerts over business firms and labor unions has varied in different corporate states. Some, such as Sweden and Britain, are more democratic, open, and inclusionary; others, such as Nazi Germany, Fascist Italy, and the contemporary military dictatorships of Brazil, Chile, and Argentina, have pursued a more dictatorial, closed, and exclusionary strategy, especially toward trade unions.

In Sweden and Britain, government officials follow pluralist patterns of decision making. Several political parties compete for political power. Trade unions retain the autonomy to press their claims before government agencies and private business corporations. Particularly in Sweden, highly organized unions take an active part in making economic decisions. Through the works councils, union officials consult with company managers about a wide range of issues: working hours, wages, plant safety, recruitment of new workers, employee layoffs, personnel training, and even investment plans. The need for Swedish corporations to produce inexpensive, competitive goods for sale on the world market encourages cooperative relations between managers and union leaders. In Britain, however, the central union organization has less power over unions in each shop. The national Trades Union Congress leaders often support wage restraints opposed by local shop stewards, who initiate strike actions. Partly as a result of the fragmentation of both trade unions and business corporations, greater industrial conflict has occurred in Britain than in Sweden. Even though British union leaders preside over a faction-ridden movement, they still possess an important veto power over decisions taken by government officials and corporate executives.

In contrast to Sweden and Britain, where the government includes independent trade unions in the economic decision process, Fascist Italy, Nazi Germany, and the Latin American military dictatorships (Argentina, Brazil, and Chile) have pursued a more exclusionary strategy toward labor unions. Generally, a period of political polarization preceded the dictatorial takeovers in these countries. High inflation or unemployment exacerbated conflicts beween labor and management; organizations representing the industrial working class, including socialist parties and unions, posed a challenge to private business corporations. As a response to this polarized situation, dictatorial rulers seized power to crush the organizational strength of independent unions and socialist parties. In these corporate states, government exercises tight control over private business firms and especially unions.

Among these regimes, the Nazi state wielded the broadest scope of power over economic decision making. From the beginning of his rule in early 1933, Hitler suppressed the free trade union movements. Particularly after 1936, the state gained control of privately owned industries, including the steel, metal, chemical, and electrical industries that rearmed Germany.

In Italy and Latin America, however, private corporations retained greater autonomy than in Nazi Germany. Mussolini and the Latin American dictators, like Hitler, excluded unions from political or economic power. Yet they allowed private industrialists some freedom to make their own economic decisions. Especially in contemporary Brazil and Chile, multinational corporations and large-scale domestic private industries play a key role. Although welcoming capitalist investment, these military dictators reject not only communist collectivism but also the individualism and pluralism associated with classical liberalism. Instead, they support an organic, corporatist state based on order, hierarchy, elitism, paternalism, and social harmony. Opposed to anarchical class conflict, the state coordinates private group activity so as to maximize economic production.[3]

State Socialism

Of all four politico-economic systems, state socialism establishes the greatest government domination over the economic process. The communist party-state basically steers economic society; it not only controls economic decision making but also owns the major means of production, including most land and industrial capital. Through their centralized direction, party and government officials try to mobilize the work force to fulfill high production objectives outlined in the state plan. State socialist societies are thus development dictatorships; by industrializing their underdeveloped nations, the communist elite aims to create a new society.

The major techniques for engineering rapid economic development involve guidance by the government, Communist party, and mass associations linked to the Party. In the Soviet Union, the state planning committee reconciles the economic demands made by different government economic ministries; these in turn supervise the operation of state enterprises, state farms, and collective farms. The Communist party checks the performance of the state planning committee, economic ministries, and state enterprises. At the initial stage of policy formulation, the Party gathers needed information from technical experts, government ministers, and trade union officials. Then it oversees the fulfillment of the economic plans.

Guided by the Party, the mass associations, including trade unions and farm organizations, play a key role in the attainment of economic goals. These associations operate as transmission belts between the top party–state elite and the individual citizens. They stimulate higher production, encourage greater labor discipline, teach rational, secular norms, and help implement social services such as health benefits, vacations, recreational opportunities, access to housing, and social insurance. Although unions claim to represent the worker's interests, they lack the right to strike; in economic decision making, they play a subordinate role to government officials, party activists, and directors of state enterprises.

Under state socialism, the public interest dominates private interests. Claiming to know the long-range general interests of the industrial proletariat better than do the factory workers themselves, the Communist party elite imposes its concept of the public good on the society. Downgrading the pursuit of private interests, government and party institutions politicize social life; public agencies penetrate the individual's private life. The Communist party and its mass associations, rather than voluntary associations and elected legislators, take prime responsibility for representing individual economic interests. Although in the Soviet Union the legislative bodies—the Supreme Soviet and local soviets—do voice some popular criticisms about specific economic policies, their impact on public policymaking seems relatively limited. Instead, most citizens rely on party-dominated organizations to press their economic claims.[4]

Not all nations ruled by a Communist party experience the powerful state domination over the economy found in the Soviet Union. China features greater decentralization of economic decision making to the provincial and local levels; Chinese peasants possess greater freedom than peasants on the Soviet collective or state farms. In Poland, most farms come under private ownership. Under the Hungarian New Economic Mechanism and the Yugoslav workers' management system, enterprises retain considerable autonomy from direct government control. Market considerations, not a centralized economic plan, determine key economic decisions. Although dominated by a communist party, Hungary and especially Yugoslavia exemplify a market socialist type of politico-economic system.[5]

Market Socialism

Unlike the state socialist policies followed in the Soviet Union, market socialism as practiced by the Yugoslavs involves greater economic and political decentralization. The central government and communist party (League of Communists) play a less dominant role in economic decision making. Whereas in the USSR the state owns the major means of production, in Yugoslavia the general society, not the state, legally owns nearly all enterprises. The workers control the operation of the enterprises through elected workers' councils, which operate in enterprises employing at least thirty persons. They decide the type and amount of production, prices for goods, wage levels, and distribution of profits. Along with the local government agency—the people's committee of the commune—the workers' council hires and fires the director of the enterprise. The director, managing board, and technical staff make the key decisions, subject to workers' council supervision.

In Yugoslavia, the state administration places few restrictions on either the enterprise's managers or the workers' council. The central government formulates a highly general economic plan, coordinates interactions among the enterprises, levies taxes, determines the money supply and exchange rates, and imposes some price controls. Commercial banks that do not fall under state ownership supply most investment funds. Each enterprise carries out the remaining aspects of economic decision making. Through the market's operation, individuals enjoy the freedom to choose a job and to buy consumer goods. Consistent with a market system, the price mechanism determines the details of producing a particular good.

In the Yugoslav version of market socialism, political decentralization reinforces the autonomy wielded by the publicly owned enterprise and workers' council. Composed of diverse ethnic groups—Serbs, Croatians, Slovenes, Macedonians, Albanians, Montenegrins—Yugoslavia is a multinational federal system with six republics and two autonomous regions. In the federal government organs, each ethnic group secures representation corresponding to its proportion of the national population. To satisfy ethnic group demands for political, economic, and cultural autonomy, the central government leaders have delegated crucial responsibilities to the republic, provincial, and communal governments, which retain the power to shape economic decision making. Within these governments below the federal level, the legislatures—republic assemblies, provincial assemblies, communal assemblies—wield greater influence than the legislative bodies found in the Soviet Union. Through these parliamentary organs, individuals press for the satisfaction of their economic interests.

In contrast to the Soviet elite, the Yugoslavs accept the legitimacy of private interests. Some private ownership does exist, including not only 85 percent of the land but also small-scale enterprises employing fewer than five persons outside the family. The market system enables individuals to express their demands for consumer goods. A variety of territorial and functional agencies represent individual economic interests. Through the Federal Assembly, republic assemblies, and communal assemblies, people can articulate their economic claims on public policies. At the national level, unions press for greater allocation of resources to consumption; at the enterprise level, they try to satisfy workers' economic demands for higher wages and better working conditions.

Faced with this interest diversity, Yugoslav leaders have established complex methods for reconciling public and private interests. Unlike competitive capitalists, who assume that an "unseen hand" will transform the pursuit of private gain into the public good, market socialists in Yugoslavia perceive the need to establish institutions that accommodate private interests with the general welfare. At the workplace level, leaders have organized workers' councils in enterprises and self-managing councils in school and cultural institutions.

Through active participation in these self-managing agencies, individuals supposedly view their private interests from a public perspective.

The dominant party in Yugoslavia—the League of Communists—also attempts to coordinate the divergent individual, enterprise, ethnic, and regional interests into general public policies. League members dominate government organizations; yet they wield less power over economic decision making than do Communist party bureaucrats in the Soviet Union. Although the League represses political dissent, it allows considerable economic freedom to unions and enterprises. Unions have some limited autonomy from the party. In each enterprise, the director makes the key economic decisions; the League seems to carry less weight than the managing board, technical staff, and workers' council. Today the League has the primary responsibility to cope with the economic problems facing Yugoslavia—high inflation, high unemployment, low productivity, and economic inequalities dividing wealthy regions and enterprises from the poorer ones. By trying to reconcile competing claims from workers, managers, technocrats, national government officials, and regional leaders, the League of Communists, not the state, operates as the basic steering mechanism that guides the Yugoslav nation.[6]

Notes

1. R. E. Pahl and J. T. Winkler, "The Coming Corporatism," *Challenge* 18 (March–April 1975): 31; J. T. Winkler, "Corporatism," *Archives Européennes de Sociologie* 17, no. 1 (1976): 113.
2. Norman H. Keehn, "A World of Becoming: From Pluralism to Corporatism," *Polity* 9 (Fall 1976): 19–39; Alfred Stepan, *The State and Society: Peru in Comparative Perspective* (Princeton, N.J.: Princeton University Press, 1978), pp. 7–17.
3. For analyses of corporatism in the Western world, see Alfred Diamant, "Bureaucracy and Public Policy in Neocorporatist Settings: Some European Lessons," *Comparative Politics* 14 (October 1981): 101–124; Pahl and Winkler, "The Coming Corporatism," pp. 28–35; Winkler, "Corporatism," pp. 100–136; Alan Cawson, "Pluralism, Corporatism and the Role of the State," *Government and Opposition* 13 (Spring 1978): 178–198; Andrew Cox, "Corporatism as Reductionism: The Analytic Limits of the Corporatist Thesis," *Government and Opposition* 16 (Winter 1981): 78–95; Harold L. Wilensky, *The "New Corporatism," Centralization, and the Welfare State*, Sage Professional Papers in Contemporary Political Sociology, vol. 2, series no. 06-020 (Beverly Hills, Calif.: Sage, 1976), pp. 21–23. Studies of the corporate state in Fascist Italy and Nazi Germany appear in Edward R. Tannenbaum, *The Fascist Experience* (New York: Basic Books, 1972), pp. 89–112; S. Lombardini, "Italian Fascism and the Economy," in *The Nature of Fascism*, ed. S. J. Woolf (New York: Vintage Books, 1969), pp. 152–164; T. W. Mason, "The Primacy of Politics—Politics and Economics in National Socialist Germany," in Woolf, *The Nature of Fascism*, pp. 165–195. For discussions of Latin American corporatism, see Stepan, *The State and Society*, pp. 46–113; Howard J. Wiarda, "Toward a Framework for the Study of Political Change in the Iberic-Latin Tradition: The Corporative Model," *World Politics* 25 (January 1973): 206–235; David M. Landry, "Resurrection of the Corporate Model in Latin American Politics," *Studies in Comparative International Development* 11 (Fall 1976): 70–83; Guillermo A. O'Donnell, "Corporatism and the Question of the State," in *Authoritarianism and Corpora-*

tism in Latin America, ed. James M. Malloy (Pittsburgh, Penn.: University of Pittsburgh Press, 1977), pp. 47–87; Paul W. Drake, "Corporatism and Functionalism in Modern Chilean Politics," *Journal of Latin American Studies* 10 (May 1978): 83–116.

4. See David Lane, *The Socialist Industrial State: Towards a Political Sociology of State Socialism* (London: George Allen and Unwin, 1976), pp. 13–14, 73–119; Jerry Hough and Merle Fainsod, *How the Soviet Union Is Governed* (Cambridge, Mass.: Harvard University Press, 1979), pp. 362–408; Gregory Grossman, *Economic Systems*, 2d ed. (Englewood Cliffs, N.J.: Prentice-Hall, 1974), pp. 93–122; Martin C. Schnitzer and James W. Nordyke, *Comparative Economic Systems*, 2d ed. (Cincinnati, Ohio: South-Western, 1977), pp. 367–428.

5. Grossman, *Economic Systems*, pp. 123–167.

6. Ibid., pp. 153–160; Schnitzer and Nordyke, *Comparative Economic Systems*, pp. 477–509; Charles E. Lindblom, *Politics and Markets* (New York: Basic Books, 1977), pp. 330–343; Bogdan Denis Denitch, *The Legitimation of a Revolution: The Yugoslav Case* (New Haven, Conn.: Yale University Press, 1976), esp. pp. 149–184; Sidney Verba and Goldie Shabad, "Workers' Councils and Political Stratification: The Yugoslav Experience," *American Political Science Review* 72 (March 1978): 80–95; Sidney Verba, Norman Nie, and Jae-on Kim, *Participation and Political Equality: A Seven-Nation Comparison* (London: Cambridge University Press, 1978), pp. 215–233; Branka Magas, "Tito's Deluge," *New Statesman* 99 (January 25, 1980): 122-123; Ellen T. Comisso, "The Logic of Worker (Non) Participation in Yugoslav Self-Management," *Review of Radical Political Economics* 13 (Summer 1981): 11–22.

CHAPTER

8

Political Parties in Constitutional Systems

What, in fact, is the modern party? It is the methodical organization of the electoral masses.
—ROBERT MICHELS

The party is alive only during election periods.
—MAX WEBER

In 1911, throughout the Austro-Hungarian empire, elections took place for seats in the Chamber of Deputies, the central parliament that met in Vienna. Although during the late nineteenth century only property owners had held the franchise, gradually more men gained the right to vote. By 1906, all men, regardless of property ownership, could choose representatives to provincial assemblies and to the central Chamber of Deputies. A bewildering array of political parties competed for electoral support. Originally, the young Czechs battled the old Czechs. National Socialists and the Czech Agrarian party later strove to win the peasants' vote. Social Democrats attracted the urban working class. Poking fun at all these parties, the Czech author Jaroslav Hasek and his friends in 1911 formed the Party of Moderate Progress within the Limits of the Law. The party's manifesto proclaimed:

> Czechs! In the Czech nation there are many parties which maintain that everything can be accomplished all at once—suddenly! Other parties will tell you that nothing can be done at all! Then whom should you trust?

Trust those who bring before you the successful, time-honored formula of moderate progress within the limits of the law.[1]

Unfortunately for the party's cause, only thirty-eight men succumbed to the manifesto's appeals and voted for the Party of Moderate Progress. But like all unsuccessful candidates, Hasek concluded that its political defeat really meant a moral victory: "As the realists say, we got a drubbing but gained a moral victory."[2]

Governments have operated as long as societies have functioned; yet political parties arose only during the last 200 years. Compared with government legislatures and bureaucracies, parties are a more "modern" organization associated with the rise of mass participation in politics. As party developments in the Austro-Hungarian empire indicate, parties originated in those countries where the electoral franchise expanded and representative government gained legitimacy. The first modern political parties were the Hamiltonians and Jeffersonians, who campaigned for seats to the newly established House of Representatives at the end of the eighteenth century in the United States. In Europe, as in America, the expansion of the franchise stimulated the organization of political parties with a mass base. In England, the Liberal and Conservative parties originally represented factions in the House of Commons, rather than electoral machines. After 1867, however, both the Liberals and the Conservatives began to build a mass electoral base. Just as in the United States, the widening of the suffrage motivated the legislative elite to organize political parties that would strengthen their chances for reelection.[3]

Because political parties originated with the expansion of the franchise and mass political participation, their electoral function is crucial. Accordingly, I view a political party as a relatively cohesive organization whose candidates seek election to government offices. This conception has the greatest relevance to pluralistic party systems, where each party forms a part of the whole system. In modern constitutional societies, competition among political parties animates the struggle for government office.[4] This chapter concentrates on political parties in seven constitutional governments: the United States, Canada, Britain, Sweden, West Germany, France, and Italy.

The following discussion explores three variables that characterize political parties' operation: party *ideologies* (programs for public policy), the *voting behavior* of social groups, and the *activities* the parties perform. The policy goals of party activists and the structural context in which they operate tend to influence the types of activities. We assume that if party leaders view ideology as highly important and if the party structure links the elite to the masses in complex, explicit, and powerful ways, then the party activities become highly comprehensive.

Party Ideologies

In the campaign for elected office, most political parties take stands on various specific issues. Although the desire to win the election may be primary, few candidates seek government office just for the power, wealth, and status that supposedly spring from electoral success. Instead, political party leaders, both government officeholders and activists who hold no formal offices, articulate proposals for public policies that revolve around attitudes toward government promotion of freedom and equality. Two important aspects of freedom include civil liberties (right to express opposition toward government policies, leaders, and institutional arrangements) and the degree of government management of the economy, specifically, the economic freedoms private enterprises enjoy. The equality issue focuses on the role of government action in promoting greater economic and ethnic equality.

Throughout the contemporary Western world, political parties have differed primarily over the issues of freedom for private enterprises and economic equality. Left-wing parties (Socialists and especially Communists) support government actions to realize greater economic equality for workers and consumers. The leftist parties want to increase government management of the economy, either through nationalizing more privately owned firms or through expanding state regulations over the private economic sector. In contrast, right-wing parties (conservatives and Christian Democrats) show a weaker commitment to government promotion of economic equality and state management of the economy. Fewer disagreements between leftist and rightist parties have occurred over the pursuit of political freedom. Although the democratic socialists and liberal democrats display slightly greater support for civil liberties, the interparty differences are not extensive.

PARTISAN ATTITUDES TOWARD EQUALITY

Since the 1930s, the Republican and Democratic parties in the United States have taken divergent attitudes toward government actions to promote economic equality. The Democrats support tax, expenditure, and government regulatory programs to secure greater economic equality, both equality of incomes and especially equality of opportunities to achieve wealth. For instance, Democratic voters and particularly party activists favor progressive taxes, including higher taxes on inherited property and capital gains. Democratic attitudes toward government expenditures also express a commitment to egalitarian values. Democrats want to increase spending for medical care, education, and job programs. To realize these egalitarian objectives, Democrats support an activist role for the federal government in managing the economy. They want to implement antitrust legislation, policies to prevent economic recessions, and government programs that promote healthier, safer working conditions. Republicans generally show less enthusiasm for these equalitarian public policies.[5]

Compared with policies toward economic equality, the issue of racial equality has produced less polarization between the two American parties. Particularly during the 1950s, Democrats and Republicans took similar stands. Regional differences overwhelmed party differences, with the Republicans occupying an intermediate position between northern and southern Democrats.

Yet beginning with the 1964 election, the two parties began to advocate divergent programs toward racial equality. The Republican candidate for president, Senator Barry Goldwater, was one of six Republican senators who voted against the passage of the final 1964 civil rights bill. President Lyndon Johnson made frequent public speeches upholding equal rights for Blacks; he strengthened the civil rights bill that President Kennedy had originally submitted to Congress. As expected, in 1964, Democrats showed stronger support than Republicans for government policies to realize equality of racial opportunity in schools, public accommodations, housing, and employment. Democratic white- and blue-collar workers looked more favorably on racial equality than did Republicans with the same occupational background. Whereas middle-class Democrats most enthusiastically supported government actions to secure equal rights for Blacks, working-class Republicans voiced the most opposition to racial equality. Similarly, white-collar workers voting for President Johnson expressed strongest support for racial equality; blue-collar workers preferring Senator Goldwater displayed the greatest antipathy toward civil rights policies.

During the 1968 and 1972 elections, different approaches to racial matters continued to divide the two parties. With a "southern strategy," the Republicans hoped to consolidate their popularity throughout the states of the Old Confederacy and the Southwest. Not surprisingly, those two elections saw both Democratic activists and voters look more sympathetically on policies to expand the rights of racial minorities. Even among the white people outside the South, partisan differences remained, with the middle-class Democratic activists expressing the strongest support for equalitarian measures. By the late 1970s, the regional differences over racial equality had largely disappeared.[6]

In Britain, the Conservative and Labour parties reveal somewhat similar policy disagreements over equality as in the United States. Labour voters and leaders prefer more equalitarian programs, such as higher taxes on the wealthy and increased government expenditures for welfare services, old-age pensions, and public housing. The Labour party also has campaigned more strongly for comprehensive schools, an educational policy intended to provide equal opportunities for secondary school students of all social classes. British parties showed fewer disagreements over the issue of racial equality. Compared with the Conservative members of Parliament, the Labour MPs have shown somewhat greater support for the rights of coloured immigrants from the West Indies, Pakistan, and India to remain in Britain and to enjoy equal opportunities with the Whites. However, survey evidence gives an ambiguous, conflicting portrait of English voters. Some surveys indicate that Labour voters, compared with Conservatives, are more racially equalitarian. Other studies suggest that Liberal voters express greatest support for coloured immigration and Labour voters show the least support, with the Conservatives taking an intermediate position.[7] In short, economic issues, rather than racial matters, more strongly divide the British parties.

Because Sweden has a high degree of ethnic homogeneity, economic issues divide the major political parties. As in Britain, the leftist parties, particularly the Communists and to a lesser extent the Social Democrats, most strongly favor government actions to secure greater income equality. They want to increase government expenditures for social services, raise the inheritance tax, lower poor people's taxes, lessen pay differences among workers, and narrow income differentials. The more conservative parties—conservative, liberal, and center—express greater opposition to these equalitarian measures.[8]

Similarly, the French and Italian political parties take different stands on egalitarian issues, with the left-wing parties (Communists and Socialists) highly disposed to expand equality. At the local government level, a comparison of PCI *(Partito Comunista Italiano)* and Christian Democratic activists showed the PCI more enthusiastic about measures to redistribute wealth to the poor and thus secure greater economic equality. In France, the Communist party also voices the strongest commitment to social and economic equality. To a greater extent than the Socialist party, the PCF *(Parti communiste français)* prefers a higher minimum wage, a greater narrowing of salary differences among government employees, higher taxes on the wealthy, and larger increases in old-age pensions.[9]

PARTISAN ATTITUDES TOWARD FREEDOM

Although the left-wing parties in France and Italy prefer greater equality, do they also uphold political freedom? In the Italian Chamber of Deputies, leftist parliamentarians voice greater support for civil liberties than do neofascists. Among Italian deputies, the Socialists appear most favorably disposed to political liberties. Communist and Christian Democratic deputies offer less support. The right-wing legislators—namely, the neofascists—rank the lowest on a civil liberties scale. Somewhat similar attitudes among party leaders occurred when they answered a "dogmatism" questionnaire. As formulated by Milton Rokeach, the dogmatism scale measures the extent to which a person has a closed mind—that is, a mind that evaluates information not on its own merits but on irrelevant internal pressures, such as acute anxieties, or on external conditions, such as actions of authority figures. On this dogmatism scale, the Communist and Socialist deputies attained the lowest scores; the Christian Democrats received an intermediate score; and the neofascist *Movimento Sociale Italiano* leaders expressed the highest dogmatism.

In France, the different attitudes held by Communist (PCF) and Socialist (PS) party leaders toward civil liberties seem as striking as the positions separating the leftist partisans from their more conservative colleagues. Although the PCF has renounced the dictatorship of the proletariat, accepted the need for a pluralist party system, and made a verbal commitment to political liberty, it still wants to play a vanguard role among both the left-wing parties and the working class. Compared with the Socialist party, the Communist party expresses a weaker commitment to party turnover in government and a weaker faith in electoral competition as the best way to achieve socialism. PCF leaders appear less open than PS activists to alternative sources of political information, such as conservative newspapers, Catholic friends, and right-wing government officials. Certainly, the top PCF leaders manage a more autocratically organized party than do Socialist leaders. Committed to a Leninist organizational pattern, members of the Communist elite take a less democratic attitude toward the presence of factions within the Party; PCF leaders want to decide issues in a secret caucus. The Socialists, however, more warmly accept several party factions, which openly debate party policies.

Generally, the Italian Communist party leaders accord greater importance to maintaining political freedoms than do their French communist brethren. Although both Communist parties have come out against single-party control and the dictatorship of the proletariat, the PCI takes a more flexible view of the political world. Its leaders want to retain diversity within Italian society. It upholds dissent, decentralization, multi-party competition, reconciliation of diverse views, and alliances with both the Socialists and the Christian Democrats. By contrast, the PCF leaders perceive the world through more rigid lenses. For them, a bipolar struggle, not diversity, faces society. Although top party leaders stress the need for explaining their decisions to subordinate party activists, the PCF elite still believes in party discipline and democratic centralism as essential to maintain party solidarity. In sum, among left-wing party leaders in

France and Italy, the Socialists express the greatest commitment to freedom, and the Italian Communists hold more libertarian views than do the French Communists. Thus, divergence within the ideological Left appears as pronounced as the differences between leftist and rightist parties.

French and Italian Communists also articulate divergent views toward government management of the economy and economic freedom for private business firms. Both France and Italy already have extensive public ownership of the economy. The Italian Communists reject any proposals to further extend the nationalized and state-holding sectors. By contrast, the French Communist party has campaigned for more state ownership of private firms than has any other party.

French Socialists and especially Gaullists oppose extensive nationalization of private businesses. When PS leaders gained government power in 1981, they supported nationalizing large steel corporations, aircraft producers, weapons manufacturers, electrical–electronics companies, and some private banks and insurance firms. According to the PS view, state participation in the management of other large corporations, not government ownership, would secure more desirable results. On the Right, Gaullist parties have rejected expanded nationalization and greater state control of industry, viewing both measures as threats to the economic freedom of private entrepreneurs.[10]

In Sweden and Britain as well, the conservative parties equate expanded government management of the economy with a loss of economic freedom. The Swedish conservative, liberal, and center parties—the three dominant "bourgeois" parties—oppose greater government control of the economy and more nationalization of domestic natural resources, large corporations, private insurance companies, and commercial banks. These parties believe that greater state control over the economy will increase unemployment among the workers, reduce economic efficiency, and endanger the freedom of the private business enterprise. The British Conservative party takes a similar position toward government management of the economy. In their successful 1979 election campaign, the Tories rejected policies to extend nationalization, to expand wage and price controls, and to increase government participation in the collective bargaining process between labor unions and business firms. From the Conservative perspective, freedom means not only free speech but also freedom to operate a business and to own private property. In contrast, the Labour members of Parliament perceive freedom primarily in civil liberties terms—as the right to express opinions with no fear of censorship. For them, freedom for the private capitalist assumes lower priority than social equality for all people.[11]

Compared with the view toward socioeconomic equality, support for political freedom reveals greater agreement by British and American leaders from all parties. Although the differences are small, the left-wing activists take a somewhat stronger stand for civil liberties. For example, in England, local Labour party members are less authoritarian than Conservative party members. In the House of Commons, Labour parliamentarians give slightly more support to political liberties. Relative to the Conservative MPs, they seem less willing to impose government controls on organizational activities.

In the United States, Democratic delegates to the national convention uphold civil liberties more enthusiastically than do Republican delegates; Democratic delegates show greater concern for protecting the rights of the accused and greater opposition to government wiretapping. Republican delegates rank lower on such pro–civil liberties measures as tolerance, procedural rights, and faith in democracy. Among college-educated party activists, Republicans appear less disposed than Democrats to uphold freedom of the press, respect the rights of the accused, grant communist professors the right to teach, and allow protest meetings and marches.

Mass attitudes toward civil liberties in Britain and America show fewer differences than stands taken by the party elite. Middle-class citizens preferring left-wing parties usually express slightly stronger support for political freedom. Thus, middle-class Labourites place greater value on freedom of speech than do working-class Labourites or middle-class Tories; the latter group appears the least libertarian. Conservative voters also are a bit more willing than Labour voters to impose censorship and to place stricter controls on political demonstrations.

In the United States as well, left-wing partisans show the greater preference for extending civil liberties. Especially among Democrats, the differences between party *voters* emerge as more pronounced than between party *identifiers*. Compared with identifiers, Democratic voters more strongly support the rights of the accused to have a fair trial, protestors to hold meetings, Communists to teach in a college, and newspaper reporters to withhold information about their sources. Republicans, both identifiers and voters, express the greatest opposition to these four civil liberties.[12] Nevertheless, the issues of economic equality, rather than political freedom, still polarize the two groups of partisan supporters to a greater extent.

PARTISAN IDEOLOGICAL CONFLICTS OVER PUBLIC POLICIES

As we have seen, ideological conflicts over the pursuit of freedom and equality enliven the electoral scene in most Western democratic countries. These ideological disputes divide not only different political parties but also factions within each party. In exploring the two types of ideological conflicts, this section probes two basic questions: To what extent do activists, government officeholders, and supporters in the *same* party hold similar views of political issues? During the last sixty years, why has there occurred a decline of ideological polarization between *different* parties in West Europe?

Political activism and ideological commitments. Of the three key groups in a political party—*government officeholders, activists* who work for the party but who hold no government position, and more passive *supporters* (either voters or psychological identifiers)—the activists are generally the most "ideological" in both style and substance. From the stylistic standpoint, activist ideologues use abstract, deductive reasoning. They link particular details (life in a slum) to general principles of freedom and equality. They perceive concrete events in light of abstract ideas. Activists also deduce specific conclusions from general theoretical principles. In terms of ideological content, partisan activists also take more polarized views than do either government officeholders or the mass of voters. For instance, left-wing activists most strongly support government policies to enlarge income equality and to extend state control over the economy; right-wing party activists remain highly opposed to these two measures.

In contrast to the activists, few passive supporters, either voters or especially psychological identifiers, engage in ideological (abstract, deductive) thinking. In most Western countries, probably no more than 20 percent of the electorate views political activities from a left versus right perspective. Few voters interpret electoral campaigns through an ideological prism or can articulate the meaning of Right and Left. Most do not assess political events in terms of a comprehensive set of ideological principles that systematically relate several diverse issues. The majority of voters lacks detailed political information about complex issues, holds vague preferences, and changes policy views over time. Not only in the United States but also abroad, most citizens base their electoral choices on their party identification, image of the candidate, and past government performance, rather than on explicit ideological principles.[13]

Why do partisan activists take a more ideological view of politics than the mass of voters? Compared with passive voters, party activists are by definition highly involved in political life. They have achieved more formal education. Generally, they also seek more changes in the existing situation—either the creation of a new, more equalitarian social order or the restoration of a previously operating situation where laissez-faire principles guided government activities. Both advanced education and support for social change lead activists to regard a programmatic ideology as a political requirement.[14]

Throughout the Western democratic world, people with middle-class occupations—business executives and professionals (lawyers, journalists, writers, teachers, civil servants)—actively participate in both left-wing and right-wing political parties. The ideological conflicts between parties and within the same party stem from the attitudinal splits within this college-educated middle class. In the United States, Britain, Sweden, and Italy, middle-class activists within the leftist parties take more equalitarian stands on issues than do the passive rank-and-file party supporters. Compared with party followers, activists from different parties also adopt more polarized positions.

For example, in the United States, the middle-class Democratic activists take more equalitarian stands than the Democratic masses; that is, the activists display greater support for public policies promoting economic and racial equality. Although party activists in both parties have middle-class backgrounds, the Democrats come from the "new middle class" composed of government employees, teachers, public interest lawyers, writers, mass media figures, and scientists. Republican activists better represent the interests of corporation executives, managers, small business owners, company lawyers, realtors, and doctors. These groups seem less committed to public policies upholding stronger government efforts to realize economic and racial equality. These diverse attitudes splitting the American middle class have thus become incorporated into the two major parties' policy positions. As a result, on such issues as increased government spending for jobs, education, and medical care, middle-class Democrats express the greatest support and middle-class Republicans articulate the strongest opposition. Working-class Republicans and Democrats assume intermediate positions between the polarized party activists.[15]

In Britain, Sweden, and Italy as well, middle-class activists in the left-wing parties express a stronger commitment to equalitarian values than do the partisan followers. For instance, in England, Labour voters have shown less support for antidiscrimination legislation, trade union rights, increased welfare benefits, and increased public expenditures than have middle-class Labour activists—teachers, lecturers, social workers, and government employees. Whereas party activists interpret socialism primarily to mean social equality and public ownership of production, Labour members playing a more passive role within the party view socialism mainly as rising standards of living, rather than as an extension of economic equality. In Sweden, most Social Democrats elected to city councils come from white-collar backgrounds; compared with Social Democratic voters, they favor higher public expenditures for equalitarian measures. In Italy, middle-class activists working for the Communist party place greater importance on the equal distribution of national income than do PCI voters; the latter perceive capitalism as less threatening to Italian life. On these two issues, leaders from different parties express more divergent views than do the masses of voters.[16]

In sum, the ideological conflicts occurring both within and between political parties have stemmed from the divergent stands taken by middle-class party activists. Those on the Left support more equalitarian public policies, increased government spending on social services, and greater state management of the economy. By contrast, middle-class activists in the rightist parties oppose income equality, seek reduced government expenditures for social services, and reject an extension of government control over private business firms. Among the more passive working-class identifiers of different parties, greater ideological convergence prevails.

Declining ideological polarization in West Europe. Despite these ideological disputes still separating leftist from rightist political parties, during the last sixty years ideological polarization has declined in West Europe. Because ideology assumes the greatest functional importance during times of drastic social change, the most intense ideological struggles between parties have occurred when societies experienced institutional disintegration, challenges to established authority, and rapid industrialization.

In West Europe, ideological polarization reached a peak between 1860 and 1940, when European societies faced rapid economic growth, challenges to monarchical rule, war, disillusionment with orthodox religion and conventional morality, and economic depression. After 1860, the Industrial Revolution began to accelerate. As capitalism became more entrenched, socialist parties formed to articulate working-class demands. Established churches often sided with the employers against the workers; as a result, the leftist parties gained their primary support from the most secularized, nonreligious segments of the population. The First World War fragmented the European socialist movement. Whereas the German Social Democrats abandoned their pacifist heritage to support the Kaiser's war effort, some Socialists refused to participate in the war. After 1917, the socialist movement split into two antagonistic parties. In France and Italy, those Socialists opposing the war and supporting the new Soviet state in Russia organized a separate Communist party. With the coming of the economic depression in the 1930s, the conflicts between the left-wing parties and the conservative forces intensified; the Communists stressed the class struggle, and the conservatives often allied with the fascists to protect the rights to private ownership of property.

During the post–World War II era, ideological polarization declined throughout West Europe. The Second World War saw a broad alliance emerge between left-wing and right-wing parties opposed to Nazi Germany and Fascist Italy. However, after the war this coalition broke up as Soviet troops helped communist parties gain political power in East Europe. Yet in France and Italy, communist party leaders won control of city and regional governments, often in a coalition with socialist parties. There, as elsewhere in Europe, the thaw in the cold war, the postwar prosperity, the expansion of the middle class, the growing separation between the Catholic church and the state, and the left-wing parties' participation in government all decreased the historical ideological cleavages.

Exploring in detail this decreased polarization, John C. Thomas carried out a content analysis of political party literature between 1910 and 1976. Two policy issues dealt with government actions to stimulate economic equality; these included the desirable extent of social welfare services and government actions to promote greater equality of wealth. Two other issues focused on government management of the economy, including nationalization (public ownership of industries) and an active government role in economic planning. According to the findings of this historical content analysis, between 1910 and 1976 the major parties in Britain, West Germany, Sweden, France, and Italy have all ideologically converged. Especially on the issues of social welfare and wealth distribution, all parties have moved "left"—that is, become more equalitarian. Cleavages on the nationalization issue remain more acute; yet the Social Democratic parties in Germany and Sweden have become less enthusiastic about extending state ownership.

On the European continent today, the French and Italian parties remain the most ideologically polarized, followed by the German and Swedish. Although the Swedish "bourgeois" parties oppose greater government regulation of the economy, all parties support the welfare state. Like the Social Democrats and Communists, the other more conservative parties seek increased government spending for old-age pensions, child allowances, and housing. The three largest antisocialist parties promise to implement these programs with greater efficiency and lower taxes. Although the German Christian Democrats campaign on the issue of "socialism versus freedom," in office the CDU and the socialists enact somewhat similar policies, especially toward economic matters. In France and Italy, strong communist parties provide some ideological distinctiveness. Yet even though these two societies experienced the most intense ideological polarization in the late 1950s, recently the PCF and especially the PCI have adopted essentially reformist policy positions.[17]

Compared with the French Communist party, the Italian Communist party upholds a more reformist outlook toward political life. Rather than mobilizing organizations for a total system change, PCI leaders have tried to reconcile the diverse views with Italy. Instead of behaving like an "antisystem" party, the PCI functions as an established part of the existing system. It seeks essentially reformist goals: free health care, free child care centers, more public housing, assistance to small farmers, higher unemployment insurance lasting over a longer time period, and free higher education. True, the French Communists running local governments also pursue reformist policies, such as more low-income housing, higher family welfare services, and larger old-age state pensions. Yet the PCF has shown a reluctance to abandon its Leninist heritage and its revolutionary doctrines; it still remains committed to the vanguard role of the Communist party in building a socialist society.[18] Compared with French political parties, the Italian parties have thus demonstrated greater ideological convergence.

Even the economic crisis of the late 1970s, which brought high unemployment, high inflation, and declining production, failed to revive ideological polarization between the major Italian parties. Rather than demanding increased state ownership of the economy as a move toward a revolutionary economic transformation, PCI leaders have adopted an austerity policy somewhat similar to the programs pursued by the ruling Christian Democrats. According to this policy, high economic growth should take priority over wage gains that exceed the growth in labor output per hour. Wage restraints on highly paid workers and opposition to strikes are major features of this austerity program. As unemployment in Italy has grown and the PCI leaders, along with top union officials in the procommunist CGIL *(Confederazione Generale Italiana del Lavoro)*, have supported these austerity measures, worker discontent with the PCI has mounted.

During the 1979 parliamentary elections, the PCI won only 30 percent of the popular vote to the Chamber of Deputies—a 4 percent decline from its 1976 record high. Disenchanted with unemployment, inflation, and declining real income, some workers either abstained from voting or else switched to the Christian Democrats. Unemployed university graduates and some students bolted the PCI to vote for more antiestablishment parties such as the Radical party. Other middle-class radical youth left the PCI to join either terrorist organizations (Red Brigades) or small-scale organizations that called for extensive public ownership of firms and the establishment of workers' councils to operate the factories.

In short, for the PCI, the reconciliation strategy with the Christian Democrats brings a political dilemma. If the PCI coalesces with the Christian Democrats, favors an austerity program, and undertakes an accommodating, reformist strategy, then it loses support from workers, trade unionists, radical youth, and party activists who seek faster transformations of Italian society. Yet if the PCI pursues a more aggressive, revolutionary strategy for gaining political power, it loses middle-class support as a "responsible" party qualified to govern Italy.[19]

In other Western democracies as well, left-wing parties have faced a similar dilemma: Ideological convergence with more conservative parties has meant growing discontent from youth, trade unionists, and party activists. Unless leftist governing parties manage to maintain low unemployment and inflation rates, ideological convergence with right-wing parties cannot avert a loss of electoral support.

Growing ideological polarization in Britain and the United States. During the 1970s and 1980s, this ideological dilemma particularly faced the more left-wing parties in Britain and the United States, where economic stagnation produced a rise in ideological polarization that split middle-class party activists. The Labour party held government power from 1974 through 1979, at a time when high inflation, high unemployment, and declining productivity plagued Britain. Responding to these economic crises, the Labour party government officials adopted many deflationary policies that the Conservative party also favored, including lower government spending for some social services, higher interest rates, lower increases in the money supply, wage restraints, and opposition to strikes. As the jobless rate grew and price increases still hovered around 10 percent a year, the Labour government fell from power in 1979, defeated in the election by the Tories, who attracted skilled workers, trade unionists, and youth away from the Labour party.

Led by Prime Minister Margaret Thatcher, the Conservative government sought to abandon the consensus politics that had united the Labour and Conservative approaches since World War II. Whereas both major parties had formerly supported government economic planning, limited state ownership, progressive taxes, and extensive social services provided by the government, Prime Minister Thatcher tried to implement some laissez-faire economic policies advocated by Friedrich Hayek and Milton Friedman. These policies included higher interest rates, lower taxes on the wealthy, reduced government expenditures for social services, and lower unemployment compensation to strikers.

As the Conservative party moved toward a more laissez-faire position, the Labour party shifted leftward. Opposed to the accommodationist policies preferred by former Labour government officials, middle-class Labour activists who gained control of the constituency party organizations came out for greater nationalization of private firms, expanded economic planning by the government, and an extension of government-provided social services. These activists also rejected policies that imposed wage restraints on trade unionists. The

Thatcher government strongly opposed all these measures.[20] Hence, as economic conditions worsened in Britain, the Labour and Conservative parties became more ideologically polarized.

Similarly, in the United States, the period from 1964 through 1980 marked a sharpening of ideological differences between Democratic and Republican party activists. Several changes, such as the struggle for racial equality, opposition to American involvement in the Vietnam War, rising inflation, declining productivity, and movements for acceptance of diverse lifestyles, sharpened the ideological dialogue. Democratic and Republican party activists took divergent stands on a variety of economic and cultural issues. Particularly after 1967, Democratic activists became more "liberal." Republicans remained "conservative." Different attitudes toward freedom and equality separated the party activists, mainly highly educated, middle-class professionals and business executives. The liberal Democrats stressed cultural freedom for the individual; they favored the freedom to smoke marijuana and choose abortion. By contrast, the conservative Republicans were more opposed to these lifestyle freedoms and instead focused on the rights of the private entrepreneur to remain free from government regulation. Liberal Democrats called for greater economic, racial, and sexual equality; they wanted the government to assume a more active role in providing social services to the poor, securing civil rights for Blacks, and attaining equal rights for women. Conservative Republicans, however, rejected this egalitarian role for the national government.

In 1980, high inflation, combined with increasing unemployment in the auto, steel, and construction industries, led to the defeat of the Democratic president, Jimmy Carter, and the election of Ronald Reagan, the first self-styled "conservative" president since the pre–New Deal days. Unlike previous Republican presidents—Eisenhower, Nixon, and Ford—Reagan strongly identified with the conservative wing of the Republican party and took conservative stands on most economic and cultural issues. For instance, he favored tax reductions for the wealthy, decreased government regulation of private business, and lower government expenditures on egalitarian social service programs. On cultural issues, President Reagan opposed the Equal Rights Amendment, abortion, and Supreme Court restrictions on prayer in public schools. Most Democratic party activists, especially the middle-class, highly educated delegates who attend Democratic conventions, rejected President Reagan's conservative stands on these issues. At the beginning of the 1980s, the two major American political parties thus stood more ideologically divided than most continental European parties.[21]

In sum, both Britain and the United States have experienced growing ideological polarization during the last decade. In both nations, the more left-wing governing party—American Democratic and British Labour—proved unable to reduce the rising inflation and jobless rates. A gap emerged between government officials, who favored austerity programs to dampen inflationary pressures, and middle-class, left-wing party activists, who supported an extension of egalitarian social service policies and continued government regulation of the economy. Largely because voters perceived the leftist party government as incompetent to manage the economy, the British Conservatives and American Republicans scored electoral victories during 1979 and 1980. In these elections, the rightist parties received greater backing than in the past from skilled manual workers and union members, social groups that formerly gave key support to leftist parties. Thus, the rise of ideological polarization between middle-class activists in the two major parties accompanied the decline of class polarization at the polls.

Voting Behavior of Social Groups

The structural relationships between political parties and social groups affect not only the public policies party leaders voice but also the parties' success at the polls. As we have seen, political parties play a direct role in the electoral process. Arising during the period when the franchise expanded, they continue to provide one channel for popular participation in political life. Their continuing electoral success depends upon the ability to rally a variety of groups behind their banner.

Political scientists have devoted more recent attention to voting behavior than to any other topic; part of this fascination with elections stems from the market economies present in Western democratic societies. Concentrating on the United States, Canada, and West Europe, most political scientists perceive an analogy between the economic market and the political system. Group competition and exchange relationships occur in both. Particularly during elections, voter sovereignty resembles consumer sovereignty on the market. Just as consumers voice demands for certain goods, so citizens register their demands for particular policies. Votes form the equivalent of dollars; citizens provide votes in exchange for leadership. In this exchange process, the voter resembles a buyer; political party candidates running for office act like sellers. Like business firms, political parties compete for popular support. Just as the firm in a market economy seeks to maximize profits, so the political party, especially in a two-party system, wants to maximize votes.[22]

When measuring group support for a party, survey analysts have used several indicators, including a person's expressed intention to vote for a party, the vote actually cast for a party's candidate, and party identification—that is, the sense of subjective attachment to a party. I shall use mainly the first two behavioral indicators as measures for party support, giving less attention to party identification. The following discussions of ethnic, religious, and class voting consider several related dimensions: nations where each type of group voting predominates, patterns of group support during the 1960s and 1970s, changes in group support over time, and degree of group polarization behind opposing political parties.

POLITICAL PARTIES AND SOCIAL CLEAVAGES

During the last 200 years, three primary structural cleavages have influenced the development of political parties in the Western world.[23] First, the primordial cleavage centers on the relationships among diverse ethnic, linguistic, and regional groups. Where different primordial groups occupy a national territory, which among them will be perceived as an integral part of the nation? This general issue encompasses the more specific problems of political representation. For example, which ethnic groups should be represented in the national political institutions? Which language should become the national language? Which region will dominate the nation, especially its three sectors—the economy, culture, and polity? Primordial groups have employed diverse strategies to gain greater representation. Usually, they initially demand a voice in the already established organizations, including both government and political parties. Those groups that do not feel represented may form a separate party. Less often, a malrepresented regional group may attempt to secede from the nation and establish its own political institutions, as did the Southern states during the American Civil War or as some contemporary French-speaking leaders in Quebec have threatened. Because the United States and Canada have the greatest ethnic-linguistic-regional heterogeneity among the seven Western countries, primordial groups have exerted a pervasive influence in these two nations. Yet even in Britain, where the politics of class has long overwhelmed the politics of ethnicity, ethnic–regional parties in Wales and Scotland have shown electoral strength.

A second important basis of political party conflict revolves around religious cleavages. Like the primordial cleavage, the religious issue also involves matters of political representation and public policy: Which religious groups will control the government? What rights will religious minorities have? Who will take primary responsibility for moral behavior? Will secular government officials or the clergy operate the public schools? If a separation between church and public education occurs, will the religious schools receive government economic assistance? The group support behind different parties reflects several dimensions of the religious cleavages. Generally, left-wing parties, especially socialist and communist, gain votes from members of nonestablished churches and from persons not actively involved in religious activities. Christian Democratic parties have emerged during the twentieth century to articulate the values of Catholics, as in Germany and Italy, or fundamentalist denominations not linked with the established Lutheran church, as in Sweden.

Third, the economic cleavage highlights the twin issues of production and distribution. How will productivity be maximized? How will the resulting goods and services be distributed? The issue of maximizing economic production influenced the political party conflicts during the nineteenth century at the beginning of the industrialization process. Representing the interests of landowners, the conservative parties originally were reluctant to support either a laissez-faire economic policy or active government assistance to promote industrialization. Influenced by industrialists and business executives, the liberal parties placed greater emphasis than the conservatives on rapid economic expansion, either through government financial aid to private business or through reliance on a "free" market.

The socialist parties that emerged at the end of the nineteenth century stressed distribution, rather than production, as the key political issue. Throughout West Europe, they voiced the demands of the factory working class for a larger, more equal share of the economic pie. After 1917, when the Bolsheviks triumphed in Russia, socialists sympathetic with the Soviet Union split away from the socialist parties and formed communist parties. Usually, whereas the socialist parties expanded their electoral base into the middle classes, especially teachers and civil servants, the communists attracted main support from the factory workers. Especially in Scandinavia, the small farmers felt unrepresented in the already established parties—conservative, liberal, socialist, communist. Therefore, in Sweden, they established an Agrarian party in 1921 to secure government economic policies favorable to their farm interests.

Today these three group cleavages—primordial, religious, and economic—continue to influence political party developments. By exploring ethnic, religious, and class voting, we hope to understand better the government policies formulated by different political parties.

ETHNIC VOTING

In countries where high ethnic heterogeneity divides the national population and where political party leaders make strong appeals to ethnic loyalties, ethnic group support for parties becomes especially polarized. If the established national parties ignore ethnic group demands, then the educated members of the ethnic group that feels relatively deprived may organize an ethnic party at the regional level. These conditions hold particularly true in the United States, Canada, and Britain. Among the seven Western industrial societies, these three nations contain the highest degree of ethnic–linguistic heterogeneity. American Blacks comprise around 12 percent of the population. Spanish-speaking citizens, including Mexican Americans and Puerto Ricans, make up over 6 percent. Indians and Asians constitute nearly 2 percent. The remaining 80 percent or so come from a variety of European countries, including England, Ireland, France, Scandinavia, Germany, Italy, Poland, and Canada.

The Canadian population also contains a mosaic of ethnic groups. Nearly 45 percent originally came from Britain, 29 percent from France, 20 percent from other European countries, and 1 percent from Asia. Indians and Eskimos comprise about 1 percent. Whereas in America the main ethnic conflicts have pitted Blacks against Whites, in Canada the struggle between the French- and English-speaking citizens has animated political life since the 1700s. Today about 67 percent speak only English; 18 percent speak only French; and just 13 percent are bilingual. Both the French-speaking and the bilingual population live in Quebec; few persons in other provinces, except Ontario, can speak French.

Compared with the United States and Canada, Britain contains a more ethnically homogeneous population. The English make up about 85 percent of the total British population; the Scots, 10 percent; and the Welsh, only 3 percent. Slightly over 2 percent have emigrated to Britain from India, Pakistan, and the West Indies.[24]

Members of a particular ethnic group often live in a single region; for this reason, ethnic parties have appeared at the regional level in Canada, the United States, and Britain. For example, the Parti Québécois, which advocates greater political independence for Quebec and more French control over the economy, in 1976 became the governing party in Quebec by winning 41 percent of the popular vote and nearly two-thirds of the seats in the provincial legislature. Five years later the Parti Québécois retained government control when it secured 49 percent of the votes and two-thirds of the seats. Particularly in local elections in Texas, California, Colorado, New Mexico, and Arizona, where most Mexican Americans reside, La Raza Unida party has won a few seats to school boards and city councils; Crystal City, Texas, represents the best known example. Even in Great Britain, where the politics of class has long submerged ethnic appeals, ethnic parties—the Welsh Plaid Cymru and the Scottish National party—have gained electoral strength in Wales and Scotland. Both these ethnic–regional parties articulate demands for greater regional autonomy, economic resources, and cultural recognition—demands generally ignored by the Labour and especially the Conservative party.[25]

Although no national ethnic political parties have arisen in the United States, leaders of the two major established parties still make ethnic appeals. Since the 1964 American presidential election, the Republican party has followed a "southern strategy" aimed at securing the support of white voters in the South. During the 1960s and 1970s, poorer southern whites, and particularly the wealthier white population, became increasingly Republican in their presidential voting. Unlike the Republicans, the Democrats have concentrated on securing black voters in both the North and South. As a result of these opposed strategies, racial polarization as expressed in group support for the two parties has increased. For example, in 1960, 68 percent of the Blacks and 49 percent of the Whites voted for John F. Kennedy. During 1980, President Jimmy Carter, a Democrat, gained votes from 86 percent of Blacks; however, his electoral support among Whites was only 36 percent, a sign of heightened racial cleavages.[26]

In Canada as well, ethnicity and religion, rather than occupation, account for the group support received by the two major parties, the Liberals and Progressive-Conservatives. Since the late nineteenth century, the Liberal party has succeeded in attracting votes from both French-speaking Quebec and the rest of Canada. Although the Progressive-Conservatives have rarely issued anti-French appeals, they have made few efforts to gain electoral supporters in Quebec. As a result, the Conservative party attracts few French voters. For instance, in the 1980 election to the House of Commons, the Progressive-Conservatives won only one seat in Quebec. Generally, their major electoral support came from English-speaking people who live in Ontario and the western provinces. Similarly, the socialist New Democratic party gained seats from Ontario and the western provinces of British Columbia, Saskatchewan, and Manitoba but not from Quebec or the four English-speaking Maritime provinces. Although during past elections the Liberal party achieved greater success in attracting diverse linguistic groups, in 1980 it obtained only two seats west of Ontario; half its seats in the House of Commons came from French-speaking Quebec.[27] As in the past, today ethnic–linguistic cleavages threaten Canadian national unity.

Even in Britain, ethnic cleavages now divide the electorate. The Conservative party secures its greatest support among the English in the south of Britain. Welsh and Scottish voters favor either the regional parties—the Plaid Cymru and the Scottish National party—or the Labour party. Other non-English ethnic groups—Asians, Africans, West Indians, Irish—also prefer the Labourites. Among the coloured population (Pakistanis, Indians, West Indians), ethnic ties overwhelm economic position; that is, regardless of economic class, nearly all Coloureds vote for the Labour party. However, among the Whites, occupation becomes a more important guide to voting behavior. Upper-class Whites (managers, employers, administrators, some professionals) clearly back the Tories; by contrast, manual workers lean toward the Labour party.[28]

RELIGIOUS VOTING

Although no national ethnic party has emerged in any of these seven Western countries to exacerbate ethnic tensions, Christian Democratic parties have achieved a wide territorial base, especially in Italy and Germany. These parties articulate campaign appeals that transcend the interests of a single occupational group. As a result, they gain support from people of diverse economic backgrounds.

From the survey data gathered about voter preferences, three generalizations emerge about the effect of religious involvement on electoral support for political parties.[29] First, as religious involvement (measured by frequency of church attendance) increases, support for a conservative party also rises. In Italy, West Germany, and France, active church attenders vote overwhelmingly for conservative parties such as the Italian Christian Democrats, the German Christian Democratic Union, and Rassemblement pour la République. By contrast, the left-wing parties in these three countries as well as Sweden win greater support from those people, especially men and youth, who rarely or never go to church services.

Second, the greater the involvement in an established church, the stronger the support for a conservative party. This generalization particularly explains patterns of religious voting in societies where both Catholics and Protestants attract sizable numbers of adherents. Catholics comprise 46 percent of the total population in Germany, 44 percent in Canada, 27 percent in the United States, and 9 percent in Britain. Except in Germany, where the Catholic church, allied with the landed nobility, formed a key prop upholding the feudal system, the Protestants have operated the more establishment-oriented church. Whereas German Protestants have voted for the Social Democrats, in the United States, Britain, and Canada, Protestants have supported the conservative parties. Catholic citizens of these three nations, however, lean toward the more liberal party—American Democratic, British Labour, and Canadian Liberal.

Except in Northern Ireland, religious disputes have declined in most Western countries since the nineteenth century. As a consequence, the struggles between Catholics and Protestants now seem less likely to become expressed in political party conflicts. Certainly, the early 1970s witnessed less religious voting than an earlier period.

For instance, in the 1960 American presidential election, when the main issue revolved around the Catholic affiliation of John F. Kennedy, 78 percent of Catholics and only 38 percent of Protestants voted for the Democratic candidate. However, by 1980 the gap between the two denominations in their support for the Democratic party's nominee had declined to seven percentage points. (Jimmy Carter received 46 percent of the Catholic vote and 39 percent of the Protestant vote.) Religious differences have also decreased in political importance throughout Canada. In Britain, voters born since World War II make fewer connections between their religious preferences and their party preferences than do individuals who grew up during the early twentieth century; hence, Catholics, Anglicans, and nonconformist Protestants not linked to the established Church of England less often choose political parties according to church membership. In Germany as well, the Social Democrats have broadened their electoral base to include greater numbers of Catholics.[30]

Third, among both the European middle and working classes, the higher the religious involvement, the greater the support for conservative parties. In most countries, middle-class persons appear more religiously involved. They attend church services more often than working-class individuals. They also accept a more theologically orthodox interpretation of religious issues, such as belief in God, life after death, and the divinity of Christ. The middle classes prefer that churches concentrate on matters, such as birth control and abortion, that involve their private personal lives. By contrast, the European workers want churches to become more actively engaged in general political and economic issues, such as social reform. Yet because the established churches have shown a reluctance to intervene actively on behalf of political causes, workers have leaned toward government policies, rather than religious action, as the more effective method for resolving their personal problems. Consequently, in Europe members of the working class with a weak religious commitment—for example, ones who never attend church—vote most frequently for the Socialist and Communist parties. However, workers who resemble middle-class persons in their higher religiosity give stronger support to the Conservative and Christian Democratic parties.[31]

CLASS VOTING

In *Political Man: The Social Bases of Politics*, Seymour Martin Lipset entitled two of his chapters "Elections: The Expression of the Democratic Class Struggle."[32] To what extent does this vivid description accurately characterize popular support for left-wing and right-wing political parties? Do those at the top of the social stratification system always vote for the conservative party and those at the bottom support the liberal party? How strong is class voting, compared with ethnic and religious voting? Answering these questions, social scientists have used two indicators of social class: subjective class identification and occupation (the objective measure).

What is the impact of class identification on voting behavior? Generally, individuals who strongly identify with the working class give greater support to a left-wing party. Professionals who hold middle-class occupations (teachers, journalists, social workers, government civil servants) but who view themselves as members of the working class vote for the leftist party. Finally, persons denying the realities of class stratification and refusing to identify with any particular class usually lean toward conservative parties. Traditionally, the right-wing parties have appealed to voters who feel that they belong to a classless society.

Of the two measures of class, occupation generally shows a stronger relationship with electoral support for a political party. Within the industrial sector, people employed in more prestigious and financially remunerative occupations vote for the conservative party. Among nonmanual workers, the upper middle class—business executives, industrialists, managers, professionals, administrators—most strongly support right-wing parties. Composed of white-collar employees, salespeople, clerks, and shopkeepers, the lower middle class votes less frequently for conservative parties. Manual workers—skilled, semiskilled, and unskilled—provide left-wing parties with their greatest source of support. Independent farmers, except the tenant farmers in Italy who lean toward the Communists, usually vote for the conservative parties.[33]

Despite this correlation between occupation and party voting, the strength of the relationship tends to be rather weak, at least compared with the effects of religion. Using Robert Alford's indicator, we can measure class voting as the difference between the percentage of persons in manual occupations voting for left-wing parties and the percentage of persons in upper, nonmanual occupations voting for the leftist party. Similarly, religious voting indicates the percentage of Catholics (Protestants in Germany) or low church attenders who voted for the left-wing party minus the proportion of Protestants (German Catholics) or high church attenders who voted leftist.[34]

According to these measures, occupation has the greatest impact on voting behavior in Britain and especially Sweden, the two most religiously homogeneous societies. In West Germany, both occupational ties and religious affiliations have strongly affected partisan choices. Whereas class voting prevailed over religious voting during the 1950s and 1960s, in the 1970s religious affiliation became a more important factor behind the German electorate's votes for representatives to the Bundestag. In France and Italy, the nations with the largest proportion of Catholics, religious involvement, as measured by frequency of church attendance, more strongly influences party voting than does occupation.

The United States and Canada show a complex interaction among occupation, religious affiliation, and electoral behavior. In the United States, the 1972 presidential election produced the lowest class voting of the last fifty years; a plurality of all occupational groups, including professionals, business managers, white-collar employees, and manual workers, supported Richard Nixon. In 1976 and 1980, wider voting cleavages separated professionals and business executives from manual workers than divided Protestants and Catholics. In Canada, the effect of occupational class on partisan choice depends on the ideological classification of the Liberal and the New Democratic parties. If we consider the Liberals the left-wing party, class voting seems weaker than religious voting because the Liberals gain support from Catholics, middle-class people, and many workers, too. Although the Progressive-Conservatives recruit their followers from the middle class, they appeal mainly to Protestants. However, if we classify the socialist New Democratic party (NDP) as the leftist party, class voting becomes more pronounced because votes for the NDP come primarily from non-Catholic manual workers who belong to unions.[35]

The degree of class voting in a nation primarily depends on the strength of socialist parties and trade unions. During the late nineteenth century in Sweden, Britain, and Germany, socialist political parties and unions established close cooperation; both struggled for the expansion of the suffrage and for an improvement in the workers' living conditions. Except in England, where the unions created the Labour party in 1900, the socialist party usually organized the union movement, as happened in Germany during the 1880s and in Sweden in 1898. Since that time, union members have strongly supported the socialist parties. For example, in Britain today, the Labour party receives its greatest support from unionized manual workers employed in state enterprises and large private industries. By contrast, Conservative votes come mainly from nonunionized, nonmanual employees working in private industries, both large and small.[36]

In France, Italy, Canada, and the United States, socialist parties and trade unions have less political strength. Compared with Swedish, British, and German unions, the union movements in France and Italy are more politically fragmented. After World War II, communist and noncommunist parties organized separate unions. In Italy, the Christian Democrats and Republicans formed two unions independent from the General Confederation of Italian Labor, long dominated by an alliance of Communists and Socialists. In France, the socialists and left-wing Catholics refused to participate in the *Confédération Générale du Travail*, which after the war came under Communist party influence. Only recently have the French and especially Italian unions begun to adopt an essentially nonpartisan stance. The split among the left-wing parties parallels the divisions within the union movement. The Italian Christian Democrats and the French Gaullists benefit from the division between the Socialist and Communist parties. By supporting the conservative parties, the influential Catholic church blunts class appeals; as a result, religiously involved Catholic workers support the right-wing parties. Thus, the power of the Catholic church, the divisions between clerical and anticlerical workers, the weak trade unions, and the split between the two left-wing parties all help reduce class voting among the French and Italian electorates.[37]

In the United States and Canada, neither unions nor socialist parties exercise dominant political power. Although giving greater electoral support to the Democrats, American unions attempt to maintain good terms with both parties. Indeed, the largest union, the Teamsters, has developed close ties with the Republicans. The American and Canadian economies are closely interlocked; American corporations make extensive investments in Canada. Partly for this reason, over half the Canadian trade unionists belong to the Canadian Labour Congress, which is affiliated with the AFL-CIO. Rather than attaching themselves to a major Canadian party, they have aligned with an American union. Some Canadian unions have established links with the socialist New Democratic party; yet in recent elections, it has failed to gain more than 20 percent of the total national vote. The various U.S. socialist parties receive minuscule support from the electorate.

Since the end of World War II, class voting has declined somewhat in the United States and other Western industrial nations. Less-intense occupational cleavages now separate supporters of diverse political parties than before the war. For example, over the last fifty years in the United States, class voting reached its highest levels during the period from the 1930s through the 1948 election. Between 1952 and 1980, class voting was lower. In the 1972 presidential election, class had a particularly weak influence on electoral behavior. In 1976 and 1980, however, the correlation between occupation and partisan choice was slightly higher.

The political issues stressed by presidential candidates, along with economic conditions facing the country, partly explain these changing patterns of U.S. class voting. When political party leaders concentrate on economic issues, especially on ways for government to reduce unemployment, guarantee jobs, and provide low-cost health care, then class voting increases. These issues dominated the 1936, 1940, 1948, 1976, and 1980 elections. Voters perceived that the presidential candidates took opposed stands on these issues, with the Democratic nominee, compared with the Republican candidate, preferring more progressive taxes and greater government assistance for expanded employment opportunities and a comprehensive public health care system.

From the mid 1950s through the early 1970s, economic issues declined somewhat in importance; cultural issues—racial equality, women's rights, campus protests against the Vietnam War, urban unrest, abortion, marijuana—came to the fore. Especially in the 1972 election, these issues dominated the electoral agenda. Voters perceived clear differences between Senator McGovern and President Nixon on a variety of diverse issues: the war in Vietnam, busing for racial integration, the legal right to smoke marijuana, and ways to cope with campus disturbances. More voters, including manual workers, preferred President Nixon's position on these issues than favored Senator McGovern's stand. Yet especially in the North, many young, college-educated, middle-class persons—teachers, college professors, government civil servants, journalists, public interest lawyers—aligned themselves with McGovern's positions and voted Democratic. In 1972, class polarization thus declined as these cultural issues overwhelmed the New Deal economic issues.

For both cultural and economic reasons, class polarization in voting behavior decreased slightly between the 1976 and 1980 presidential elections. During the 1980 campaign, Ronald Reagan's stands on cultural issues—namely, his opposition to abortion and the Equal Rights Amendment—impelled some traditionally Democratic voters, such as working-class southerners and middle-class Catholics, to support the Republican candidate. In 1980, inflation was the key economic issue troubling voters. Most Americans held the Carter administration accountable for the rising prices and believed that Reagan could better control the inflationary surge. Because inflation affects all economic groups, Reagan attracted broad support from various occupations. In particular, blue-collar workers who perceived that their financial situation had worsened during 1980 voted heavily for Reagan. President Carter lost votes from key groups, including manual workers and union members, who had strongly backed him in 1976.[38]

A similar trend toward declining class voting has occurred in European nations as well. Although conservative parties obtain a higher percentage of votes from the manual workers than the socialist or communist parties secure from the upper middle class, the leftist parties have recently attempted to broaden their appeal to all occupational groups. Rather than class parties, "catch-all" or "catch-as-catch-can" parties have become increasingly important. Just as in the United States, teachers and government civil servants are increasing their power within the union movement. These middle-class groups often support socialist or communist parties. The three most powerful socialist parties—the Swedish Social Democrats, the German SPD, and the English Labourites—have attracted around 40 percent of the lower middle class, including white-collar employees, salespersons, and clerks. Recently, the Swedish Social Democrats have lost electoral support among the working class but increased their popularity with middle-class voters, especially those under thirty years of age. In Germany during the late 1960s and 1970s, the SPD gained growing middle-class support, particularly from the new middle class of government civil servants, salaried employees, and clerical personnel. Similarly in Britain, class voting has decreased since before World War II. In the 1979 election, about 50 percent of skilled workers supported the Conservative party. To a lesser extent, France and Italy have experienced the same trend; the conservative parties have mounted a broad appeal to all social classes. The socialist parties secure as much electoral support from the lower middle class as from the manual workers. Even the Communist party, especially in Italy, has recently attempted to expand its electoral base beyond the proletariat.

What variables explain the decline in class voting throughout West Europe? As in the United States, three reasons—historical economic conditions, contemporary social mobility, and party policy positions—seem particularly important. First, class cleavages were far more acute before the Second World War. The periods between 1880 and 1920, when the industrialization process began, and during the 1930s, when an economic depression plagued Europe, accentuated conflicts between business owners and workers. Today these class struggles have receded. The post–World War II era has seen the declining importance of the old middle class, including self-employed business persons and independent professionals. By contrast, the new middle class—salaried personnel, clerical employees, highly educated professionals, and government civil servants—has become a larger share of the labor force. These groups, especially the youths, vote for more left-wing parties than does the old middle class. They also show greater support for promoting environmental protection, nuclear disarmament, women's equality, abortion, and minority rights. Although the leftist parties, rather than the rightist ones, more closely identify with these noneconomic issues, factory workers reveal a weaker commitment to these measures than both the old and especially the new middle class. As a result, left-wing parties have lost some working-class support but gained greater middle-class backing. Hence, class polarization in voting behavior has declined.

Second, social mobility reduces class division among the parties. Data for Britain, Sweden, and Italy indicate that mobile persons take positions between the stationary groups. For example, the stationary middle class gives greatest support to a nonsocialist party. The stationary working class votes most heavily for the socialists. The downwardly and upwardly mobile are less socialist than the stable workers but more socialist than the stable middle class.

Third, political party leaders since the war have downplayed class appeals. European conservative parties have always stressed religion and nationalism as key campaign issues; to win the workers, they uphold the need for moderate welfare benefits and promise to administer social service policies more efficiently than left-wing parties. In turn, the socialist and communist parties have tried to reassure the middle-class voter by emphasizing their allegiance to the nation and by muting any hostility to the established churches. Their domestic economic programs reflect a reformist approach to social change. All these policy appeals represent an attempt to secure electoral support from diverse occupational groups.[39]

Table 8-1 summarizes the relative influence of occupational and religious voting in seven industrial countries. Although winning the majority of votes from middle-class business people and farmers, conservative party leaders also direct their appeals to the religiously involved working class. The other middle-class party, the liberal, manages to secure sizable support from members of all social classes, especially in the United States and Canada, where liberal parties have historically exercised the greatest power. Unlike the American Democratic party, liberal parties in Canada, Germany, Britain, and Sweden gain more votes from the middle than the working class; these four parties must campaign against a socialist party further to the left. Except in Germany, liberal parties attract more electoral support from members of the nonestablished churches, such as Catholics and non-state-church Protestants. Compared with socialists, communists have failed to build as wide a coalition of group support. Socialist parties win a higher proportion of votes from religiously involved persons and from middle-class persons, such as civil servants, teachers, and other young professionals. Despite their attempts to broaden their class base and win clerical voters in France and Italy, the communist parties there still attract predominant support from manual workers and the nonreligious, as well as from some intellectuals.

POLITICAL PARTIES AND GROUP SUPPORT

Several conclusions emerge from this estimation of social group support for political parties. First, primordial values have become more politically important. After 1960 in the United States, Blacks and

TABLE 8-1 The group bases of party support

Country	Religious behavior	Occupation	Trade union membership	Party support
United States	Catholic, Jew	manual worker	yes	Democrat
	Protestant	manager	no	Republican
Canada	Catholic	nonmanual worker		Liberal
	United Church	farmer		Progressive-Conservative
Britain	Catholic	unskilled worker	yes	Labour
	Anglican	professional	no	Conservative
Germany	Protestant, nonchurchgoing	manual worker	yes	SPD (Social Democrat)
	Catholic, churchgoing	self-employed middle classs	no	Christian Democrat
Sweden	state church, nonattender	worker	LO	Socialist
	state church, attender	upper nonmanual	none or SACO	Conservative
France	non–church attender	manual worker	CGT	Communist
	Catholic church attender	nonmanual worker	no	Gaullist
Italy	non–church attender	manual worker	CGIL	Communist
	Catholic church attender	nonmanual worker, independent farmer	no	Christian Democrat

Whites showed far more divergent voting patterns than did religious or occupational groups. Britain has witnessed strong ethnic regional parties in Wales and especially Scotland; the Scottish National party now calls for political independence from England. In Canada, ethnic tensions between French and English continue to separate supporters of both major parties. Second, although religious voting has declined slightly, church affiliation and attendance still strongly influence party voting. Third, since World War II, the association between occupation and partisan choice has decreased in nearly every country. What variables explain these trends behind electoral behavior? Three structural factors appear crucial.[40]

During the twentieth century, especially the period after World War II, the social structure has become less rigid. Feudal ties, which helped stimulate the rise of class-related socialist parties at the end of the 1880s, have certainly declined. The conflicts between an industrial proletariat and the capitalist bourgeoisie have also become less acute. Leftist parties no longer seek to gain just a working-class base but now attempt to expand their support into the new middle class. Throughout Europe, as in America, young white-collar employees, civil servants, intellectuals, students, teachers, journalists, and writers have begun to play a more active role within leftist parties. As they move toward the left in their voting patterns, parties lose their distinctive class base. Along with the decline of feudalism and less intense struggles between workers and employers has gone a moderate degree of social mobility. As residential environments become more heterogeneous, people encounter individuals with diverse class backgrounds and political viewpoints. The exposure to a growing variety of political stimuli and cross-pressures weakens traditional class voting.

The most effective socializing media tend to downplay the importance of class considerations, choosing instead to appeal to the mass. In the United States, the partisan, class-related press prominent between 1860 and 1900 has largely disappeared. Forswearing class polarization, television broadcasts multiclass messages. Candidates' ethnic origins, religious affiliation, and personality receive greater attention than their class background or stands on class-related issues. The schools also minimize divisive class appeals and concentrate instead on consensual themes based on religion and nationalism.

Perhaps the major reason for the weak effects of class on voting behavior revolves around the need for concrete organizations to articulate class appeals and to provide concrete benefits. Unlike a church or an ethnic association, a class is more a categorical group than a membership group. Unless all factory workers live in the same neighborhood and work in similar plants, they rarely gain a strong sense of community that can be translated into support for a particular party. More than a religion or an ethnic group, a class needs a political organization to articulate its demands for public policies. Rather than the class struggle shaping political behavior, political organizations, including parties, influence class behavior at the polls. As Giovanni Sartori reminds us, political organization, not social group ties, may offer the better explanation for a person's partisan choices:

> It is not the "objective" class (class condition) that creates the party, but the party that creates the "subjective" class (class consciousness). More carefully put, whenever parties reflect social classes, this signifies *more* about the party end than about the class end of the interaction. The party is not a "consequence" of the class. Rather, and before, it is the class that receives its identity from the party. . . . Large collectivities become less class structured only if they are class persuaded; and the most likely and apt "persuader" is the party (or the union) playing on class-appeal.[41]

Class voting has reached its highest levels in those three countries—Britain, Germany, and particularly Sweden—where both socialist parties and allied trade unions have established the strongest base of power and the closest working relationships. These twin organizations articulate values and norms important to the socializing process. Besides forming a center of social solidarity, they also dispense concrete rewards. All these values and incentives help swing the members behind the party at election time.

Yet even in Sweden, Germany, and Britain, as elsewhere, class voting has recently decreased. The major parties appeal to several groups, not just one. Trade unions concentrate on securing higher wages and better working conditions, not on pressing their political demands. Union leaders seek free collective bargaining, tax reductions for the workers, and anti-inflation policies to restrain price increases. Thus, trade union consciousness, rather than political consciousness, animates most Western workers. They seem more willing to vote for whatever party chooses to implement these demands. Besides the decline of interlocking relationships between party and union, the growing importance of middle-class persons, such as teachers and government civil servants, within the union movement also has caused a decline in class voting.[42]

Finally, churches and ethnic associations are concrete organizations that voice predominantly nonclass appeals. Members of one ethnic group often live in a single region, such as the French-speaking Canadian citizens in Quebec and the Scots in Scotland. Because they belong to a membership group rather than a statistical category, they can more easily organize a political party to express their policy preferences. Similarly, members of a religious denomination also participate in an organizational network. Given the issues before the country, such as divorce, abortion, and government aid to church schools, the clergy may decide to support a political party, such as the Christian Democrats in Germany and Italy, or to oppose a party, such as the Communist party in France. For these structural reasons, even in highly industrialized societies, religion and ethnicity continue to remain significant bases of electoral support for diverse political parties.

Party Activities

Political activities refer to structures in operation. Motivated by certain objectives and working through such organizations as parties, political participants strive to realize consequences that affect the whole society. The following sections examine four primary activities of Western political parties. *Political education* concerns the interaction between party leaders and party supporters. *Political recruitment* also deals with the relations between party leaders and members. *Interest aggregation* involves the reconciliation process among party leaders, party factions, and other parties. The *management of government* denotes the interaction between party heads and government officials. In this analysis, we want to ascertain the extent to which political parties in seven Western countries actually carry out these activities. To what degree have other structures, such as the civil service, interest groups, and the mass media, undertaken the performance of these four activities?

POLITICAL EDUCATION

Because political parties link citizens with their government, one key activity revolves around political education. By this process, party members learn the most effective ways to press policy demands on the government. Political education implies the existence of both a teacher and a learner—that is, media of communication as well as members to receive the educational messages. Generally, party leaders who take ideology seriously place a greater emphasis on political education. Thus, European socialist and communist parties regard political education as more important than do American or Canadian parties. Leftist parties organize several media of communication, such as party newspapers and party training schools, to articulate values and information. For example, the PCI publishes *L'Unità;* the PCF prints *L'Humanité*. Each week the left-wing Labourites issue *The Tribune*. All these newspapers provide a forum for the party leaders to educate their members. The success of the party's educational activities depends on its ability to reach a mass membership.

Since World War II, political education activities have declined throughout Europe. All parties, including the left-wing ones, have declined in membership. In 1977, the French Communist party enrolled only three-fourths the number of members that it had around 1945. Similarly, the Italian Communist party attracted fewer members in 1976 than twenty years earlier. The British Labourites have also experienced a declining membership. During the middle 1970s, only 4 percent of Labour party voters enrolled as party members. Less than 10 percent of the members participated in party activities. Lacking a mass base, the Labour party performed few electoral activities. For example, in the 1979 parliamentary elections, only seventy-five full-time Labour party agents worked for the party; hence, most Labour voters were never contacted by a party representative. Now the local Labour organizations serve mainly as social clubs for middle-class members.

In the United States and Canada, party membership has little meaning. People identify with or support a party, but the organizations are too weak for them to "belong" to a party. Nevertheless, the dominant liberal and conservative parties have managed to wage skillful electoral campaigns and gain control of government office.

In short, throughout the Western democratic world, political parties no longer concentrate on political education except during elec-

CHAPTER 8 POLITICAL PARTIES IN CONSTITUTIONAL SYSTEMS 261

toral campaigns. Other structures, such as the mass media, interest groups, and broad social movements, now perform vital educational activities.[43]

POLITICAL RECRUITMENT

Political recruitment also involves interaction between party leaders and party members. Like political education, this activity seems limited in importance. Certainly, the whole membership of the party rarely selects candidates for local office. Local party activists or perhaps some nonparty group, such as a trade union or a business firm, usually choose the candidate. The candidate often selects himself or herself and then the party ratifies this self-selection. Unlike the United States, no European society holds party primaries; thus, local leaders have great scope for exercising the recruitment function. Even in the United States, party members' control over candidate selection in the primaries seems limited, mainly because some states allow nonpartisans to vote in a party's primary. Yet, compared with Europeans, American voters do get more opportunity to decide which party will govern the legislative branch. If one party wins a majority of seats in the legislature, then it organizes the legislature. In the European parliamentary systems, several parties, not just two, compete for power; therefore, various parties have to form a coalition government. The party leaders in the legislature, not the party's members among the electorate, select ministers for the cabinet.

Political recruitment refers mainly to the selection of legislators. Except for the French and Italian communist parties, which exercise greater centralized control over the selection process, local party activists usually undertake the initial choice. Within the parliament, central party leaders select the cabinet ministers. Except in West Germany, where the party patronage system governs recruitment to the civil service, nonpartisan criteria generally influence appointment to government bureaucracies. In this recruitment process, party members thus play only a limited role.[44]

INTEREST AGGREGATION

In a democratic system, where competing political organizations have to reconcile their differences, interest aggregation probably constitutes the most important activity political parties perform, especially during the election campaign. To win elections and implement some legislative program, party leaders must combine or "aggregate" the diverse views within a party and between different parties. Most parties, especially those on the Left, contain several organized groups. For example, members within the PCI belong to such allied organizations as associations for women, resistance (World War II antifascist) veterans, small farmers, athletes, and youth. Besides these formally organized groups, several informal factions make up all political parties. In the United States, these factions center around regional, ethnic, religious, economic, ideological, and personalistic ties. Southerners, Blacks, Jews, Catholics, trade union officials, liberals, and followers of dominant personalities all form caucuses within the Democratic party. As we have seen, regional factions comprise the dominant informal group within Canadian parties. Elsewhere, factions form around age groups, regions, personalities, ideological *tendances*, and so forth. To get their candidates elected to office and to evolve a public policy when in office, party leaders bargain, form coalitions, try to reconcile differences, and build alliances among these diverse social groups.[45]

Particularly in a multiparty parliamentary system where no party ever gets a majority of seats, the task of building coalitions among different parties becomes absolutely necessary. Except for the United States, few among these seven Western countries have two-party systems; parties build coalitions after elections, rather than before. Hence, the largest party usually must unite with smaller ones to form a majority in the lower house of the legislature. For instance, minority governments are common in Canada; the dominant Liberal party has allied with the smaller New Democratic party. The British Liberal party has established a loose electoral coalition with the Social Democratic party. The Swedish Social Democrats have often joined forces with such disparate parties as the Center party to its right and the Communist party to its left. German Social Democrats govern in alliance with either the CDU or the Free Democrats. Confronting the most divided multiparty system, the Italian Christian Democrats choose to form a government with nearly every party except the Communists; these included such disparate parties as the neofascists, Liberals, Republicans, and Socialists. In Italy and France, a key issue confronting the Socialist parties focuses on the relationships with the Communist party. Some Socialist leaders prefer to align with noncommunist parties. Others are more willing to join the Communists in an electoral alliance and coalition government. The process of forming this alliance obviously takes considerable political skills of reconciling divergent interests. Leaders of other parties also need to demonstrate these same skills of interest aggregation for the effective operation of multiparty coalition governments.

MANAGEMENT OF GOVERNMENT

Managing government means formulating and implementing public policy. Unlike the situation in the Soviet Union, where the Communist party decides basic policy and supervises its execution, political parties in Western democratic societies play a more limited role. Certainly, parties exercise little *structural* control over the policy process. Yet their *attitudinal* influence is greater in the sense that they shape policy moods, set priorities, and suggest solutions to pressing social problems. By exploring the relationships between the party leaders and legislators, we will investigate this disjunction between strong attitudinal influence and weaker structural control.

In the Western democracies, the legislators and civil servants, not the party leaders, formulate the basic policies. For instance, the British Labour party historically stressed the crucial role party members should play in strictly controlling actions taken by the Labour members of Parliament. Despite this injunction, neither the Labour party's annual conference nor even the National Executive Committee made basic decisions. Instead, the parliamentary Labour party, specifically the top ministers when the party holds office, together with the senior civil servants, formulated policies, sometimes in opposition to party activists' preferences. In the Federal Republic of Germany, the Social Democratic party organization cannot control the operations of the SPD parliamentary group. Similarly, in Sweden, another country with a strong Social Democratic party, the socialists do not really formulate policy but rather respond to policy proposals government civil servants initiate. As in other countries, the dominant party exercises only weak control over the government bureaucracy.[46]

Party influence on government leaders' behavior. Despite this lack of structural control, political parties do influence policy by shaping legislators' voting behavior and political leaders' attitudes toward specific issues. The attitudinal effects of parties thus appear stronger than their structural control over government officials.

Membership in a political party produces some degree of cohesion when legislators vote for bills. Generally, the left-wing parties in continental Europe demonstrate a higher degree of party cohesion in legislative voting behavior than do right-wing parties, partly because Socialists and Communists take ideology more seriously. Thus, the German Social Democrats, the French Communists, and the Italian Communists all have greater party unity in the legislature than their conservative colleagues. In Britain and the United States, the conservative parties have demonstrated stronger legislative party cohesion than the more leftist parties. Compared with Tory members of Parliament, Labour MPs have split into more divisive policy-based factions. Indeed, in 1981, this factionalism even led to a partial disintegration of the Labour party as thirteen Labour MPs formed a new Social Democratic party. This new party opposed the nationalization of more industries and supported an incomes policy that would restrain union members' wage hikes. It also rejected the Labour party proposal for an electoral college, composed of parliamentarians, unionists, and local constituency party members, that would select the top party leaders. Instead, the Social Democratic party wanted the parliamentary party to continue choosing the party leadership.

In the United States, political party structures are relatively weak; thus, few legislators feel intense voting pressures from party organizations outside the legislature. During the 1970s, the Republicans developed a stronger national party headquarters, with a more professional staff, than did the Democrats. Taking ideology more seriously, conservative Republican legislators, especially in the House of Representatives, showed greater party cohesion when voting for bills. Despite these differences between the two parties, both Republicans and Democrats have revealed weaker legislative cohesion than do Canadian or West European parties, mainly because the parliamentary system necessitates strong party discipline to maintain the government in office. If the dominant parties lose a vote of confidence, then new elections will take place. This desire to avoid several elections a year before Parliament's term elapses, usually lasting from three to five years, stimulates high party cohesion. In the United States, only two parties hold seats in Congress. Members of the House serve for fixed two-year terms; senators hold tenure for six years. Because the executive governs a separate institution, the presidency, the system does not require high legislative party cohesion to maintain the government in power. Therefore, both congressional parties, especially the Democrats, are split by regional and ideological cleavages.[47]

Party membership also affects attitudes toward policy issues. The more liberal party supports an expansion of economic equality and civil liberties. For example, in the United States, Democratic members of Congress, compared to Republicans, more often vote for bills designed to implement tax reforms—that is, to make the tax system more progressive so that the rich pay a larger percentage of their total income in taxes than do the poor. To attain economic equality and to offset the power exerted by private corporations, Democratic legislators also favor more active government management of the economy and the extension of social welfare benefits. Thus, the poor tend to benefit when the Democrats hold office; the rich gain advantages when both parties are weak or when the Republicans exercise power. As Benjamin Page notes: "There *are* some significant differences between the American parties.... These differences are not confined to campaign rhetoric but appear also in presidential action and in congressional voting and legislation, as well as party platforms. The alternation of parties in power makes a difference in policy."[48]

The election of Republican Ronald Reagan to the presidency in

1980 brought significant economic policy changes. Although both President Carter and President Reagan favored reduced budget expenditures, tax cuts for business, lower increases in the money supply, and some government deregulation of private business firms, the Reagan economic program brought greater benefits to the wealthy than to the poor. Compared with the 1980 Carter budget, the 1982 Reagan budget proposals decreased expenditures for consumer and housing credit, mass transportation, community development, public education, public service jobs, employment training, and social services. Increased spending for defense benefited the arms manufacturers. Reagan's tax proposals—lower capital gains taxes, reduced taxes for persons in high-income brackets, and decreases in the windfall profits tax—also meant greater economic advantages for the wealthy. Programs that encouraged private economic corporations to exploit publicly owned lands for oil, minerals, and timber also enlarged the resources of the rich.

In the West European parliamentary systems, governing nonsocialist parties pursue somewhat different economic policies than those preferred by the socialist parties controlling government power. Nonsocialist parliamentarians place greater emphasis on decreasing government expenditures on social services, reducing taxes on the wealthy, and lowering public employment. Government spending priorities diverge. For instance, the Conservative government led by Prime Minister Margaret Thatcher reduced public expenditures for education (school meals, school transportation), day-care centers, health services for the disabled, family support services (home assistance, home meals, social workers), job training, unemployment benefits, public transportation, and social security benefits. Compared with the previous Labour government, the Tory administration increased spending on defense projects, the military, and the police. In Germany between 1950 and 1976, the Social Democrats controlling the federal government spent a higher percentage of total revenues for transportation and education, but the governing Christian Democrats allocated more funds to defense and agriculture.

Democratic socialists in Germany and Britain, compared with their conservative party colleagues, also made slightly different policy responses to changes in inflation and jobless levels between 1950 and 1975. When prices rose, the governing German Social Democrats opted for higher interest rates and for a budget surplus. When unemployment increased, they resorted to lower interest rates and a budget deficit. Christian Democratic governments, however, showed less willingness to actively intervene in the market to resolve these twin economic problems. In Britain, whereas the Labour party government used interest rates to curb inflation and budget deficits to reduce unemployment, the Conservative party in power relied on monetary policy to cope with both inflation and unemployment.[49] In sum, socialist and nonsocialist parties pursue somewhat divergent economic policies; yet the differences between these West European parties remain moderate.

Disparities between party goals and government policies. Despite the influence of party affiliation on policy preferences, legislators often fail to translate their party's positions into public policies, especially at the local government level. Even though German city governments controlled by the Christian Democrats generally spend less for social services such as health and education, the policies the CDU and the SPD enact are not greatly different. Indeed, blue-collar and white-collar cities dominated by the Social Democrats diverge just as much. Whereas city governments in working-class areas spend more money on welfare and public housing, middle-class urban governments enact higher taxes and vote higher public expenditures, particularly for such local government employees as teachers, police officers, and other municipal workers.

In France and Italy, local governments controlled by the Communist party try to implement not revolutionary policies but moderate, reformist policies. For example, when the Communists administer French city governments in coalition with the Socialists, the left-wing governments spend more on schools, canteens, swimming pools, day-care centers, and other social services for youth than do noncommunist municipal administrations, which give higher priority to road repairs, clean streets, and parking garages. Similarly, in Italy, local coalition governments of Communists and Socialists have stressed balanced budgets, honest and efficient management, higher unemployment compensation, increased public service jobs for unemployed youth, and the establishment of public housing, city planning bureaus, credit bureaus, day-care centers, and better city transportation. Contrary to expectations, the Italian Christian Democrats controlling city governments have enacted more expansionary fiscal policies than have the Communists.[50]

Even at the national government level in the United States, Britain, and Sweden, the major parties' spending priorities showed only slight differences, at least until Prime Minister Thatcher and President Reagan assumed government power. Between 1950 and 1976, the Labour party governments stressed expenditures for employment services and for comprehensive schools; however, the Conservative party governments allocated greater public funds for housing, research, and the environment. In the United States between 1941 and 1976, changes in party control of Congress and the executive branch produced only minor changes in the level of expenditures and in the types of programs funded. The major difference was that the Democrats spent less money on agriculture than did the Republicans. When the three nonsocialist parties in Sweden formed a coalition government during 1976, they proceeded to expand social service programs and the number of workers employed in the public sector. Departing from their ideological promises, they even increased the state-owned share of the economy. Striving to rescue some private firms from bankruptcy, the government nationalized some steel, mining, shipbuilding, paper, and pulp industries.[51] In short, nearly all political parties have muted their ideological differences when they wield executive power.

Three general reasons explain the gap between a party's ideological positions and its government policies. First, in the United States and elsewhere, party activists take programmatic ideology more seriously than do elected officeholders. Everywhere candidates running for elective office have a broader constituency; they must gain rapport not just with a few party ideologues but with a plurality of voters, who generally regard abstract ideology as less important than do party activists. All candidates view success at the polls as the crucial instrumental objective, for without electoral victory they will be unable to implement their programs. The overriding desire to win office hence discourages complete ideological consistency. In contrast, party activists more fully enjoy the symbolic, expressive benefits that derive from working for a candidate who takes similar ideological positions, even if the candidate loses the election.

Second, all policymaking has important incremental qualities. No party ever imposes its will on a political vacuum; rather, past experiences condition present policies. Contemporary governments often make minor adjustments to the existing policies, not fundamentally different decisions.

Third, organizations other than a government official's own political party shape the policy process. Especially in Europe, few parties ever gain a majority in the legislature at either the national or the local level. All parties need to form coalition governments; this process requires the compromise of policy positions. Even in the United States, Republicans and Democrats often establish a coalition government, particularly at the local level. Whereas in the American "nonpartisan" governments both parties frequently oppose extensive government activities to promote greater equality, in the continental European multiparty governments nearly all parties, whether of the Right or the Left, favor activist government. Indeed, in European countries, conservative parties established government enterprises and social welfare services prior to World War I, before socialist parties came to office. Hence, rather similar policies have flowed from different parties. Besides political parties, other organizations, such as interest groups and especially the civil service, participate in the policy process. They play a crucial role in formulating and implementing government decisions.

THE DECLINING INFLUENCE OF POLITICAL PARTIES

Political parties performed the most diffuse activities during the late nineteenth and early twentieth centuries, when the industrialization process was "taking off" and the mass of voters began to secure the vote. In the United States, the period between the end of the Civil War and the 1896 election marked the high point of party activity. As Robert Merton has observed, before the growth of bureaucratic government, the two parties carried out a number of activities unfulfilled by other organizations.[52] Rapid industrialization attracted millions of European immigrants to the American cities. To these disadvantaged people looking for work in the urban areas, parties provided several concrete benefits, such as food, jobs, legal advice, and scholarships for the workers' children. Work within the party provided disadvantaged persons with alternative channels of upward social mobility. The more advantaged business owners also received practical benefits from the local party "machine," including contracts, licenses, special zoning regulations, and tax subsidies.

During the pre–World War I era, left-wing European parties performed even more extensive activities than American party organizations. Unlike the electoral situation in the United States, where nearly all white males had gained the suffrage by the 1840s, most European workers did not have the right to vote at the end of the nineteenth century. Socialist parties were organized as social movements. They pressed for both political and economic rights to the working class—the right for all to vote and the right to organize trade unions that would improve working conditions. Where the existing governments provided few comprehensive social services, the socialist parties took steps to grant these concrete benefits in a personal, humanistic way. After World War I, however, a number of social welfare programs administered by the national civil service began. As other concrete structures fulfilled these social needs, the diffuse activities formerly carried out by political parties gradually declined.

Since the early 1950s, party activities have become less important. As parties' mass memberships decline, they no longer carry out extensive political education. Interest aggregation occurs mainly before elections, when the various factions within a party must coalesce to score a victory at the polls, and after the election, when several parties in a multiparty system need to form a coalition government. Few political parties exert strong structural control over the policy process, even though legislators' partisan affiliations shape their policy views. Thus, during the post–World War II era, the declining power of political parties has meant the growing influence of interest group leaders and civil servants over the policy process.[53]

Most Western parties, whether liberal, conservative, Christian democrat, socialist, or even communist, now assume a specialized electoral role. Active mainly around elections, they devote most of their attention to winning control of government office. Other structures perform the activities that parties used to fulfill. For instance, schools and the mass media carry out political education. The rising costs of publishing have recently caused several European party newspapers to discontinue, as happened in the United States seventy years ago. Newspaper publishing has become primarily a business enterprise concerned with reaching a large, diverse audience. As a result, the papers are more nonpartisan than previously. Television replaces the party press as a source of political education.[54] Interest groups increasingly cater to people's specialized needs. For example, European trade unions have become independent of party control as they concentrate on collective bargaining, rather than more explicicitly political activities.

The rise of the welfare state administered by professionalized civil servants means that parties no longer provide various concrete benefits to needy citizens. Significantly, only in Italy, where an inefficient, unwieldy, corrupt bureaucracy dominates the political process, have political parties retained their diffuse role. As we have seen, the PCI provides needed personal services to people in the northern industrial cities; more effectively than other parties, except the Christian Democrats, it has managed to pry concessions from the bureaucrats.[55] Elsewhere, political party activities revolve mainly around the winning of elections, not the implementing of public policies.

Despite their limited structural control over the policy process, parties still organize elections, provide citizens a choice of candidates, influence voters' attitudes toward political issues, and shape government leaders' policy positions. From this attitudinal perspective, they continue to play a politically important role in constitutional governments.

Notes

1. Jaroslav Hasek, "From the History of the Party of Moderate Progress within the Limits of the Law," trans. Peter Kussi, *Harper's* 257 (August 1978): 38.
2. Ibid., p. 40.
3. See William N. Chambers, "Parties and Nation-Building in America," in *Political Parties and Political Development*, ed. Joseph LaPalombara and Myron Weiner (Princeton, N.J.: Princeton University Press, 1966), pp. 79–106; Samuel P. Huntington, *Political Order in Changing Societies* (New Haven, Conn.: Yale University Press, 1968), pp. 89–90; Richard Rose,

Politics in England, 2d ed. (Boston: Little, Brown, 1974), pp. 41–45.
4. See the conceptions of Leon D. Epstein, "Political Parties," in *Handbook of Political Science*, vol. 4, ed. Fred I. Greenstein and Nelson W. Polsby (Reading, Mass.: Addison-Wesley, 1975), p. 230; Giovanni Sartori, *Parties and Party Systems: A Framework for Analysis*, vol. 1 (London: Cambridge University Press, 1976), pp. 39–66.
5. The literature is voluminous. See the following studies of Republican and Democratic voters: Warren E. Miller, Arthur H. Miller, and Edward J. Schneider, *American National Election Studies Data Sourcebook, 1952–1978* (Cambridge, Mass.: Harvard University Press, 1980), pp. 186, 190; Edward G. Carmines and J. David Gopoian, "Issue Coalitions, Issueless Campaigns: The Paradox of Rationality in American Presidential Elections," *Journal of Politics* 43 (November 1981): 1170–1189; Stephen D. Shaffer, "The Policy Biases of Political Activists," *American Politics Quarterly* 8 (January 1980): 15–33; Everett Carll Ladd, Jr., and Charles D. Hadley, *Political Parties and Political Issues: Patterns in Differentiation Since the New Deal*, Sage Professional Papers in American Politics, vol. 1, series no. 04-010 (Beverly Hills, Calif.: Sage, 1973), pp. 21–24; Everett Carll Ladd, Jr., and Charles D. Hadley, "Party Definition and Party Differentiation," *Public Opinion Quarterly* 37 (Spring 1973): 24–25; Gerald Pomper, *Voters' Choice: Varieties of American Electoral Behavior* (New York: Harper & Row, 1975), pp. 167–168; Benjamin I. Page, *Choices and Echoes in Presidential Elections: Rational Man and Electoral Democracy* (Chicago: University of Chicago Press, 1978), pp. 62–108. The following essays report information about the views of delegates to national party conventions: Herbert McClosky, Paul J. Hoffmann, and Rosemary O'Hara, "Issue Conflict and Consensus among Party Leaders and Followers," *American Political Science Review* 54 (June 1960): 407–427; John W. Soule and James W. Clarke, "Issue Conflict and Consensus: A Comparative Study of Democratic and Republican Delegates to the 1968 National Conventions," *Journal of Politics* 33 (February 1971): 72–91; John W. Soule and Wilma E. McGrath, "A Comparative Study of Presidential Nomination Conventions: The Democrats 1968 and 1972," *American Journal of Political Science* 19 (August 1975): 501–517; John W. Soule, Wilma E. McGrath, and Deborah Dunkle, "A Comparative Study of Five National Party Conventions: 1968–1976" (mimeographed). For other analyses of Democratic and Republican elites, see Allen H. Barton, "Consensus and Conflict among American Leaders," *Public Opinion Quarterly* 38 (Winter 1974–1975): 507–530; Aage R. Clausen, *How Congressmen Decide: A Policy Focus* (New York: St. Martin's Press, 1973).
6. Information about the 1964 election comes from my analysis of the national survey data made available by the Inter-University Consortium for Political and Social Research and originally collected by the Survey Research Center of the University of Michigan. For data pertaining to the period between 1968 and 1976, see Ladd and Hadley, *Political Parties and Political Issues*, pp. 32–37; *Gallup Opinion Index* no. 127 (February 1976): 10; Miller, Miller, and Schneider, *American National Election Studies Data Sourcebook*, p. 210; Shaffer, "The Policy Biases of Political Activists," pp. 24–26.
7. Rose, *Politics in England*, pp. 304–312; Richard Rose, "Resistance to Moral Change," *New Society* 48 (April 12, 1979): 90; "The Policies of the Parties," *New Society* 48 (April 19, 1978): 142–144; Ivor Crewe, Bo Särlvik, and James Alt, "Partisan Dealignment in Britain, 1964–1974," *British Journal of Political Science* 7 (April 1977): 129–190; Donald D. Searing, "Measuring Politicians' Values: Administration and Assessment of a Ranking Technique in the British House of Commons," *American Political Science Review* 72 (March 1978): 76–77; Donley T. Studlar, "Policy Voting in Britain: The Colored Immigration Issue in the 1964, 1966, and 1970 General Elections," *American Political Science Review* 72 (March 1978): 46–64; Bob Jessop, *Traditionalism, Conservatism, and British Political Culture* (London: George Allen and Unwin, 1974), p. 98; Glenn Wilson, "The Liberal Extremists," *New Society* 26 (November 1, 1973): 263.
8. See Bo Särlvik, "Recent Electoral Trends in Sweden," in *Scandinavia at the Polls*, ed. Karl H. Cerny (Washington, D.C.: American Enterprise Institute, 1977), p. 108; Michael Lindén, "Political Dimensions and Relative Party Positions: A Factor Analytic Study of Swedish Attitude Data," *Scandinavian Journal of Psychology* 16, no. 2 (1975): 97–107; Olof Petersson and Henry Valen, "Political Cleavages in Sweden and Norway," *Scandinavian Polit-*

ical Studies 2, new series, no. 4 (1979): 325.
9. Robert D. Putnam, *The Beliefs of Politicians: Ideology, Conflict, and Democracy in Britain and Italy* (New Haven, Conn.: Yale University Press, 1973), pp. 199, 216; Alan J. Stern, "Rudimentary Political Belief Systems in Four Italian Communities," *Journal of Politics* 37 (February 1975): 241–243; Denis Lacorne, "On the Fringe of the French Political System: The Beliefs of Communist Municipal Elites," *Comparative Politics* 9 (July 1977): 421–441.
10. Putnam, *The Beliefs of Politicians*, p. 216; Milton Rokeach, *The Open and Closed Mind* (New York: Basic Books, 1960), p. 57; Gordon J. DiRenzo, *Personality, Power and Politics* (Notre Dame, Ind.: University of Notre Dame Press, 1967), p. 97; John Ardagh, "The War within the French Left," *New Society* 35 (February 19, 1976): 375–377; Ronald Tiersky, "French Communism in 1976," *Problems of Communism* 25 (January–February 1976): 20–47; Lacorne, "On the Fringe of the French Political System," pp. 421–441. For comparisons of the views held by French and Italian Communist Party leaders, see also the following essays in *Communism in Italy and France*, ed. Donald L. M. Blackmer and Sidney Tarrow (Princeton, N.J.: Princeton University Press, 1975): Robert D. Putnam, "The Italian Communist Politician," pp. 186–198; Georges Lavau, "The PCF, the State, and the Revolution: An Analysis of Party Policies, Communications, and Popular Culture," pp. 96–99; Denis Lacorne, "Left-Wing Unity at the Grass Roots: Picardy and Languedoc," p. 320; Sidney Tarrow, "Communism in Italy and France: Adaptation and Change," pp. 619–623.
11. Lindén, "Political Dimensions and Relative Party Positions," pp. 101–102; Särlvik, "Recent Electoral Trends in Sweden," pp. 108–109; Crewe et al., "Partisan Dealignment in Britain," p. 151; Searing, "Measuring Politicians' Values," pp. 76–77; "The Policies of the Parties," pp. 142–144; Petersson and Valen, "Political Cleavages in Sweden and Norway," p. 325.
12. For Americans' policy positions, see Ladd and Hadley, *Political Parties and Political Issues*, pp. 34–38, 52–54; McClosky et al., "Issue Conflict and Consensus among Party Leaders and Followers," p. 416; Soule and Clarke, "Issue Conflict and Consensus," p. 78; Soule, McGrath, and Dunkle, "A Comparative Study of Five National Party Conventions," table 2. For the policy attitudes of the British, see David Berry, *The Sociology of Grass Roots Politics: A Study of Party Membership* (New York: St. Martin's Press, 1970), pp. 106–107; Rose, *Politics in England*, p. 395; Wilson, "The Liberal Extremists," p. 263; Mark Abrams, "The British Middle-Class Socialist," *Encounter* 44 (March 1975): 13–15; Putnam, *The Beliefs of Politicians*, p. 216.
13. See Putnam, *The Beliefs of Politicians*, pp. 34–48; Philip E. Converse, "Some Mass-Elite Contrasts in the Perception of Political Spaces," *Social Science Information* 14, nos. 3–4 (1975): 49–83; Philip E. Converse and Gregory B. Markus, "Plus ça change...: The New CPS Election Study Panel," *American Political Science Review* 73 (March 1979): 32–49; Benjamin I. Page, "Elections and Social Choice: The State of the Evidence," *American Journal of Political Science* 21 (August 1977): 639–668; Norman Nie, Sidney Verba, and John Petrocik, *The Changing American Voter*, enlarged ed. (Cambridge, Mass.: Harvard University Press, 1979), pp. 20–21, 110–122, 361–372; David Butler and Donald Stokes, *Political Change in Britain: The Evolution of Electoral Choice*, 2d ed. (New York: St. Martin's Press, 1974), pp. 329–337.
14. Joseph A. Schlesinger, "The Primary Goals of Political Parties: A Clarification of Positive Theory," *American Political Science Review* 69 (September 1975): 840–849.
15. Nie, Verba, and Petrocik, *The Changing American Voter*, pp. 194–205; Ladd and Hadley, *Political Parties and Political Issues*, pp. 46–54; Ladd and Hadley, "Party Definition and Party Differentiation," pp. 21–34; Shaffer, "The Policy Biases of Political Activists," pp. 21–24.
16. Paul Whitely and Ian Gordon, "The Labour Party: Middle Class, Militant and Male," *New Statesman* 99 (January 11, 1980): 41–42; Paul Whitely, "Who Are the Labour Activists?" *Political Quarterly* 52 (April–June 1981): 160–170; Patrick Seyd and Lewis Minkin, "The Labour Party and Its Members," *New Society* 49 (September 20, 1979), 613–615; Paul Britten Austin and Jörgen Westerståhl, "How Local Is Government?" *Sweden Now* 9, no. 2 (1975): 42–43; Samuel H. Barnes, "Left, Right, and the Italian Voter," *Comparative Political Studies* 4 (July 1971): 170–173.
17. For content analyses of political parties' ideological stands, see the following works by John Clayton Thomas: "Policy

Convergence among Political Parties and Societies in Developed Nations: A Synthesis and Partial Testing of Two Theories," *Western Political Quarterly* 33 (June 1980): 233–246; "Ideological Trends in Western Political Parties," in *Western European Party Systems; Trends and Prospects,* ed. Peter H. Merkl (New York: Free Press, 1980), pp. 348–366; "The Changing Nature of Partisan Divisions in the West: Trends in Domestic Policy Orientations in Ten Party Systems," *European Journal of Political Research* 7 (December 1979): 397–413; *The Decline of Ideology in Western Political Parties: A Study of Changing Policy Orientations,* Sage Professional Papers in Contemporary Political Sociology, vol. 1, series no. 06-012 (Beverly Hills, Calif.: Sage, 1975), esp. pp. 8–19. See also Seymour Martin Lipset, *Political Man: The Social Bases of Politics,* expanded and updated ed. (Baltimore, Md.: Johns Hopkins University Press, 1981), pp. 64–79, 439–456, 524–565.

18. For comparisons of the programs articulated by PCF and PCI leaders, see the following essays in Blackmer and Tarrow, *Communism in Italy and France*: Sidney Tarrow, "Party Activists in Public Office: Comparisons at the Local Level in Italy and France," pp. 143–172; Tarrow, "Communism in Italy and France," pp. 575–640. See also Thomas H. Greene, "Non-Ruling Communist Parties and Political Adaptation," *Studies in Comparative Communism* 6 (Winter 1973): 331–361; Norman Kogan, "The French Communists—and Their Italian Comrades," *Studies in Comparative Communism* (Spring–Summer 1973): 184–195; Martha H. Good, "The Italian Communist Party and Local Government Coalitions," *Studies in Comparative Communism* 13 (Summer–Autumn 1980): 197–219; Samuel H. Barnes, *Representation in Italy: Institutionalized Tradition and Electoral Choice* (Chicago: University of Chicago Press, 1977), pp. 58–60; Tiersky, "French Communism in 1976," pp. 28, 44; Frank L. Wilson, "The French CP's Dilemma," *Problems of Communism* 27 (July–August 1978): 12–14. Giovanni Sartori, "European Political Parties: The Case of Polarized Pluralism," in La Palombara and Weiner, *Political Parties and Political Development,* p. 148, categorizes the PCI as an "antisystem" party. For a critique of this position, see Sidney Tarrow, "The Italian Party System between Crisis and Transition," *American Journal of Political Science* 21 (May 1977): 193–224.

19. Stephen Hellman, "The Italian CP: Stumbling on the Threshold?" *Problems of Communism* 27 (November–December 1978): 31–48; Paolo Farnetti, "The Troubled Partnership: Trade Unions and Working-Class Parties in Italy, 1948–78," *Government and Opposition* 13 (Autumn 1978): 416–436; Michael J. Sodaro, "The Italian Communists and the Politics of Austerity," *Studies in Comparative Communism* 13 (Summer–Autumn 1980): 220–249; Peter Lange, "Crisis and Consent, Change and Compromise: Dilemmas of Italian Communism in the 1970s," *West European Politics* 2 (October 1979): 110–132; Judith Chubb, "Naples under the Left: The Limits of Local Change," *Comparative Politics* 13 (October 1980): 53–78.

20. Whitely and Gordon, "The Labour Party," pp. 41–42; Seyd and Minkin, "The Labour Party and Its Members," pp. 613–615; Whitely, "Who Are the Labour Activists?" pp. 165–170; Lewis Minkin, "The Party Connection: Divergence and Convergence in the British Labour Movement," *Government and Opposition* 13 (Autumn 1978): 458–484; Suzanne Berger, "Politics and Antipolitics in Western Europe in the Seventies," *Daedalus* 108 (Winter 1979): 27–50; William Schneider, "The Mistress of Downing Street: Why She Won," *Public Opinion* 2 (June–July 1979): 51–54.

21. Thomas, "The Changing Nature of Partisan Divisions in the West," pp. 403–404; Frederick Hartwig, William R. Jenkins, and Earl M. Temchin, "Variability in Electoral Behavior: The 1960, 1968, and 1976 Elections," *American Journal of Political Science* 24 (August 1980): 553–558; Nie, Verba, and Petrocik, *The Changing American Voter,* pp. 357–386; Everett Carll Ladd, Jr., and Seymour Martin Lipset, "Anatomy of a Decade," *Public Opinion* 3 (December 1979–January 1980): 2–9; *Public Opinion* 3 (December 1980–January 1981): 36–37; *New York Times,* November 9, 1980, p. 18; Shaffer, "The Policy Biases of Political Activists," pp. 21–31; Anne N. Costain, "Changes in the Role of Ideology in American National Nominating Conventions and among Party Identifiers," *Western Political Quarterly* 33 (March 1980): 73–86.

22. For analogies between the market system and the political system, see Talcott Parsons, " 'Voting' and the Equilibrium of the American Political System," *American

Voting Behavior, ed. Eugene Burdick and Arthur Brodbeck (New York: Free Press, 1959), pp. 80–120; Anthony Downs, *An Economic Theory of Democracy* (New York: Harper & Row, 1957).

23. See Seymour Martin Lipset and Stein Rokkan, "Cleavage Structures, Party Systems, and Voter Alignments: An Introduction," in *Party Systems and Voter Alignments*, ed. Seymour M. Lipset and Stein Rokkan (New York: Free Press, 1967), pp. 1–64, esp. pp. 13–50.

24. Sar A. Levitan, William B. Johnston, and Robert Taggart, *Minorities in the United States* (Washington, D.C.: Public Affairs Press, 1975), p. 3; Minister of Industry, Trade, and Commerce, *Perspective Canada: A Compendium of Social Statistics* (Ottawa: Statistics Canada, 1974), pp. 225, 230, 257; Richard Rose and Derek Urwin, "Social Cohesion, Political Parties and Strains in Regimes," *Comparative Political Studies* 2 (April 1969): 54.

25. John Saywell, *The Rise of the Parti Québécois, 1967–76* (Toronto: University of Toronto Press, 1977), p. 168; Armando G. Gutiérrez and Herbert Hirsch, "Political Maturation and Political Awareness: The Case of the Crystal City Chicano," *Aztlán* 5 (Spring and Fall 1974): 295–312; Armando Gutiérrez, "Hispanics and the Sunbelt," *Dissent* 27 (Fall 1980): 494–495; Anthony Fusaro, "Two Faces of British Nationalism: The Scottish National Party and Plaid Cymru Compared," *Polity* 11 (Spring 1979): 362–386; Joseph R. Rudolph, Jr., "Ethnonational Parties and Politics in Britain and Belgium: Political Mobilization and Party-Building in the Multinational States of Western Europe," paper presented at the 1975 annual meeting of the Western Political Science Association, Seattle, Washington, March 20–22, 1975.

26. *Gallup Opinion Index* no. 183 (December 1980): 6–7; Charles D. Hadley, "Survey Research and Southern Politics: The Implications of Data Management," *Public Opinion Quarterly* 45 (Fall 1981): 393–401.

27. John Meisel, *Working Papers on Canadian Politics*, 2d ed. (Montreal: McGill-Queen's University Press, 1975), pp. 259, 268–269, appendix table II; John Meisel, *Cleavages, Parties, and Values in Canada*, Sage Professional Papers in Contemporary Political Sociology, vol. 1, series no. 06-003 (Beverly Hills, Calif.: Sage, 1974); *Maclean's* 93 (February 25, 1980): 20.

28. Ivor Crewe, "The Black, Brown, and Green Votes," *New Society* 48 (April 12, 1979): 76–78.

29. See Vincent Wright, "The French General Election of March 1978: 'La Divine Surprise,'" *West European Politics* 1 (October 1978): 39; *Sondages* 35, no. 1 (1973): 26; Jean-Claude Rabier, "On the Political Behaviour of French Workers," *Acta Sociologica* 21, no. 4 (1978): 367–370; Peter H. Merkl, "The Sociology of European Parties: Members, Voters, and Social Groups," in Merkl, *Western European Party Systems*, pp. 649–650; Kendall L. Baker, Russell J. Dalton, and Kai Hildebrandt, *Germany Transformed: Political Culture and the New Politics* (Cambridge, Mass.: Harvard University Press, 1981), pp. 180–186, 282–283; Giacomo Sani, "The Italian Electorate in the Mid-1970s: Beyond Tradition?" in *Italy at the Polls: The Parliamentary Elections of 1976*, ed. Howard R. Penniman (Washington, D.C.: American Enterprise Institute, 1977), p. 114; Meisel, *Working Papers on Canadian Politics*, p. 259; and the following essays in *Electoral Behavior: A Comparative Handbook*, ed. Richard Rose (New York: Free Press, 1974): Richard Rose, "Britain: Simple Abstractions and Complex Realities," pp. 517–518; Derek W. Urwin, "Germany: Continuity and Change in Electoral Politics," pp. 147–150; Bo Särlvik, "Sweden: The Social Bases of the Parties in a Developmental Perspective," pp. 415–419.

30. For data on the United States, see Seymour Martin Lipset, *Revolution and Counterrevolution: Change and Persistence in Social Structures* (New York: Basic Books, 1968), pp. 246–303; *Gallup Opinion Index* no. 183 (December 1980): 6–7; Everett Carll Ladd, Jr., "The Brittle Mandate: Electoral Dealignment and the 1980 Presidential Election," *Political Science Quarterly* 96 (Spring 1981): 11–18; and the following articles by Robert Axelrod: "Where the Votes Come From: An Analysis of Electoral Coalitions, 1952–1968," *American Political Science Review* 66 (March 1972): 14–18; "Communication on the 1972 Election," *American Political Science Review* 68 (June 1974): 717–720; "Communication: 1976 Update," *American Political Science Review* 72 (June 1978, September 1978): 622–624, 1010–1011; "Communication," *American Political Science Review* 76 (June 1982): 393–396. In *Working Papers on Canadian Politics*, pp. 253–274, and *Cleavages, Parties, and Values in Canada*, pp. 15–17, Meisel

discusses the relationship between politics and religion in Canada. For information about Britain, see Butler and Stokes, *Political Change in Britain*, pp. 155–166. German data can be found in Baker et al., *Germany Transformed*, p. 182.

31. See Rodney Stark, "Class, Radicalism, and Religious Involvement in Great Britain," *American Sociological Review* 29 (October 1964): 698–706; Anthony King, "A Sociological Portrait: Politics," *New Society* 19 (January 13, 1972): 59; Butler and Stokes, *Political Change in Britain*, pp. 155–166; Bo Särlvik, "Socioeconomic Position, Religious Behavior, and Voting in the Swedish Electorate," *Quality and Quantity* 4 (June 1970): 95–116; François A. Isambert, "Les ouvriers et l'Église catholique," *Revue française de sociologie* 15 (Octobre–Décembre 1974): 529–551; Alan Stern, "Political Legitimacy in Local Politics: The Communist Party in Northeastern Italy," in Blackmer and Tarrow, *Communism in Italy and France*, pp. 225–235.

32. Lipset, *Political Man*, pp. 230–300. As Lipset notes, he took this chapter title from a book by Dewey Anderson and Percy Davidson, *Ballots and the Democratic Class Struggle* (Stanford, Calif.: Stanford University Press, 1943).

33. Ronald Rogowski, "Social Class and Partisanship in European Electorates: A Re-Assessment," *World Politics* 33 (July 1981): 639–649; Alan Zuckerman and Mark Irving Lichbach, "Stability and Change in European Electorates," *World Politics* 29 (July 1977): 541; Avery M. Guest, "Class Consciousness and American Political Attitudes," *Social Forces* 52 (June 1974): 504–509; Pomper, *Voters' Choice*, p. 48; Butler and Stokes, *Political Change in Britain*, pp. 91–93; Reeve D. Vanneman, "U.S. and British Perceptions of Class," *American Journal of Sociology* 85 (January 1980): 780–785; Rick Ogmundson, "Party Class Images and the Class Vote in Canada," *American Sociological Review* 40 (August 1975): 510; Meisel, *Working Papers on Canadian Politics*, pp. 5–7, 71, appendix, table II; James D. Wright and Daniel Holub, "Social Cleavage and Party Affiliation Revisited: A Comparison of West Germany and the United States," *Sociology and Social Research* 63 (July 1979): 671–697; Wright, "The French General Election of March 1978," p. 39; Guy Michelat and Michel Simon, "Classe sociale objective, classe social subjective et comportement électoral," *Revue française de sociologie* 12 (Octobre–Décembre 1971): 492, 519; Barnes, *Representation in Italy*, pp. 60–63; Giacomo Sani, "Mass-Level Response to Party Strategy: The Italian Electorate and the Communist Party," in Blackmer and Tarrow, *Communism in Italy and France*, p. 469; and the following essays in Rose, *Electoral Behavior*: Rose, "Britain," pp. 500–507; Urwin, "Germany," pp. 146–153; Särlvik, "Sweden," pp. 400–415.

34. See Robert R. Alford, *Party and Society* (Chicago: Rand McNally, 1963), pp. 79–80, 91–92; Robert R. Alford, "Class Voting in the Anglo-American Political Systems," *Party Systems and Voter Alignments*, pp. 67–93; Paul R. Abramson, *Generational Change in American Politics* (Lexington, Mass.: Lexington Books, 1975), pp. 13–14; Torben Worre, "Class Parties and Class Voting in the Scandinavian Countries," *Scandinavian Political Studies* 3, no. 4 (1980): 317–319.

35. Barnes, *Representation in Italy*, pp. 43–64; Sani, "The Italian Electorate in the Mid-1970s," pp. 109–115; Guy Michelat and Michel Simon, "Religion, Class, and Politics," *Comparative Politics* 10 (October 1977): 159–186; Baker et al., *Germany Transformed*, pp. 190–283; Colin S. Rallings and Rudy B. Andeweg, "The Changing Class Structure and Political Behavior—A Comparative Analysis of Lower Middle-Class Politics in Britain and the Netherlands," *European Journal of Political Research* 7 (March 1979): 27–47; W. L. Miller, "Social Class and Party Choice in England: A New Analysis," *British Journal of Political Science* 8 (July 1978): 257–284; W. L. Miller, "The Religious Alignment in England at the General Elections of 1974," *Parliamentary Affairs* 30 (Summer 1977): 258–268; Rick Ogmundson, "On the Measurement of Party Class Positions: The Case of Canadian Federal Political Parties," *Canadian Review of Sociology and Anthropology*, pt. 2, 12 (November 1975): 565–576; John F. Zipp, "Left-Right Dimensions of Canadian Federal Party Identification: A Discriminant Analysis," *Canadian Journal of Political Science* 11 (June 1978): 251–277; John F. Zipp and Joel Smith, "A Structural Analysis of Class Voting," *Social Forces* 60 (March 1982): 738–759; John F. Myles, "Differences in the Canadian and American Class Vote: Fact or Pseudofact?" *American Journal of Sociology* 84 (March 1979): 1232–1237; *Gallup Opinion Index* no. 183 (December 1980): 6–7; *Public Opinion* 3

(December 1980–January 1981): 39.
36. See Klaus von Beyme, "The Changing Relations between Trade Unions and the Social Democratic Party in West Germany," *Government and Opposition* 13 (Autumn 1978): 399–415; Patrick Dunleavy, "The Political Implications of Sectoral Cleavages and the Growth of State Employment: Part 2, Cleavage Structures and Political Alignment," *Political Studies* 28 (December 1980): 527–549; Colin Crouch, "Varieties of Trade Union Weakness: Organized Labour and Capital Formation in Britain, Federal Germany, and Sweden," *West European Politics* 3 (January 1980): 87–106; A. W. J. Thompson, "Trade Unions and the Corporate State in Britain," *Industrial and Labor Relations Review* 33 (October 1979): 36–54; John D. Stephens, "Class Formation and Class Consciousness: A Theoretical and Empirical Analysis with Reference to Britain and Sweden," *British Journal of Sociology* 30 (December 1979): 389–414.
37. Walter Korpi and Michael Shalev, "Strikes, Industrial Relations and Class Conflict in Capitalist Societies," *British Journal of Sociology* 30 (June 1979): 178–179; Jack Hayward, "Trade Union Movements and Their Politico-Economic Environments: A Preliminary Framework," *West European Politics* 3 (January 1980): 1–9; Marino Regini and Gösta Esping-Andersen, "Trade Union Strategies and Social Policy in Italy and Sweden," *West European Politics* 3 (January 1981): 107–123; Georges Lavau, "The Changing Relations between Trade Unions and Working-Class Parties in France," *Government and Opposition* 13 (Autumn 1978): 437–457.
38. Paul R. Abramson, John H. Aldrich, and David W. Rohde, *Change and Continuity in the 1980 Elections* (Washington, D.C.: Congressional Quarterly Press, 1982), pp. 95–184; *Gallup Opinion Index* no. 183 (December 1980): 6–7; *Public Opinion* 3 (December 1980–January 1981): 27–28, 36; Alden S. Raine, *Change in the Political Agenda: Social and Cultural Conflict in the American Electorate*, Sage Professional Papers in American Politics, vol. 3, series no. 04-035 (Beverly Hills, Calif.: Sage, 1977); Page, *Choices and Echoes in Presidential Elections*, pp. 62–107.
39. For analyses of class voting in West European societies, see the following studies: Lipset, *Political Man*. pp. 503–521; Paul R. Abramson, "Social Class and Political Change in Western Europe: A Cross-National Analysis," *Comparative Political Studies* 4 (July 1971): 131–155; Paul R. Abramson, "Intergenerational Social Mobility and Partisan Preference in Britain and Italy: A Cross-National Comparison," *Comparative Political Studies* 6 (July 1973): 221–234; John W. Books and JoAnn B. Reynolds, "A Note on Class Voting in Great Britain and the United States," *Comparative Political Studies* 8 (October 1975): 360–376; Schneider, "The Mistress of Downing Street," pp. 51–54; Tom Forester, "The Tale of the Working Class Tory," *New Society* 58 (October 15, 1981): 97–99; Phyllis Thorburn, "Political Generations: The Case of Class and Party in Britain," *European Journal of Political Research* 6 (June 1977): 135–148; Mark N. Franklin and Anthony Mughan, "The Decline of Class Voting in Britain: Problems of Analysis and Interpretation," *American Political Science Review* 72 (June 1978): 523–534; Crewe, Särlvik, and Alt, "Partisan Dealignment in Britain," pp. 168–181; Richard Rose, "From Simple Determinism to Interactive Models of Voting: Britain as an Example," *Comparative Political Studies* 15 (July 1982): 146–156; Olof Petersson, "The 1976 Election: New Trends in the Swedish Electorate," *Scandinavian Political Studies* 1, nos. 2–3 (1978): 116–119; Worre, "Class Parties and Class Voting in the Scandinavian Countries," pp. 303–307; John D. Stephens, "The Changing Swedish Electorate: Class Voting, Contextual Effects, and Voter Volatility," *Comparative Political Studies* 14 (July 1981): 163–204; Baker et al., *Germany Transformed*, pp. 165–179, 190, 282–283; Michael S. Lewis-Beck, "The Electoral Politics of the French Peasantry: 1946–1978," *Political Studies* 29 (December 1981): 529. Otto Kirchheimer, "The Transformation of the Western European Party System," *Political Parties and Political Development*, pp. 177–200, coined the term *catch-all* party. Sidney Tarrow, "Italy: Political Integration in a Fragmented Political System," paper presented to the 1975 annual meeting of the American Political Science Association, San Francisco, September 2–5, 1975, pp. 21–22, referred to the Italian Christian Democratic party as a "catch-as-catch-can party."
40. See the analysis of Jessop, *Traditionalism, Conservatism, and British Political Culture*, pp. 42–44, 193–194, 253–260.
41. Giovanni Sartori, "From the Sociology of Politics to Political Sociology," in *Politics and the Social Sciences*, ed. Seymour Mar-

tin Lipset (New York: Oxford University Press, 1969), pp. 84–85.

42. See William H. Form, "Job vs. Political Unionism: A Cross-National Comparison," *Industrial Relations* 12 (May 1973): 224–238; Timothy May and Michael Moran, "Trade Unions as Pressure Groups," *New Society* 25 (September 6, 1973): 570–573; and the articles on English, Swedish, German, Italian, and French unions in *Industrial and Labor Relations Review* 38 (October 1974 and January 1975); *West European Politics* 3 (January 1980); George Ross, "What is Progressive about Unions? Reflections on Trade Unions and Economic Crisis," *Theory and Society* 10 (September 1981): 609–643.

43. For reviews of party membership and forms of political education carried out by parties, see the classic study of Maurice Duverger, *Political Parties*, trans. Barbara and Robert North (New York: Wiley Science Editions, 1963), pp. 61–123; Leon D. Epstein, *Political Parties in Western Democracies* (New York: Praeger, 1967), pp. 112–113, 164, 253–254; Epstein, "Political Parties," pp. 250–270; Merkl, "The Sociology of European Parties," p. 617; Colin Martin and Dick Martin, "The Decline of Labour Party Membership," *Political Quarterly* 48 (October–December 1977): 459–471; Peter Kellner, "Labour's Culture of Illusions," *New Statesman* 98 (September 28, 1979): 447; Whitely, "Who Are the Labour Activists?" pp. 161–162; Tom Forester, "Labour's Local Parties," *New Society* 33 (September 25, 1975): 695–696; Frank L. Wilson, "The Revitalization of French Parties," *Comparative Political Studies* 12 (April 1979): 87–89; Kay Lawson, *The Comparative Study of Political Parties* (New York: St. Martin's Press, 1976), pp. 145–159; Donald L. M. Blackmer, "Continuity and Change in Postwar Italian Communism," in Blackmer and Tarrow, *Communism in Italy and France*, p. 35.

44. See Epstein, *Political Parties in Western Democracies*, pp. 201–232; Epstein, "Political Parties," pp. 257–259; Lawson, *The Comparative Study of Political Parties*, p. 122; Tarrow, "Communism in Italy and France," pp. 612–621; Barnes, *Representation in Italy*, p. 135; Kenneth H. F. Dyson, *Party, State, and Bureaucracy in Western Germany*, Sage Professional Papers in Comparative Politics, vol. 6, series no. 01-063 (Beverly Hills, Calif.: Sage, 1977).

45. Gabriel Almond, "Introduction: A Functional Approach to Comparative Politics," in *The Politics of the Developing Areas*, ed. Gabriel A. Almond and James S. Coleman (Princeton, N.J.: Princeton University Press, 1960), pp. 38–45, coined the term *interest aggregation*.

46. See Epstein, "Political Parties," pp. 260–266; Epstein, *Political Parties in Western Democracies*, pp. 294–305; Rose, *Politics in England*, pp. 323–342; Samuel H. Beer, *British Politics in the Collectivist Age* (New York: Knopf, 1965), pp. 228–234; Nils Elvander, "The Politics of Taxation in Sweden 1945–1970: A Study of the Functions of Parties and Organizations," *Scandinavian Political Studies* 7 (1972): 63–82; Dyson, *Party, State, and Bureaucracy in Western Germany*, pp. 12–13.

47. For analyses of party cohesion in legislative voting behavior, see Nelson W. Polsby, "Legislatures," in Greenstein and Polsby, *Handbook of Political Science*, vol. 5, p. 293; Roland Cayrol, Jean-Luc Parodi, and Colette Ysmal, "French Deputies and the Political System," *Legislative Studies Quarterly* 1 (February 1976): 67–99; Frank L. Wilson and Richard Wiste, "Party Cohesion in the French National Assembly: 1958–1973," *Legislative Studies Quarterly* 1 (November 1976): 467–490; Wilson, "The Revitalization of French Parties," p. 91; Giuseppe Di Palma, *Surviving Without Governing: The Italian Parties in Parliament* (Berkeley: University of California Press, 1977), pp. 163–175; Walter Dean Burnham, "Insulation and Responsiveness in Congressional Elections," *Political Science Quarterly* 90 (Fall 1975): 427; Barbara Deckard Sinclair, "Who Wins in the House of Representatives: The Effect of Declining Party Cohesion on Policy Outputs, 1959–1970," *Social Science Quarterly* 58 (June 1977): 121–128; *Congressional Quarterly Almanac*, vol. 16–36 (Washington, D.C.: Congressional Quarterly, Inc., 1961–1980); Jeffrey Cohen, "The Dynamics of Party Voting in Congress, 1955–78: A Cohort Model," *Political Behavior* 3, no. 3 (1981): 224; Edward W. Crowe, "Cross-Voting in the British House of Commons: 1945–1974," *Journal of Politics* 42 (May 1980): 487–510; Leon D. Epstein, "What Happened to the British Party Model?" *American Political Science Review* 74 (March 1980): 9–22; John E. Schwarz, "Exploring a New Role in Policy Making: The British House of Commons in the 1970s," *American Political Science Review* 74 (March 1980): 23–37. For information about the split in the Labour Party and the formation of the

new Social Democratic Party, see Peter Kellner, "'Moderate' Hopes Confused," *New Statesman* 101 (March 20, 1981): 3; "The Appeal of the Centre," *New Society* 55 (March 19, 1981): 508.

48. Page, *Choices and Echoes in Presidential Elections*, p. 105. For data, see Clausen, *How Congressmen Decide*, p. 149; Thomas J. Reese, *Tax Reform Scores of Senators and Representatives* (Washington, D.C.: Taxation with Representation, 1975), esp. pp. 2–7.

49. See Alan Walker, "A Right Turn for the British Welfare State?" *Social Policy* 10 (March–April 1980): 46–51; Stuart Weier and Robin Simpson, "Are the Local Authority Social Services Being Bled Dry?" *New Society* 53 (July 10, 1980): 59–62; David Walker, "Queen Canute's State," *New Society* 55 (March 19, 1981): 504; "The Hundred Days' War," *New Statesman* 98 (August 10, 1979): 192–195; "An Anatomy of Thatcherism," *New Society* 57 (September 1981): 519–522; Rose, *Politics in England*, pp. 310–311; Manfred G. Schmidt, "The Politics of Domestic Reform in the Federal Republic of Germany," *Politics and Society* 8, no. 2 (1978): 165–200; Bruno S. Frey, "Keynesian Thinking in Politico-Economic Models," *Journal of Post Keynesian Economics* 1 (Fall 1978): 76–77; David R. Cameron, "The Expansion of the Public Economy: A Comparative Analysis," *American Political Science Review* 72 (December 1978): 1243–1261; David R. Cameron, "On the Limits of the Public Economy," *Annals of the American Academy of Political and Social Science* 459 (January 1982): 46–62; Andrew T. Cowart, "The Economic Policies of European Governments, Part I: Monetary Policy," *British Journal of Political Science* 8 (July 1978): 285–311; Andrew T. Cowart, "The Economic Policies of European Governments, Part II: Fiscal Policy," *British Journal of Political Science* 8 (October 1978): 425–439.

50. See Gerhard Lehmbruch, "Party and Federation in Germany: A Developmental Dilemma," *Government and Opposition* 13 (Spring 1978): 151–177; Robert C. Fried, "Party and Policy in West German Cities," *American Political Science Review* 70 (March 1976): 11–24; Robert C. Fried, "Comparative Urban Policy and Performance," in Greenstein and Polsby, *Handbook of Political Science*, vol. 6, pp. 323–324, 343–346; Tarrow, "Communism in Italy and France," p. 624; Martin A. Schain, "Communist Control of Municipal Councils and Urban Political Change in France," *Studies in Comparative Communism* 12 (Winter 1979): 351–370; Chubb, "Naples under the Left," pp. 53–78.

51. See Frank Gould and Barbara Roweth, "Politics and Public Spending," *Political Quarterly* 49 (April–June 1978): 222–227; Paul Burstein, "Party Balance, Replacement of Legislators, and Federal Government Expenditures, 1941–1976," *Western Political Quarterly* 32 (June 1979): 203–208; Marquis Childs, *Sweden: The Middle Way on Trial* (New Haven, Conn.: Yale University Press, 1980), pp. 78–79, 169.

52. Robert K. Merton, *Social Theory and Social Structure*, rev. and enlarged ed. (Glencoe, Illinois: The Free Press, 1957), pp. 74–78.

53. See the review of party activities by Anthony King, "Political Parties in Western Democracies—Some Skeptical Reflections," in *Comparative Political Systems*, ed. Louis J. Cantori (Boston: Holbrook Press, 1974), pp. 296–323. For analyses of the decline of political parties' power in the United States and Europe, see Morris P. Fiorina, "The Decline of Collective Responsibility in American Politics," *Daedalus* 109 (Summer 1980): 25–45; Crewe, Särlvik, and Alt, "Partisan Dealignment in Britain," pp. 129–190; Berger, "Politics and Antipolitics in Western Europe in the Seventies," pp. 42–47.

54. See Svennik Høyer, Stig Hadenius, and Lennart Weibull, *The Politics and Economics of the Press: A Developmental Perspective*, Sage Professional Papers in Contemporary Political Sociology, vol. 1, series no. 06-009 (Beverly Hills, Calif.: Sage, 1975).

55. See Berger, "Politics and Antipolitics in Western Europe in the Seventies," p. 41; Sidney Tarrow, *Between Center and Periphery: Grassroots Politicians in Italy and France* (New Haven, Conn.: Yale University Press, 1977), pp. 175–202.

PART

IV

Political Legitimacy and System Stability

Political system stability derives from the interaction among its three major foundations: social stratification, political organization, and beliefs. First, the degree of change that takes place in political systems reflects conditions within the social stratification system, notably the power and values of primordial, religious, and economic groups. Particularly in conflict-prone situations, if government leaders fail to gain support from powerful social groups, then the political system may undergo change.

Second, a system's stability also depends on the power of governments and dominant political parties to control groups that threaten to undermine the system. In this regard, political organizations' skillful exercise of both coercive and consensual power becomes important.

Third, the beliefs about the legitimacy of a political system shape the degree of stability in different nations. Legitimacy means that groups, including both the powerful and the powerless, accept justifications of the right to exercise political power as morally binding on them. These perceptions of legitimacy stem from both material and moral sources. When people expect mainly concrete benefits from the political system and the leaders actually deliver these tangible goods—employment opportunities, inexpensive consumer products, cheap credit, education, housing, sanitation facilities, access to health care—then the political system has won material legitimacy. Yet many groups also seek such moral–spiritual values as justice, righteousness, and public virtue. In this case, people evaluate the political system, its leaders, and public policies on ethical criteria. Systems that demonstrate a strong commitment to civic virtue gain moral legitimacy.

In part IV, we shall examine how policy performance and perceptions of policies shape the degree of political stability in the United States, Britain, Germany, and Russia. These four case studies illustrate the impact of social groups, political organizations, and legitimating beliefs on systemic continuity in the United States and Britain but greater change of governmental systems in Germany and Russia during the last hundred years.

CHAPTER
9

The Concept of Political Legitimacy

> *All human activity, political and religious, stems from an undivided root. As a rule, the first impulse for . . . social action comes from tangible interests, political or economic. . . . Ideal interests elevate and animate these tangible interests and lend them justification. Man does not live by bread alone; he wants to have a good conscience when he pursues his vital interests.*
> —OTTO HINTZE

> *In God we trust. All others pay cash.*
> —JEAN SHEPHERD

During revolutionary upheavals, questions about political legitimacy come to the fore. Rather than accepting the political status quo, people begin to question political leaders, institutional arrangements, and public policies. Why should certain rulers govern a society? What moral principles and concrete benefits justify the right of particular leaders to make binding public decisions? The French Revolution of the 1790s marked such a time when people doubted the legitimacy of the monarchical system. In a play entitled *Marat/Sade*, Peter Weiss explored the reasons for the downfall of the monarchical regime. Taunting Jean-Paul Marat, a defender of the revolution, the Marquis de Sade claimed that most people rejected the old political order not because it denied certain idealistic values—liberty, equality, fraternity. Instead, it failed to provide concrete benefits, such as edible fish, comfortable shoes, and "the best soup in the world."[1] Thus, according to de Sade, popular support for the revolution stemmed primarily from the promises to satisfy material interests—the loaves and the fishes.

Yet, as Otto Hintze reminds us, people do not live by bread alone; they also pursue certain moral–spiritual values that give a transcendent meaning to human existence. In Russia fifty years before the Soviet revolutionaries seized political power, the novelist Fyodor Dostoyevsky perceived that spiritual values provided the basic legitimacy upholding the czarist regime. His novel, *The Possessed*, appeared in the turbulent days of the early 1870s when socialists began to organize opposition to the czarist political system. Attacking the atheistic principles of revolutionary leaders, Dostoyevsky considered socialists to be possessed by demons. From his perspective, no lasting political movement can ever be based just on reason and science, as the French revolutionaries and Russian Socialists avowed. Instead, the most powerful, durable organizations rest on a spiritual foundation. In particular, the nation enjoys a divine legitimacy. True nationalists recognize only national gods:

> The objective of any nationalist movement in any people at any time is actually a search for God, for their own national God—and it must, above all, be their own God—and belief in Him as the only true God. God's personality is a synthesis of the entire nation from the beginning of its existence to its end. . . . If a great nation does not believe that it alone to the exclusion of any other possesses the sole truth, if it does not believe that it alone is destined to and can regenerate and save the rest of the world through the truth it holds, it immediately ceases to be a great nation and becomes merely an ethnographical designation. . . . Now, the only God-bearing nation is the Russian nation.[2]

For Dostoyevsky, the Russian Orthodox church legitimized the Russian nation and the czarist government. According to him, revolutionary socialists who took an atheistic position and attacked the church were undermining the legitimacy of the czarist political system and thereby plunging the Russian nation into social chaos. He predicted in 1871 that amid the disorder that would accompany the disintegration of the czarist regime, the socialist revolutionaries would construct a new authority "such as the world has never before heard of."[3] Nearly fifty years later, with the triumph of the Soviet government, his predictions seemed to come true.

Political legitimacy expresses the mutual relationship between the leaders who govern a society and those who obey. When leaders justify their right to rule a people, they assert their political authority. These justifications may rest on appeals to sacred values, laws, traditions, extraordinary personal attractiveness, or concrete benefits provided the populace. In turn, when the nonleaders accept these justifications of the right to exercise political power as morally right and binding on them, they grant their leaders legitimacy. Authority thus proceeds from the top downward; it involves political leaders justifying their role over other persons, either the whole population or leaders of powerful groups. Legitimacy proceeds from the bottom upward; it means that the nonleaders consent to the justifications their rulers voice.

Political decision makers seek to justify not only their own personal rule but also other parts of the political system, including the regime and public policies. A political regime comprises three basic components:

1. Fundamental values, such as freedom, equality, and justice
2. A fundamental law (a constitution) that regulates the exercise of power
3. Institutional arrangements, such as parliamentary democracy, party–state dictatorship, federalism, and the balance of powers between the president and the legislature

Operating through political structures and influenced by basic values and rules, political leaders enact certain public policies for a society. When implemented, these policies exert certain consequences on individuals and social groups. For example, tax and spending policies may reduce or increase the inflation rate. The building of more public schools may affect children's values, skills, and information. The training of more doctors in government-financed medical schools influences infant mortality and life expectancy rates of various social groups.[4] In short, people may accord differential legitimacy to several aspects of a political system: values, rules, institutional arrangements, government officeholders, public policies, and policy results. Crises of political legitimacy arise especially when popular support for political leaders, policies, and policy consequences begins to wane. Under conditions of growing political alienation and disintegration of a government's coercive mechanisms, the political regime may come under attack, as happened during the French and Soviet revolutions.

Sources of Legitimacy

The relationship between expectations and benefits affects the degree of legitimacy that people accord a political system. According to Saint Augustine, "A people is an assemblage of reasonable beings bound together by a common agreement as to the objects of their love. . . . In order to discover the character of any people, we have only to observe what they love."[5] When people expect mainly *concrete benefits* from the political system, they seek to satisfy their interests—that is, their demands for greater wealth and status.

Motivated by their interests, people pursue such things as well-paying jobs, opportunity for economic advancement, low-priced consumer goods, housing, paved roads, sewage facilities, and access to health care. If the political system responds to these demands for concrete benefits, people grant the political system pragmatic acceptance. They evaluate political institutions, laws, officeholders, and public policies on pragmatic criteria; efficiency, success, and technical reason assume highest importance. People accept the political system because they see no alternative to the existing one that would provide more concrete benefits.

Yet in most societies, people expect more than just comfortable shoes, tasty soup, and edible fish from their political system; many persons also seek *moral–spiritual values*: justice, freedom, and righteousness. In this case, people acknowledge the primacy of conscience as the proper end of a political system. Rather than evaluating leaders and policies on pragmatic criteria, they use ethical criteria to make political judgments. The display of civic virtue (the behavioral commitment to certain ultimate ends) takes precedence over practical efficiency. A mystical understanding of the political universe becomes as important as technical reason. When the search for moral–spiritual values assumes primacy, people grant the political system normative acceptance if it embodies certain ethical values, such as freedom, equality, equity, and justice.[6]

Of course, people in all political systems show a commitment to both moral and material benefits; yet the priority given to each type varies among different individuals, societies, and historical eras. To the extent that the benefits provided by the political system correspond to the dominant type of expectations, especially those powerful groups articulate, we assume that the system will attain a relatively high legitimacy.

Political legitimacy also depends on the strength of individualist and collectivist orientations within a society. Who should receive the benefits political leaders allocate? If a society places a high priority on individualism, a system that allocates benefits to the individual will win legitimacy. For example, in the United States, individuals receive concrete benefits such as social security payments, food stamps, and unemployment compensation. Most people expect that the political system will guarantee personal freedom, civil liberties, equal opportunity, and justice to the individual. However, particularly where ideologies of classical conservatism and communism are powerful, collectivist values shape popular attitudes toward public policies. Under these conditions, people expect government to provide moral and material benefits to the collectivity—the nation, economic class, religious group, ethnic group, or extended family. If public policies improve the status of the group, the political system attains legitimacy.

Political Alienation

As I use the term, *political alienation* implies distrust of political leaders and their public policies. If citizens perceive that incumbent officeholders are incompetent, ignorant, and indecisive, then popular confidence in these leaders declines. Political alienation means that a government has lost legitimacy, largely because it fails to provide moral and material benefits. Particularly in contemporary industrial societies, the populace judges leaders according to their success in dealing with economic affairs and the issues of war and peace. When government fails to lower unemployment, reduce inflation, increase personal disposable income, and keep the nation at peace with other states, its leaders suffer a loss of support.

Evaluations of the political system also rest on moral–spiritual values. Political leaders who do not embody certain moral values may incur growing distrust. If officeholders lack personal friendliness, warmth, compassion, morality, and public honesty, they may lose their political legitimacy.[7] Similarly, people judge public policies as well as political leaders on moral and material criteria. Take abortion policy as one example. Opponents of government-funded abortions perceive abortion as murder; it violates God's moral law. From this perspective, public expenditures for abortions represent an immoral use of taxpayers' money. Hence, as abortion laws become widely implemented, political alienation grows. By contrast, supporters of abortion believe that legislation allowing abortions increases women's reproductive freedom—a desirable value for them. Government-financed abortions allow poor women the same rights enjoyed by wealthier women. Accordingly, when government moves to restrict abortions, either by disallowing them or by restricting their funding, it loses legitimacy from abortion supporters. In sum, one dimension of political alienation includes *distrust*—a perception that government leaders and the public policies associated with them do not respond to individuals' moral and material expectations.

Another dimension of political alienation is *efficacy*, meaning the perceived ability of the individual, group, or government to deal successfully with a problem. When widespread suffering occurs in a society, whom do people blame for their problems, such as ill health, high inflation, unemployment, and poverty? They may blame fate, the individual, or the collectivity (group, government, social system). Especially in a feudal society, people attributed their misfortunes to fate, chance, luck, God, or the devil—that is, to conditions beyond the individual's control. Plagued by a fatalistic, resigned attitude, people lacked the perceived effectiveness to overcome their problems.

Capitalism places a greater responsibility on the individual for his or her destiny. Individuals blame themselves for their lot in life. Whatever their position in the social stratification system, people feel that through individual hard work, education, and self-discipline, they can improve their life conditions. Thus, capitalism brings a more optimistic feeling about overcoming hardships; compared with the feudal situation, personal efficacy tends to increase.

Socialist ideology stresses the collective reasons for social and personal problems. Socialists blame powerful social groups, especially the corporate capitalists, for severe economic crises. Socialists also blame the government, which implements policies designed to protect the interests of the capitalist class. Attributing blame to these collective sources of personal grievances, socialists emphasize collective methods to overcome their alienation. Reliance on union solidarity represents a form of group efficacy. By cooperating with fellow workers in strong union organizations, they hope to win favorable settlements from business corporations. Through participation in socialist political parties and trade unions, workers try to influence government policy. By gaining desired tax, spending, health care, education, and housing policies, they demonstrate their political effectiveness.[8]

Challenges to Legitimacy: Political System Stability

A political system that gains widespread legitimacy—both from the whole population and especially from leaders of powerful groups in the social stratification system—will show greater stability over time. Even if public policies change and political leaders hold office for only a short time, the political regime (basic values, fundamental laws, and institutional arrangements) continues. Leaders win office through peaceful methods; no military coups d'etat interrupt the decision process.

Four factors seem especially crucial for attaining political stability. First, the population and powerful leaders trust the political system, which ranks high on both moral and material legitimacy. Political rule thus rests on consensus. Second, the government elite wields effective coercive power against dissident groups. In few systems does everyone consent to the status quo. Even in a relatively legitimate regime, some citizens reject the policies, leaders, and perhaps the institutional arrangements. Particularly if these citizens have high feelings of political efficacy and move to challenge the system, political stability may depend on the efficient exercise of coercion against them. Certainly, in dictatorial regimes, where leaders lack legitimacy, they remain in power by their skillful use of coercion against opponents. Third, when most individuals have low political efficacy, prospects for political stability increase. Low political effectiveness results in political apathy. Fourth, individuals blame fate or themselves for their personal problems. Feeling either resigned to their personal misfortunes or else committed to individual methods for coping with grievances, they show little inclination to participate in political affairs to change the status quo.

The opposite set of factors—low trust, inefficient use of coercion, high political efficacy, and the collective attribution of blame for personal problems—engenders political instability. First, when a political system ranks low on both moral and material legitimacy, distrust of incumbent leaders increases. Popular distrust may lead to challenges of the political regime.

Second, lack of widespread consensus means a reliance on coercion to preserve the regime's stability; if the military and police use coercion inconsistently over time and against groups, then stability is threatened. Those countries employing an intermediate degree of coercion seem especially vulnerable to violent attacks against the government because moderate coercion strengthens resentment toward the existing regime but also reduces fear of punishment. By contrast, low coercion minimizes resentment, but high levels of repression make people fearful of opposing the government. As happened in Russia during 1917, the state's declining ability to apply high levels of coercion increases political instability. When desertions from the army accelerate and the police no longer seem willing to defend the old regime, the state's coercive mechanisms disintegrate. As a result, organized revolutionary forces, such as the Russian Bolsheviks, gain the structural opportunity to seize state power.

Third, if people blame their personal problems on a collective source (the government), seek a collective solution to their grievances, and demonstrate high political efficacy, political instability will increase. No society lacks frustrated individuals. When people fatalistically accept their deprivations or pursue individual solutions to these frustrations, the political system faces few challenges. Only when people blame their discontent on such collective factors as government indifference to the poor, government's failure to provide equal opportunities, and political leaders' alliances with the wealthy do widespread frustrations stimulate organized opposition to public policies, incumbent officeholders, and perhaps even the political regime itself. Particularly if the organized opposition overcomes resignation, transcends individualistic solutions, and demonstrates high political efficacy, prospects improve for a fundamental change in the political system.[9]

In summary, political stability depends on the following four conditions:

1. High trust in the political system—a trust based on moral and material legitimacy

2. The tendency to blame fate or the individual for personal problems
3. High political efficacy among the trusting and low political efficacy among the distrustful, who resign themselves to their misfortunes or else seek individual solutions to personal grievances
4. The efficient use of coercion against distrustful groups that regard the system as illegitimate and take political actions to express their grievances

Political instability will most likely occur under these conditions:

1. Low trust in the political system—a distrust based on the failure of political leaders and their public policies to satisfy moral and material expectations
2. The tendency to blame government leaders and public policies for personal misfortunes
3. High political efficacy felt by the distrustful, who seek collective political solutions to individual grievances
4. The inefficient use of government coercion against groups taking political actions against a regime regarded as illegitimate

The following chapters explore these hypotheses by looking at political legitimacy in four countries: the United States, Britain, Germany, and Russia. Over the last 200 years, Americans and British have experienced a high degree of structural continuity in their political systems. In contrast, during the last century, Germans have lived under four different political systems: the Second Reich, the Weimar Republic, the Nazi regime of the Third Reich, and, after World War II, the German Federal Republic and the German Democratic Republic. Since the early seventeenth century, Russia has maintained the same political system except for one fundamental transformation—the establishment of the Soviet revolutionary regime in 1917, a development that has profoundly changed world history during the twentieth century. Why have the American and British political systems remained more legitimate than those in Germany and Russia? As we shall see, evaluations of public policies and policy results constitute a crucial explanation.

Notes

1. Peter Weiss, *Persecution and Assassination of Jean-Paul Marat as Performed by the Inmates of the Asylum of Charenton under the Direction of the Marquis de Sade*, English version by Geoffrey Skelton (New York: Atheneum, 1973), p. 61.
2. Fyodor Dostoyevsky, *The Possessed*, trans. Andrew R. MacAndrew (New York: New American Library, 1962), pp. 237–238.
3. Ibid., p. 403.
4. For analyses of the concept of political authority and legitimacy, see Charles F.

Andrain, *Political Life and Social Change*, 2d ed. (Belmont, Calif.: Wadsworth, 1975), pp. 141–159. Peter G. Stillman, "The Concept of Legitimacy," *Polity* 7 (Fall 1974): 32–56, stresses the importance of policy results as a fundamental basis of legitimacy. The definition of political regime comes from David Easton, *A Systems Analysis of Political Life* (New York: Wiley, 1965), pp. 193–211.

5. Saint Augustine, *The City of God* (New York: Random House Modern Library, 1950), p. 706.
6. For distinctions between moral and material benefits, see David E. Apter, *Choice and the Politics of Allocation* (New Haven, Conn.: Yale University Press, 1971), pp. 21–23; Michael Mann, "The Social Cohesion of Liberal Democracy," *American Sociological Review* 35 (June 1970): 423–439.
7. See Benjamin I. Page, *Choices and Echoes in Presidential Elections: Rational Man and Electoral Democracy* (Chicago: University of Chicago Press, 1978), pp. 222–265.
8. William A. Gamson, *Power and Discontent* (Homewood, Ill.: Dorsey, 1968), p. 42; Patricia Gurin, Gerald Gurin, and Betty Morrison, "Personal and Ideological Aspects of Internal and External Control," *Social Psychology* 41 (December 1978): 275–296; Patricia Gurin, Arthur H. Miller, and Gerald Gurin, "Stratum Identification and Consciousness," *Social Psychology Quarterly* 43 (March 1980): 30–47; Joe R. Feagin, "God Helps Those Who Help Themselves," *Psychology Today* 6 (November 1972): 101–110, 129.
9. For analyses of political stability, see James D. Wright, *The Dissent of the Governed: Alienation and Democracy in America* (New York: Academic Press, 1976), pp. 253–279; Richard Boyd with Herbert Hyman, "Survey Research," in *Handbook of Political Science*, vol. 7, ed. Fred I. Greenstein and Nelson W. Polsby (Reading, Mass.: Addison-Wesley, 1975), p. 277; Ivo K. Feierabend, Betty Nesvold, and Rosalind L. Feierabend, "Political Coerciveness and Turmoil: A Cross-National Inquiry," *Law and Society Review* 5 (August 1970): 93–118; Theda Skocpol, *States and Social Revolutions* (Cambridge, England: Cambridge University Press, 1979), pp. 50–51, 80–81, 99; D. E. H. Russell, *Rebellion, Revolution, and Armed Force* (New York: Academic Press, 1974), p. 87; Alejandro Portes and Adreain Ross, "A Model for the Prediction of Leftist Radicalism," *Journal of Political and Military Sociology* 2 (Spring 1974): 33–56.

CHAPTER
10

Puritanism and Madisonianism in America

Whereas the central term for understanding individual motivation in the [Puritan] biblical tradition was "conscience," the central term in the [Madisonian] utilitarian tradition was "interest." The biblical understanding of national life was based on the notion of community with charity for all the members, a community supported by public and private virtue. The utilitarian tradition believed in a neutral state in which individuals would be allowed to pursue the maximization of their self-interest and the product would be public and private prosperity.

—ROBERT BELLAH

Political legitimacy in the United States has historically stemmed from two dominant belief systems: Puritanism and Madisonianism. Both were present at the country's creation. Puritanism came to Massachusetts and other New England colonies during the early seventeenth century. The political elite in New York and Virginia articulated utilitarian principles associated with early classical liberalism. The two main writers of *The Federalist Papers*, written in 1787–1788 to secure the ratification of the United States federal Constitution, were Alexander Hamilton, a New Yorker, and James Madison, a Virginian. Puritanism expressed the dominance of moral conscience. Madisonianism focused on the pursuit of material interests. Although these two belief systems were formulated over 200 years ago, they continue to influence American life today and help explain the continuity of political legitimacy in the United States.

Puritanism and Madisonianism

As originally formulated, Puritanism and Madisonianism expressed divergent philosophical values and conceptions of the political system.[1] Early Puritan thinkers affirmed the primacy of moral values. Individuals exist on earth to pursue spiritual virtue—God, not Mammon. From the Puritan viewpoint, excessive affluence and widespread poverty interfere with the pursuit of conscience. Freedom means liberation from sin, not the right to accumulate material goods. Puritans interpreted equality as the individual's identical status before God; all people have sinned and alienated themselves from God. Despite this universal fall, God loves everyone. Thus, in the earthly life, everybody has the responsibility to love each other within a community fellowship.

A stress on the church community, rather than on individualism, characterized the early Puritan society. According to Puritan beliefs, individualism represents love of the self and alienation from God. The individual should deny the self and love God instead. Yet only in a community setting, not in isolation, can the individual pursue spiritual virtues. In early Massachusetts, this community solidarity rested on a common commitment to shared religious values. By serving as active members of the Puritan churches, individuals gained the right to participate in political affairs at the town meetings.

The Puritans' conception of the political system derived from their religious beliefs. They perceived the polity as a church, an organic body bound by shared spiritual values. Articulating an organic view, Puritans drew parallels among the human body, the *corpus mysticum*, and the body politic. Just as the brain directs the human body, so Christ heads the church and the polity. The interdependence of bodily organs resembles the functional interdependence of members within society. The goal of the human body is the harmonious functioning of the parts; similarly, harmony, order, and fraternal solidarity constitute the primary social objectives. Just as blood gives life to the human body, so shared values provide life to the religious and political communities.

In the early Puritan community, government performed vital educational functions. Puritan churches and the Massachusetts Bay Commonwealth were united; both promoted moral values—spiritual and civic virtue. The political magistrates educated the citizens by promoting virtue and punishing vice. The Puritan ministers taught religious virtues to their congregations. Although not holding government office, they did determine the eligibility of church members. Significantly, only church members had the right to vote for elected officials—governors, deputies, magistrates—and to participate in town meetings, where political and religious issues were discussed.

Both the religious and the political officials stressed the need for widespread education. Indeed, knowledge of religious principles constituted one visible sign of a "saint." Many ministers had attended Cambridge University in England and had won acclaim for their intellectual achievements. After settling in New England, they encouraged school construction. During the 1640s, the Massachusetts Bay Colony became the first American colony to establish a public school system.

Although the Massachusetts Puritans attempted to establish a tightly knit, homogeneous community where all held the same spiritual values, neither the ministers nor the magistrates governed in a tyrannical manner. True, they showed intolerance toward those who did not accept the Puritan way; they valued freedom from sin over freedom of religious dissent. Yet the law restrained the actions of those in authority. According to the Puritan conceptions, the law assumed sacred value; it represented the covenant relationship between God and His people. Originally, God had made a covenant with Abraham. He had chosen the Hebrews to articulate His divine mission to the world; in turn, they pledged to obey God's will. Similarly, Puritans formulated a covenant—the Mayflower Compact—between the rulers and the ruled. Under this covenant, the minister served as an impersonal agent of the Bible, the word of God. Rather than glorifying the minister, the congregations should glorify God, who alone held full sovereignty. Magistrates also had the obligation to abide by the laws of Scripture. If a political ruler, like a tyrannical monarch, violated these holy laws, the people had the right to overthrow him, as the English Puritans beheaded King Charles I during the mid seventeenth century. Thus, by mediating between the political leader and the citizens, the law established constraints on his power.

The Puritan conception of public policy, both the decision-making processes and the policy contents, reflected a commitment to pursue civic virtue. The policy process involved public participation in town meetings. Through discussions about building schools, repairing roads, helping the poor, and choosing a minister, citizens reached a public decision based on a transcendent standard—the perceived will of God as revealed in the Bible. Although Max Weber perceived that the Puritan stress on asceticism, frugality, self-control, temperance, hard work, and methodical techniques contributed to the rise of capitalism, Puritans in seventeenth-century Massachusetts did not practice laissez-faire economic policies.[2] True, Puritan ministers condemned laziness and warned against rendering too much charity to the idle poor. Yet the Puritan ethos led the magistrates to assist the destitute. The Massachusetts commonwealth regulated economic affairs by controlling prices, limiting wealth, providing employment opportunities, and providing economic assistance to the needy when natural disasters struck. Political action, rather than reliance on the "free market," represented the early Puritan way for dealing with social crises.

Madisonian beliefs expressed different conceptions of philosophical objectives and political practices. Whereas the Puritans sought moral virtue, the Madisonians pursued material interests. James Madison realistically accepted the tendency for individuals to engage in "self-love." By nature, people want to increase their wealth and status. Because all societies feature an unequal distribution of property, conflicting interests arise. Debtors clash with creditors. Landowners compete with manufacturers. Because individuals naturally seek to advance their own interests, government attempts to suppress these interest conflicts will cause greater harm than actions to control the effects of interest group struggles. If diverse interests control different branches of government, so that an effective checks and balances system operates, then freedom will thrive. Under these conditions, the multiplicity of interests in a representative government guarantees public rights. Each group must have the right to satisfy its own interests without fearing that either tyranny or anarchy will disrupt the society. Freedom gives all individuals equal opportunity to gain greater wealth and status. In short, interest, rather than conscience, binds the society. From Madison's perspective, constitutional government rests on competing interests and divided powers. External structural controls, not internal moral–spiritual restraints, guarantee liberty:

> It is vain to say that enlightened statesmen will be able to adjust these clashing interests and render them all subservient to the public good. Enlightened statesmen will not always be at the helm. . . . Neither moral nor religious motives can be relied on as an adequate control.[3]

By placing interest rather than conscience at the center of political society, Madisonianism undermined the basis for community solidarity. The early Puritans regarded conscience as an objective standard; they found moral virtue in a public document—the Bible. Public commitment to biblical truths brought unity to the society. In contrast, Madisonians gave higher priority to individual and group interests than to communal solidarity. As each individual and faction gained the right to advance its own interests, people became alienated from each other. Each individual, not the church or the state, became the best judge of his or her own unique interests. Interest group conflicts pervaded social intercourse. Even though the individual gained religious freedom and the freedom to pursue private economic interests, economic freedom and religious tolerance triumphed at the expense of collective solidarity.

Whereas the Puritans made an analogy between the polity and the church, the Madisonians interpreted the political system in economic terms. For them, the polity resembled the market. In the economic sphere, individual buyers use money to demand goods sellers supply through the market mechanism, which links buyers with sellers. The goal of the free market is to establish an equilibrium between supply and demand. Excessive demands or insufficient supplies disturb the equilibrium. Similarly, in the political sphere, individual citizens (buyers) with votes (money) demand public policies (goods) supplied by political officials (sellers) through legal institutions (market institutions). Representative institutions, especially Congress and the presidency, connect citizens with their leaders. The goal of free government is to establish an equilibrium between popular demands and public policies. Political disorder results if citizens demand too much from their government or if government lacks the resources to meet public expectations. According to Madison, government officials must regulate the interest group struggle; by transforming several partial interests into general public policies, political leaders temper demands for government payoffs. Government also has the responsibility to encourage increased economic productivity, thereby enlarging the supply of resources.

The Madisonian conception of government and laws also diverged from the Puritan interpretation. According to the Puritans, government performs a vital educational role; it promotes civic virtue and punishes vice. Laws assume a sacred value, for they derive from God and express a covenant relation between the rulers and the ruled. By contrast, Madisonianism advocates more limited functions for government. Government institutions, particularly the legislature and the judiciary, set forth general rules to regulate the interest group struggle. From this perspective, laws have a more utilitarian than sacred value; they are useful in protecting individuals against concentrated, arbitrary power. Because individuals and factional groups naturally seek to advance their interests, institutional and legal checks are necessary for restraining this factional struggle for greater power. Given the weakness of religious and moral virtues in limiting interest group competition, Madison perceived that a written constitution was necessary for averting the descent into anarchy or tyranny.

According to the Madisonian framework, the policy process resembles market conditions. Through the free market, individual consumers translate their private economic wants into public demands. Similarly, through political institutions, citizens transform their private interests into public policies. Government agencies represent the interests of different groups: landowners, small farmers, merchants, manufacturers, bankers, artisans, skilled workers. In pluralist fashion, these interest groups retain the freedom to express their claims on the government. Officials in the legislative and executive branches then reconcile these private interests into a more general public policy. Compared with the early Massachusetts Puritans, the late eighteenth-century Madisonians adopted a more laissez faire approach toward policy contents. Unlike the Puritans, they viewed neither poverty nor excessive wealth as a sin. Indeed, they perceived economic inequality as a necessary incentive for encouraging hard work and productivity. Those who worked hardest and produced the most deserve the highest rewards. Under Madisonian principles, government thus does not promote economic equality; rather, its public policies remove restraints on free trade within the United States, promote commerce, encourage national productivity, and establish the infrastructure (financial, transportation, and communication facilities) needed to maximize prosperity.

The Revolutionary War: Emergence of an American Civil Religion

Although Puritans and Madisonians articulated somewhat divergent principles of political legitimacy, both groups rejected the monarchical authority of the British colonial system. Asserting the absolute sovereignty of God, Puritans wanted the Bible, the word of God, not the king or the state, to serve as the source of all authority. In this Puritan view, the law should check the power of both rulers and citizens. If a political leader, especially a monarch, violated the laws of Scripture and the covenant between the rulers and the ruled, then the people had the right to dislodge the leader from power. During the 1640s, the Puritans in England had brought about the downfall of the monarchical regime led by Charles I. During the 1770s, their descendants in New England spearheaded the revolt against King George III; Puritan clergy led the revolutionary movement, charging that colonial rule was illegitimate.

The Madisonians in Virginia and New York also campaigned against monarchical authority. Like the Puritans, the Madisonians supported republican rule—that is, nonmonarchical government. Rather than a person—either the monarch or the pope—exercising authority, an impersonal source—the law—should guide political decision making. Basing their ideas on Lockean classical liberalism, the Madisonians assumed that government and laws function primarily to preserve personal security and to protect private property (life, liberty, and estate). According to Locke, government should issue rules, settle conflicts, and punish those who threaten the security of private property. If a ruler, especially a monarch, exercises arbitrary authority, violates the law, and betrays his trust with the governed, the people as a collective agency have the right to change the government.[4] During the mid 1770s, the Madisonians perceived that the government of King George III threatened the colonists' right to preserve their private property and thereby interfered with the freedom to satisfy their economic interests. Because the king had violated his contract with the people, the Madisonians declared their political independence from him.

With the breakdown of monarchical authority, the American revolutionaries formulated a new political legitimacy based on both Puritan and Madisonian beliefs. Whereas during the seventeenth century the Puritans had secured a tight alliance between the political commonwealth and the church, the Madisonians insisted on a separation of church from state. As classical liberals, they assumed that just as many competing interest groups guarantee political liberty, so many different religious denominations guarantee religious freedom. Because various churches with divergent theologies functioned in late eighteenth-century America, a single belief system such as Calvinism could no longer serve as the basis of political authority.

The civil religion that emerged after the end of the Revolutionary War became a more inclusive belief system: It included not just the Bible Commonwealth of Massachusetts Bay Colony but the whole American nation. Unlike the established religions of Europe, America's civil religion transcended distinctive theological creeds; it remained free from control by the state or a particular church denomination.[5] In effect, Puritanism became Americanism. At the end of the eighteenth century, some Americans perceived the American nation as a community of righteousness, the new Israel gaining independence from the Egyptian house of bondage (decadent Europe). George Washington acted as the second Moses, the divine agent of political salvation who guided the exodus from British imperial rule. Early Americans saw the United States as a model for the world, a vanguard chosen people who had the duty to proclaim the gospel of liberty to others. Freedom rested on the practice of civic virtue and a commitment to abide by the covenant—the new written constitution that guaranteed the free exercise of religion but also banned religious tests as requirements for public office.

From the early nineteenth century onward, political rituals reaffirmed these values of America's civil religion. On certain holy days, such as Thanksgiving, Americans have expressed appreciation for their forefathers' sacrifices. Presidents' inaugural addresses offer an opportunity to proclaim America's distinctive national heritage. For instance, in 1805 Thomas Jefferson affirmed: "I shall need, too, the favor of that Being in whose hands we are, who led our fathers, as

Israel of old, from their native land and planted them in a country flowing with all the necessities and comforts of life."[6] In this passage, Jefferson sketched the combined heritage of Puritanism and Madisonianism. America represented the new Israel, the promised land, the center of political virtue. The legitimacy of American political institutions also rested on their ability to allow individuals to satisfy material interests—that is, the "necessities and comforts of life."

The Civil War: Crisis of Political Legitimacy

Despite the popularity of America's civil religion, the bases of authority for the new republican government remained fragile in early America. True, most supporters of monarchical colonial rule either reluctantly accepted the new regime or else fled to Canada, the West Indies, or back to England. Hence, defenders of the *ancien régime* posed no serious danger to the republican political institutions. Yet both moral and material conflicts continued to divide American groups; by the late 1850s, these issues threatened to destroy the American political community. As the legitimacy of national institutions declined, secession and civil war erupted. Both Puritanism and Madisonianism underlay the declining political legitimacy.

The moral issue of slavery versus abolition divided North from South. The early Puritans sought to free the world from sin; they judged public policies and political leaders by moral criteria. Beginning in the 1820s and 1830s, Christian evangelists, such as Charles Finney, began attacking the slave system as a violation of the human liberty proclaimed in America's civil religion. Viewing slavery as a collective sin, they demanded not just a change in individual slaveholders but also a change in the existing society and political institutions. From their perspective, the incumbent politicians who occupied the presidency, Congress, and Supreme Court sought merely to accommodate and compromise pragmatic interests. Preserving the existing institutions, including the Southern slavocracy, took precedence over affirming ethical virtue and making decisions based on sacred ends.

Along with evangelist Charles Finney, abolitionists William Lloyd Garrison and Theodore Dwight Weld functioned as Hebrew prophets, proclaiming the gospel of liberty to a wicked generation. Garrison even called the Constitution "a covenant with death and an agreement with hell." Demanding the dissolution of the union, he urged Americans to separate themselves from an unclean government that upheld slavery.

In reaction to these abolitionist attacks against the slave system, Southern ministers began to defend slavery on moral grounds. During the 1840s and 1850s, Southern Baptists, Southern Methodists, and Southern Presbyterians seceded from national organizations to form separate regional branches. Secession from the national government seemed the natural next step. Thus, the moral polarization dividing the abolitionists and defenders of slavery accelerated the decline of political legitimacy granted the political system.[7]

Clashing economic interests also weakened support for the federal institutions. The Madisonian authors of the Constitution based the authority of the republican institutions on utilitarian grounds; government and laws were intended to facilitate the satisfaction of interests. People should accept the Constitution because it established institutions and procedures to regulate conflicts over scarce resources. By the 1840s, however, powerful economic groups began to doubt the validity of the federal institutions.

Three regional groups—Southern slaveholders who grew cotton, northeastern industrialists, and western and midwestern farmers—struggled to secure dominance in the national institutions. Initially, Southerners usually controlled the presidency, held the balance of power in Congress, and dominated the Supreme Court. Yet the admission of new states to the Union threatened Southern power, especially if western territories entered the federal system as free states. As the western farmers expanded their food trade with the North and sought free lands out west to raise wheat, they came into conflict with Southern slaveholders, who wanted to grow cotton in the western territories. In the Southern view, these territories should be admitted to the Union as slave, not free, states. During this period, Northern industrialists also developed economic conflicts with Southern planters. Experiencing sharp competition from English manufacturers, American industrialists wanted to implement protective tariffs that would encourage American development of textile, iron, and steel industries. In contrast, the Southern planters, who needed to sell their cotton overseas, demanded that free trade policies continue. The growing alliance between Northern industrialists and western farmers led to the establishment of the Republican party in 1856. Both economic groups opposed admitting western territories as slave states. Fearing that they could no longer control the presidency and Congress if slavery were banned in the West, the thirteen Southern states, led by the slaveholders, seceded from the Union after Republican candidate Abraham Lincoln was elected president in late 1860.[8]

The failure of Northern industrialists, Southern planters, and midwestern and western farmers to reconcile their economic interests within the existing institutions led to a disintegration of the federal political system. When their economic interests could no longer be satisfied, Southerners withdrew their legitimacy from the

United States Constitution and political institutions. Clashing economic interests thus produced political polarization. Civil war resulted from the decline of political legitimacy.

During the Civil War, the national political religion became reformulated. Viewing the nation from a Puritan perspective, President Abraham Lincoln saw America as a righteous community whose members had the obligation to maintain the covenants expressed in the Declaration of Independence and the Constitution. So long as Americans adhered to the principles of liberty and equal opportunity found in these covenants, the nation deserved respect. According to Lincoln, slavery and civil war had violated these ideas. To preserve the union, he called on Americans to make the supreme sacrifice for national salvation. After Lincoln's assassination in 1865, he joined the Parthenon as a new national saint. At least to some Northerners and freed slaves in the South, he represented the founder of the reborn American nation, a Christ-like martyr who had given his life for the cause of liberty and equality.

Lincoln interpreted national destiny not only in moral–spiritual terms but also from an economic perspective. He urged the American people to support national institutions as the best mechanisms for providing equal economic opportunities to all citizens:

> While we don't propose any war upon capital, we do wish to allow the humblest man an equal chance to get rich with everybody else. When one starts poor, as most do in the race of life, free society is such that he knows he can better his condition; he knows that there is no fixed condition of labor for his whole life. . . . I want every man to have a chance—and I believe a black man is entitled to it—in which he can better his condition. . . . That is the true system.[9]

After the Civil War ended, the material bases of legitimacy took precedence over the moral criteria. Whereas Lincoln saw America as a righteous community destined to realize ethical aims, later political and business leaders judged the political system on more utilitarian grounds: its success in stimulating economic productivity. As the nation entered the industrial era, the national government played a key role in stimulating economic development. During the late nineteenth century, the federal government, largely influenced by northern Republican manufacturers, implemented protective tariffs that encouraged domestic industries. It established a new national banking system, granted subsidies to railroad firms, and sold publicly owned lands to private enterprises so they could profit from the mineral and timber resources. To help the western farmers, the federal government provided land grants to agricultural colleges, which later became major state universities. Under the Homestead Act, small farmers received land at low prices. A contract labor law implemented by the national government enabled business executives to recruit labor from overseas. Between 1870 and 1914, millions of European immigrants flocked to America seeking work at higher wages than they had earned in their home countries. Madisonianism was in full bloom. Government functioned to satisfy economic interests.

As Vernon Louis Parrington suggests, the policy process in the immediate post–Civil War era resembled a great barbecue:

> Congress had rich gifts to bestow—in lands, tariffs, subsidies, favors of all sorts; and when influential citizens made their wishes known to the reigning statesmen, the sympathetic politicians were quick to turn the government into the fairy godmother the voters wanted it to be. A huge barbecue was spread to which all presumably were invited. Not quite all, to be sure; inconspicuous persons, those who were at home on the farm or at work in the mills and offices, were overlooked.... But all the important persons, leading bankers and promoters and business men, received invitations. There wasn't room for everybody and these were presumed to represent the whole.[10]

Even though not all citizens gained equal portions at the great barbecue, the political institutions appeared to provide most white citizens some opportunities to secure a share of the expanding economic pie.

Economic Crisis of the Depression

Despite government's commitment to support an expanding economy, not everyone benefited equally from economic growth. Government policies were unable to regulate the business cycles of boom and bust, of overproduction and recession. When the bust periods occurred, widespread unemployment resulted. For instance, the unemployment rate soared to over 10 percent between 1893 and 1898, in 1921, and from 1931 through 1940. During the depression years of the 1930s, the jobless rate never fell below 14 percent; in 1933, it reached one-quarter of the work force. Given these dire economic circumstances, why did the American political system remain legitimate? After all, in the German Weimar Republic, the Nazi leader Hitler became chancellor largely because of the severe economic depression. Yet American voters in 1932 elected Franklin Roosevelt president. As a candidate of the established Democratic party, Roosevelt campaigned for a balanced federal budget, reduced government expenditures, and state government assistance to the unemployed—a program not radically different from the policies espoused by the incumbent Republican president Herbert Hoover.[11]

Americans' commitment to individualistic values partly explains their continuing support for the structural arrangements and constitutional procedures of the political system, if not for the administration of President Hoover. National sample surveys conducted during the 1930s indicate most American voters held individualistic attitudes toward their economic situation and also showed a weak collective consciousness. The percentage of factory wage workers and unemployed persons who identified with the working class and who perceived a fundamental class conflict between labor and management represented less than 3 percent of the total work force. A majority of factory laborers and unemployed workers sought individual mobility within the existing economic system; they preferred self-employment to working for others. For them, individual opportunities for advancement took priority over economic security. They also remained optimistic about their future economic prospects and especially about the opportunities for their children.

Because most Americans, even the unemployed, held individualistic, optimistic attitudes, they hardly seemed likely to reject the political system as illegitimate. Instead, economic discontent focused on the incumbent leader, President Hoover. In the 1932 election, Franklin Roosevelt, the Democratic party challenger, received 57 percent of the popular vote. Together, all the radical opposition parties—Socialist, Socialist Labor, and Communist—that sought more fundamental changes in the American politico-economic system secured less than 3 percent of the vote.[12] In sum, popular attitudes, combined with the historical stability of the two major political parties, accounted for the failure of radical movements to successfully challenge the established regime, even at a time of severe economic crisis.

Political Legitimacy in Contemporary America

Despite the continuity of American political institutions, several recent crises have weakened citizens' trust in government's performance. Especially during the 1960s and 1970s, several crises challenged the political leadership: race relations, the Vietnam War, the Watergate scandals, and economic stagnation. Partly stemming from popular dissatisfaction with the ways political leaders have handled these problems, trust in government has declined since 1964. For example, in 1966 about 40 percent of the American population expressed a great deal of confidence in the federal executive and the Congress. By 1978, however, only 14 percent trusted the executive; only 10 percent held the same high view of Congress. Similarly, between 1958 and 1978, agreement with the following two statements rose from around 25 percent to nearly 70 percent: "Government is run for the benefit of a few big interests"; "You cannot trust the government to do what is right most of the time."

A decline in political efficacy went along with decreasing trust in government. Over this time period, more and more people doubted their ability to influence government leaders and public policies.[13] What variables explain this declining political trust and efficacy? To what extent do these survey results indicate a fundamental challenge to the legitimacy of the American political system, especially the political regime (values, laws, and structural arrangements)?

Probes into American popular beliefs suggest that declining trust stems primarily from dissatisfaction with political leaders' performance, certain public policies, and policy results, not from a widespread disenchantment with the political regime. In 1977, slightly over 70 percent of Americans perceived the political system as basically sound, with a need for only a few improvements. Only 7 percent perceived that the political system is basically unsound and therefore needs fundamental structural changes. Certainly, belief in the sanctity of the Constitution remains strong. Americans also continue to uphold such values as personal freedom and equal opportunity.

Despite growing distrust of "big government," popular support for government regulatory and social service policies remains high. In 1976, more than 60 percent of Americans preferred federal government regulation of the automobile, chemical, steel, and oil industries; around one-third even favored *increased* regulation of chemical, steel, and auto corporations. One-half wanted government to increase its regulatory powers over oil companies. Yet support for government ownership of these four industries is weak. In 1977, less than 10 percent favored government either nationalizing these industries or else establishing a government-run company to compete with these private enterprises.

The American public still wants government to play a strong role in improving health care, providing education to children, and guaranteeing a job to everyone. For example, in 1978, over 80 percent agreed that the government should help people secure doctors and hospital care at low cost; nearly three-fourths believed that the federal government has the responsibility to ensure that everybody who wants to work can gain employment. In 1982, over half the national population supported increased federal government expenditures for job training, health care, and education; only between 10 percent and 20 percent believed that the federal government should reduce spending on these programs. As the survey results suggest, Americans want the government to continue regulating the private sector, refereeing the interest group struggle, and providing such desired public services as health care, education, and employment opportunities.[14]

Popular dissatisfaction with racial policies, the war in Vietnam, Watergate, and programs to deal with economic stagnation largely explains the declining political trust since 1966. As Warren Miller and Teresa Levitin point out:

> Trust in government . . . is primarily based on satisfaction with how well the government is performing. The [survey] items do not tap feelings of loyalty or patriotism, abstract philosophical theories about government, or existential states of alienation or helplessness as directly as they indicate satisfaction with the performance of the party in power. As voters have become more concerned with issues, and as their demands for policy alternatives have become increasingly polarized, cynicism or lack of trust in government to meet those demands has increased correspondingly.[15]

During the 1960s and 1970s, this dissatisfaction with policy performance and policy impacts derived from both ethical and utilitarian standards; however, Americans primarily used moral criteria to evaluate race relations, the Vietnam War, and Watergate while relying on more pragmatic economic criteria to judge public policies that dealt with inflation and unemployment.

RACE RELATIONS

The polarized attitudes produced by the struggles over racial equality and the Vietnam War led to declining trust in government during the late 1960s. Just as slavery had been the dominant ethical issue in the mid nineteenth century, so black–white relations became a central moral problem after World War II. Like the early Puritans who campaigned for the abolition of slavery, leaders of the civil rights movement—black students, black ministers, and liberal white students and professionals—sought greater freedom and equality for black people. For them, integration meant that Blacks would gain equal respect and equal opportunities with Whites. Voting rights legislation would bring political freedom to southern Blacks. Integrated education, housing, employment, and public accommodations would give Blacks the freedom to secure upward mobility and the equal chance to improve their life conditions. Civil rights laws would also provide needed economic improvements to those ethnic minorities who had suffered from unfair discrimination. As in the nineteenth century, groups opposed to racial equality and integration took an opposite moral stand. For the segregationists, civil rights laws passed by Congress violated the rights of each state government to regulate race relations. Laws implemented by the federal government also meant special economic privileges for ethnic minorities; "affirmative action" laws seemed a form of reverse discrimination.

As a result of these conflicts over the proper scope of federal government authority over race relations, Americans at both ends of the policy poles expressed the greatest alienation from government. In both 1964 and 1970, segregationists showed the highest political distrust. In 1970 but not in 1964, integrationists and groups that supported government policies to improve Blacks' conditions also felt alienated from government. Presumably, the change in national administrations between 1964, when Democratic president Lyndon Johnson favored civil rights laws, and 1970, when the Nixon administration showed less enthusiasm for racial equality policies, produced integrationists' rising distrust.

VIETNAM WAR

The attitudinal polarization the Vietnam War produced also explains declining trust in government. Opponents of the administration's military policy attacked the war on both moral and pragmatic grounds. Calling the war unjust and immoral, "doves" demanded immediate withdrawal of American troops from Vietnam. From the doves' perspective, the Saigon government hardly represented the bastion of the "free world." On the contrary, U.S. involvement was enslaving Vietnamese to American firepower, rather than freeing them. The war also brought economic hardships, particularly rampant inflation, to both Americans and South Vietnamese. The "hawks" sought a complete military victory in Vietnam. For them, freedom meant liberation from communist enslavement. To maintain this freedom for the South Vietnamese, they wanted the American government to escalate military power and secure total victory over the communist enemy.

In 1964 and 1970, doves and hawks both expressed the lowest trust in government, with the doves somewhat more alienated, especially during 1970. Groups supporting the existing administration's war policy took the least cynical attitude toward government. Like the racial equality struggle, the Vietnam War polarized attitudes; so groups at opposite ends of the policy scale showed the greatest alienation from government.[16]

WATERGATE

Just as growing popular opposition to the Vietnam War reflected a weakened belief in the sacred mission of the United States to save the world for freedom, so the Watergate events of the early 1970s signaled a decline in civil religion and civic virtue. In 1972, five men working for the Committee to Re-Elect the President broke into the Democratic National Committee's headquarters in Washington, D.C. Two years later the House Judiciary Committee voted to impeach President Nixon, charging that he had delayed, impeded, and obstructed investigations into the Watergate scandal and had covered up his own role in this illegal entry. According to the Judiciary Committee report, President Nixon had subverted constitutional government and had violated citizens' constitutional rights. Although most Americans condemned the Watergate break-in, Nixon supporters blamed his advisors, rather than the president himself. Some cynically suggested that all politicians were crooks; Nixon, however, had the misfortune to get caught for his crimes. Whatever their reaction to Watergate, nearly all Americans tended to blame particular leaders in office, rather than the political system. Even though discontent with incumbent politicians increased, support for the system remained high.

In retrospect, the Watergate events reflect the historic tensions between Puritanism and Madisonianism. During the Nixon administration, interest triumphed over conscience (civic virtue). President Nixon rejected Puritan notions about the sacred value of law and the need for government leaders to abide by the law. Instead, for him, the pursuit of self-interest took precedence over legal restraints on political behavior. A self-made man from a humble background, Nixon embodied certain Madisonian values. From his perspective, the goal of human struggle is to secure greater material welfare and status for the individual. To advance one's self-interests, pragmatism and prudence become necessary requirements. As in a football game, secrecy, shrewdness, and deception are the most effective techniques for gaining political victory. For Nixon, constitutional rules represented not normative checks on presidential power but obstacles blocking the way to political victory. By encouraging Americans to pursue their private interests, Nixon hoped to deflect attention away from the conduct of public policy. Although he attempted to rule as a presidential monarch who had supposedly transcended the interest group struggle, his violations of the law eventually aroused the opposition of both Congress and the Supreme Court.

The Madisonian checks and balances system eventually prevented the triumph of the imperial presidency. The Supreme Court ordered President Nixon to release certain Watergate tapes to special Watergate prosecutor Leon Jaworski. After hearing these tapes, the House Judiciary Committee recommended that the House of Representatives impeach the president for obstructing the Watergate investigation and concealing illegal activities. As a result of institutional opposition to him and his waning constitutional legitimacy, Nixon resigned from the presidency in August 1974.[17] According to constitutional provisions, Vice-President Gerald Ford then became the president. Unlike most Latin American nations, the United States experienced a peaceful change of officeholders. Despite the constitutional crisis, the political regime retained continuity with the original structural arrangements established in 1787.

ECONOMIC STAGNATION

The popular support accorded political leaders derives not only from their adherence to constitutional standards but also from their success in handling such crucial economic issues as inflation and unemployment. From a Madisonian perspective, government exists to satisfy individual interests, to provide concrete benefits. As the incumbent administration fails to reduce unemployment, decrease inflation, and raise real disposable income, its popular appeal declines. Between 1953 and 1975, a 1 percent gain in the unemployment rate meant a 4 percent decline in the president's popularity, as measured by national Gallup polls. As prices rose by 1 percent a year, presidential popularity fell by about the same amount. When people's real disposable income grew by 1 percent, the president's popularity increased by .5 percent. During the administration of Jimmy Carter, inflation rates increased each successive year of his presidency. Real disposable income declined in 1979 and 1980. Although the jobless rate fell from 1977 through 1979, it rose in 1980. Thus, President Carter lost the election to challenger Ronald Reagan mainly because most voters perceived that Carter had incompetently managed the economy.

Policy impacts also affect trust in government. Most Americans blame the government, not labor unions or business corporations, for rising prices and jobless rates. As expected, those citizens who perceive that government policies have not reduced unemployment or stemmed inflationary pressures express the least confidence in government. Particularly during the 1970s, when rising inflation accompanied high jobless rates, disenchantment with government grew. Americans feeling the greatest distrust toward government expressed the strongest support for reducing taxes and curtailing government spending programs.[18]

Political Stability in America

Despite the growing economic crises, the United States has experienced considerable political stability. Even if Americans became alienated from particular political leaders, policies, and policy impacts, the basic values, constitutional arrangements, and political institutions remained stable. Why? Five reasons seem especially crucial.

First, the American political system has enjoyed comparatively high legitimacy. Except during the Civil War, most Americans have granted the institutional arrangements both normative and pragmatic acceptance. They have perceived no alternative system that would either provide greater concrete benefits or embody a morally superior set of values. Support for the Constitution, the values of freedom and equal opportunity, and the political institutions (federalism, balance of powers among Congress, the presidency, and the courts) has remained strong, even while Americans have recently shown declining trust in the behavior of incumbent officeholders and the responsiveness of public policies to popular needs.

Elections of the president and members of Congress, which have occurred regularly since the late eighteenth century, give voters the opportunity to express their discontent with public officials, government policies, and policy results. In this electoral game, politicians try to anticipate the reactions of voters, who reward incumbents for results perceived as "good" (low inflation, low unemployment, low crime, world peace) but vote the "rascals" out of office if conditions deteriorate.[19] Thus, institutional continuity accompanies change in leadership and perhaps some policy modifications.

Second, the important role played by orthodox churches in Americans' personal lives has constituted a vital source of political stability. According to cross-national surveys taken in the United States and West Europe, Americans are more likely than Europeans to attend a church service each week, to regard religious beliefs as very important, and to accept orthodox theological principles, such as belief in a personal God, the devil, heaven, hell, and life after death. In the United States, individuals who affirm these orthodox beliefs also prefer a literal interpretation of the Bible, make a commitment to Jesus Christ as their personal savior, express the greatest confidence in organized religion, and assert that religion plays a very important part in their lives. People holding these orthodox beliefs come predominantly from the less wealthy, less formally educated sectors of American society. Attracted to fundamentalist–evangelical churches, they prefer that government concentrate on such problems as crime, drug addiction, alcoholism, obscenity, and sexual deviance. For them, individual sin, not society, causes the key problems facing contemporary America. Only widespread personal conversions can free society from its sins. Yet fundamentalists despair that individuals will ever achieve great success in resolving social problems. Basic changes can occur only through divine intervention, not through government policies. From the fundamentalist perspective, Christians should hence concentrate on achieving moral purity, self-control, and personal immortality, not on transforming society.[20]

The widespread acceptance of orthodox theological beliefs and the influence of fundamentalist churches, especially among groups at the bottom of the social stratification system, partly lead to political stability. The poor and uneducated look mainly to evangelical churches, not the government, to satisfy their spiritual and pragmatic needs. By involving the laity in church services, fundamentalist churches provide spiritual solace and moral guidance. By teaching certain Puritan virtues—hard work, perseverance, self-control, frugality, sacrifice, methodical habits, temperance—fundamentalist ministers may even help parishioners improve their economic positions in this world. Because many Americans view the church as an appropriate institution for fulfilling their moral and material needs, the low expectations placed on government help maintain political stability.

Third, the dominance of individualistic, rather than collectivist, attitudes in the American culture also explains the continuity of political institutions, mainly because most persons do not expect the government to solve all their personal problems. In 1975, sample surveyors asked people in the United States and West Europe to state the main cause of unemployment. Americans cited three major reasons: world economics (40 percent), lazy people (22 percent), and government (21 percent). Only British citizens showed a greater tendency than Americans to blame unemployment on individual laziness.[21]

Polls conducted solely in the United States reach similar conclusions about the widespread American belief in individual failings as the main cause of social problems. For example, in 1969 slightly more than half a national sample chose as the main explanations for poverty certain individualistic reasons: lack of thrift and hard work by poor people, loose morals, and drunkenness. A majority of Americans thus remain committed to an ethic of self-reliance and individualism. They believe in hard work, competition, and the allocation of economic rewards based on individual initiative and performance. According to these optimistic assumptions, personal success results from individual virtue; personal failures stem from a defective character. Generally, those groups at the top of the social stratification system, especially older white Protestant Republicans, most strongly affirm these individualistic values.

Fewer Americans—mainly Blacks, younger persons, Jews, and northern Democrats—blame poverty on collective sources: low wages, exploitation by the rich, failure of private industry to provide jobs, ethnic discrimination, and low-quality education for poor people. Those groups locating the source of their personal problems in social-structural conditions want these problems handled by government actions—for example, by public policies that provide a guaranteed annual income, income equality, and a government-administered, comprehensive health care program.

By contrast, individualistic Americans deny that the government should help them resolve their personal problems, especially those affecting their personal quality of life, their family's life conditions, their own health, and their economic fortunes. Because these self-reliant individuals constitute a majority of the population, expectations about government action remain low, thereby maintaining political stability.[22]

Fourth, Americans at the bottom of the social stratification system feel the greatest economic grievances yet express the highest fatalism and political powerlessness; therefore, they represent little threat to political stability. Fatalistic individuals attribute such personal difficulties as poverty to circumstances beyond their individual control: bad luck, innate lack of abilities, ill health, and physical handicaps. Generally, the groups holding these fatalistic assumptions have the lowest incomes, the least formal education, and the least skilled jobs. These fatalistic Americans also reveal low political efficacy. Although they want the government to play a more active role in securing a universal health care program, full employment, and greater economic equality, they doubt their ability to affect the public policy process. Indeed, Americans most severely plagued by personal economic problems—especially by unemployment, poverty, and growing financial adversity—have the lowest political involvement, political awareness, participation in organizations, and voting records. Because their expectations of effective government actions remain low, they lack the motivation to become organized for political change. Moreover, their low incomes and low educational attainments deny them the resources to engage in effective political participation.

Groups at the top of the social stratification system express the least fatalistic beliefs. As formal education and income rise, fatalism declines but political efficacy increases. These well-educated, wealthy Americans participate actively in political life. Satisfied with their own life conditions, they pose little challenge to the legitimacy of the political system.[23]

Fifth, although the American political system has rested mainly on a consensual base, the political elite has not refrained from using coercion against groups it regards as a threat to political stability. Historically, certain ethnic groups—Blacks, Indians, Asians, and Mexican Americans—have been the object of political repression, especially before the World War II era. Moreover, left-wing movements showing a high distrust of government policy, high political efficacy, and active political participation also appeared a threat to those leaders operating the political system. State governments, the federal government, and private corporations used coercion to suppress the activities of such groups as the Western Federation of Miners, the Industrial Workers of the World, the Communist party, the

Socialist party, and the Socialist Workers' party. Particularly when war, international crises, depressions, and strikes threatened political stability, government repression increased against dissident movements.[24] Although government coercion does not represent the major source of U.S. political stability, it has deterred opposition groups seeking radical, fundamental changes in American political and economic institutions.

Notes

1. See Robert Bellah, "New Religious Consciousness," *New Republic* 171 (November 23, 1974): 33–41; Robert Bellah, *The Broken Covenant: American Civil Religion in Time of Trial* (New York: Seabury Press, 1975), pp. 1–35; Sheldon S. Wolin, *Politics and Vision* (Boston: Little, Brown, 1960), pp. 165–194, 338–342; John M. Mulder, "Calvinism, Politics, and the Ironies of History," *Religion in Life* 47 (Summer 1978): 148–161; Thomas Jefferson Wertenbaker, *The Puritan Oligarchy* (New York: Scribner's, 1947); Sacvan Bercovitch, *The Puritan Origins of the American Self* (New Haven, Conn.: Yale University Press, 1975); Sydney E. Ahlstrom, *A Religious History of the United States* (New Haven, Conn.: Yale University Press, 1972), pp. 78–81, 124–165; Wilson Carey McWilliams, *The Idea of Fraternity in America* (Berkeley: University of California Press, 1973), pp. 112–145, 170–193; Haven Bradford Gow, "Society Is the Human Condition," *Nation* 221 (September 6, 1975): 185–186; John H. Schaar and Francis M. Carney, "The Circles of Watergate Hell," *American Review* no. 21 (October 1974): 1–41; Joyce Appleby, "Modernization Theory and the Formation of Modern Social Theories in England and America," *Comparative Studies in Society and History* 20 (April 1978): 259–285; Jean Yarbrough, "Thoughts on *The Federalist's* View of Representation," *Polity* 12 (Fall 1979): 65–82.
2. Max Weber, *The Protestant Ethic and the Spirit of Capitalism*, trans. Talcott Parsons (New York: Scribner's, 1958), pp. 98–128.
3. Alexander Hamilton, James Madison, and John Jay, *The Federalist Papers*, ed. Clinton Rossiter (New York: New American Library, 1961), pp. 80–81; see also pp. 78–79, 320–325, as well as Robert J. Morgan, "Madison's Analysis of the Sources of Political Authority," *American Political Science Review* 75 (September 1981): 613–625; William A. Schambra, "The Roots of the American Public Philosophy," *The Public Interest* no. 67 (Spring 1982): 36–48.
4. John Locke, *The Second Treatise of Government*, ed. Thomas P. Peardon (New York: Liberal Arts Press, 1952), pp. 49, 139.
5. See Robert Bellah, "Civil Religion in America," *Daedalus* 96 (Winter 1967): 1–21; Robert N. Bellah, "Religion and Legitimation in the American Republic," *Society* 15 (May–June 1978): 16–23; Gail Gehrig, "The American Civil Religion Debate: A Source for Theory Construction,'" *Journal for the Scientific Study of Religion* 20 (March 1981): 51–63.
6. Quoted in W. Lance Bennett, "Political Sanctification: The Civil Religion and American Politics," *Social Science Information* 14, no. 6 (1975): 86.
7. John L. Hammond, "Revivals, Consensus, and American Political Culture," *Journal of the American Academy of Religion* 46 (September 1978): 293–314; Bellah, *The Broken Covenant*, pp. 49–60; Ahlstrom, *A Religious History of the United States*, pp. 648–689; Vernon Louis Parrington, *Main Currents in American Thought*, vol. 2 (New York: Harcourt, Brace, and Company, 1930), pp. 352–361.
8. Richard Rubinson, "Political Transformation in Germany and the United States," in *Social Change in the Capitalist World Economy*, ed. Barbara Hockey Kaplan (Beverly Hills, Calif.: Sage, 1978), pp. 54–61; Robert A. Dahl, *Democracy in the United States: Promise and Performance*, 3d ed. (Chicago: Rand McNally, 1976), pp. 420–442.
9. Quoted in Parrington, *Main Currents in American Thought*, vol. 2, p. 154. See also Dwight G. Anderson, *Abraham Lincoln: The Quest for Immortality* (New York: Knopf, 1982), esp. pp. 136–207; John H. Schaar, "The Case for Patriotism," *Amer-

ican Review no. 17 (May 1973): 69–74; Yehoshua Arieli, *Individualism and Nationalism in American Ideology* (Baltimore, Md.: Penguin Books, 1966), pp. 311–314.

10. Parrington, *Main Currents in American Thought*, vol. 3, p. 23. See also Rubinson, "Political Transformation in Germany and the United States," pp. 61–71; Dahl, *Democracy in the United States*, pp. 429–436.

11. Ray C. Fair, "The Effect of Economic Events on Votes for President," *Review of Economics and Statistics* 60 (May 1978): 172; Benjamin I. Page, *Choices and Echoes in Presidential Elections: Rational Man and Electoral Democracy* (Chicago: University of Chicago Press, 1978), p. 69.

12. Sidney Verba and Kay L. Schlozman, "Unemployment, Class Consciousness, and Radical Politics: What Didn't Happen in the Thirties," *Journal of Politics* 39 (May 1977): 291–323; U.S. Department of Commerce, Bureau of the Census, *The Statistical Abstract of the United States, 1977* (Washington, D.C.: Government Printing Office, 1977), p. 490.

13. James D. Wright, *The Dissent of the Governed: Alienation and Democracy in America* (New York: Academic Press, 1976), pp. 172–176; Seymour Martin Lipset and William Schneider, "How's Business? What the Public Thinks," *Public Opinion* 1 (July–August 1978): 42–43; *Public Opinion* 2 (January–February 1979): 24; Avery M. Guest, "Subjective Powerlessness in the United States: Some Longitudinal Trends," *Social Science Quarterly* 54 (March 1974): 827–842; Morris P. Fiorina, "The Decline of Collective Responsibility in American Politics," *Daedalus* 109 (Summer 1980): 42; Warren E. Miller, Arthur H. Miller, and Edward J. Schneider, *American National Election Studies Data Sourcebook 1952–1978* (Cambridge, Mass.: Harvard University Press, 1980), pp. 257, 268, 273, 278.

14. Seymour Martin Lipset and William Schneider, "The Public View of Regulation," *Public Opinion* 2 (January–February 1979); 6–13; *Public Opinion* 2 (January–February 1979): 26; *Public Opinion* 1 (September–October 1978): 35; Daniel Yankelovich, "A Crisis of Moral Legitimacy," *Dissent* 21 (Fall 1974): 526–533; David M. Alpern, "Polarizing the Nation?" *Newsweek*, February 8, 1982, pp. 33–34; Kathleen Maurer Smith and William Spinrad, "The Popular Political Mood," *Social Policy* 11 (March–April 1981): 37–45.

15. Warren E. Miller and Teresa E. Levitin, *Leadership and Change: The New Politics and the American Electorate* (Cambridge, Mass.: Winthrop, 1976), p. 227. For a similar interpretation of the positive relationship between political trust and perceived policy performance, see Alan I. Abramowitz, "The United States: Political Culture under Stress," in *The Civic Culture Revisited*, ed. Gabriel Almond and Sidney Verba (Boston: Little, Brown, 1980), pp. 177–207.

16. Arthur H. Miller, "Political Issues and Trust in Government 1964–1970," *American Political Science Review* 68 (September 1974): 951–972; Jack Citrin, "Comment: The Political Relevance of Trust in Government," *American Political Science Review* 68 (September 1974): 973–988; Arthur H. Miller and Warren E. Miller, "Issues, Candidates and Partisan Divisions in the 1972 American Presidential Election," *British Journal of Political Science* 5 (October 1975): 404–407; James S. House and William M. Mason, "Political Alienation in America, 1952–1968," *American Sociological Review* 40 (April 1975): 123–147.

17. Paul M. Sniderman, W. Russell Neuman, Jack Citrin, Herbert McClosky, and J. Merrill Shanks, "Stability of Support for the Political System: The Initial Impact of Watergate," *American Politics Quarterly* 3 (October 1975): 437–457; Schaar and Carney, "The Circles of Watergate Hell"; Dahl, *Democracy in the United States*, pp. 153–179; Arthur J. Vidich, "Political Legitimacy in Bureaucratic Society: An Analysis of Watergate," *Social Research* 42 (Winter 1975): 779–811.

18. Bruno S. Frey, "Keynesian Thinking in Politico-Economic Models," *Journal of Post Keynesian Economics* 1 (Fall 1978): 74–75; Bruno S. Frey and Friedrich Schneider, "An Empirical Study of Politico-Economic Interaction in the United States," *Review of Economics and Statistics* 60 (May 1978): 174–183; David Caplovitz, "Making Ends Meet: How Families Cope with Inflation and Recession," *Public Opinion* 1 (May–June 1978): 54; Anne Statham Macke, "Trends in Aggregate-Level Political Alienation," *Sociological Quarterly* 20 (Winter 1979): 77–87; Arthur H. Miller, "Current Trends in Political Trust," *Economic Outlook USA* 6 (Summer 1979): 58–59; *Public Opinion* 3 (December 1979–January 1980): 41; Kay Lehman Schlozman and Sidney Verba, *Injury*

to Insult: Unemployment, Class, and Political Response (Cambridge, Mass.: Harvard University Press, 1979), p. 348. For data on the 1980 presidential election and economic conditions between 1976 and 1980, see Paul R. Abramson, John H. Aldrich, and David W. Rohde, *Change and Continuity in the 1980 Elections* (Washington, D.C.: Congressional Quarterly Press, 1982), esp. pp. 119–158; *OECD Economic Outlook* no. 30 (December 1981): 140, 142; Patricia Capdevielle and Donato Alvarez, "International Comparisons of Trends in Productivity and Labor Costs," *Monthly Labor Review* 104 (December 1981): 17.

19. Michael Mann, "The Social Cohesion of Liberal Democracy," *American Sociological Review* 35 (June 1970): 423–439; Jack Citrin, Herbert McClosky, J. Merrill Shanks, and Paul M. Sniderman, "Personal and Political Sources of Political Alienation," *British Journal of Political Science* 5 (January 1975): 13; Page, *Choices and Echoes in Presidential Elections*, pp. 220–231, 284.

20. *Gallup Opinion Index* no. 44 (February 1969): 3, 15–20; *Gallup Opinion Index* no. 130 (May 1976): 8–21; *Gallup Opinion Index* no. 140 (March 1977): 19; *Gallup Opinion Index* no. 145 (August 1977): 43–44; *World Opinion Update* 1 (November 1977): 27; Everett Carll Ladd, Jr., "The New Divisions in U.S. Politics," *Fortune* 99 (March 26, 1979): 92; Rodney Stark and Charles Y. Glock, *American Piety: The Nature of Religious Commitment* (Berkeley: University of California Press, 1968), pp. 177–182; James D. Davidson, "Religious Belief as an Independent Variable," *Journal for the Scientific Study of Religion* 11 (March 1972): 73–74; Harold E. Quinley, "The Dilemma of an Activist Church: Protestant Religion in the Sixties," *Journal for the Scientific Study of Religion* 13 (March 1974): 1–22; Rodney Stark, "Rokeach, Religion, and Keeping an Open Mind," *Review of Religious Research* 11 (Winter 1970): 153–154; Peter L. Benson, "Religion on Capitol Hill: How Beliefs Affect Voting Behavior in the U.S. Congress," *Psychology Today* 15 (December 1981): 46–57; Sheldon S. Wolin, "America's Civil Religion," *Democracy* 2 (April 1982): 7–17.

21. *Gallup Opinion Index* no. 126 (January 1976): 10.

22. Joe R. Feagin, "God Helps Those Who Help Themselves," *Psychology Today* 6 (November 1972): 101–110, 129; Joe R. Feagin, "America's Welfare Stereotypes," *Social Science Quarterly* 52 (March 1972): 921–933; N. T. Feather, "Explanations of Poverty in Australian and American Samples: The Person, Society, or Fate?" *Australian Journal of Psychology* 26 (December 1974): 199–216; Paul M. Sniderman and Richard A. Brody, "Coping: The Ethic of Self-Reliance," *American Journal of Political Science* 21 (August 1977): 501–521; Richard A. Brody and Paul M. Sniderman, "From Life Space to Polling Place: The Relevance of Personal Concerns for Voting Behavior," *British Journal of Political Science* 7 (July 1977): 337–360; Everett C. Ladd, Jr., "Traditional Values Regnant," *Public Opinion* 1 (March–April 1978): 45–49; Michael E. Schlitz, *Public Attitudes toward Social Security 1935–1965*, research report no. 33 (Washington, D.C.: U.S. Social Security Administration, Office of Research and Statistics, 1970), pp. 160–161, 176; Richard M. Coughlin, *Ideology and Public Policy: A Comparative Study of the Structure of Public Opinion in Eight Rich Nations* (Ph.D. dissertation, Department of Sociology, University of California at Berkeley, 1977), pp. 74–76; Alan J. Stern and Donald D. Searing, "The Stratification Beliefs of English and American Adolescents," *British Journal of Political Science* 6 (April 1976): 177–201; Schlozman and Verba, *Injury to Insult*, pp. 89, 238, 348; Linda Burzotta Nilson, "Reconsidering Ideological Lines: Beliefs about Poverty in America," *Sociological Quarterly* 22 (Autumn 1981): 531–548. According to Patricia Gurin, Gerald Gurin, and Arthur H. Miller, "Stratum Identification and Consciousness," *Social Psychology Quarterly* 43 (March 1980): 30–47, working-class individuals, like middle-class persons, blame the individual, rather than the political system or other collective sources, for poverty.

23. Wright, *The Dissent of the Governed*, pp. 137, 227; Marc Fried, *The World of the Urban Working Class* (Cambridge, Mass.: Harvard University Press, 1973), pp. 194–196; Feagin, "God Helps Those Who Help Themselves"; Brody and Sniderman, "From Life Space to Polling Place," pp. 344–357; Schlozman and Verba, *Injury to Insult*, pp. 235–277; Macke, "Trends in Aggregate-Level Political Alienation," p. 86; Wilbur J. Scott and Alan C. Acock, "Socioeconomic Status, Unemployment Experience, and Political Participation: A Disentangling of Main and Interaction Effects," *Political Behavior* 1, no. 4 (1979):

361–381; Raymond E. Wolfinger and Steven J. Rosenstone, *Who Votes?* (New Haven, Conn.: Yale University Press, 1980), esp. pp. 102–108; Miller et al., *American National Election Studies Data Sourcebook*, pp. 274, 279; Steven J. Rosenstone, "Economic Adversity and Voter Turnout," *American Journal of Political Science* 26 (February 1982): 25–46.

24. See Robert J. Goldstein, *Political Repression in Modern America* (Cambridge, Mass.: Schenkman, 1978), esp. pp. 547–574.

CHAPTER
11

The Mixed Constitution in Britain

> *Every constitution must first gain authority, and then use authority; it must first win the loyalty and confidence of mankind, and then employ that homage in the work of government. . . . The dignified parts of Government are those which bring it force—which attract its motive power. The efficient parts only employ that power.*
>
> —WALTER BAGEHOT

Like the United States, Britain has enjoyed a long period of system continuity. The last fundamental challenge to the system occurred during the Civil War period of the 1640s, when the Puritan opposition deposed the monarch and instituted a republican form of government. Although the Puritans executed Charles I in 1648, they did not rule England for long. The monarchical system was restored when Charles II ascended the throne in 1660. Nearly thirty years later, in 1688, the landed gentry in Parliament successfully established a parliamentary system. The king no longer ruled as an "absolute sovereign." Instead, Parliament became sovereign; it placed strict constitutional checks on the monarch's right to make binding public policy. Since that time, the British political system has retained its structural continuity. The powers of the House of Lords and the monarch have declined; the House of Commons, the cabinet, and political parties have gained greater influence over political decision making; yet the parliamentary system remains.[1]

The Dignified and Efficient Institutions

The major reason for the continuity of British political structures stems from the political elite's ability to reconcile diverse values in complementary institutions. The British political system mixes opposite values in distinct institutions so that value conflicts become peacefully accommodated, rather than remain antagonistic. Distinct yet complementary institutions embody material and moral values as well as collectivism and individualism. The result is a "mixed constitution" or style of political governing. According to Walter Bagehot, who analyzed the British political system in 1865, the "dignified" institutions—the monarchy, House of Lords, Anglican church, and common law—embody the moral-spiritual values; they help the political system gain and maintain its legitimacy. In turn, the "efficient" institutions—the prime ministry, House of Commons, cabinet, political parties, and agencies for economic policymaking—make the binding political decisions. If public policies secure concrete benefits for the citizenry, these successful policy results will reinforce systemic legitimacy.[2]

Today in Britain the dignified institutions strengthen the personal, sacred, and legal sources of political legitimacy. The monarchy represents certain moral values: family virtues, dignity, and national solidarity. With a lifelong tenure, Queen Elizabeth II serves as a symbol of continuity. Refusing to become actively involved in political decision making, she reigns rather than rules. A representative of national political consensus, she performs important ceremonial, ritualistic duties. As a result of her role performance, the British people take a warm, sympathetic view of the queen. The House of Lords also plays a largely ceremonial role. Whereas vital political decisions take place in the House of Commons, especially the cabinet, the House of Lords represents mainly a place where gentlemen can discuss political matters at leisure.

Unlike the United States, where church and state are formally divided, Britain has an established church—the Church of England. Just as the monarchy and the House of Lords embody personal values, so the Church of England represents basic sacred values. Despite their established status, the high Anglican clergy do not participate in political decision making. All churches can exercise religious freedom; the Church of England displays a tolerant attitude toward Protestant nonconformists and Catholics, who together make up about 40 percent of the British population.

The common law also serves to maintain the moral legitimacy of the British political system. Whereas the British assume a pragmatic attitude toward specific policies, they regard the common law with greater reverence. For them, the law, which dates back to the medieval period, enjoys sacred value, for it has historically served to restrain the power of the political elite.

As a complement to the dignified or ritualistic institutions, the efficient institutions contribute to political legitimacy by supplying concrete benefits to the people. Whereas the queen and the House of Lords reign, the prime minister, cabinet, civil service, and House of Commons rule—that is, formulate the public policies affecting all British citizens. The queen holds office for life; she embodies continuity and consensus. The prime minister governs only while his or her party enjoys majority support in the House of Commons. As a transitory political figure, the prime minister symbolizes change and conflict, especially the conflicts between the Conservative and Labour parties. Although the British express warm feelings toward the queen, they take a more cool, detached view of the prime minister, who retains their support so long as the government secures such benefits as low unemployment, low inflation, high disposable income, a favorable balance of payments, and reduced crime.

Assisting the prime minister in government decision making are the cabinet (composed of leading ministers recruited largely from the House of Commons), the senior civil servants, who advise the ministers, and the top political party officials. The House of Commons as a collective agency functions mainly to elect the governing party or parties, to question the ministers about policy implementation, to discuss political issues, and to vote on bills the cabinet proposes. Like the British population, members of the political elite take a pragmatic attitude toward public policies. Rather than assume a doctrinaire position, they show a willingness to experiment with different policies to ascertain those measures that most effectively achieve desired results.

The British political system has also blended individualistic values with more collectivist beliefs. Whether of Tory, Liberal, Social Democratic, or Labour party persuasion, nearly all political leaders uphold the need for group consultation in decision making. The modern "social contract" assumes that cabinet ministers, senior civil servants, top party leaders, trade union officials, private corporate executives, and other interested groups will participate in the policy process.

Despite this corporate stress on collective decision making, the English also value individual liberty. Even Walter Bagehot in 1865 acknowledged the English tendency to resist political authority, particularly that exercised by police, bureaucrats, and court justices. Historically, the English have maintained a respect for individual privacy, dissent, and eccentricity; in their view, adherence to the common law represents an effective guarantee of individual liberty.

A stress on self-reliance also characterizes the British population.

The values of classical liberalism originated in England with the writings of John Locke, Adam Smith, David Ricardo, Thomas Malthus, and Jeremy Bentham. Although popular support for these individualist principles is stronger today in the United States than in Britain, the English still expect the individual to take some responsibility for his or her welfare. These values appeal especially to leaders of the Conservative party, such as Prime Minister Margaret Thatcher, Geoffrey Howe, and Keith Joseph, who as classical liberals reject the collectivist attitudes associated with previous Conservative governments and instead support more laissez-faire policies.

Despite this recent revival of economic individualism, historically all major political parties have supported an activist government that provides for the collective welfare. They stressed the need for a strong government, a social service state, and a managed economy. As far back as 1875, the Tory government led by Disraeli passed legislation establishing public health services, urban renewal for workers, and the rights of labor unions to engage in collective bargaining. During the twentieth century, Liberal and Conservative administrations, as well as Labour governments, extended social service programs.[3] By providing these concrete benefits to the whole population, all political parties hoped to strengthen their own fortunes at the polls and to reinforce the legitimacy of the political system.

Decline of Deference and Rise of Political Alienation

Despite Britain's historic success at blending opposite values—dignity and efficiency, individualism and collectivism—in complementary institutions, political legitimacy has declined during the post–World War II era. Especially during the 1970s, a large proportion of the British citizens regarded their political system as neither efficient nor dignified. Several surveys conducted in Britain during the 1970s uncovered widespread distrust and feelings of political powerlessness. For example, at the beginning of the 1970s, the British showed lower political efficacy and slightly lower trust in government than did Americans. During 1973 and 1975, sample surveys in nine West European nations explored the degree of popular satisfaction with the performance of democracy; in both years, the British and Italians expressed the most dissatisfaction. In 1976, the British people rated the honesty and ethical standards of twelve occupational groups. Members of Parliament, along with trade union leaders, received the least favorable evaluations.[4] What are the reasons for the growing political alienation in Britain?

Both normative and pragmatic support for the political system has recently begun to wane. Citizens reveal less deference (normative acceptance) than before; they also doubt that government can continue to provide as many concrete benefits, especially low-priced goods, full employment, and steady increases in personal disposable income—all signs of pragmatic acceptance. Although previous studies exaggerated the degree of deference the British people showed toward their political elite, today no more than 20 percent at a maximum take a deferential attitude, that is, show uncritical respect for their "betters." Deference encompasses three attitudes:

1. Support for an ascriptive elite whose members were born into the peerage and aristocracy
2. Admiration for political leaders' personal qualities, specifically, their benevolence and generosity
3. Reverence for the monarchy, the royal family, and the House of Lords—a belief that these institutions play an exalted, essential role in modern society

The main people holding these deferential beliefs are elderly, middle-class women who live in rural areas and identify with the Conservative party.

Most individuals take a more pragmatic, detached view of their political leaders and institutions. The nondeferential public, which judges officials according to their personal merit and political performance, respects leaders who attain beneficial policy outcomes. Although perceiving that the monarchy and House of Lords perform important ritualistic, ceremonial functions, these nondeferential individuals refuse to acknowledge the exalted role of the queen or lords. These rather skeptical attitudes are held primarily by young male Labour supporters who live in the city, work in large factories, and either attend the Catholic church or do not attach themselves to any religious denomination.[5] For these citizens, government attains greatest legitimacy when it secures concrete benefits, not merely when it embodies certain moral–spiritual values associated with a deferential political culture.

The poor economic performance Britain has shown since the end of World War II has also led to growing political alienation. After the Second World War, imports nearly always exceeded exports. The failure to spend money for fixed capital investment meant technological inefficiency. Because manufacturing workers received fairly high wage increases yet secured low gains in output per hour, unit labor costs were higher than in most European countries. The low capital investment, combined with high labor costs, resulted in low productivity, thus dampening the market for British exports. From 1961 through 1980, Britain secured a lower real growth rate than any other Western country. During this period, both unemployment and inflation rates soared above the levels found in most West European nations.

Because neither major party seemed able to manage the economy, distrust of government grew. For instance, between 1959 and 1974, as unemployment rates increased by 1 percent, the popularity of the party holding government office declined by 6 percent. When the inflation rate grew by 1 percent, the incumbent party's Gallup poll support decreased by about .5 percent. A 1 percent growth rate of real disposable income led to a 1 percent gain in the governing party's popularity.

After the Conservative party won control of the government in 1979, economic conditions failed to improve. Partly as a result of the Thatcher government's deflationary policies—higher interest rates, lower increases in the money supply, higher value-added taxes, lower wage increases for unionized workers, and reduced expenditures for social service programs—the unemployment rate rose to 7.4 percent in 1980 and then soared to over 10 percent in 1981. Growth rates in industrial production fell. Consumer prices still increased by double-digit figures: 18 percent in 1980 and 12 percent a year later. As a consequence of the dire economic situation, Prime Minister Thatcher experienced a sharp drop in her national survey popularity from early 1980 through late 1981.[6]

The basic dilemma facing Britain today revolves around ways to satisfy demands for higher consumption while stimulating greater investment and productivity. High jobless rates strengthen popular pressures for increased government expenditures to expand employment opportunities. Severe inflation, however, leads some citizens to call for reduced government expenditures that will lower aggregate demand. The slow economic growth rate means that government lacks the resources to supply concrete benefits and social services. When the economy expands slowly and inflation reduces the purchasing power of money, the pursuit of individual gain takes precedence over the search for the collective welfare. As individuals concentrate on satisfying their economic interests, popular indifference to government mounts. The normative restraints regulating the pursuit of greater material payoffs become weaker. When British governments follow a strategy of incorporating more and more groups—unions, domestic enterprises, multinational corporations—in the process of making economic policy, the political leaders lose their power to enforce their will on all these varied groups. Poor management of the economy results. Political immobility accompanies economic stagnation. As a consequence of the less effective policy performance, government legitimacy declines.[7]

Political Stability in Britain

Despite the rising political alienation, the political regime in Britain remains fairly stable. Predictions of a military coup, a communist takeover, and a fascist seizure of government power have so far proven false. Why has the parliamentary system enjoyed such a long historical continuity? Three reasons explain the structural stability. First, British citizens have lowered their expectations about government performance. As political leaders appear less able to cope with inflation and unemployment, individuals come to rely on themselves, not the government, to overcome economic misfortunes. Rather than blaming the government for poverty, most people attribute the main cause of personal poverty to individual failings: laziness, financial mismanagement, wasteful spending, reluctance to save money, and lack of willpower.[8] Because popular expectations about government's policy performance have fallen, Britain's economic decline does not produce demands for fundamental changes in the parliamentary system. Instead, as happened in 1979, voters elect to office a Conservative party promising less government intervention in the economy, a curb on trade union power, and greater reliance on individual initiative.

Second, as economic conditions have declined, the British public has become more politically apathetic; a relatively low percentage of the population expresses the high distrust and political efficacy that motivate individuals to organize active opposition to the existing system. About a third of the citizens display strong allegiance to the system; they rank high on trust and efficacy. Another third express high distrust and high powerlessness. Although alienated from the political system, they fail to participate to challenge the institutional arrangements or even the policies. Instead, they fatalistically resign themselves to the present conditions. As we have seen, about 20 percent adopt deferential attitudes; high trust coexists with low efficacy. This group gives passive support to the political regime. Less than 20 percent show the combination of low trust and high political effectiveness needed to organize political protests. These dissidents comprise mainly ideologically aware young male leftists who belong to unions. Rather than repudiating the parliamentary, democratic system, they seek changes in public policies and political leadership. Hence, their challenges do not threaten the political regime—that is, institutional arrangements, values, and rules.[9]

Third, the British political elite has historically met challenges to authority in a consensual, rather than coercive, manner. The English leaders tried to incorporate the Scots and Welsh into the existing British system. Local political autonomy and representation in the British Parliament gave the Scots and Welsh opportunities to express regional demands. Although the Church of England became the established church in 1688, since that time it has extended considerable religious freedom to Catholics, Protestant nonconformists, and non-Christians.

Most important, the political elite maintained a relatively open social stratification system. The landed aristocracy admitted successful entrepreneurs to its ranks. By marrying into an aristocratic family, a wealthy business executive gained high status and access to political decision making. During the late nineteenth century, the political elite also incorporated left-wing socialists and labor leaders into the existing political institutions. True, all working-class men did not gain the right to vote until 1918, almost eighty years later than American white males won the suffrage in the United States. Yet compared with American leaders, the British elite before World War I granted more civil liberties to left-wing organizations, especially labor unions and socialist political parties. By 1874, the British government had ended persecution of labor leaders and began to allow them freedom to bargain collectively with employers. British socialist parties freely operated. British left-wingers also showed respect for conservative sentiments. When they came to power, they retained the conservative symbols and institutions—the monarchy, the House of Lords, and the Church of England—identified with English traditionalists.[10]

In sum, leaders of all political persuasions—Conservatives, Liberals, and Labourites—have accepted the bargaining political culture. To gain working-class support, the Conservatives implemented social welfare programs and granted civil liberties to trade unions and socialist parties. In exchange for conservative support, the left-wingers in power maintained the symbols and institutions of traditional authority. Although these institutions lost decision-making power, they remained symbolically important. Through these pragmatic exchanges, British leaders helped stabilize the political system.

Notes

1. See Keith Thomas, "The United Kingdom," in *Crises of Political Development in Europe and the United States*, ed. Raymond Grew (Princeton, N.J.: Princeton University Press, 1978), pp. 41–94.
2. Walter Bagehot, *The English Constitution* (Ithaca, N.Y.: Cornell University Press, 1963).
3. For analyses of Britain's mixed political culture, see Herbert J. Spiro, *Politics as the Master Science: From Plato to Mao* (New York: Harper & Row, 1970), pp. 59–81; Richard Rose, *Politics in England*, 2d ed. (Boston: Little, Brown, 1974), pp. 53–112; Richard Rose, "England: A Traditionally Modern Political Culture," in *Political Culture and Political Development*, ed. Lucian W. Pye and Sidney Verba (Princeton, N.J.: Princeton University Press, 1965), pp. 83–105; Harry Eckstein, "The British Political System," in *Patterns of Government*, 2d ed., ed. Samuel H. Beer

and Adam B. Ulam (New York: Random House, 1962), pp. 75–101; Samuel H. Beer, "The British Political System," in *Patterns of Government*, 3d ed., ed. Samuel H. Beer and Adam B. Ulam (New York: Random House, 1973), pp. 121–141, 261–303; Samuel H. Beer, *British Politics in the Collectivist Age* (New York: Knopf, 1965), esp. pp. 263–264, 271, 278, 353–377; Fred I. Greenstein, Valentine Herman, Robert N. Stradling, and Elia Zureik, "The Child's Conception of the Queen and the Prime Minister," *British Journal of Political Science* 4 (July 1974): 257–287; Joseph Adelson and Lynnette Beall, "Adolescent Perspectives on Law and Government," *Law and Society Review* 4 (May 1970): 495–504; Alan J. Stern and Donald D. Searing, "The Stratification Beliefs of English and American Adolescents," *British Journal of Political Science* 6 (April 1976): 198; Richard M. Coughlin, *Ideology and Public Policy: A Comparative Study of the Structure of Public Opinion in Eight Rich Nations* (Ph.D. dissertation, Department of Sociology, University of California at Berkeley, 1977), p. 112; Bagehot, *The English Constitution*, p. 263; Howard Newby, "The Deferential Dialectic," *Comparative Studies in Society and History* 17 (April 1975): 139–164; Dennis Kavanagh, "The Deferential English: A Comparative Critique," *Government and Opposition* 6 (Summer 1971): 346–347; Paul Barker, "Whistling in the Dark: Social Attitudes as We Enter the 80s," *New Society* 50 (November 29, 1979): 481.

4. *Current Opinion* 5 (February 1977): 21–22; David Butler and Donald Stokes, *Political Change in Britain: The Evolution of Electoral Choice*, 2d ed. (New York: St. Martin's Press, 1974), pp. 454, 466; Richard Rose and Dennis Kavanagh, "The Monarchy in Contemporary Political Culture," *Comparative Politics* 8 (July 1976): 548–576; Ronald Inglehart, *The Silent Revolution: Changing Values and Political Styles among Western Publics* (Princeton, N.J.: Princeton University Press, 1977), p. 169; James D. Wright, *The Dissent of the Governed: Alienation and Democracy in America* (New York: Academic Press, 1976), pp. 169–170; Alan Marsh, *Protest and Political Consciousness* (Beverly Hills, Calif.: Sage, 1977), pp. 114–118; Jack Dennis, Leon Lindberg, and Donald McCrone, "Support for Nation and Government among English Children," *British Journal of Political Science* 1 (January 1971): 25–48.

5. Kavanagh, "The Deferential English," pp. 333–360; Robert McKenzie and Allan Silver, *Angels in Marble* (London: Heinemann, 1968), esp. pp. 166–167, 189–191, 242–261; Bob Jessop, *Traditionalism, Conservatism, and British Political Culture* (London: George Allen and Unwin, 1974); R. D. Jessop, "Civility and Traditionalism in English Political Culture," *British Journal of Political Science* 1 (January 1971): 1–24.

6. Ivor Crewe, "Do Butler and Stokes Really Explain Political Change in Britain?" *European Journal of Political Research* 2 (March 1974): 82–83; Bruno S. Frey, "Keynesian thinking in Politico-Economic Models," *Journal of Post Keynesian Economics* 1 (Fall 1978): 74–75; Bruno S. Frey and Friedrich Schneider, "A Politico Economic Model of the United Kingdom," *Economic Journal* 88 (June 1978): 243–253; *Public Opinion* 4 (October–November 1981): 27–28; C. F. Pratten, "Mrs. Thatcher's Economic Experiment," *Lloyds Bank Review* no. 143 (January 1982): 36–51; Ken Coutts, Roger Tarling, Terry Ward, and Frank Wilkinson, "The Economic Consequences of Mrs. Thatcher," *Cambridge Journal of Economics* 5 (March 1981): 81–93; Willem H. Buiter and Marcus Miller, "The Thatcher Experiment: The First Two Years," in *Brookings Papers on Economic Activity*, no. 2, ed. William C. Brainard and George L. Perry (Washington, D.C.: Brookings Institution, 1981), pp. 315–367; *International Financial Statistics* 35 (March 1982): 44–47; *OECD Economic Outlook* no. 30 (December 1982): 44, 131, 140, 142.

7. See Norman H. Keehn, "Great Britain: The Illusion of Governmental Authority," *World Politics* 30 (July 1978): 538–562; Peter T. Ewell, *A Structural Analysis of an Industrial Society: The Case of Britain* (Ph.D. dissertation, Department of Political Science, Yale University, 1976), pp. 111–136; Richard Rose, "Ungovernability: Is There Fire Behind the Smoke?" *Political Studies* 27 (September 1979): 351–370; Dennis Kavanagh, "Political Culture in Great Britain: The Decline of the Civic Culture," in *The Civic Culture Revisited*, ed. Gabriel Almond and Sidney Verba (Boston: Little, Brown, 1980), pp. 124–176.

8. Peter Golding, "It's the Poor What Gets the Blame," *New Society* 60 (April 1, 1982): 12–13; David Lipsey, "The Reforms People Want," *New Society* 50 (October 1979):

12–14; Peter Townsend, *Poverty in the United Kingdom* (Berkeley: University of California Press, 1979), pp. 428–431; Tom Forester, "Do the British Sincerely Want to be Rich?" *New Society* 40 (April 28, 1977): 158–161; J.-R. Rabier, "European Surveys and Social Research," *European Journal of Political Research* 6 (September 1978): 333; *World Opinion Update* 1 (November 1977): 31.
9. Marsh, *Protest and Political Consciousness.*
10. Seymour Martin Lipset, *The First New Nation* (New York: Basic Books, 1963), pp. 215–217, 239–245; Robert Goldstein, "Political Repression and Political Development: The United States and Europe, 1789–1917," paper presented at the Western Political Science Association convention, Los Angeles, California, March 17, 1978; H. F. Moorhouse, "The Political Incorporation of the British Working Class: An Interpretation," *Sociology* 7 (September 1973): 341–359.

CHAPTER
12

Pragmatism and Absolutism in Germany

Law, peace, and order cannot spring from the manifold and clashing interests of society but from the power that stands above it, armed with the strength to restrain its wild passions. Here we first get a clear idea of what we may call the moral sanctity of the State. It is the State that brings justice and mercy into this struggling world.
—HEINRICH VON TREITSCHKE

Like the social contract, the contract of government is problematical in Germany. The state is nothing but the man-made authority that permits some to exercise power over others, that is, convert interests into valid norms.
—RALF DAHRENDORF

Compared with Britain, Germany has experienced greater changes in political systems. Since the late seventeenth century, Britain has maintained a parliamentary system. During the last hundred years, however, Germans have lived under several different political systems: the Second Reich (1871–1918), the Weimar Republic (1919–1933), the Nazi regime (1933–1945), and, after World War II, the German Federal Republic (West Germany) and the German Democratic Republic (East Germany). Why have Britain and Germany pursued different paths of political development? Unlike British leaders, who have tried to reconcile opposing values in complementary institutions, the German political elite attempted to suppress value conflicts. Because the political system never gained widespread legitimacy from the key elite and important social groups, a high degree of structural discontinuity has plagued Germany.

Rise and Fall of the Second Reich

GROUP CONFLICTS

Established by Chancellor Bismarck in 1871, the Second Reich (empire) began on a shaky foundation of legitimacy because the German elite failed to reconcile conflicts among the diverse ethnic, religious, and economic groups. In contrast to Britain, which has enjoyed a long period of national identity, the German principalities united into a single nation-state only during the last part of the nineteenth century. With two-thirds of the territory and 60 percent of the population, Prussia dominated the state. Other ethnoregional groups, such as Bavarians, Saxons, and Hanoverians, who exercised less political and economic power, resented Prussian dominance of the bureaucracy, military, and courts.

Unlike England, where the Church of England tolerated the Catholic minority, in Germany conflicts between Catholics and Protestants plagued the Second Reich. About equal proportions of the German population identified with each Christian denomination. During the 1870s, Bismarck feared a Catholic alliance of France and Austria-Hungary against Germany. As a Protestant, he favored the Protestants at the expense of the Catholics. Faced with this hostility, the German Catholics formed their own religious political party, the Zentrum or Center party.

Economic conflicts also endangered the political stability of the Second Reich. The *Junker* landed aristocrats from Prussia dominated the key state organs, including the civil service, the military bureaucracy, and the judiciary. They upheld the absolutist monarchical system. Liberal democrats, primarily some industrialists, manufacturers, intellectuals, and professionals, failed to establish a constitutional, democratic state where parliamentary leaders effectively controlled the military, the bureaucracy, and the kaiser. Alarmed by the growing support that the working class gave the Social Democratic party, the manufacturers and industrialists, especially in the iron and steel industries, allied with the *Junker* landowners to crush the factory workers. Although the *Junker* aristocrats retained political control of the state, the industrialists gained certain policy concessions: state financial assistance to promote industrialization, high tariffs that protected domestic manufacturers, state control of wages, and government repression of the Socialist party and trade unions.

Between 1878 and 1890, Bismarck tried to suppress the activities of the Social Democratic party and the Free Trade Unions, mainly by curtailing their newspapers and journals, firing their supporters, and persecuting their leaders. Nevertheless, during this period, they still retained the right to compete in elections to the Reichstag (the lower house of parliament) and to hold some seats there.

While repressing the Social Democrats' political activities, Bismarck sought working-class legitimacy for the Second Reich by granting the workers some welfare services, such as insurance providing health care, protection against accidents, and old-age pensions. Even under these social service programs, the workers remained politically and economically subordinate to the employers, who paid a relatively small share of the insurance funds. Unlike the English government, the German state failed to implement public policies that shortened the work week, protected working women and children, or provided for state inspections of factory conditions.[1]

In short, Bismarck's state-sponsored "marriage of iron and rye" between industrialists and *Junker* landlords took place at the expense of the emerging working class. Although the industrialists gained some economic privileges from the state, the *Junkers* still exercised political power and maintained a rigid status system. The workers secured some paternalistic welfare benefits; yet Bismarck denied them extensive political rights and trade union freedom. The Second Reich largely excluded all but the *Junker* aristocrats from active participation in political decision making. Political absolutism thus accompanied economic pragmatism.

In contrast, the British elite operated a more open stratification system. The landed gentry opened the system to merchants and industrialists who gained access to political power and entrance into high-status groups. The workers won the right to vote, to organize socialist parties, and to join trade unions that bargained collectively with employers. The more peaceful reconciliation of economic conflicts in Britain than in Germany brought greater legitimacy and stability to the British political system.

VALUE CONFLICTS

The Germans' failure to accommodate group conflicts parallels their difficulty in reconciling opposed values. Whereas the British blended opposite values in complementary institutions, the German elite could not easily harmonize such conflicting values as idealism versus materialism and individualism versus collectivism. German political beliefs stressed the need for a rigid stratification system and an authoritarian, absolutist state, rather than widespread political participation and representation of diverse groups in decision-making institutions. As a result, excluded groups accorded the political system only weak legitimacy. Let us examine the importance of the law, the personal leader, and sacred values in securing support for the system.

Unlike Britain, where the Parliament and courts embodied the common law, in Germany the state civil service represented the legal orientations toward authority. Whereas Parliament exercised greater power than the professionalized bureaucracy in England, the opposite tendency existed in Germany. Here, the legal traditions demanded explicit, detailed, comprehensive rules to govern political decision making. Rather than restraining political absolutism, the law immobilized the decision process. Frustrated by bureaucratic rigidities, German rulers sought a charismatic hero, a feudal warring knight who would overcome procedural immobility to attain great miracles. Thus, during the Second Reich, an ultralegalistic orientation alternated with arbitrary personal rule.

In contrast to the German elite of the Second Reich, British officials secured a more harmonious relationship between ceremonial and policymaking leadership. In Britain, the monarch reigned, but the prime minister and the cabinet ruled. During the first decade of the twentieth century, King Edward VII refrained from actively interfering in public policymaking. Although he advised parliamentary leaders about ways to maintain European peace, the prime minister and cabinet made the final decisions. The political party gaining the most seats in the House of Commons selected the prime minister, who governed as long as he retained support in Commons.

The Second Reich never achieved such a complementary separation of dignified and efficient personal leadership. From 1871 to 1890, Bismarck ruled Germany as chancellor; the kaiser served as emperor. Bismarck took the main responsibility for governing German society until Kaiser Wilhelm died in 1888. When his grandson, Wilhelm II, assumed the throne in 1888, however, he wanted to play the dominant role in asserting Germany's imperial destiny. Seeking both to reign and to rule, the kaiser in 1890 forced Bismarck to resign as chancellor. Until Wilhelm II's abdication in 1918, he, not the Reichstag, selected the chancellor. While Edward VII gained widespread admiration for his dignity, responsibility, and conscientious role as king, his nephew, Kaiser Wilhelm II, ruled as "an irresponsible maniac on the throne endowed with supreme authority over the government and the army."[2] As twentieth-century developments in Germany and Russia indicate, monarchs who chose to rule rather than just reign found themselves toppled from office.

Idealism versus materialism. The German elite faced greater difficulties than British leaders in reconciling idealism with materialism. In Britain, the Church of England functioned as the established yet tolerant church; its clergy, who affirmed the sacred solidarity of the nation, also challenged political leaders to pursue ethical ends. The Puritan minority asserted the need for civic virtue and rule by law; for the Puritans, the law held sacred value in restraining both the rulers and the citizens. Thus, the British blended pragmatism and idealism. Sacred beliefs and the law regulated the pursuit of material benefits; yet a tolerant, pragmatic attitude weakened tendencies toward ideological absolutism and rejection of political compromises.

In Germany, no such complementary balance occurred between idealism and materialism. The economic and moral–spiritual realms remained sharply separated but not complementary. Especially between 1895 and 1914, the Second Reich attained rapid industrialization. Instead of adopting a laissez-faire position, the German state actively encouraged rapid economic growth; it established factories, built mines, imported machinery and technicians from Britain, and subsidized private industries. By the late nineteenth century, Germany, along with Japan and the United States, began to capture the world markets formerly dominated by Great Britain. This rapid growth rate brought some benefits to the workers. Unemployment and inflation remained low. Real disposable income showed a rapid rise. All these material benefits legitimized the political system of the Second Reich. Despite these economic achievements, German intellectuals and perhaps some of the masses as well disdained the mundane, material world. Spiritual absolutes—the State, the World Spirit, Faith—took precedence over pragmatic actions. Mysticism triumphed at the expense of a matter-of-fact, skeptical attitude toward political affairs. Unlike Britain, where ethical ideals tempered the pursuit of material gain and pragmatism weakened any tendencies toward spiritual absolutism, Germany under Kaiser Wilhelm II never secured a harmonious blend of the idealistic and materialist strands of the human condition.[3]

The influence of Lutheranism on modern German political culture partly explains the difficulty in harmonizing the moral and material bases of legitimacy. In contrast to John Calvin, another leader of the Protestant Reformation, Martin Luther drew a stark contrast between the spiritual realm (the Kingdom of God) and the secular domain (the kingdoms of the world). For Luther, the Kingdom of God rests on a personal faith in Christ and his gospel; only faith in God, not reason, law, or education, can lead people to salvation. In the Kingdom of God, people live in community and brotherhood, united by their faith in God's grace. The political kingdoms of this world, however, rule by coercion. Because people are naturally anarchic, sinful, and selfish, the state wields coercive power to restrain their evil tendencies. Rather than checking the rulers' actions, the law primarily curbs the wicked, maintains political order, and promotes mass discipline.

Drawing a parallel between the irrational wonder of God and irrational secular authority, Luther upheld a repressive role for the state:

> Such [earthly] authorities carry the sword in order to overawe those who do not abide by godly teachings and to give other people peace and quietness.... God ordains that the lowliest must suffer at the hands of the worldly upper classes, in order to make it plain that our salvation is not due to any man but to God's power and works.[4]

Leading the revolt against the Roman Catholic church, Luther removed any intermediaries between rulers and ruled. Just as the individual stands in a direct relationship to God, so neither church nor law should intervene between the people and their sovereign. Spiritual faith takes precedence over secular law. Luther perceived the church as an invisible assembly of the faithful, not a visible ecclesiastical institution with power to check the state. Obedience to sovereign authority, rather than political participation, became the German norm for conduct in the secular realm. Faith in God, not "good works" on earth, became the standard for good spiritual behavior. These Lutheran beliefs reinforced the trends toward political absolutism in Germany.

Individualism versus collectivism. Just as the Germans failed to harmonize the conflicting moral and material bases of legitimacy, so they never resolved the tensions between individualism and collectivism. In England, both individual liberty and collective consultation among diverse groups in the public policy process remained strong. In Germany, however, collective values and structures—the state, the nation, the *Volk*—took precedence over the freedom of the individual. From this collectivist perspective, the state guaranteed the individual's freedom and well-being. Seeking an identification with the collectivity, some Germans became attracted to a warrior elite that promised individual fulfillment in service to the nation, *Volk*, and state.[5] For the German military officers, war represented the most effective means for reconciling the conflicting demands of individualism and collectivism. By sacrificing themselves to the national cause, individuals were supposed to find a collective meaning that transcended their private lives.

Although participation in World War I stimulated collective identification with state and nation, the German defeat in 1918 led to the disintegration of the Second Reich. After two years of severe warfare, by late 1916 German strength began to deteriorate. Military desertions escalated. Food shortages were common. When the government reduced food rations in 1918, mass strikes and food riots erupted. After the United States troops entered the war in the spring of 1918, the Germans suffered military defeats. When the power of the German armed forces collapsed, the kaiser no longer seemed an effective warring knight who could attain a miraculous military victory. Pressured to resign, Wilhelm II abdicated the throne in October 1918. After Social Democrats, left-wing socialists (the Spartacists), liberal democrats, and conservative defenders of the empire struggled for power, in early 1919 Social Democrats, liberals, and a few conservatives succeeded in establishing the Weimar Republic, a parliamentary system that represented a sharp break with the previous monarchical regime.

Political Illegitimacy of the Weimar Republic

Throughout its fourteen-year history, the Weimar Republic failed to gain widespread pragmatic or normative acceptance. Neither the elite nor the masses enthusiastically supported the new parliamentary system. The moral–spiritual bases of legitimacy remained weak. After the destruction of the monarchy, no authoritative personal leader remained to embody German national solidarity. True, the Weimar constitution provided for an elected president; yet the ineffectiveness of the chancellor encouraged the president to become the primary decision maker. As political and economic crises mounted and the government seemed unable to resolve them, the president's personal authority waned. Moreover, no state religion united Protestants and Catholics behind the Weimar government. Even though the Catholic Center party participated in most coalition governments, the public schools became nondenominational; this secularization of public education alienated some Catholics from the regime. Protestants, especially those in the rural areas who opposed the Marxist parties, also gave weak support to the Weimar governments; indeed, Protestant farmers strongly backed the Nazi party's rise to power. Finally, the Weimar constitution inspired no widespread veneration because the victorious Allied powers, mainly the United States, England, and France, imposed the constitutional arrangements on the defeated German nation.

The various Weimar governments lacked political effectiveness in handling the severe political and economic crises that confronted German leaders from the beginning. From a political standpoint, German defeat in the First World War weakened its national power. Many Germans felt humiliated by the Treaty of Versailles, under which Germany lost population, territory, foreign investments, and other forms of wealth. The reparations agreements imposed severe economic burdens. French and Belgians occupied the Rhineland area after the war ended; in 1923, the French army invaded the territories on the left bank of the Rhine. These conditions aggravated German hostility to foreigners. Many war veterans who returned from the front lines felt betrayed by those parties supporting the peace treaty, especially the Social Democrats, Communists, and Catholic Centrists. War orphans also became deeply alienated from the Weimar political system. Longing for a father figure and a new community identity, they supported Hitler's Nazi movement.

The severe postwar conditions brought political and personal violence to the Weimar Republic. Both the left-wingers and the right-wingers staged numerous coups d'etat: The left-wing Spartacists and Communists between 1918 and 1920 attempted to establish a revolutionary workers and peasants socialist republic. From the Right originated the Kapp putsch of 1920 and the abortive Hitler Munich putsch three years later. Particularly after the depression struck Germany in 1929, political violence escalated. Armed bands of Nazi stormtroopers terrorized Jews, Social Democrats, and Communists.

Severe economic crises, both inflation and unemployment, also plagued the Weimar Republic. During the five-year period after the war, hyperinflation brought economic ruin to millions. Whereas in 1922 the wholesale price index was 101, by late 1923 it had reached 750 billion. Unemployment accompanied the soaring price increases. After the currency stabilized in early 1924, the economy prospered until 1929, when the depression led to rising unemployment rates. Closely tied to the American economy, Germany endured severe hardships. After the U.S. Congress passed the Smoot-Hawley Tariff in 1930, German exports to America drastically declined. When American loans to Germany ceased, the German government could no longer make reparations to France and Britain; these two nations thus stopped buying imported goods from Germany. Partly as a result of these crises in the world capitalist economy, over 40 percent of the German labor force was unemployed by 1932.

The Weimar governments and political parties proved unable to resolve these political and economic crises. Competition among rival parties, factions, and government institutions led to political immobilism, which hindered effective policymaking. Between 1919 and 1933, seven different political parties each gained at least 10 percent of the vote at some election to the Reichstag. Until 1930, the Social Democrats (SPD) won the most votes, followed by the Catholic Center party and the conservative German National People's party. Along with the Center party, smaller middle-class parties (mainly the German Democratic party and the German People's party) usually formed the government. Even though the SPD legislators held the most seats, they remained out of government coalitions except from 1919 to 1923 and 1928 to 1930. As the coalitions became more prone to disintegration, support for the parliamentary system waned. By the time Hitler became chancellor in January 1933, the Weimar Republic had seen over twenty different coalition governments.

The frequent change of governments and the difficulty of reconciling competing parties weakened political democracy. Playing an ineffective role, the chancellor yielded power to the president, an elected official who had authority to appoint and dismiss the chancellor, to dissolve the Reichstag, and to wield emergency powers. As the political–economic crises grew more severe, the Reichstag abandoned its decision-making authority and the president ruled largely by decree. Three conservative groups within the state institutions—the military, the bureaucracy, and the judicial officials—began to exercise more independent power, unchecked by either the Reichstag or the chancellor. Thus, as political immobilization plagued the political parties and the coalition governments, autocratic power reverted to groups hostile to the Weimar Republic, including both the Nazis and the conservative defenders of the Second Reich.

Hitler and the Nazis profited from all these political and economic crises that weakened the legitimacy of the Weimar system. As unemployment grew, Nazi electoral support rose. In 1928, the Nazi party won less than 3 percent of votes to the Reichstag. Of the seven major parties, it held the fewest seats in parliament. In the 1930 election, however, it gained 18 percent, becoming the second largest party. In the two 1932 elections, the Nazis secured 33 percent and 37 percent of the vote; they then held the most seats in the Reichstag. In 1933, President Hindenburg, a Prussian general during World War I, appointed Hitler chancellor.

How did the Nazis score these electoral successes? They appealed primarily to those groups expressing the greatest discontent with the Weimar system. Hitler promised the war veterans a resurrected, militarily powerful German state. To the war orphans, he became a substitute father figure heading a new national community. Those who had been ruined by the earlier inflation—self-employed persons, pensioners, and retired people—voted for the Nazis. The Nazi party also appealed to various groups suffering from the depression: unemployed government employees and entrepreneurs, the Protestant lower middle class (self-employed traders, shopkeepers, artisans), Protestant farmers, and young unskilled workers who belonged to no union and who held jobs in small-scale firms.

Particularly after 1929, Hitler received support from the German economic elite, both the *Junker* landowners and corporate executives who ran the coal, iron, steel, machinery, electrical, and chemical industries. No longer able to sell their goods on the domestic or world market, these industrialists backed Hitler's policies for German rearmament and economic autarky. Opposed to the power wielded by labor unions and the Social Democratic party during the Weimar Republic, the industrialists welcomed the Nazi determination to curtail wage increases, independent unions, collective bargaining, labor councils, and state arbitration that favored working-class interests.

The groups most strongly identified with the two major political parties supporting the Weimar Republic—the Social Democrats and the Catholic Center—generally rejected Nazi electoral appeals. These groups included urban industrial factory workers, unionists, farm workers, Catholics, and women.[6]

In sum, the Weimar Republic fell because it gained neither moral nor material legitimacy. Its political institutions received little normative acceptance. The parties and coalition governments proved unsuccessful at resolving key problems. With a weak attachment to the collective values and institutions of the Weimar Republic, German citizens concentrated on satisfying their individual interests. Yet the German inflation and unemployment rates—higher than in either Britain or the United States at this time—made it impossible for a large segment of the population to secure desired economic benefits. In desperation, nearly 40 percent voted for the Nazi party.

Third Reich: The Cult of the Führer

With the downfall of the Weimar Republic, Hitler moved quickly to establish a new basis of legitimacy for his regime. He tried to synthesize opposing values—collectivism versus individualism, pragmatic materialism versus spiritual absolutism—a goal that had eluded Second Reich and Weimar Republic leaders. The Third Reich stressed the expansion of material benefits. Determined to secure German rearmament, the Nazi state encouraged rapid industrial growth, especially in the iron and steel industries. Unemployment rates declined from the high levels of 1932. Until the late 1930s, when Germany began its expansionary drive to conquer Europe, price increases remained moderate. Even though by 1937 gross per capita income was still lower than in 1928, economic conditions appeared brighter than during the depression years. By purging the civil service of some highly educated persons and by lowering educational requirements for professional jobs, the Nazi government granted less well educated German male youth greater opportunities for upward social mobility. The stress on military service, athletic skill, Nazi party loyalty, and racial purity as requirements for employment and university attendance opened up the system to less advantaged persons. By curbing the economic power of labor unions, socialist and communist parties, international financiers, and Jewish owners of large department stores, Hitler appealed to German entrepreneurs, who sought protection against working-class organizations, Marxist parties, foreign capitalist enterprises, and Jews.

According to national sample surveys conducted after World War II, the depressed economic situation of Germany in 1932 constituted the major reason for the Nazi rise to power. Most people perceived the Weimar Republic as the least prosperous system between 1871 and 1945. The Second and Third Reichs were regarded as bringing the greatest prosperity. These polls indicate that more individuals supported Hitler's domestic economic policies than his aggressive foreign policies.[7]

Hitler also tried to incarnate certain nonmaterial, irrational, mystical values of German political culture. A personal cult of *der Führer* emerged. After the death of President Hindenburg in 1934, Hitler ruled as both president and chancellor. He not only made the key political decisions but also claimed to embody the German national spirit. At mass rallies, festivals, nationalist ceremonies, rituals, and demonstrations, the Nazi party mobilized Germans to demonstrate their personal loyalty to the absolute leader. Recalling Luther's teachings, Hitler encouraged German Christian churches to concentrate solely on matters of faith, doctrine, and the inner spiritual, private life. Rather than actively participating in politics and criticizing government policies, German Christians were urged to obey their ruler, Adolf Hitler, who fancied himself the redeemer of the Reich, saving Germany from Jews, Marxists, and foreign powers that looked down on the German nation. As Nazi Germany became more militarily aggressive during the late 1930s, the mystical feudal cult of blood and soil exhorted German youth to sacrifice their lives for national glory.

A cult of irrational violence, rather than veneration for the law, animated Nazi Germany. From Hitler's perspective, war represented the best means for youth to express their German manhood and dedication to the Aryan race. Just as the ancient warrior-vassals had served their feudal lord, so Nazi soldiers should commit themselves to *der Führer* and fight for Aryan hegemony over the world. In this struggle for racial supremacy in Germany and Aryan domination overseas, Hitler rejected any legal restraints on his personal rule. Although he never abolished the Weimar constitution, a special enabling act the Reichstag passed in 1933 subordinated the law to the will of the Führer, who ruled mainly by decree.

In the Nazi society, collectivist values took precedence over individualism. Hitler promised to transcend the individual and group interest conflicts that had characterized the Weimar Republic—for example, the conflicts separating the landed *Junker* gentry from small farmers, the large-scale steel industrialists from the small shopkeepers and merchants. According to Hitler, harmony of interests would replace individualistic economic conflicts. Service to the nation would bring material rewards to the individual. For Hitler, national socialism meant collective labor discipline and hard work for the national cause, not individual economic equality.

As Germany struggled to expand its military power during the late 1930s, the collective values were more forcefully emphasized. Nazi leaders urged the German citizen to live and die for national values. Conceiving of the nation as an organic people's community—the *Volksgemeinschaft*—they established a cult of the German *Volk*, the Aryan race, and the Nazi state. As Nazi armies moved through West and East Europe, nationalism became transformed into imperialism.[8] By these military conquests, Hitler hoped to reinforce his charismatic legitimacy as a modern hero and miracle worker, a twentieth-century warring knight.

Even though Hitler promised a thousand-year reich, his regime lasted only twelve years. When Russian, British, American, and French armies defeated Nazi Germany in 1945, the Third Reich came to an end. Rather than purifying the nation, Hitler destroyed it. At the end of the war, the German nation was divided into two states: the Federal Republic of Germany, allied to the United States, and the German Democratic Republic, supervised by the USSR. Hitler's attempts to expand the German nation thus ended in national disintegration.

Federal Republic of Germany: The Economic Foundations of Political Legitimacy

Although Hitler's policies led to the destruction of millions of people—Jews and Christians, Germans and non-Germans—the war did establish a democratic foundation for the new Federal Republic of Germany (FRG). The Nazi stress on a classless society had undermined the power of the *Junker* aristocracy in the civil service; young German males from less-privileged backgrounds gained the opportunity to join the bureaucracy. As a result of Nazi defeat in World War II, the rigid social stratification system further disintegrated. Nazi army officers and civil servants lost their power. Those areas of eastern Germany formerly dominated by the autocratic Prussian aristocracy became part of the German Democratic Republic. The regions that had voted for more democratic political parties during the Weimar era were included in the West German political system.

Led by the United States, the victorious Allied powers determined to avoid the mistakes of the World War I era, when the peace settlement had produced national resentment and economic devastation for most Germans. Particularly after the Soviet Union became the dominant power in East Europe and states there came under Communist party control, the United States moved to rebuild the West

German economy. The Marshall Plan, under which West Germans gained over $3 billion in loans, helped engineer a speedy economic recovery. With the establishment of the North Atlantic Treaty Organization, West Germany became a close military ally of Western democratic states. Supervised by American constitutional experts, the FRG's constitution or "Basic Law" legitimized a federal system with numerous checks and balances against absolutist state power.[9] Unlike the Weimar Republic, the Federal Republic of Germany hence began its existence with more favorable prospects for democratic stability.

Like the Weimar leaders, West German politicians have stressed the material and individualist bases of political legitimacy; yet, compared with the Weimar Republic, the Federal Republic has scored more striking economic successes, thus strengthening its legitimacy. Between 1950 and 1970, annual price increases averaged less than 3 percent, a low inflation rate relative to other countries in Europe and the world. From 1960 through 1973, unemployment rates were less than 1 percent a year. Even after 1973, when economic conditions in most Western nations began to deteriorate, West Germany still maintained comparatively low inflation and unemployment records. In 1978, a survey evaluated the "quality of life" in fourteen European countries. The study compared their performance on such measures as economic productivity, efficient organization of industries, rights of the work force, health care, cultural attainments, opportunities for leisure, and environmental conditions. On this quality of life scale, West Germany ranked third, behind Sweden and Denmark, which gained the top scores.[10]

From the standpoint of political performance, contemporary West German officials have also demonstrated greater successes than their Weimar predecessors. Numerous political parties fragmented coalition building in the Weimar Republic. Because party leaders could not easily form coalitions, governments rose and fell, leading to considerable political instability. Because the chancellor and parliament could not govern effectively, decision-making power reverted to the civil service and the president, who ruled by decree. In the Federal Republic, however, only three major political parties—the Social Democrats (SPD), the Christian Democrats (CDU), and the Free Democrats (FDP)—compete for power. As a small swing party, the Free Democrats allied first with the CDU and later with the SPD. The chancellor functions as an effective decision maker; yet other parliamentarians and leaders of the *Länder* (state) governments establish checks on his power so that he cannot rule as a dictator. The president performs mainly ceremonial roles. Purged of Nazi officials, the German civil service operates in a more democratic manner than during either the Weimar Republic or the Third Reich.

National sample surveys indicate that the West German public grants legitimacy to the Federal Republic because of its effective economic and political performance. Germans evaluate their political leaders according to their success in securing concrete benefits for the individual. Between 1951 and 1975, as the rate of unemployment and inflation each increased by 1 percent, the popularity of the governing parties, as measured by national polls, declined about 1 percent. Increases in the growth of real disposable income raised the government's standing in the polls by about .5 percent. According to sample surveys, most Germans perceive their political elite as effective. In 1973, 44 percent of both the German and the British publics expressed great satisfaction with the way democracy functioned in their country; however, by 1977, the German percentage had risen to 78 percent, the most favorable evaluation in nine European nations. The British, along with the French and Italians, took the least favorable view of the way democracy worked in their society.

Compared with British citizens, Germans now rank higher on measures linked to political participation. During the 1970s, West Germans had stronger feelings of political effectiveness; they felt greater confidence in their ability to shape public policies. A higher percentage of the citizenry voted in FRG elections than in British elections. Membership in consumer protection organizations included a larger share of the population in West Germany. The Germans also expressed higher trust in government than did the Britons.[11] Undoubtedly, these attitudes of political efficacy and trust in government stem from the responsiveness of the West German political system in providing desired concrete benefits. Political stability thus rests on policy effectiveness.

The moral–spiritual legitimacy of the FRG rests on a weaker foundation. Although people favorably evaluate the political system for its concrete benefits and efficient performance, the personal, sacred, and legal aspects of legitimacy arouse less enthusiasm. After German defeat in World War II, the nation became fragmented into two opposed parts. The West German government rules only half the divided nation. The history of political instability and the authoritarian heritage have given both the German elite and the masses feelings of psychological insecurity about threats to the regime. Few institutions like the monarchy and Church of England in Britain operate in West Germany to symbolize the values of national identity. The president acts as a ceremonial leader and does not enjoy the widespread respect shown toward the Queen of England. No established church functions to transcend the political party conflicts between the Catholics, who participate mainly in the Christian Democratic Union, and the Protestants, who dominate the Social Democratic and Free Democratic parties.

Most important, the attachment to procedural legitimacy and civil liberties seems weaker in West Germany than in most other West European nations except Spain and Portugal. Called the Basic Law, the FRG constitution has a rather temporary status because in 1949 West German leaders looked forward to the early reunification of the German nation and the incorporation of Germany into a wider European community. For this reason, the West German public displays less veneration for constitutional documents than do British and Americans.

The main challenges to civil liberties in West Germany arise more from elite behavior than from mass attitudes. In 1977, sample surveys conducted in several European nations asked people to state the main goals for their country during the next ten years. Twenty-seven percent of the West Germans and British named "protecting freedom of expression" as their first or second choice. One-third of the sample in both countries wanted to give people greater influence over government decisions. More British than Germans—64 percent versus 57 percent—stressed the need to maintain law and order as a primary national objective. During 1977, public opinion polls in Britain, West Germany, France, and Italy listed several different freedoms and asked samples to classify these liberties as either a basic human right or a privilege granted by the state. On nearly all the *political* freedoms—freedom from arbitrary arrest or imprisonment, freedom from censorship of the mass media, freedom to emigrate, and equal legal treatment of racial and national minorities—West Germans secured a higher ranking than did other Europeans; that is, a larger percentage of Germans regarded these political liberties as basic human rights, rather than as privileges granted by the state. National sample surveys conducted only in West Germany also indicate widespread popular support for civil liberties, the Basic Law, procedural democracy, equality before the law, and institutionalized political competition.[12]

Yet FRG government officials feel threatened by the communist-controlled German Democratic Republic, by left-wing terrorists, and by youth sympathetic to left-wing policies. As a response, city and state governments have required loyalty oaths and security checks for civil servants; the Constitutional Court has ruled that government employees may not "attack the state." Teachers and other civil servants have been fired for belonging to leftist organizations or living with "anarchists." One man who edited a book criticizing the prison system was charged with "defaming the state and its officials." The political police have raided printers, publishing houses, and bookstores. State governments have censored television broadcasts. In 1976, the federal legislature passed an antiterrorist law giving government officials the right to read letters and written communications passed between accused terrorists and their attorneys. This law reflects the historic German assumption that the state guarantees freedom to the individual, who possesses no rights independent of the state. Hence, although the Federal Republic is far more democratic than any of the three preceding political systems, elite actions to curtail civil liberties reveal an insecure attitude toward political opposition.[13]

In conclusion, West German political stability has stemmed from its efficient economic performance. Because the West German public perceives that the government institutions under the Bonn republic have brought favorable economic and political results, generalized support for the Federal Republic has grown stronger since the early 1950s. Mass participation in political decision making has recently increased. For example, voluntary groups have formed to support nuclear disarmament, peace with the Soviet Union, ecology, and the removal of government restraints on political freedom. Despite these participatory developments, the FRG still remains a political system in which a political elite, especially party leaders and civil servants, dominates public policymaking and the mass media. Citizens perceive that they have limited control over their leaders, who form coalitions and bargain over policy contents. So long as unemployment and inflation rates remain low and political officials govern efficiently, the system will retain its stability. However, if economic performance declines and the elite cannot resolve social problems, the pragmatic legitimacy may weaken, thereby leading to a loss of normative acceptance shown toward the political system.[14]

Notes

1. See Volker Rittberger, "Revolution and Pseudo-Democratization: The Formation of the Weimar Republic," in *Crisis, Choice, and Change: Historical Studies of Political Development*, ed. Gabriel A. Almond, Scott C. Flanagan, and Robert J. Mundt (Boston: Little, Brown, 1973), pp. 291–299; Richard Rubinson, "Political Transformation in Germany and the United States," in *Social Change in the Capitalist World Economy*, ed. Barbara Hockey Kaplan (Beverly Hills, Calif.: Sage, 1978), pp. 50–54; Guido Goldman, "The German Political System," in *Patterns of Government*, 3d ed., ed. Samuel H. Beer and Adam B. Ulam (New York: Random House, 1973), pp. 473–482; John R. Gillis, "Germany," in *Crises of Political Development in Europe and the United States*, ed. Raymond Grew (Princeton, N.J.: Princeton University Press, 1978), pp. 323–332; Seymour Martin Lipset, *The First New Nation* (New York: Basic Books, 1963), pp. 232–242.

2. Alexander Gerschenkron, *Bread and Democracy in Germany* (Berkeley: University of California Press, 1943), p. 88. For a study of Edward VII's reign, see Philip Magnus, *King Edward VII* (New York: Penguin Books, 1964), pp. 335–559.

3. Goldman, "The German Political System," p. 478; Rittberger, "Revolution and Pseudo-Democratization," pp. 298–302; A. F. K. Organski, *The Stages of Political Development* (New York: Knopf, 1965), p. 67; Enid Greenberg Bloch, *The Inverse Cultures: Politics versus Philosophy in America and Germany* (Ph.D. dissertation, Department of Political Science, Cornell University, 1973).

4. Bertram Lee Woolf, *Reformation Writings of Martin Luther*, vol. 2 (London: Lutterworth Press, 1956), pp. 236, 245. See also Sheldon S. Wolin, *Politics and Vision* (Boston: Little, Brown, 1960), pp. 141–164; J. M. Porter, "Luther and Political Millenarianism: The Case of the Peasants' War," *Journal of the History of Ideas* 42 (July–September 1981): 389–406; Richard Lowenthal, "Why German Stability Is So Insecure," *Encounter* 51 (December 1978): 36.
5. Bloch, *The Inverse Cultures*, pp. 55–82; Barrington Moore, Jr., *Injustice: The Social Bases of Obedience and Revolt* (White Plains, N.Y.: Sharpe, 1978), pp. 213–220.
6. For analyses of the Nazi vote, see Goldman, "The German Political System," pp. 489–496; Rittberger, "Revolution and Pseudo-Democratization," pp. 366–382; Peter H. Merkl, *Political Violence under the Swastika: 581 Early Nazis* (Princeton, N.J.: Princeton University Press, 1975); Loren K. Waldman, "Mass-Society Theory and Religion: The Case of the Nazis," *American Journal of Political Science* 20 (May 1976): 319–326; Thomas Childers, "The Social Bases of the Nationalist Vote," *Journal of Contemporary History* 11 (October 1976): 17–42; David Abraham, "State and Classes in Weimar Germany," *Politics and Society* 7, no. 3 (1977): 229–266; David Abraham, *The Collapse of the Weimar Republic: Political Economy and Crisis* (Princeton, N.J.: Princeton University Press, 1981); Jürgen W. Falter, "Radicalization of the Middle Classes or Mobilization of the Unpolitical?" *Social Science Information* 20 (May 1981): 389–430; R. I. McKibbin, "The Myth of the Unemployed: Who Did Vote for the Nazis?" *Australian Journal of Politics and History* 25 (August 1969): 25–40; Lewis E. Hill, Charles E. Butler, and Stephen A. Lorenzen, "Inflation and the Destruction of Democracy: The Case of the Weimar Republic," *Journal of Economic Issues* 11 (June 1977): 299–313; *The Path to Dictatorship: 1918–1933* (Garden City, N.Y.: Doubleday Anchor, 1966), pp. 203–210; Moore, *Injustice*, pp. 400–410; James R. Kurth, "Industrial Change and Political Change: A European Perspective," in *The New Authoritarianism in Latin America*, ed. David Collier (Princeton, N.J.: Princeton University Press, 1979), pp. 346–349; Tim Mason, "National Socialism and the Working Class, 1925–May, 1933," *New German Critique* 4 (Spring 1977): 49–93.
7. David P. Conradt, "Changing German Political Culture," in *The Civic Culture Revisited*, ed. Gabriel Almond and Sidney Verba (Boston: Little, Brown, 1980), p. 226; Elisabeth Noelle and Erich Peter Neumann, eds., *The Germans: Public Opinion Polls 1947–1966*, trans. Gerard Finan (Allensbach and Bonn: Verlag Für Demoskopie, 1967), pp. 195–197; Goldman, "The German Political System," p. 499; William Jannen, Jr., "National Socialists and Social Mobility," *Journal of Social History* 9 (Spring 1976): 339–366.
8. J. P. Stern, *Hitler: The Führer and the People* (Berkeley: University of California Press, 1975); Simon Taylor, "Symbol and Ritual under National Socialism," *British Journal of Sociology* 32 (December 1981): 504–520; Heimrich August Winkler, "German Society, Hitler, and the Illusion of Restoration, 1930–33," *Journal of Contemporary History* 11 (October 1976): 1–16; Robert H. Keyserlingk, "Hitler and German Nationalism Before 1933," *Canadian Review of Studies in Nationalism* 5 (Spring 1978): 24–44; Norman H. Baynes, ed., *The Speeches of Adolf Hitler, April 1922–August 1939*, vol. 1 (London: Oxford University Press, 1942), pp. 375–390.
9. Lipset, *The First New Nation*, pp. 237–238; Ralf Dahrendorf, *Society and Democracy in Germany* (New York: Doubleday Anchor, 1969), pp. 381–396; Goldman, "The German Political System," pp. 510–518, 566.
10. "Quality of Life in the Next Decade," *Vision* no. 92–93 (July–August 1978): 28–40; *OECD Economic Outlook* no. 30 (December 1981): 140, 142; Charles F. Andrain, *Politics and Economic Policy in Western Democracies* (North Scituate, Mass.: Duxbury Press, 1980).
11. Bruno S. Frey and Werner W. Pommerehne, "Toward a More Theoretical Foundation for Empirical Policy Analysis," *Comparative Political Studies* 11 (October 1978): 327; Bruno S. Frey, "Keynesian Thinking in Politico-Economic Models," *Journal of Post Keynesian Economics* 1 (Fall 1978): 74; Rudolf Wildenmann, "Towards a Sociopolitical Model of the German Federal Republic," *Sozialwissenschaftliches Jahrbuch für Politik* 4 (1975): 296; *World Opinion Update* 2 (January 1978): 11; James D. Wright, *The Dissent of the Governed: Alienation and Democracy in America* (New York: Academic Press, 1976), p. 121; Alan Marsh, *Protest and Political Consciousness* (Beverly Hills, Calif.:

Sage, 1977), p. 115; "Quality of Life in the Next Decade," p. 37; Conradt, "Changing German Political Culture," pp. 212–265.
12. Lowenthal, "Why German Stability Is So Insecure," pp. 31–37; Lewis J. Edinger, *Politics in West Germany*, 2d ed. (Boston: Little, Brown, 1977), pp. 7–12; *World Opinion Update* 2 (January 1978): 11; *World Opinion Update* 2 (July 1978): 85–86; David P. Conradt, "Political Culture, Legitimacy and Participation," *West European Politics* 4 (May 1981): 18–34.
13. Ivo K. Feierabend., Betty Nesvold, and Rosalind L. Feierabend, "Political Coerciveness and Turmoil: A Cross-National Inquiry," *Law and Society Review* 5 (August 1970): 105; Charles Lam Markmann, "Civil Liberties? Vas Ist Das? A Report from the German Federal Republic," *Civil Liberties Review* 1 (Fall 1974): 42–53; Martin Oppenheimer, "The New German Repression," *Nation* 223 (September 11, 1976): 201–202; Martin Oppenheimer, "West German McCarthyism," *Nation* 228 (March 17, 1979): 267–270; E. J. Hobsbawm, "The West German Witch Hunt," *New Society* 37 (July 22, 1976): 166–168; Melanie Phillips, "The German Pursuit of Law and Order," *New Society* 37 (July 29, 1976): 232–233; Kenneth A. Bollen, "Issues in the Comparative Measurement of Political Democracy," *American Sociological Review* 45 (June 1980): 387.
14. Wildenmann, "Towards a Sociopolitical Model of the German Federal Republic," pp. 283–285, 297–298; Sidney Verba, "Germany: The Remaking of Political Culture," in *Political Culture and Political Development*, ed. Lucian W. Pye and Sidney Verba (Princeton, N.J.: Princeton University Press, 1965), pp. 130–154; Conradt, "Political Culture, Legitimacy and Participation," pp. 24–26, 29–32; Kendall L. Baker, Russell J. Dalton, and Kai Hildebrandt, *Germany Transformed: Political Culture and the New Politics* (Cambridge, Mass.: Harvard University Press, 1981), pp. 21–57, 261–276.

CHAPTER
13

Orthodoxy and Revolution in Russia

> *The Supreme, Autocratic power belongs to the All-Russian Emperor. . . . Obedience to his authority, not only for wrath but also for conscience sake, is ordained by God Himself.*
> —CZAR NICHOLAS II

> *The task of the Communist Party (Bolsheviks), which is the class-conscious spokesman for the strivings of the exploited for emancipation, is to . . . understand that it is necessary to stand at the head of the exhausted people who are wearily seeking a way out and lead them along the true path, along the path of labor discipline, along the path of coordinating the task of arguing at mass meetings about the conditions of work with the task of unquestioningly obeying the will of the Soviet leader, of the dictator, during the work.*
> —V. I. LENIN

For the last 500 years, various Russian political elites have combined coercion and consensus to maintain their absolutist rule. Both before and after the Soviet revolution of 1917, sharp value cleavages fragmented elite solidarity and also divided the elite from the masses. Whether czarist officials or Communist party leaders, the top rulers centralized their authority in a powerful state bureaucracy. They relied on a comprehensive political religion, either Russian Orthodoxy or Marxism-Leninism, to legitimate their authority. Yet international warfare and foreign economic pressures threatened to undermine the elite's legitimacy. When challenged by workers' strikes, peasant revolts, and protests by Western-oriented intelligentsia, the central leaders strengthened state coercion to maintain the stability of the existing system.

Despite the frequent demands for system change since the consolidation of the Muscovite state in the mid fifteenth century, Russians have experienced long periods of systematic stability. Except for a brief time at the beginning of the 1600s, the czarist monarchical state lasted until 1917, when the Bolsheviks seized political power.[1] However great the international and domestic pressures faced by the Soviet elite during the last seventy years, the communist political system has so far remained intact.

Political Legitimacy in Czarist Russia

By stressing moral–spiritual values and a collectivist ethos, the traditional Russian elite attempted to legitimate czarist rule. Although the personal and sacred sources of legitimacy were strong, the legal bases remained weak. The czar (caesar) perceived himself as the supreme, absolute sovereign emperor of all the Russias. Unlike the situation in West Europe, where the Roman Catholic church secured autonomy from the state, in Russia the czar early gained control over the Russian Orthodox church. Rather than the church checking the state's power, the czar dominated the church. The Orthodox clergy acclaimed the divine nature of the czar, urged his subjects to obey him, and justified the centralization of the state's rule over dispersed areas. The universalist beliefs associated with the Roman Catholic church became subordinated to national values. The czar embodied Russian national identity; the Russian Orthodox church identified with the Russian national cause and promoted political unity. Thus, both czar and Russian Orthodox clergy merged secular with sacred values. As a secular ruler, the czar claimed to be the representative of God on earth. According to this rationale, God sent the czar to punish people for their sins; hence, the coercive power exercised by the state was legitimate. Because people were irrational and evil, government by impersonal laws was not possible. To guarantee obedience, the Russian elite supported rule by a coercive state and a powerful personality such as the czar, who embodied the conscience of the nation. Because the czar derived his authority from God, no legal or constitutional restraints curbed his power.[2]

From the czarist perspective, collectivist values assumed priority over an individualist ethos. Equating individualism with the materialistic, decadent pursuit of self-interest, the Russian Orthodox clergy denounced classical liberalism. For them, the individual right to pursue happiness, as stressed by English and American theorists, meant the liberty to unleash individual instincts and passions. Rather than seeking individual human rights, the people should demonstrate their obligation to God, society, and Holy Mother Russia. As interpreted by the Orthodox clergy, national conscience embodied in the czar took precedence over individual self-interest. National collective values, not individual rights to concrete benefits, thus legitimized the czarist political system.

Downfall of the Czarist State and the Provisional Government

Having lasted for over 500 years, the monarchical Russian system finally collapsed in early 1917. Why? Both foreign economic pressures and defeats in war weakened the political power as well as the legitimacy of the czarist state. Foreign investment in Russia, greater incorporation of Russia into the world economic market, and Russian army defeats during World War I all exacerbated the economic and political-economic grievances felt by key social groups—intelligentsia, factory workers, peasants, and soldiers. As the wartime situation grew more severe, trust in the czar weakened. The coercive power wielded by army and police declined. When the coercive mechanisms of the state disintegrated, the power to repress distrustful opposition groups waned. Blaming their personal misfortunes on a collective source—the government—revolutionary groups felt high political efficacy about their ability to transform the political system, including its leaders, policies, and decision-making structures. As a result of these conditions, Czar Nicholas II abdicated in February 1917.

A dual system of power emerged, with the provisional government and the soviets, mainly in Petrograd and Moscow, struggling to exercise the dominant authority. Continued defeats of Russian troops by superior German forces led to further deterioration of political and economic conditions. In October 1917, the Bolsheviks, who had superior organization and a comprehensive ideology, led the movement to topple the provisional government. After a bitter civil war lasting from mid 1918 through 1921, the Bolsheviks emerged triumphant.

DISAFFECTION OF KEY GROUPS

One reason for the political system change in 1917 involved the failure of the existing governments to retain the legitimacy of key social groups. Initially, the international economic pressures and later Russian defeats in World War I aggravated political distrust. During 1917, four groups—the radical intelligentsia, factory workers, peasants, and soldiers—played an especially important role in toppling the czarist and provisional governments. Each group expressed moral and material grievances that the incumbent authorities could not resolve.

The radical intelligentsia—primarily teachers, students, writers, lawyers, and lower-ranking bureaucrats—perceived Russia as backward vis-a-vis West Europe. They sought rapid modernization of the society, including a greater stress on secularization, rationality, and science. In the economic sphere, they wanted rapid industrialization, which they associated with enlightenment. Deprived of high positions in the state bureaucracy, radical intellectuals believed that only a fundamental change in the existing political system would enable them to play a decisive role in reshaping Russian society. Some intellectuals tried to institute a liberal constitutional regime modeled after the parliamentary governments of Scandinavia and Britain. Other segments of the intelligentsia took a more revolutionary position, preferring either a democratic socialist republic or a more radical "proletarian dictatorship." But all these intellectuals—constitutional liberals, democratic socialists, and communists—supported the overthrow of the czarist government in early 1917.

The industrial factory workers in Moscow and Petrograd also helped secure the downfall of both the czarist regime and later the provisional government. Economically backward compared with West European countries, Russia under czarist rule experienced rapid industrialization between 1890 and 1914. Like the Prussians in Germany, the czarist elite used the state to expand the industrial base: The government built railroads, operated mines, subsidized private industries, and stimulated foreign investment. French, Belgian, British, and German capitalists invested in mining, oil production, chemical operations, and electrical engineering. As the government secured foreign loans for these investment projects, the Russian debt owed Germany, Britain, and particularly France soared. The economic conditions suffered by the factory workers weakened their support for the czarist government. Low wages, long working hours, lack of social services, and government opposition to trade union freedoms made the workers increasingly militant. Although industrial workers by 1914 constituted only about 5 percent of the labor force, they were concentrated in large factories and therefore readily available for political mobilization.

Wartime economic pressures intensified working-class discontents. As the czarist government faced continual defeats on the battlefield, its officials pushed the workers harder to expand production for the war effort. The movement of peasants to the cities resulted in overcrowded housing. Wartime defeats led to food and fuel shortages. Accelerating inflation meant that real wages declined; workers lacked the money to purchase even those goods that were available.

Business owners who could not obtain raw materials laid off more and more workers. Even after the czar abdicated, the economic situation failed to improve as the war situation worsened. Particularly in Petrograd and Moscow, the core cities of Russia, factory workers rallied to those left-wing parties promising peace, bread, and workers' control of industry.

Both before and during the First World War, the peasantry felt economic grievances that eventually motivated them to withdraw their support from the established government. Not only the factory workers but also the peasants bore the burdens of the czar's rapid industrialization policies. To finance heavy industries, the government levied high regressive taxes on the peasants and forced them to sell their grain to the state at low prices. The government then exported the grain to other countries, mainly England and Germany. When the prices for agricultural exports fell on the world market, the peasantry suffered severe losses.

Although the czar had freed the peasants from serfdom in 1861, they did not secure favorable economic benefits from the emancipation. The peasants gained more land; yet they had to pay high rents to the landlords and high interest rates to the state banks. The czar and the landed nobility still retained extensive fertile landholdings. Determined to promote rapid industrialization, the government elite did not devote enough resources to expand agricultural productivity. Agricultural technology remained primitive. As late as 1914, most peasants still practiced subsistence agriculture. The distribution of food between urban and rural areas never became efficient. Faced with high taxes, debts, and rents, the peasants remained poor, deeply resenting the czarist officials and heads of the landed estates.

The war intensified the peasants' economic suffering. As young farmers left to join the army, labor shortages developed. The Imperial army forced the peasants to sell their horses at a low price. The state also requisitioned grain, meat, and dairy products for use by soldiers and urban residents; yet the prices granted the peasants for their produce were low. After the czar's downfall, the provisional government failed to improve economic conditions for the peasantry. It did not expropriate land from the Crown and landed nobility. Although it used some military force to deter peasant-sponsored land seizures, central control over the peasantry remained ineffective. The futile attempts to requisition grain at low prices also weakened rural enthusiasm for the provisional government. By the summer of 1917, peasant discontent with the incumbent authorities had escalated. Perceiving the central government in Petrograd as distant and uncaring, the peasants sought land equality, economic security, an end to the war, and decentralization of power to rural assemblies.

DISINTEGRATION OF STATE CONTROL

The most fundamental immediate cause explaining the downfall of the czarist regime and the provisional government is that the mechanisms of state coercive control disintegrated. As Russian troops experienced increasingly severe defeats in the war, desertions from the Imperial forces mounted. A large number of soldiers returned to their rural homes, where they supported peasant land seizures and opposed the government's military and economic policies. Other soldiers, who remained in their garrisons, resisted government efforts to send them to the front lines. By early 1917, the Imperial army and navy had largely collapsed. After several army mutinies occurred, the czar abdicated the throne.

Later in 1917, the provisional government also faced desertions and mutinies. Calling for the overthrow of the provisional government, the Bolsheviks rallied several armed forces around the capital, Petrograd: a workers' militia or Red Guard of 20,000 workers, the sailors of Kronstadt and the Baltic fleet, and soldiers within the Petrograd garrison. Combined with sympathetic soldiers in Moscow, these armed forces staged a successful seizure of political power.

MOBILIZATION OF KEY GROUPS

The revolutionaries succeeded in overthrowing the established governments not only because state coercive power had disintegrated but also because they mobilized key social groups against the incumbent authorities. Whereas in the past individuals had blamed God or themselves for their personal suffering, now they blamed the central government. Because the czarist state had played the key role in the industrialization process and in the abortive prosecution of the war against Germany, its legitimacy declined when military defeats increased. Peasant soldiers became more politically aware. They had formerly perceived the war as a necessary evil sent by God; now they regarded it as the product of cunning government officials who managed the war for their selfish ends.

A growing political efficacy accompanied the tendency to blame the government for personal misfortunes. Peasants, workers, soldiers, and radical intellectuals all mobilized to change the established political system. The peasants established rural soviets, district committees, land committees, and peasant unions. Through these political organizations, peasants staged land seizures, refused to give grain to the state purchasing organizations (supply committees), and demanded higher prices for grain but lower prices for farm tools. Opposing the central government in Petrograd, they worked through local associations, mainly village communes and peasant committees. The urban factory workers cooperated with the soldiers in Petrograd to organize violent resistance against the state. Operating in soviets, unions, factory committees, and workers' militia, the workers campaigned for higher wages, an eight-hour work day, trade union freedom, workers' control of factories, and an end to inflation.

The radical intellectuals played the leading role in socialist political parties and the urban soviets. Three left-wing parties competed for dominance. The Socialist Revolutionaries, who had greatest strength in agricultural regions, articulated the need for more equal land ownership. The Mensheviks, a democratic socialist party, won some support in urban unions and in such regions as Georgia and the Caucasus. Along with the Constitutional Democrats (Kadets), the Socialist Revolutionaries and Mensheviks dominated the provisional government. The third left-wing party, the Bolsheviks, refused to participate in the provisional regime. Of all the political parties, they most strongly supported immediate Russian withdrawal from the war. They also advocated a progressive income tax, limits on war profits, land equality, and workers' control of industry.

The less well educated factory workers, primarily those employed in chemical industries and metal works, voted in city elections for the Bolsheviks, whose base of support lay in the northern cities of Petrograd and Moscow, the core areas of Russia. In the August 1917 elections to the Petrograd Duma (assembly), the Bolsheviks gained 33 percent of the total vote, only 4 percent less than the Socialist Revolutionaries, who obtained the most seats. The next month the Bolsheviks won 51 percent of the popular vote to the Moscow Duma; the second largest party, the Constitutional Democrats, secured 26 percent. Besides obtaining extensive electoral support in these two cities, the Bolshevik party rallied to its cause sailors in the Baltic fleet, soldiers stationed on the central and western fronts, and some peasants who lived in central and western provinces.

A successful coup against the provisional government occurred in October 1917. Even though in November 1917 the Bolsheviks gained only 25 percent of the national votes for the constituent assembly, the party's control of the heartland of Russia enabled it to maintain government power. Access to the railroads and telegraph lines gave the Bolsheviks an advantage over their opposition in the civil war, for they could transport the soldiers and supplies needed to win the war.

In conclusion, the Bolsheviks emerged the dominant party because they undermined both the legitimacy and the power of the provisional government. Their ideology appealed to important social groups, especially in the core areas of Russia. Lenin's slogan of "peace, land, and bread" attracted support from soldiers, sailors, factory workers, and some peasants who suffered from war defeats, inflation, unemployment, and food shortages. Although the Bolshevik party scarcely operated in the monolithic way outlined by Lenin in 1903, it did have a stronger, better funded organization than either the Mensheviks or the Socialist Revolutionaries. Unlike the organizational apparatus that emerged after the Bolsheviks seized power, the party's structure during 1917 showed decentralization, free debate, and factional arguments about the best policies to pursue. This flexible mode of organizational operation increased the party's support among workers, soldiers, sailors, and intellectuals around Petrograd and Moscow, thereby enabling the Bolsheviks to consolidate their political power.[3]

Stability of the Soviet Union

After destroying the old regime's authority, the Bolshevik leaders began to create a new base of power and legitimacy. Soviet officials sought to industrialize the economy, modernize society, but maintain the stability of the political system. Since Lenin assumed control in late 1917, the Soviet elite has employed both coercion and consensus to realize its objectives.

COERCIVE POWER

In the political sphere, the Communist party centralized state power throughout Russia, gained extensive control over voluntary associations, and ruled through coercion. Although in 1917 the Bolsheviks had promised greater decentralization, power to the soviets, worker control of industries, trade union freedom, and equality of land ownership, they abandoned these goals during the civil war period (1918–1921). A highly centralized party–state dictatorship emerged. The Communist elite in Moscow strengthened its centralized power. After repressing opposition parties, the CPSU also curtailed the autonomy of trade unions, factory committees, soviets, rural communes, and village assemblies. As early as two months after seizing power, Lenin ordered the Cheka (the All-Russian Extraordinary Commission for Combating Counter-Revolution, Sabotage, and Speculation—the security police) to arrest opposition leaders from the Socialist Revolutionary and Menshevik parties.

After the civil war ended in 1921, the government allowed greater freedom, especially in the economic and cultural spheres. The New Economic Policy retained state ownership of large-scale industries, transportation, banking, and foreign trade; yet it allowed private ownership of light industries and trading firms. Privately owned farms and farm cooperatives carried out agricultural production. In the cultural sector, intellectuals secured greater freedom to express their ideas. Youth and women gained more rights. Educational innovations modeled after John Dewey's progressive ideas gave the school system new vitality. Artists and writers presented new works to the public. Even in the political sphere, party and government organizations debated about the best ways to socialize the economy. Although Lenin discouraged organized factions in the CPSU, factional arguments still enlivened party meetings. All these policies helped legitimize the new Soviet regime.

After Stalin consolidated his rule in 1928, the Soviet political system became more coercively organized than when Lenin had guided the state. During the 1930s, Stalin strengthened the power of the central state, especially the power wielded by the secret police and the professional military. The Communist party came to dominate all social groups, including trade unions, cooperatives, and neighborhood associations. Factional discussions within the Party ended; Stalin and his close associates made all the key decisions. Particularly between 1936 and 1938, political terror became common. During the purge of top Communist party leaders, 70 percent of the Party's Central Committee members died. More than 100,000 lower-ranking party leaders also perished in the purge.

The state-induced program of rapid industrialization under Stalin brought widespread economic suffering. Heavy industry—steel, iron, chemicals, petroleum, electrical engineering—took priority over the manufacture of consumer goods. As Stalin concentrated all resources on industrial investment, rather than consumption, workers' real wages declined. Managers, professionals, and technical experts gained higher status and pay. Wages thus became more unequal. To supply grain and workers to the new urban industrial centers, Stalin ordered the collectivization of agriculture in 1928. Private ownership of farms ended; collective farms and state farms became the dominant mode of agricultural production. Government officials forced the peasants to surrender to the state a specified quota of grain at low prices. Peasants received low incomes, few government social services, and few educational opportunities.

In the cultural sphere, the free experimentation of the 1920s ended. As in the czarist years, schools once again stressed the need for hierarchy and discipline. Women and youth lost their rights. Artists, writers, and intellectuals no longer had the freedom to discuss their ideas or to engage in spontaneous expression.[4] In short, under Stalin, repressive policies permeated all sectors of society: the polity, economy, and culture.

Naturally, this harsh repression alienated wide segments of the Soviet citizenry. A sharp value cleavage emerged between the party–state elite and the masses, especially peasants and unskilled factory workers. Elite and masses expressed divergent attitudes toward both concrete benefits and moral–spiritual values. Whereas the elite supported rapid industrialization and the allocation of resources for production (investment), the masses favored expanded social services and consumer goods. The elite regarded the Russian nation as the instrument to realize an eventual world revolution. Participating in a cult of Marxist-Leninist ideology, party leaders viewed the Communist Party of the Soviet Union as the embodiment of ideological ends. In contrast, the masses saw Russian nationalism as an ultimate end in itself. Bored with Marxist-Leninist political education, they perceived Mother Russia as the embodiment of collective values.

Attitudes toward collectivism and individualism also reflected a partial elite–mass gap. True, both the leaders and citizens agreed on certain collective values: social order, central control, firm political leadership, state supervision of moral behavior, government planning, and government provision of social services. All Russians, regardless of their political status, felt a strong need for a group identification and affiliation. Yet in other respects, especially the value of collective organization versus individual spontaneity, the elite and masses took different positions. The party–state officials asserted the dominance of political organization over the individual. Because Party and government controlled social groups, especially churches, family, and personal networks, individuals felt constricted. Opposed to the elite stress on the supremacy of politics, the masses rejected the harsh, demanding, punitive, bureaucratic authority the elite imposed. Rank-and-file citizens have sought more freedom to assert their individual spontaneity and to express their emotions fully. They desired more autonomy for their private lives, particularly in their family, neighborhood, church, and peer group. From their perspective, political authorities should function in a sympathetic, nurturant, supportive, warm, and informal way, not in a harsh, depriving, punitive, cold, bureaucratic manner.

In short, coercive authority has led to outward compliance but inner attitudinal resistance. Although the application of coercive power under Stalinist rule did maintain the stability of the Soviet system, individuals tried to withdraw from active political participation.[5]

CONSENSUAL POWER

Despite the extensive coercion in the Soviet Union, no Soviet leader, including Stalin, has overlooked the need for consensual power to maintain political stability. All Communist party leaders have attempted to legitimate their rule by ideological and material means. Even though Lenin discouraged a cult of the Party, Stalin during the 1930s established a secular political religion that paralleled the operation of the Russian Orthodox church. In effect, the revolution became orthodox. Under the czars, the Orthodox church functioned as a charismatic institution closely linked to the Russian state. The sacred beliefs rested on Orthodox theology. Serving as the key decision makers, the priests had the responsibility to guard against a loss of faith and to save the people from sin, corruption, and exploitation. A tension between universalism and nationalism plagued Orthodox religious leaders. Although they participated in a universalist Christian faith, they also regarded Holy Mother Russia as the center of Christendom and viewed Moscow as the Third Rome. Thus, the Russian state and church had the national destiny to redeem the world.

By contrast, Soviet leaders articulated atheistic beliefs and struggled to curb the power of the Russian Orthodox church; however, the revolutionary secular political religion under Stalin resembled the old orthodoxy. The Communist party operated as a charismatic institution directing the central state. Marxist-Leninist ideology became the center of new sacred beliefs. Party cadres functioned as the key decision makers. Trying to avert a loss of ideological enthusiasm among the masses, they strove to redeem Russian society from economic backwardness and capitalist oppression. Like the Orthodox clergy, the Communist leaders also have faced a tension between nationalism and universalism. Marxism constituted a set of universalistic beliefs; Marx wanted the workers of the world to unite against capitalist oppression. Despite this universalist ethos, Soviet leaders have also affirmed nationalistic values. Opposed to the concept of polycentrism, under which many centers of communism retain their autonomy, they perceive Moscow as the center of world communism. For them, the CPSU has the duty to redeem the world from economic backwardness and capitalist exploitation.[6]

Stalin not only relied on ideological orthodoxy to consolidate his rule but also tried to gain greater pragmatic legitimacy. Soviet victories over the Nazis in World War II reinforced Stalin's support. Survey studies conducted among Russian refugees who left the Soviet Union during World War II indicate that they also supported certain government economic and social policies, especially state ownership of heavy industry, the mass public education program, low-cost public housing, the comprehensive health care system, widespread opportunities for employment, and such cultural facilities as libraries, theaters, operas, and museums. These refugees, however, strongly attacked the Stalinist terror, political oppression, collective farm system, harsh labor discipline, forced pace of industrialization, lack of consumer goods, and low living standards.[7]

Since the death of Stalin in 1953, Soviet leaders have moved to abandon some repressive features of Stalinist rule and to expand the concrete benefits granted by the government. Terror and the coercive power of the secret police have declined. Yet the elite still curtails civil liberties, practices censorship, suppresses demands for regional independence, opposes the free discussion of political issues even within the Party, and deters dissidents' activities. The importance of secular political religion has also waned. Soviet leaders now concentrate on providing material benefits as the primary way to legitimate the system. During the 1970s, wage equality increased; inflation and unemployment rates remained low. The average citizens, especially state and collective farmers, gained higher income, more social services, and greater access to consumer goods. Through the mass education program and the rapid industrialization policies, the Party provided opportunities for upward mobility to workers, peasants, and non-Russian nationalities. By joining the Party and gaining an advanced education, members of these groups have become engineers, administrators, and party officials—the people with the highest status and pay.[8]

Today the degree of political trust and efficacy felt by various groups in the social stratification partly explains the stability of the Soviet political system. Groups at the bottom of the social stratification hierarchy—the collective farmers and unskilled workers—express the greatest alienation. Although distrusting the system, they will hardly lead a revolt because they lack confidence in their political effectiveness. Fatalistic and resigned to the status quo, they withdraw into their private worlds. The skilled industrial workers, compared with the collective farmers, grant the system more trust and legitimacy; yet these workers also feel politically ineffective.

Communist party leaders, government officials, and managers of state enterprises comprise the Soviet elite. They dominate political decision making, earn the highest income, and receive the most status. Basically satisfied with most aspects of the system, they demonstrate high trust in government and high political efficacy.

Some professionals—academicians, artists, writers, journalists, scientists—lead the main dissident movements. Feeling politically effective yet distrustful of party–state officials and certain public policies, they constitute the greatest challenge to Soviet legitimacy. Through incorporating them into party-guided organizations, censoring their work, imprisoning them, and occasionally exiling them, the Communist elite tries to silence their protests.[9]

Given the weakness of dissident groups, the Communist party leaders will likely maintain the basic aspects of the current Soviet system: the single party dictatorship, centralized planned economy, and restrictions on cultural freedom. In the contemporary USSR, political orthodoxy has thus triumphed over revolutionary experimentation.

Notes

1. Walter M. Pintner, "Russia," in *Crises of Political Development in Europe and the United States,* ed. Raymond Grew (Princeton, N.J.: Princeton University Press, 1978), pp. 347–380.
2. See Jerry F. Hough and Merle Fainsod, *How the Soviet Union Is Governed* (Cambridge, Mass.: Harvard University Press, 1979), pp. 3–9; Stephen White, *Political Culture and Soviet Politics* (New York: St. Martin's Press, 1979), pp. 22–63; Reinhard Bendix, *Kings or People: Power and the Mandate to Rule* (Berkeley: University of California Press, 1978), pp. 88–127.
3. For analyses of the Russian revolutions of 1917, see Hough and Fainsod, *How the Soviet Union Is Governed,* pp. 38–73; Theda Skocpol, *States and Social Revolutions* (Cambridge, England: Cambridge University Press, 1979), pp. 87–99, 128–140, 206–213; Mary McAuley, *Politics and the Soviet Union* (New York: Penguin Books, 1977), pp. 21–79; Arthur L. Stinchcombe, *Theoretical Methods in Social History* (New York: Academic Press, 1978), pp. 31–76; John L. H. Keep, *The Russian Revolution: A Study in Mass Mobilization* (New York: Norton, 1976); Alexander Rabinowitch, *The Bolsheviks Come to Power: The Revolution of 1917 in Petrograd* (New York: Norton, 1976); Graeme J. Gill, "The Mainsprings of Peasant Action in 1917," *Soviet Studies* 30 (January 1978): 63–86; William G. Rosenberg, "The Russian Municipal Elections of 1917: A Preliminary Computation of Returns," *Soviet Studies* 21 (July 1969): 131–163, esp. 161; Diane Koenker, "The Evolution of Party Consciousness in 1917: The Case of the Moscow Workers," *Soviet Studies* 30 (January 1978): 38–62.
4. Hough and Fainsod, *How the Soviet Union Is Governed,* pp. 74–191; Skocpol, *States and Social Revolutions,* pp. 213–235; Keep, *The Russian Revolution,* pp. 464–471.
5. See Raymond A. Bauer, Alex Inkeles, and Clyde Kluckhohn, *How the Soviet System Works* (New York: Vintage Books, 1956); Alex Inkeles, Eugenia Hanfmann, and Helen Beier, "Modal Personality and Adjustment to the Soviet Socio-Political System," *Human Relations* 11, no. 1 (1958): 3–22; Zvi Gitelman, "Soviet Political Culture: Insights from Jewish Emigrés," *Soviet Studies* 29 (October 1977): 543–564; Stephen White, "Continuity and Change in Soviet Political Culture: An Emigré Study," *Comparative Political Studies* 11 (October 1978): 381–395; White, *Political Culture and Soviet Politics,* pp. 113–142, 166–190.
6. Frederick O. Bonkovsky, "American Civil Religion—and Others," *Worldview* 19 (October 1976): 14–17; Reinhard Meier, "The Power of Russian Tradition," *Swiss Review of World Affairs* 28 (March 1979): 21–25.
7. Bauer, Inkeles, and Kluckhohn, *How the Soviet System Works,* pp. 248–257.
8. Hough and Fainsod, *How the Soviet Union Is Governed,* pp. 237–268, 291–293, 561–567.
9. Jeffrey W. Hahn, "Stability and Change in the Soviet Union: A Developmental Perspective," *Polity* 10 (Summer 1978): 542–567.

CHAPTER
14

Conclusion: Political Legitimacy, Policy Performance, and System Change

> *People's definition of the situation they are in is powerfully determined by what situation they are in, and that is an institutional product. . . . What an army consists of is a system for maintaining the definition of the situation, in each soldier's mind, that says he had better obey—the way armies break down in revolutions cannot be understood otherwise.*
> —ARTHUR L. STINCHCOMBE

The analysis of political stability in the United States, Britain, Germany, and Russia has explained how beliefs about legitimacy combine with the structural situation to shape the degree of systemic change. As we have seen, during the last 200 years, the United States and Britain have maintained greater continuity of their political regimes, including the basic values, fundamental laws, and institutional arrangements. Although leaders, public policies, and policy results have changed over this period, the political regime has undergone fewer alterations. By contrast, Germans and Russians have experienced far greater transformations of the political regime. The Soviet revolution of 1917 marked a dramatic change in fundamental values, rules for making public decisions, and ways of exercising political power. During the last century, Germany also witnessed several regime changes: the Second Reich, the Weimar Republic, the Nazi Third Reich, and the Federal Republic. How do attitudes toward political legitimacy interact with the power of political organizations and social groups to influence greater regime change in Russia and Germany?

As Arthur L. Stinchcombe suggests, the structural situation—the power of political organizations vis-a-vis social groups, the network of economic relations, the geopolitical location of a nation—shapes motivations, purposes, perceptions of political reality, interpretations of legitimate authority, definitions of the existing situation, and visions of alternative political regimes. In turn, these beliefs stimulate discontented social group leaders and political activists to press for changes in the political regime. Particularly when public policies enacted by the existing government fail to alleviate grievances felt by powerful social groups and political organizations and when the government lacks the power to crush the opposition, the prospects for a regime change become greater.[1] Thus, to understand systemic changes, we need to examine both the beliefs and the resources of social groups and political organizations.

Structural Crises and Political Legitimacy

From a general perspective, the causes of systemic changes stem from the interaction among structural crises, structural opportunities for change, incentives to change the political regime, policy responses to the crises, and attitudes toward political legitimacy. National crises include such problems as high unemployment, high inflation rates, low growth rates, economic inequalities, gaps between wealthier urban areas and poorer rural regions, floods, earthquakes, famines, and civil wars. These crises usually involve conflict relationships between the state and social groups and among different antagonistic groups—for example, peasants versus landlords, Catholics versus Protestants, Irish versus English. International crises pit one state against another state. Foreign invasions, colonial domination, and international wars create destabilizing tendencies within a country. Similarly, worldwide economic pressures—depressions, recessions, oil price hikes, falling prices for agricultural produce on the world market—may also weaken a government's power at home.

National and international crises affect both the structural opportunities and the attitudinal incentives for systemic change. Because crises weaken the state's coercive and consensual power, they expand the structural opportunities for opposition movements to overthrow the established political regime. If the civilian government, army, and police can neither use coercion effectively nor form a consensus, the system becomes more open to change. From the structural perspective, subordinate social groups and opposition political movements gain greater independence from the state and the dominant elite. As a result, opposition leaders raise their expectations about the possibility of mounting a successful challenge against the old regime. The crises, such as war and economic pressures, also intensify the grievances felt by antiregime organizations. From the attitudinal standpoint, these expectations and grievances act as powerful incentives to change the existing political regime.[2]

The chances for toppling a political regime depend on policy officials' responses to the crises and grievances. If their policies are ineffective in coping with the structural crises and widespread grievances, the prospects for a systemic change grow more favorable. Yet ineffective policy performance by itself does not necessarily lead to fundamental changes in the political regime. Only when policy ineffectiveness combines with a disintegration of state power and a loss of legitimacy can the opposition threaten the regime's stability. As the established leaders lose control over society, they can less easily formulate and implement policies that will mollify the opposition. When the incumbent government officials make ineffective policies, belief in the regime's legitimacy often declines, thereby increasing the prospects for a systemic breakdown.

Particularly when the politically mobilized sectors of a society view the existing regime as illegitimate, this loss of legitimacy usually signals the disintegration of the old regime. As part IV has indicated, beliefs about legitimate authority comprise four key dimensions:

1. Political efficacy
2. Trust
3. Attribution of blame for personal grievances
4. The vision of a new alternative political system that promises to allay these grievances

Most often, political systems remain fairly stable because people at the bottom of the social stratification system—groups with the greatest objective grievances—feel politically ineffective, powerless to change the status quo. As Barrington Moore has observed: "Those who are the worst off are generally the last to organize and make their voices heard. Those at the bottom of the social heap are generally the last ones to hear the news that there has been a change in the capacity of human society to cope with the miseries of human existence."[3] Resigned to their fate, they fear taking steps that will bring severe state repression. Yet when structural crises weaken the coercive power of the state, subordinate groups often become aroused from their political slumber. As their political efficacy grows stronger, they join opposition movements led by aspiring political leaders who feel efficacious to change the existing regime. These leaders usually come from such relatively well educated professions as teaching, religion, literature, journalism, law, medicine, and the lower ranks of the civil service. Combined with their strong political efficacy, their high distrust of the political regimes makes these groups pose a severe challenge to the existing government.

Political regimes undergo systemic change when they lose the trust of powerful social groups and such political agencies as the armed forces, police, and segments of the civilian bureaucracy. Political trust stems from both material and moral sources. When the established government can no longer provide either material satisfactions (employment opportunities, low inflation rates, education, health services, physical security) or moral benefits (righteousness, justice, dignity, decent human treatment), its legitimacy may plummet. If the opposition can offer desired moral and material benefits to aggrieved groups, this transference of legitimacy to the opposition may trigger the overthrow of the old regime.

The attribution of blame for personal grievances also affects the degree of political stability. Grievances, frustrations, and relative deprivations pervade all societies. If subordinate groups blame God, the devil, fate, luck, or the individual for their deprived conditions, the political system enjoys greater stability. Only when opposition leaders convince discontented individuals that the political regime bears the blame for personal grievances does a system breakdown become likely. Under these conditions, the existing political regime no longer appears legitimate because it cannot make policies that resolve the grievances. Opposition leaders assert that only new basic values, new fundamental rules for making political decisions, and transformed institutional arrangements will remedy current problems.

Finally, the likelihood of systemic change increases when a powerful opposition holds a vision of an alternative political regime that will supposedly resolve structural crises and widespread personal grievances. Ideologues usually sketch a vision of a transformed political system. Through political education, propaganda, and mass mobilization, they try to convince members of deprived groups to share this political vision. In turn, the shared vision of an alternative political regime serves as a magnet that pulls alienated individuals toward participation in an opposition movement to change the political system.

Political Change in Four Nations

These general perspectives on the reasons for systemic change explain the greater political continuity in the United States and Britain than in Germany and Russia during the last hundred years. Because of their geographical locations, Germany and Russia have experienced more vulnerability to international structural crises, especially war. As land powers located in continental Europe, these two states frequently faced foreign invasions. Wars threatened the disintegration of the states' coercive power. Geopolitically vulnerable, German and Russian elites erected strong states to maintain their political systems. Governments assumed crucial responsibilities to make policies that affected the lives of all citizens. Aggrieved groups naturally focused on the established regime as the main source of blame for their deprivations.

Yet when a grave structural crisis, such as war or economic pressures, undermined the state's legitimacy, the collapse of state power expanded the possibilities for fundamental changes in the political regime. For example, the Second Reich disintegrated because its leaders lost the war to the Allied powers. Similarly, in Russia during 1917, both the czarist regime and the provisional government collapsed partly because their leaders could not wage a successful war against the invading German armies. Although war did not cause the downfall of the Weimar Republic, severe economic pressures weakened its legitimacy. Rampant inflation in 1923, followed by high unemployment from 1929 through 1932, led to widespread alienation from the Weimar political institutions. Through Nazi electoral tactics and the stormtroopers' violent activities, Hitler became chancellor and replaced the quasi-democratic Weimar regime with the dictatorial Third Reich. Like the Second Reich, it fell because of defeat in war.

The United States and Britain have faced less severe structural crises than Germany and Russia. Civil wars posed a weaker threat to established institutions in England and America. Britain's civil war took place in the seventeenth century; the Americans fought their civil war during the 1860s. After these civil wars ended, the defeated sides—the English royalists and the white Southerners—regained entry into the political decision process. As a result of this accommodating strategy, they came to accept the political regime's legitimacy. Internationally, the United States and Britain remained less geopolitically vulnerable to invasions by armies from enemy states. As naval powers, they conducted most wars overseas, not on the home territory. Hence, political leaders perceived little need for a powerful state to resist foreign aggression. Influenced by classical liberal beliefs, expectations focused on the individual and on private groups to resolve grievances. The central government assumed less responsibility for meeting structural challenges. Because of the lower expectations on government institutions, fewer group pressures arose for fundamental changes in the political regime when structural crises, such as the 1930s worldwide depression, did erupt.

The Americans and British have historically granted stronger legitimacy to the dominant political institutions than have the Germans and the Russians. The governing elites successfully reconcile divergent moral and material values in complementary institutions. The most alienated individuals—especially those with the greatest grievances at the bottom of the social stratification system—show the weakest sense of political effectiveness. Rather than blaming the political regime for their personal grievances, they place the greatest responsibility on fate, bad luck, the individual, or specific government officeholders and public policies. Lacking a vision of an alternative political regime, even the most distrustful people display little willingness to transform the basic values, constitutional framework, and institutional arrangements, such as the British parliamentary system or the U.S. separation of powers system. Instead, to alleviate their grievances, they focus on changing incumbent political leaders, public policies, and the operation of government institutions so that the existing institutions become more responsive to unmet needs.[4]

By contrast, at least until the end of World War II, the basic political institutions in Russia and Germany enjoyed weaker legitimacy. Particularly during 1917 in Russia and the 1920s through the early 1930s in Germany, the incumbent authorities proved unable to provide moral and material benefits that mollified alienated groups. As the structural crises—war and economic ruin—intensified, opposition leaders became more distrustful. State repression weakened. Antiregime activists gained greater political efficacy. Group grievances escalated. Such opposition movements as the Bolsheviks in Russia and the Nazis in Germany seized the opportunity to press for a fundamental transformation of the political regime, one that would institute new values, new rules for making government decisions, and new institutional arrangements. Blaming the whole system, not just specific leaders or policies, for the grave crises, the Bolshevik and Nazi ideologues sketched a vision of an alternative political regime that rallied some alienated groups behind the opposition movements. By mobilizing key groups for a systemic change, the Bolshevik and Nazi leaders developed the coercive power needed to overthrow the *ancien régime*.

Today the Federal Republic of Germany rests on a firmer basis of legitimacy than does the Soviet Union. According to national sample surveys, most West Germans express considerable satisfaction with the functioning of their political institutions. Particularly between 1955 and 1980, Germany faced comparatively low unemployment and inflation rates. The legislature, bureaucracy, and political parties all gained credit for their effectiveness in helping engineer the "economic miracle."

Few West Germans held a vision of an alternative regime that would bring more material or moral benefits than the Federal Republic. Certainly, the German Democratic Republic in East Germany offered no widespread appeal. Even during the early 1980s, when the jobless rate soared to over 7 percent, a higher figure than at any time since 1954, no powerful movement developed to change the political regime. Blaming the incumbent officeholders for the economic problems, German citizens voted in city, state, and federal elections to replace the governing Social Democratic party with the opposition Christian Democrats. In short, the pragmatic accomplishments of the Federal Republic have strengthened general support behind the parliamentary institutions. Not even the comparatively severe recession facing West Germany in the 1980s seems likely to cause the disintegration of the democratic political regime.[5]

Although the Soviet elite governs a less legitimate state than do West German policymakers, the basic USSR political institutions appear fairly stable. True, the Soviet officials have recently faced grave economic problems: low growth rates, insufficient food production, difficulties in allocating goods. Despite these structural crises, no powerful opposition has emerged to threaten the overthrow of the Soviet regime.

Contemporary Soviet leaders blend coercive with consensual power to maintain the existing system. Although most Soviet citizens reject the collective agricultural system, the repressive power of the secret police, and the lack of personal freedom, other aspects of the system win greater support, particularly government ownership of large-scale economic firms, public educational and health services, and cultural facilities, such as museums, libraries, and artistic centers. The moral symbols associated with Mother Russia also evoke widespread acceptance among the Russian populace. Significantly, the largest groups most alienated from the Soviet political system—the collective farmers and unskilled workers—express the lowest political efficacy to change the regime. Alienated groups with higher efficacy—writers, artists, intellectuals, scientists, Jews, Baptists—meet state repression when they voice opposition to Communist party rule.

Acting on orthodox Leninist principles, the CPSU organizes social groups so that their political demands become channeled into dominant political agencies. Rather than holding the whole system responsible for their personal grievances, individuals in the party auxiliaries learn to blame lower-ranking CPSU leaders, local civil servants, managers of state enterprises, and other subordinate officials. Complaints about food shortages, inefficient management of enterprises, inferior schools, and unsatisfactory health services focus on the need to dislodge unresponsive political authorities and improve policy implementation, not on demands for a fundamental systemic change. Although some aggrieved intellectuals do have a vision of an alternative political regime based on democratic socialism, constitutional liberalism, or orthodox Russian nationalism, Communist party control of the information media impedes the communication of these political alternatives. As a result, even if social groups do not grant fervent legitimacy to Marxist-Leninist ideology or Communist party rule, the current Soviet political regime will probably remain stable.[6] Only grave structural crises, such as war or economic disaster, would create the conditions for a basic systemic change.

Notes

1. See Arthur L. Stinchcombe, *Theoretical Methods in Social History* (New York: Academic Press, 1978).
2. See Theda Skocpol, *States and Social Revolutions: A Comparative Analysis of France, Russia, and China* (Cambridge, England: Cambridge University Press, 1979); Theda Skocpol, "Review Article: What Makes Peasants Revolutionary?" *Comparative Politics* 14 (April 1982): 351–375; Harvey Waterman, "Reasons and Reason: Collective Political Activity in Comparative and Historical Perspective," *World Politics* 33 (July 1981): 554–589.
3. Barrington Moore, Jr., *Injustice: The Social Bases of Obedience and Revolt* (White Plains, N.Y.: Sharpe, 1978), p. 143.
4. For an analysis of some American evidence about political alienation and support for an alternative regime, see Paul M. Sniderman, *A Question of Loyalty* (Berkeley: University of California Press, 1981), esp. pp. 134–141, 168–169.
5. Kendall L. Baker, Russell J. Dalton, and Kai Hildebrandt, *Germany Transformed: Political Culture and the New Politics* (Cambridge, Mass.: Harvard University Press, 1981), pp. 3–37, 68–93.
6. Stephen White, *Political Culture and Soviet Politics* (New York: St. Martin's Press, 1979), esp. pp. 166–190; George W. Breslauer, *Five Images of the Soviet Future: A Critical Review and Synthesis* (Berkeley: Institute of International Studies, University of California, 1978).

INDEX

Absolutist monarchy, 181–183, 201
Activists, political, 237–239
Adenauer, Konrad, 119
African states:
    autocracy in, 181, 183–186, 201
    power of, 203, 212, 213, 214–215
Alford, Robert, 251
Alienation, political, 285–286
Allende, regime of, 90
Amin, Idi, 181, 184
Anarcho-communism, 139, 140
Anderson, Charles W., 157
Aquinas, Thomas, 213
Arab Middle East, military fascism in, 147
Argentina, military fascism in, 147, 149, 186, 189–191
Aristotle, 171–172
Arrow, Kenneth J., 103
Asia:
    civil liberties in, 159
    communism in, 139
Australia:
    civil liberties in, 158
    constitutional government in, 191
    economic equality in, 161
    socialism in, 125
Austria:
    civil liberties in, 158
    socialism in, 125
Authority, attitudes toward:
    of Americans, Japanese, and Swedes, 2–3, 20–22
    of ethnic minorities, 21
Autocracy, 181, 183–186, 201, 203, 212, 213 (*see also* Absolutist monarchy)

Barbados, civil liberties in, 158
Bagehot, Walter, 314, 315, 316
Bailey, William C., 28
Ball, John, 47
Bandura, Albert, social learning theory of, 10–15
Basic law constitution, 338
Bayley, David, 17, 21, 33
Behavior and political analysis, 8–10, 17–18 (*see also* Causal analysis; Social learning theory)
Belgium, 124
Bellah, Robert, 290
Bentham, Jeremy, 317
Bismarck, Otto von, 108, 109, 113, 325
    establishment of Second Reich by, 325–330
Black Americans, 16, 21, 31, 32, 205, 247, 256, 308, 309
    struggle for equality by, 303–304
Bolivar, Simón, 212
Bolsheviks, 59, 134, 187, 209, 246, 344, 348–349, 360
Bonald, Louis de, 109, 113
Bonaparte, Napoleon, 207
Brazil, 186, 189–191
Britain, 85, 95, 118, 125
    capitalism in, 176–178
    civil liberties in, 321
    class voting in, 251, 257–259
    constitutional government in, 192–193, 194, 195–196, 198, 199, 314–321
    corporatism and, 222
    economic equality in, 161, 162–164, 233
    ethnic voting in, 247–249, 257–258
    ideological polarization in, 238, 242–244
    monarchy in, 316, 337
    parliamentary government in, 195–196, 314–321

363

364 INDEX

Britain (continued)
    political beliefs in, 203, 210
    political change in, 358-360
    political parties in, 232-233, 235-236, 238, 242-244, 257, 262, 263-264, 265-266
    political stability in, 320-321
    public policy in, 263
    role of war in, 202, 203
    socialism in, 125
    social stratification in, 321
    social structure in building power, 203, 205-206
    welfare state socialism in, 129
Bruce-Briggs, B., 23
Bulgaria, 161
Bureaucratic dictatorship, 109, 186-191, 201 (see also Communism)
Burke, Edmund, 109, 113

Calvin, John, 328
Cambodia, 134
Canada:
    civil liberties in, 158
    class voting in, 252-253
    constitutional government in, 194, 195
    economic equality in, 161, 163, 165
    ethnic voting in, 247-248
    ideological polarization in, 238, 242-244
    political parties in, 257, 262
Capitalism, 60, 74, 82-85, 117, 119, 219, 220-222
    rise of nation-states and, 176-178
    social stratification under, 78-79, 80
Capital punishment, 27-28 (see also Criminal justice system; Homicide, deterrents to)
Carter, Jimmy, the presidency of, 243, 248, 250, 254, 265, 306
Castro, Fidel, 64
Categoric groups, 49-50
Causal analysis, 34-37
CDU, see German Christian Democrats
Centralization of power, 178, 184, 187, 189, 193-195, 201
Charles I (King of England), 206, 295, 314
Charles II (King of England), 314
Chiang Kai-shek, 71, 96, 97, 187
Chile, 65, 90, 139, 147, 149, 186, 189-191
China, 58, 59-60, 64, 65-66, 71, 78, 82, 85, 86, 87, 88, 91, 225
    communism in, 134, 186, 187-188 (see also Communism)
    social change in, 96-98
Chinese communist party (CCP), 97-98, 187
Church and state, 56-60
Churchill, Randolph, 210
Churchill, Sir Winston, 109, 113
Church of England, 49, 315
Civil liberties, 158-159, 165-166, 236, 321, 338 (see also Political freedom)
Civil War, American, and political legitimacy, 297-300
Class consciousness, 93-96
Classical conservatism, see Conservatism
Classical liberalism, see Liberalism
Classless society, 131-133
Class support, 250-256, 257
Class voting, 162, 250-259 (see also Voting)

Coercion, 184, 187, 189-190, 201, 288, 309-310, 342-343
    restraints on, 192-193
Coles, Robert, 7-8
Common law, 315-316
Communism, 59, 65, 108-110, 113 (see also Bureaucratic dictatorship; Lenin, Vladimir I.; Marx, Karl; Marxism; Marxism-Leninism):
    anarcho-communism, 139, 140
    civil liberties under, 159
    development of, 130-131, 134-136
    economic equality under, 85-87, 160-161, 231-233
    ideological principles of, 106, 108, 233, 236
    public policy under, 262
    states under, 85, 87, 159, 187-188, 201 (see also names of countries)
Communist party of the Soviet Union (CPSU), 73, 359
Communist party states, see Communism, states under
Comparative analysis, 3-6, 37-39
    analysis of data for, 19-33
    collection techniques for, 15-19
    formulation of hypotheses for, 10-15
    problems of, 34-37
    statement of problem for, 7-10
Confederazione Generale Italiano del Lavoro (CGIL), 241
Consensus, lack of, and coercion, 287, 309-310
Conservatism, 112-117
    civil liberties under, 158, 165-166
    economic equality under, 165-166
    economic freedom under, 235
    ideological principles of, 108, 109, 112-113
Constant, Benjamin, 113
Constitutional government, see Nation-state(s), types of
Corporate liberalism, 122-123
Corporate socialism, 129
Corporations, economic, 176
Corporatism, 117, 219, 221, 222-224
Correctional institutions, 25-28, 32
Costa Rica, 158, 191
Criminal justice system, 3, 15, 22-28 (see also Homicide; Police)
Cromwell, Oliver, 206
Cross-national analytic style, see Comparative analysis
Cuba, 78, 85, 88, 139, 187-188
Cult of the Führer, see Nazi regime
Cultural beliefs, 3, 11-14, 15, 19-22
Cultural equality, 112, 116, 122, 147, 151 (see also Social stratification)
Cultural freedom, 111-112, 136, 138
Cultural issues, and voting, 254-255
Cultural revolution, in China, 59-60
Cultural values, 74-75
Czarist Russia, 64, 83, 203, 204, 343-349, 359, 360 (see also Bolsheviks; Lenin; Leninism)
    centralized government of, 81, 134, 181, 211
    established church in, 57, 182, 282, 343
    provisional government following, 346-347, 359
    social system in, 208-209
Czechoslovakia, 159, 161, 230-231

Dahrendorf, Ralf, 324
Davison, Emily Wilding, 48
Deductive reasoning, 105
Democratic socialism, see Socialism, Democratic
Deng Xiaoping, 91
Denmark, 85, 158
de Oliveira, Plinio Correa, 115
Depression, American, 95–96, 125, 300–301
de Sucre, José, 212
Deterrence theory, 5, 22, 23, 25, 28 (see also Social learning theory)
Dictatorship of the proletariat, 131, 135
Disraeli, Benjamin, 109, 113, 115, 210, 317
Dogmatism, scale of, 234
Dostoyevsky, Fyodor, 282

East Europe, 139, 143, 186
Economic conditions, see Homicide rate, economic conditions; Social-structural conditions
Economic equality, 30, 112, 137–139, 151, 160–166, 231–233
and inequality, 15, 85
Economic freedom, 111–112, 114, 136
Economic groups, 60–66
Economic interests, 246, 257
Economic power, access to, 71–73
Economic resources, distribution of, 72–73
Economic rights, 207, 208–212
Education:
  political, 260–261
  and politics, 62, 63, 75, 76, 106, 238, 309
Edward VII (King of England), 327
Eisenhower, Dwight David, the presidency of, 158, 243
Embourgeoisement, 63
Engels, Frederick, 133
England, see Britain
Environment, and homicide, see Social learning theory
Equality, 151 (see also Men; Social stratification; Women):
  cultural, 112, 116, 122, 147, 151
  economic, 30, 112, 137–139, 151, 160–166, 231–233
  ideological interpretations of, 151
  meaning of, 103–105, 110–112
  racial, 232
Erhard, Ludwig, 119
Ethnic groups, 15, 16, 21, 30–33, 53–55, 56, 75, 76–77, 245, 246–249, 250, 251, 257

Fanon, Frantz, 64
Fascism (see also Hitler, Adolf; Mussolini, Benito):
  civil liberties under, 159
  economic equality under, 161
  equality under, 146
  freedom under, 143–146
  ideological principles of, 108, 109, 141–146
Federal Bureau of Investigation (FBI), 24, 158
The Federalist Papers, 172, 192, 290
Federal Republic of Germany (FRG), see Germany, West
Feudalism, 77, 78, 79, 80, 81–82
Finland, 158

Finney, Charles, 297
Firearms, 21, 22–23, 34–35, 36
Force, see Coercion
Ford, Gerald, the presidency of, 243, 305
France, 125, 159, 181
  capitalism in, 177–179
  class voting in, 252–253
  communism in, 62–63, 134
  constitutional government in, 191, 192–193, 195, 197–199
  economic equality in, 161, 165
  ideological polarization in, 240
  political beliefs in, 203, 211
  political freedom in, 233–235
  political parties in, 233–235, 240, 257, 261
  role of war in, 203, 204
  social structure in development of power, 203, 206–208
France, Anatole, 69, 84
Franco, Francisco, 149, 214
Free democrats (FDP), 336
Freedom:
  ideological interpretations of, 134–137, 150
  meaning of, 103–105, 110–112, 134–137
  and political parties, 233–236
  restraints on individuals, 113, 114–115
  types of, 111–115
Friedman, Milton, 242
Friedrich, Carl J., 105

Garrison, William Lloyd, 297
Gaullists, 235
GDR, see German Democratic Republic (East)
George III (King of England), 295, 296
Germain, Gino, 147
German Christian Democrats (CDU), 240, 241, 249, 262, 336
German Democratic Republic (East), 324, 360–361
German Federal Republic (West), see Germany, West
Germany, see German Democratic Republic (East); Germany, West; Second Reich; Third Reich; Weimar Republic
Germany, East, 324, 360–361
Germany, West, 73, 85, 95, 118–119, 125, 129, 335–339
  civil liberties in, 159, 338
  class voting in, 251, 258–259
  constitutional government in, 194–195
  economic equality in, 161, 165
  ideological polarization in, 240
  moral-spiritual values in, 327, 337
  political legitimacy in, 337
  political parties in, 240, 257, 262, 263, 265
  religious voting in, 249
Goldwater, Barry, 117, 232
Government, 171–176, 219–220
  dimensions of power, 169–170, 174
Government activities, coordination of, 180–181, 185, 187, 189, 195–198, 201
Gransci, Antonio, 109, 140–141, 159
Great Britain, see Britain
Greece, 159
Gross domestic product (GDP), 200
Gross national product (GNP), 72

Groups, *see* Social groups
Guevara, Che, 64, 88
Gurr, Ted, 32–33

Habash, George, 64
Hamilton, Alexander, 177–178, 192, 290 (*see also* Madisonianism)
Handguns, and homicide, 22–23, 34–35, 36
Hardie, Keir, 50
Hasek, Jaroslav, 229–230
Hayek, Friedrich, A., 109, 120, 242
Hegel, G. W. F., 34, 39, 172
Hindenburg, Paul von, 332
Hintze, Otto, 281, 282
Hitler, Adolf, 11, 58, 104, 108, 109, 112, 142–143, 149, 159, 214, 223, 300, 359
  beliefs of, 143–147
  economic equality under, 161
  growth of power, 331–335
Hobbes, Thomas, 8
  treatment of prisoners viewed as Hobbesian war, 27
Holistic analytical style, 37–38, 39 (*see also* Comparative analysis)
Holland, *see* the Netherlands
Homicide (*see also* Criminal justice system; Cultural beliefs; Social learning theory):
  causes of, 3, 10, 33
  deterrents to, 5, 13, 20–22, 24–28
Homicide rate:
  comparison of, in Japan, Sweden, United States, 3, 4, 15, 19–33
  economic conditions and, 15, 29, 30, 31, 36
  demographic variables and, 30–31
Hoover, Herbert, 109, 300–301
Houphouët-Boigny, Félix, 181
Howe, Geoffrey, 317
Hungary, 158, 161

Iceland, 134, 158
Ideology (*see also* Communism; Conservatism; Fascism; Liberalism; Socialism, Democratic):
  party, 231–244
  polarization of, 239–244
  political, 105–112, 157–158, 237
India, 191
Individualism, 308–309, 316, 329–330, 343
Industrialization, 61–62, 85, 87 (*see also* Revolution, Industrial)
Interest aggregation, 261–262, 268
International Working Men's Association, 133
Ireland, 56, 74, 158
Islam, 56
Italy, 106, 147, 159
  anarcho-communism in, 139, 140
  class voting in, 252–253
  communism in, 134
  constitutional government in, 193, 195
  economic equality in, 161, 165
  fascism in, 141–143 (*see also* Mussolini, Benito)
  ideological polarization in, 238, 240–244
  political parties in, 233–235, 238, 240–242, 257, 262
  religious groups in, 249

Japan, 82, 83, 191
  homicide rate in, 3, 4, 20, 33

Japan (*continued*)
  penal system in, 25–27
Jaworski, Leon, 305
Jefferson, Thomas, 296–297
Jesus Christ, 104, 116
Johnson, Lyndon B., 232, 304
  presidency of, 158
Joseph, Keith, 117, 210, 317

Kennedy, John F., the presidency of, 158, 232, 248, 250
Kenney, Annie, 47, 48, 49
Kenney, Jessie, 48
Kingdom of God, and political movements, 59, 90, 127
KRUM (Association for the Humanizing of the Penal System), 25

Labor unions, *see* Trade Unions; Unions
Labour party (British), 62–63, 162–163, 206
Laissez-faire, 84, 117, 118, 119–120, 122, 148, 177, 179 (*see also* Capitalism)
Laos, 134
Latin America, 143, 159
  dictatorships in, 189–191
  political beliefs in, 203, 213–214
  role of war in, 203, 212
  social structure in development of power, 203, 212–213
Lazarus, symbol of, 90
Left versus right, origin of, as political metaphor, 104
Left-wing parties, definition of, 231
Legitimacy, political, *see* Political legitimacy
Lenin, Vladimir I., 58–59, 64, 78, 94, 109, 130–131, 152, 187, 209, 342, 351 (*see also* Leninism; Marxism-Leninism):
  assumption of power by, 349–350
  ideology of, 134–139
Leninism, 104, 112, 140, 142–143, 159, 211, 361 (*see also* Marxism; Marxism-Leninism):
  cultural freedom, 136, 138
  economic equality and, 137–139, 160–161
  freedom, 134–137
  historical development of, 134–137
Levitin, Teresa, 303
Liberal ideologies, contemporary:
  corporate liberalism, 122–123
  libertarianism, 122
  reformist liberalism, 123–124
Liberalism, 110, 112, 117–124, 165, 209–210 (*see also* Capitalism):
  civil liberties under, 158–159, 165
  ideological principles of, 109, 110
Libertarianism, 122
Lincoln, Abraham, 298, 299
Lindblom, Charles E., 219
Lipset, Seymour Martin, 250
Locke, John, 109, 118, 295–296, 317
Lombardi, Vince, 20
Louis XIV (King of France), 181
Louis XVI (King of France), 104, 176
Luther, Martin, 328–329, 334
Luxembourg, 158

Machiavelli, Niccolò, 140, 184
Macmillan, Harold, 114–115

INDEX 367

Madison, James, 171, 172–173, 192, 290, 293
Madisonianism, 290–297
Maistre, Joseph de, 109, 113
Malthus, Thomas, 109, 317
Manifesto of Fascist Racism, 145
Mao Zedong, 59–60, 64, 71, 88, 91, 96–97, 109, 187
Marat, Jean-Paul, 281–282
Market socialism, 88, 130, 219, 220, 221, 225–227
Marx, Karl, 64, 87, 88, 89, 93, 94, 96, 109, 125, 130–131 (*see also* Marxism; Marxism-Leninism):
 compared with views of Lenin, 134–139
 ideology of, 105, 131–134
Marxism, 76, 85, 90–91, 352 (*see also* Marx, Karl; Marxism-Leninism):
 cultural equality under, 87, 132–133
 equality and, 132–133
 freedom, 131–132
Marxism-Leninism, 74, 91, 106, 130–131, 342, 352 (*see also* Leninism; Marxism)
Mass media, 17, 65, 95, 269, 338
 under Nazi regime, 144
Maurras, 109, 113
Mayflower compact, 292
McGovern, George, 254
Membership groups, 49–50
Men, status of, 74, 88, 146
Mercantilism, 177, 178, 182
Merton, Robert, 268
Mexican Americans, 16, 21, 31, 32, 77, 247, 309
Michels, Robert, 229
Military dictatorships, 189–191
Military fascism, 147–149
Miller, Warren, 303
Mobutu Sese Soko, 181
Monarch of England, as symbol, 315, 316, 337
Monarchy, absolutist, 181–183, 201
Mongolia, 134
Monism, 113–115, 188
Moore, Barrington, 357
Moral-spiritual values, 282–283, 284, 291–293, 315, 327, 340
Movimento Sociale Italiano (MSI), 141
Muller, Adam, 113
Murder, *see* Homicide; Homicide rate
Mussolini, Benito, 109, 142, 159, 214, 223 (*see also* Fascism):
 beliefs of, 143–147
 economic equality under, 161

Napoleon, 207
National assembly, 197–198
National identity symbols, 337
Nationalism, 58–60, 93
Nationalization of industry, 231–233, 235
Nation-state(s):
 centralization of power in, 179, 184
 coordination of government activities, 185, 187
 differences among, 189–191
 emergence of, 176–178
 power of, 178–181, 184, 185, 187, 197–198, 203
 role of war in, 202, 203, 204, 212
 social structure in, 203, 205–206
 types of, 181–183, 186–200, 201
Native Americans, 31, 76, 77
Nazi regime, 58 (*see also* Fascism; Hitler, Adolf):

Nazi regime (*continued*)
 development of, 144–146, 331–335
 freedom under, 143–146
Near East, 159
Netherlands, 125
 civil liberties in, 158
 constitutional government in, 195
 economic equality in, 161, 164–165
 rise of capitalism in, 83, 176–178
New Zealand, 125, 158, 191
Nicholas II (Czar of Russia), 342
 regime of, 344–349
Nisbet, Robert A., 103
Nixon, Richard M.:
 the presidency of, 158, 184, 243, 252, 254, 304
 Watergate and, 303, 304–306
Nkrumah, Kwame, 181
North America, 73, 191
North Korea, 85, 134, 186, 187–188
Norway, 85, 158, 161–162

Occupations (*see also* Social groups, occupational):
 rankings of, 75, 76, 86, 87
 and voting behavior, 251–253
O'Higgins, Bernardo, 212

Page, Benjamin, 264
Paine, Tom, 177, 178
Pankhurst family, 48–49, 50
Parliamentary government, 314–317
Parrington, Vernon Louis, 300
Parti Communiste Francais (PCF), 233, 240–241, 260
Parti Socialiste (PS), 234
Partito Comunista Italiano (PCI), 140, 141, 233, 239, 240–241, 260
Penal systems, comparisons of, 25–28, 32
People's Republic of China, *see* China
Pethick-Lawrence, Frederick, W., 50
Plato, 171–172, 173, 175
Pluralism, 113–115, 117, 140–141, 188–190, 198–199
Poland, 55–56
Police, and the police force, 23, 174, 183, 193
 attitude toward, 21–22, 32
Political activism, and ideology, 237–244
Political activities, specialization of, 180, 185, 188, 189, 201
Political beliefs:
 functions of, 101–102
 ideological values of, 103–110
 role of in growth of power, 209–212
Political change, 356–362
Political education, 260–261
Political equality, 151, 209–212
Political freedom, 111–115, 233–236
Political ideology, 105–112, 157–158, 237
Political legitimacy, 281–284, 315–317
 belief systems and, 290–295
 challenges to, 286–288
 decline of confidence in, 301, 317–319
Political parties, 229–231
 activities of, 230, 259–263
 decline in influence of, 268–269
 economic equality and, 231–233
 economic productivity and, 246

Political parties (continued)
    elections and, 230, 244
    freedom and, 233–244
    goals of, and government policy, 266–267
    groups within, 261–262
    ideology of, 231–244
    influence of, 262–266, 268–269
    political education and, 260–261
    rise of, 230, 245–246
    social groups and, 256–259, 261–262
    support indicators for, 244, 259
Political parties, support for, by:
    class interest, 250–256, 257
    economic interest, 246, 257
    ethnic groups, 245, 257
    occupation, 257
    religious groups, 245, 249–250, 251
Political power, 52–53, 70–71
    definition of, 69–70
    exercise of, 51–53, 70–71
    factors affecting, 75–78
    relationship of, to wealth and status, 75–78
    struggle for, 58–60
Political power, effect of, on:
    economic groups, 62–66
    ethnic groups, 75, 76–77
    nationalism, 58–60
    religious groups, 56–60
    social status, 73–78
    social stratification, 76–88
    wealth, 71–73, 75–78
Political recruitment, 261
Political stability, 279–284, 306–310, 320–321, 325–333
Political systems:
    alienation from, 285–286
    challenge to legitimacy of, 286–288
    economic market and, 244
    legitimacy of, 279–289
    resolving conflicts in, 315–317
Political systems, types of, see Absolutist monarchy; Anarcho-communism; Autocracy; Bureaucratic dictatorship; Communism; Conservatism; Fascism; Liberalism; Military dictatorship; Military fascism; Nation-state(s), types of; Socialism
Politico-economic systems, 221 (see also Capitalism; Corporatism; Market socialism; State socialism)
Portugal, 134, 143
Power:
    reasons for in nation-states, 203
    role of war in growth of, 202, 203, 204, 212
Prime minister of England, concept of, 316
Primordial organizations, 49, 51–52, 53, 91 (see also Ethnic groups; Social groups)
Private ownership, degrees of, 221, 225–227
Public policy, development of, 262–268
Punishment, 12–13, 24–28
Puritanism, 290, 291–297

Race relations, 303–304 (see also Black Americans; South Africa)
Racial equality, 232–233
Racism under Nazi regime, 145, 334
Reagan, Ronald, the presidency of, 117, 243, 264–265, 266, 306

Recruitment, political, 261
Reference groups, 49, 50–51
Reformist liberalism, 123–124
Religion, 90
    freedom of, 115, 120–121, 145, 296–297
    political legitimacy and, 307–308
    political parties and, 257
    political policies and, 56–57, 65
    values in, 73–75, 328–329, 337
Religious groups, 55–60, 75, 245, 249–250, 257, 259
Religious voting, 249–250
Revolution(s):
    American, 194, 295–297
    contemporary, 63–64, 65, 89, 90–91, 93, 94, 96–97 (see also China; Marxism)
    French, 58, 103–104, 112–113, 126, 207, 281
    Industrial, 61, 239
    Latin American, 212–213
    Russian, 135–136 (see also Bolsheviks; Czarist Russia)
Ricardo, David, 109, 178, 317
Right-wing parties, definition of, 231
Rokeach, Milton, 104, 112, 234
Roman Catholic Church, 49, 55, 57, 77, 104, 177
Roosevelt, Franklin D., 109, 124, 300, 301
Rumania, 161
Russia, see Czarist Russia; Union of Soviet Socialist Republics (USSR)
Russian Communist party, 347–349
Russian Orthodox Church, 55, 57, 59, 282, 351–352

Salazar of Portugal, 214
Sartori, Giovanni, 258
Scandinavian countries, 125, 195, 199
Scope of political power, 180–181, 185, 187–188, 189, 199–200, 201
Second Reich, 108, 325–330, 359 (see also Bismarck, Otto von)
Sector(s):
    public versus private, 220, 221, 223–224
    service, components of, 61
Secular political religion, 58–60
Secular-religious conflict, 56–60
Separation of church and state, 121
Shah of Iran, 55
Shaw, George Bernard, 175
Shepherd, Jean, 281
Skocpol, Theda, 64
Smith, Adam, 84, 109, 177, 178, 317
Social change, 77, 89–98
    attitude toward, 91–92
    China and, 96–98
    class consciousness and, 93–96
    conditions for, 92–93
    expansion of opportunities and, 89–90
    political power and, 92–93, 96–98
    ranking values of, 91
    rate of, 77–78
Social democrats (SPD), 331, 336
Social groups, 16, 45, 49–66, 76–77, 90–93
    categoric, 49–50
    economic, 60–66
    ethnic, 15, 16, 21, 30–33, 53–55, 56, 75, 76–77, 245, 246, 249, 250, 251, 257
    ethnoreligious, 75

Social groups (continued)
  impact of, see Social stratification
  membership, 49–50
  occupational, 75, 76, 77, 93–94
  political parties and, 256–259, 261–262
  primordial, 49, 51–52, 53, 91
  reference, 49, 50–51
  religious, 55–60, 75, 90, 245, 249–250, 257, 259
Social learning theory, 10–15, 22, 36
Social service programs, 72–74, 180–181
Social status, 80, 87–88, 112, 115
  effect on political power, 73–78
  symbols of, 74–75
Social stratification, 86–98, 115, 122, 204 (see also Social change; Social groups):
  changes in, 89–98, 321
  comparison of societies, 78–89
  dimensions of, 69–75
  inequities of, 47, 69
  political power and, 69–71, 76–78, 80
  status and, 73–75, 80, 121
  wealth and, 71–73, 80
Social-structural conditions, 4, 15, 28–32
Social structure, 204–209, 212–213
Socialism, Democratic, 108, 110, 112, 124–130 (see also State socialism):
  civil liberties under, 158–159
  development of, 124–125
  economic equality under, 125, 161–165
  equality under, 127–129
  freedom under, 109, 110, 126–127
  principles of, 109, 110, 125–129
Societies, models of, 78–89
South Africa, 51–52, 54, 76, 77, 143, 147
Soviet Union, see Union of Soviet Socialist Republics (USSR)
Spain, 134, 139, 143, 159, 161, 165, 181
Stalin, Josef, 59, 141, 159, 187, 209, 352
  assumption of power by, 350–351
State socialism, 80, 85–89, 219, 221, 224–225
Status, see Social status
Stinchcombe, Arthur L., 355, 356
Structural pluralism, 140–141
Suarez, Francisco, 213
Suffrage movement in Great Britain, 47–49, 50–51
Sweden, 85, 90, 129, 158, 182, 222
  class voting in, 251, 258–259
  constitutional government in, 193, 194
  government and public policy in, 161–165
  homicide rates in, 3, 4
  ideological polarization in, 238, 240
  penal system in, 25–27
  political parties in, 233, 235–236, 238, 240, 257, 262
Switzerland, 23, 77

Tawney, R. H., 108, 109
  principles of, 125–129, 130
Television as violent stimulus, 18 (see also Mass media)
Thatcher, Margaret, the government of, 117, 210, 242–243, 265, 266, 317, 319
Third Reich, 333–335 (see also Facism; Hitler, Adolf; Nazi regime)
Third World, 89, 96–98
Thomas, John C., 240

Thomas, W. I., 51
Tilly, Charles, 202
Tocqueville, Alexis de, 113, 114
Touré, Sékou, 181
Tracy, Destutt de, 105
Trade unions, 90, 94–96, 120, 125, 162, 164, 208, 222–223, 224–227 (see also Unions):
  and political activities, 252–253, 257, 259
Treiman, Donald J., 76
Treitschke, Heinrich von, 324
Trimberger, Ellen Kay, 64
Truman, Harry S., 158
Two-party system, 196–197

Union of Soviet Socialist Republics (USSR), 63 73, 85, 101, 227, 360–361, (see also Czarist Russia; Leninism; Marxism-Leninism; State socialism):
  civil liberties in, 159
  coercive power in, 349–351, 361
  communism in, 186–189 (see also Communism)
  consensus rule in, 351
  economic equality in, 86, 88, 161
  industrialization of, 350–351, 353
  political stability in, 349–353
  religion in, 58–59, 352
  social stratification in, 353
Unions, 65, 160 (see also Trade unions):
  labor, 60, 63, 129
  of prisoners, 25–26, 27
  of women, 48–49, 50
United Kingdom, see Britain
United States, 83, 90, 95–96, 101, 118, 158
  class voting in, 252–254
  classical liberalism in, 295–297
  constitutional government of, 191, 192, 194, 195–198, 199
  economic equality in, 161, 163
  ethnic voting in 247–248, 257–258
  homicide rates in, 3, 4, 20, 33
  ideological polarization in, 238, 242–244
  individualism in, 300–301, 308–309
  penal system in, 25–27
  political beliefs in, 203, 209
  political change in, 358–360
  political legitimacy in, 297–301, 306–308 (see also Madisonianism; Puritanism)
  political parties in, 231–232, 236, 238, 242–244, 257, 262, 263–265
  political stability in, 306–310
  political systems in, 290–309
  public policy in, 264–265
  race relations in, 303–304
  religious freedom in, 296–297, 307–308
  rise of strong national government, 177–178
  role of war in growth of, 202, 203 (see also Vietnam war)
  slavery in, 297–299
  social stratification in, 308–309
  social structure in growth of power, 203, 204, 205
Uruguay, 147, 186, 189–191
USSR, see Union of Soviet Socialist Republics

Vaison, Robert, 175
Value conflict in Germany, 326–330
Van Horne, Harriet, 2, 3–4, 33

370 INDEX

Variables in political analysis, 5, 8–9, 15, 18, 34–35, 157–158, 255
Venezuela, 191
Victoria (Queen of England), 47
Vietnam, 66, 78, 82, 85, 86–87, 88, 134, 186, 187–188
Vietnam war, 243, 301, 302, 303, 304
Violence, *see* Criminal justice system; Handguns; Homicide
Vo Nguyen Giap, 64
Voting, 244–259
  class, 162, 250–259
  ethnic, 245, 246–249
  religious, 245, 249–250

War, relationship of to state structure, 202–204, 212
Washington, George, 296
Watergate, 301, 303, 304–306
Wealth, and political power, 52, 71–73, 75–76, 79, 85–87, 91
Weber, Max, 70, 76, 173–174, 186, 229, 292
Welfare state socialism, 129–130
Weimar Republic, 144, 288, 330–333, 336
Weiss, Peter, 281

Weld, Theodore Dwight, 297
West Europe, 64–65, 73, 89
  class voting in, 254–256
  constitutional government in, 191
  ideological polarization in, 239
  political parties in, 239, 265
  rise of capitalism in, 176–178
Wildavsky, Aaron, 36
Wilhelm I (Kaiser of Germany), 327
Wilhelm II (Kaiser of Germany), 327, 328, 329–330
Wolin, Sheldon, 69
Women, 74 (*see also* Primordial organizations; Suffrage movement):
  deferential attitude of, 318
  social stratification of, 88, 112, 146
  status in USSR, 137, 160
Women's Social and Political Union (WSPU), 48–49, 50–51
Working class, 93–96, 213, 238 (*see also* Trade unions; Voting, class)

Yugoslavia, 56, 159, 225–227

Zhou Enlai, 97